WAR
BEHIND
THE WIRE

WAR BEHIND THE WIRE

Australian Prisoners of War

EDITED BY MICHAEL CAULFIELD

HACHETTE AUSTRALIA

Australian Government

Department of Veterans' Affairs

The Australians at War Film Archive was funded by the Australian Government.
Full transcripts of interviews can be found at:
http://www.australiansatwarfilmarchive.gov.au

The stories presented in this book are drawn from the Australians at War Film
Archive, commissioned by the Department of Veterans' Affairs for the Australian
Government. The intent of the archive is to record Australians' experiences of war
and its enduring impact on their lives and on Australian society. Some of the
stories may not be historically accurate, given the passage of time since the events
being recalled. Some aspects may be distressing to readers, while some of the
stories may contain offensive language, depictions of sexual matters or negative
stereotypes reflecting the culture or language of a period or place. These stories
are the memories and reflections of the people who were interviewed for the film
archive and do not reflect the views of the Department of Veterans' Affairs.

HACHETTE AUSTRALIA

Published in Australia and New Zealand in 2008
by Hachette Australia
(An imprint of Hachette Livre Australia Pty Limited)
Level 17, 207 Kent Street, Sydney NSW 2000
Website: www.hachette.com.au

National Library of Australia
Cataloguing-in-Publication data

Caulfield, Michael.
  War behind the wire / Michael Caulfield.

  ISBN: 978 0 7336 2111 6 (pbk.)

  Prisoners of war--Australia--History.
  Prisoners of war--History--20th century.

355.1130994

Text design and typesetting by Bookhouse, Sydney
Typeset in 11.85/14.92 pt BaskervilleMT and 9.25/13.92 pt Helvetica Light
Printed in Australia by Griffin Press, Adelaide

Hachette Livre Australia's policy is to use papers
that are natural, renewable and recyclable products
and made from wood grown in sustainable forests.
The logging and manufacturing processes are expected
to conform to the environmental regulations
of the country of origin.

To the wives, husbands, partners and children of the prisoners –
for without them, no healing could have begun.

Contents

Introduction

The compelling stories and inspirational lives contained in this book come from an extraordinary collection of interviews commissioned and supported by the Commonwealth government – The Australians at War Film Archive. The Archive is comprised of over two thousand interviews with Australians from all our wars, conflicts and peacekeeping missions from World War I up until the present day. It holds stories that range over the human landscape in all its glory and sadness and that detail the defeats and triumphs of many kinds of lives. And it's dauntingly vast – twelve thousand hours of material. It's awfully easy to go searching in the Archive for one person and end up becoming totally absorbed in another. Yet so often, I find myself drawn towards the interviews given by the prisoners. The Archive has over two hundred of them – men, women and children who spent years behind the wire and yet lived to tell us their stories . . . and the stories of those people they do not want forgotten.

Fifty-nine of those ex-prisoners found their way into this book; prisoners of the Japanese, the Germans, the Italians and the Chinese – soldiers, sailors, airmen, children, nurses and wives; all quite remarkable people, if not for the singular experiences they were put through, then for their truthfulness and modesty. They do not regard themselves as anyone special, perhaps luckier than most because they survived, but in reality, ordinary Australians who just happened to be in the wrong place at the wrong time. And that's true, they were. But the value of their stories does not lie in that accident of time; it is what took place afterwards that has become a matter of wonder and admiration for the rest of us.

Everyone's war is different and a war lived behind the wire is no exception. No prisoner's story is the same as another, yet clear themes emerged from these interviews and that is the way this book has been arranged. They all talk about the day they were captured, or the constant, desperate longing for food . . . and freedom. They all remember their day of liberation, and the heartbreaking diffi-culty of coming back to life and love. They all remember the deaths. They all remember their mates. I have simply linked their stories with brief, historical notes, an occasional comment, and, here and there, undisguised admiration and wonder. I hope I have done them the service they deserve.

Michael Caulfield

A Note to the Reader

This book is based on excerpts from Australians at War Film Archive interviews. Where separate moments from any interview have been joined together to maintain continuity, a series of three dots signifies the join.

The Australians at War Film Archive is a Federal government initiative through the Department of Veterans' Affairs. Its many interviews are available to all in full, in transcription form, on the website: http://www.australiansatwarfilmarchive.gov.au with the exception of those interviews conducted with currently serving members of the Australian Defence Forces.

1

'For you, the war is over'

E very frontline soldier, every sailor, every airman who takes part in a war, thinks about being wounded or killed. It's inevitable; it comes with the job. Some even consider, and then endlessly discuss with each other, which wound would be worst – face . . . ? Legs . . . ? Stomach . . . ? The overwhelming conclusion seems to be that worst by a long mile would be the loss of genitalia. But even while mulling over thoughts as grisly as these, very few of them allow the prospect of being taken prisoner to take hold. They dream, as we would all do, of a last great stand, a fight to the end, holding the enemy at bay, being saved by mates at the last moment. So when capture – or defeat, as they would have it – arrives unexpected and shocking, it is a bitter end for the warrior.

Even so, many Australian prisoners of war managed to enter their imprisonment with humour and stoicism, describing their capture as being put 'in the bag'. That was the phrase servicemen in World War II used to describe being taken prisoner: 'Did you hear about the blokes from the 8th Divvy? They're all in the bag!' It was as though it was a game of sorts, a kind of military, musical chairs that merely removed you from the battlefield for a short while. They knew better, of course, and feared being caught – or worse, surrendering. You just didn't say that aloud. It was true to the spirit of those times to pretend that the hard knocks of life would just bounce off you: 'No worries, mate. She'll be right.' But they were hurt, and some were forever broken.

Time has granted a merciful softness to the memories of some ex-prisoners of war. A kind of hazy focus mixed with a blokey humour wells up when they look back: 'All mates together we were and did I tell you the one about Slim and the crazy Jap guard?' Nonetheless, other, sharper legacies are also embedded in most of them, the pain often endured every day of their lives. They might be troubled by old wounds or bodies that have never recovered from the starvation and the beatings, the maiming and the diseases. Or it might be the desolate memories, the inescapable images of horror and loss that taunt and exhaust their emotional reserves. What *is* astonishing is that whatever their circumstances, whether they were held in Changi or Germany, Korea or Japan, the one thing they all seem to remember in minute detail is the day they were captured.

For Sergeant Malcolm Keshan, that moment came during World War II, after he'd fought his way through North Africa. He was just 21 years old when his battalion was plunged into the disastrous campaign to save Greece from the Germans. It was April 1941, and Sergeant Keshan, along with 17 099 other Australian men and women, and battalions of New Zealanders, British and the Greeks themselves, faced the all-conquering German Panzer divisions in the mountains near the Greece–Yugoslavia border. They needed a miracle – but it didn't come.

We had to walk up into the hills where we had to dig in and stop the German advance. We got up there and it started to snow. We weren't dressed for snow. We'd just come from the desert . . . We went up there and we dug in up there. Then we fought for three days.

We couldn't get anywhere. We were holding the Germans, they couldn't advance, but the trouble was with the snow; you used to dig your trenches and all this snow inside the trenches would melt . . . We had no air force. We never saw any air force. Not at any stage. The Germans, when things got tough, they just called in their air force and their Stukas would come over and they'd dive-bomb us. These Stukas used to almost be able to drop a bomb in a barrel. So you can imagine what they did with trenches.

. . . When morning came we looked over towards our left flank and the Greeks had gone. So we looked over to the right flank and the Greeks had gone there too. We were just sitting up on this hill with no one on our flanks. Eventually orders came through to evacuate the position.

. . . We came down out of the hills and you've got no idea what the bedlam was. There was blokes everywhere without rifles, they'd thrown everything away and they were just marching out. My blokes sat down for a rest. They said, 'What about this? These blokes've got nothing and we're carrying the lot!' I said, 'You can't do that. You can throw your tripods away and all the heavy stuff that you don't need, but you've got to keep your rifles. If you don't keep your rifles and you run into a German, what have you got? You've got nothing.'

So we went down to the junction on the road and there was a Major Barham there. They were just streaking up the road in disorder. So Major Barham said to our Lieutenant Copeland, 'Go up the front and stop them. We've got to get organised or we've got no chance at all!' So Copeland said to me, 'Look after Major Barham and I'll go up the front and I'll see you when you get there.' The roads were built up quite high on the side. You couldn't go up the road because you'd get bogged straight away. With the snow it was all more or less mud and there was trucks and everything bogged in the fields where they had gone off the road.

. . . All of a sudden a German came up on the side of a road. A German sergeant. He stood up. Where he came from, I don't know. The only thing I can think of, there must have been a drain under the road and he crawled up that drain and when he got out the other side he stood up. When he stood up he was in the middle of the Australians. He called on Major Barham to surrender. With which, Major Barham and him fired at the same time and they both got killed. I don't know whether it was Major Barham killed him, because everyone then fired at him. So then we were left without the officers or anything. We headed up the road again.

I was bringing up the tail. I had a Tommy gun [Thompson submachine gun] issued to me by the American Army . . . and I'm more or less walking backwards, just watching what's behind me. As I got along the road a voice said, 'Put your arms down and turn around slowly'. I looked over my shoulder and it was a German and he had his gun trained on me. It all happened in a flash. You don't realise it, but to me it was slow motion. I'm thinking, 'What do I do?' I thought, 'I can't fire at him because he's surrounded by Australians.' And he said again, and this is unusual for a German, 'Put your arms down and turn around slowly.' So I thought, 'I've got no option.' There was a creek alongside the road, so I just threw the gun out and I turned around slowly.

I was a prisoner of war.

MALCOLM KESHAN

Three hundred and twenty Australians died during the Greek campaign and 2030 were taken as prisoners of war. Sergeant Keshan would survive to endure POW camps in France and Germany for the next four years. He escaped three times, was caught and re-imprisoned, then, finally, he successfully broke out of Stalag 383 in 1945.

•

Having surrendered Greece to the Germans in just three weeks, the High Command of the British Commonwealth Force evacuated about 50 000 of the survivors to the nearby island of Crete, where another stand would be made. But the troops were battle weary and had been forced to evacuate Greece minus most of their equipment. Stocks of ammunition and food were hopelessly inadequate and they had virtually no sea or air support, no motor transport and little or no communications.

The German assault began on 20 May 1941. There was desperate and often successful fighting by Allied troops, but the Luftwaffe dominated the skies, bombing and machine-gunning anything that moved. Retreat and evacuation were the only options for the Allied soldiers and they took off across the island to the south, dodging German planes, hiding in olive groves in a desperate race to get to the beaches where they hoped to find some way, *any* way, to get off the island.

With the Germans about to overwhelm them, a 30-year-old Australian artillery officer, Lieutenant John Fitzhardinge, was heading towards the coast with his men, dragging along with them the Italian guns they had captured in the deserts of North Africa. Fitzhardinge, an architect in civilian life, knew that the Italians guns were a poor substitute for their own artillery and thought little of them. But they were all he had.

In ravines and stony hillsides, the final few pockets of Allied resistance were doing their best to delay the inevitable. An Australian infantry colonel asked Fitzhardinge to lay down a last barrage of fire to protect his troops as they evacuated. When he'd done so, John asked, 'Permission to bugger off now, Sir?' To which the commander replied, 'Go for your life, mate.' Fitzhardinge made a run for it and ended up on the coast, where, taking charge of the last men on the beach, he commandeered a leaky barge and put to sea. Exhausted, he set their course for Egypt, then collapsed.

About midnight they woke me up and said, 'One of our submarines has just come up alongside of us and shot, bang, across our bows!' So I stopped the engine and took stock, and it was an Italian submarine and they had their gun trained on us. They had a machine gun in the conning tower, so I told Big Mac, who was a New Zealand airman, I said, 'You take charge, I'm going over to negotiate with them.' So I swum across, about four guns pointing at me as I got up the side of the submarine and I spoke in schoolboy French and said, 'We have sick and wounded onboard, we don't have any arms.' Which wasn't strictly true. I said I'd tell our officers to become his prisoners if he'd let the rest go and so I called out to the officers to come aboard. One bloke, an airman, got caught between the submarine and the barge and was killed. Seven of us became prisoners and they let the rest of them go.

. . . Anyway, they took us in ambulances to the naval barracks and put us in a room under a chief petty officer. And an Italian came in that spoke good English and read us the clauses of the Geneva Convention and said that they would be kept to a word, and the next thing we knew there was a tailor came in and took our measurements and we were fitted out with Italian suits for the equivalent rank of the Italian Army! Here's me in a grey battledress or army dress coat, hangers still in the sleeves, and they were charged to our account. And then they were taken away from us after that because the *carabinieri* [Italian police] said we looked like Italian officers and it would help us to escape.

Then the chief petty officer said, 'Well, what do you want?' And we said, 'Well, we'd like some beer,' paid for it with our money. And he said, 'Would you like some women?' And we said, 'That sounds like a good idea.' And he went away and came back with some women and the *carabinieri* said, 'No way, take them away.' So we weren't allowed to have those. They were pretty sour-looking birds anyway.

JOHN FITZHARDINGE, MBE

Over 10 000 Allied troops were captured when Crete fell. They were dumped into makeshift prisoner of war compounds on the island, into a hell of starvation and disease that went on for weeks till they were transported to Greece. John Fitzhardinge would eventually be imprisoned in a number of POW camps in Germany. His men speak of him still as 'one of the best', an officer whose optimism and enterprise never failed him, or them. He was what you might call a Renaissance prisoner, using his talents on enterprises as wildly diverse as the digging of escape tunnels and the designing of sets for a prison production of *The Mikado*. For all that though, he would not see his wife and newly born son for the next six years.

•

Around 1000 Australian airmen were captured during World War II. Their biggest problem lay not necessarily in their arrest but whether they survived the fall out of the sky that preceded it. Almost 10 000 Royal Australian Air Force personnel served with the strike force called Bomber Command, flying out of Great Britain on raids across Europe and almost 3500 of them would die. They were mostly very young men, with an average age of just 22, flying those huge planes in the battles of the Ruhr, Hamburg and Berlin, the invasion of Normandy, and the final assault on Germany.

For the duration of their 'tours', which meant at least 30 flights, they had a 90 per cent chance of being among the missing. Flying a tour meant that on any given flight there was the almost certain probability of death, or, if they were fortunate, capture. For Flight Sergeant Rex Austin, a wireless air gunner (WAG) in a Lancaster bomber, both those possibilities arose suddenly in the night sky over Germany on 22 May 1944. He was twenty years old and it was his thirteenth operation.

We got attacked by a German night fighter and he put the starboard wing on fire . . . The noise, if you can remember the old blowtorches that builders used to have, that enormous sound they used to make, well it's exactly the same sort of sound with the wing on fire and an aircraft travelling along at 100-odd miles an hour and the flames coming out the back.

Our pilot, Kev McSweeney, turned round and said, 'Get out of here!' . . . and away we went. My job was to put my parachute on, run down the back, open the back door and lock it open so that the gunners could follow me out and that's exactly what took place. At the time I got there the rear gunner, Carl Reg, was coming out of his turret and sliding forward and the mid upper gunner was moving out of his turret. I went down and I locked the door . . .

and I sat on the step with the flames going past underneath me and to the side of me and Reg's comment was, 'You were a bit slow, chum, so I kicked you out!' . . . And I don't remember pulling the ripcord, but no doubt I did – well obviously I did.

And then I floated from 22 000 feet. Unfortunately the wing came off after I got out and the two gunners got out but the fellows down the front were trapped in the aircraft . . . it blew up in midair but McSweeney, the pilot, survived virtually unhurt. Fred, the navigator, survived, but he was knocked around a bit and Danny Major the bomb aimer and John Lowry were killed. It's just one of those things.

. . . I landed in a ploughed field at a little cluster of farmhouses. There would have been no more than half-a-dozen houses there, remember you're going out at half past twelve at night so it's as black as the inside of a cow, there are no lights on, on the ground, you have no points of reference to see where you're going to land and I hit the ground obviously pretty hard. My flying boots had come off when I pulled the ripcord because of the sudden jerk, so I came down without flying boots on and I didn't realise I'd been hurt until I went to stand up and then I realised that I had a broken ankle. I tried to move and, frankly, I couldn't.

I won't say that I was petrified or anything like that, but . . . when I went to stand I realised all I could do was hop, not walk. So I sat myself back down on the ground again and pulled the parachute over the top of my head and said, 'That's it, that's it'. I tried to light myself a cigarette, there was a wind blowing so that I couldn't light the cigarette, whether it was the wind or my hands shaking so much I don't know, and I wouldn't like to admit that my hand was shaking too much but I guess it probably was.

. . . It was raining gently, I was cold, wet and miserable and very lonely and thinking to myself, 'What the heck am I doing here?' You know, you tend to think to yourself, 'What's Mum and Dad going to say about this?' I had a girlfriend in England, 'What's she going to say about this?'

The following morning at dawn, two or three guys, farmers obviously, they had Wellington boots on, they arrived, they had shotguns and with them was a younger fellow, I'd guess he would have been thirteen or fourteen and he had a rifle and he insisted on pointing the rifle at me. The adults were yakking at him, but it didn't matter, he had that look in his eye, he looked as though, 'I'm going to shoot this bastard!' sort of thing and that worried me a bit . . .

These guys helped me across the field to a path alongside and there was a bicycle there and they gave me this bike and escorted me, me holding the handlebars and hopping, to a farmhouse . . . took me inside there, the woman of the house could not have been nicer. She was a typical German farm lady, fairly wide, not terribly tall and she tut-tutted, put me on a chair in front of the wood fire, put a chair for my leg and was as nice as could be. She gave me a slice of bread, brown bread, German bread, which I'd never tasted before and some butter on it I guess, which tasted foul to my palate. The whole thing wasn't very acceptable but I did my absolute utmost to make certain that I smiled and thanked her for it . . .

I stayed there for some days and became the subject of interest of everybody around the place, everybody was coming to the kitchen door and looking me up and down and then they'd disappear and somebody else would come. In due time I heard a lot of commotion outside and a little guy who was about 5 foot 4 and about 15 feet across the shoulders arrived in an impeccable uniform and with a revolver nearly as big as himself. He screamed into the house, jabbed me in the ribs with this gun again and again, oh boy, was he performing. I think he was probably abusing the farmer for being kind to me. I heard the word *terror flieger,* a couple of times, 'terror flyer' . . . About that time of the war Goebbels and his boys were brainwashing the German populace that we were killers of women and children, stirring up hatred towards Bomber Command people . . .

Bill Fordyce and Australian airmen in Stalag Luft III

Anyway, they took me out to the car, I was bundled in the back seat of this car and . . . they took me back to where the aircraft had crashed. On the way back we picked up the navigator Fred Homewood and then we went back to the crash site and it was there where he made me get out of the car and identify the bodies of Danny Major and John Lowry and I did that . . .

REX AUSTIN

•

If being taken prisoner was a challenge for servicemen, then it was far more terrifying for women, particularly when their captors were the Japanese. The Emperor's troops had already shocked the world with ruthless acts of rape and wholesale slaughter in their invasion of China. The stunning speed of their advance through South-East Asia in the first horrendous weeks of 1942 meant that they now had tens of thousands of people under their control.

Hundreds of captives, including women and children, were murdered rather than being taken prisoner. The rest were forced behind the wire. Two-thirds of all the Australians captured by the Japanese in World War II were imprisoned during that time. Thirty-six per cent of them, over 8000 men and women, would die in captivity.

One of the last cities to fall, Singapore, was close to its end when the war rolled right over the Australian Army nurses serving there. They had already refused evacuation once, determined to care for the men. Now they were to be ordered out. As the Japanese bombing increased in fury, Pat Darling was called to a meeting in her hospital.

It was the 11th of February [1942] and matron came and she said, 'I have been ordered to send half the nurses out. Those of you who are prepared to stay, move to my side.' And this we did in a body. And, of course, then she had the wretched task of choosing whom to send out and I was amongst the ones who were left behind. They left on the *Empire Star* and eventually after a very hazardous trip, got back to Australia.

Then on the 12th, one of the doctors came to me where I was working and said, 'Don't you know the sisters are leaving?' And I said, 'Nobody's told me, I'll just say goodbye to the patients.' And I can remember his tired, exasperated voice saying, 'Do you always have to do the right thing?' And I said, 'Yes, particularly this time', because we all knew the Japs were near and I couldn't let the patients think I'd just disappeared.

    . . . We were taken to a small wharf with a small ship standing beside it and it was the *Vyner Brooke*. It had been the Rajah of Sarawak's private yacht, one of his older ones . . . We set forth some time around about midnight and all next day, the captain, the ship was so tiny, he was able to hide it amongst the mangroves because he had been chased around the island by the Japanese planes for a whole week or so and had come into Singapore hoping to have a rest. Anyway, that was Friday the 13th.

    On Saturday the 14th we set off again and this poor little ship couldn't make much speed and about ten o'clock three small Japanese planes came along and machine-gunned the decks . . . they holed the lifeboats on the portside, and then about quarter to two we saw a flight of Japanese bombers coming towards us . . . We had a little 2-inch gun in the forward deck and that did its best but one of the first bombs that fell got the gun and its crew . . . another bomb went through a funnel, and of course, did a lot of damage to the engine room and the ship almost immediately lurched to the starboard, and so the order was given to abandon ship and they launched two lifeboats and Cath Noyce, Win Davis and I had gone into one of the officer's cabins and Cath said to me, 'Pat, I'm bleeding from my left hip, and I didn't have time to look at it'. And I said, 'No, well let's get you into a boat.'

    . . . So then Win and I got out of the boat and we found there were dead bodies floating around already 'cause people had jumped overboard and their lifebelts had gone up and would've broken their necks as they hit the water, and we found a spar and hung onto it for a long time. We were trying to push it to the shore, and then about four o'clock . . . a raft picked us up . . . and all night long we struggled.

    . . . At about eight o'clock next morning we were still struggling and we were probably only 200 yards from the shore at this stage, and you could see the Japs on the shore, and we didn't know which way to try and pull the thing. Anyway, they came out on a boat and they were quite kind and gentle and they pulled us on board. I was the first one they grabbed and I thought, 'Well I'm not going to be the only one', so immediately turned around to grab Win and they pushed me aside quite gently and pulled the others into the boat, and they took us ashore and they were a medical group and quite kind. They gave us food and they gave us something to drink . . . and then they took us to a house to get some dry clothes to change into.

There was a dead Indonesian lying nearby and the little Japanese, who was quite a polite little fellow, was showing us around and telling us to take what we wanted – we didn't like to take very much – and then he took from the wall a mirror, and showed me myself, and I was horrified. My hair was full of black oil. Ships have an amazing amount of oil and my face was purple, my skin, my eyes were scarlet and I sort of went, 'How terrible!' And of course he doubled up with mirth which I was relieved at because it was a normal reaction, and one just thought, you know, 'Thank goodness they're human.'

. . . Next day they walked us to Muntok, which took about two hours and at the school there we met up with the other sisters and our numbers were then 29. There were 65 of us on the ship, 65 army nurses on the ship, and some of them had been hit, kicked or slapped. Very few had been given food so we realised how lucky we had been.

PAT DARLING

In those first days of Japanese supremacy, luck was a relative matter. Richard Lloyd Cahill was a doctor in the Royal Australian Medical Corps. He was attached to the 2/19th Battalion and went into captivity with them on 16 January 1942.

I was put on a truck and I went into Singapore . . . I remember being on the back of this truck, an army truck, and we were going across one of the bridges. I looked up and there, on the lights, every one, was a head, hanging down. They'd been decapitated and they were hanging from the lights, from the lamps. And then a bit further on you'd find the whole body was hanging down. I thought, 'This is ghastly. This is the finish of the white man in here.' And then the next thing I saw was some Brits coming around a corner and they had their boots on and they had no shirts, and they were all white and pink out in the sun and they didn't have hats, and they had rope girdle things around their shoulders and they were pulling these trucks, obviously the trucks' motors must have been out or something. They were going round cleaning up Singapore and they didn't give them real trucks, they gave them these things. They had to take the garbage, all the mess, and then pull them along. They used to have these rope things with about ten men on each big rope harnessed to the carts or whatever they were pulling, through Singapore, in front of all the people. And I thought, 'This is the end, this is the end of the white man here.' Which it was. They just did everything to humiliate them, particularly the Brits.

DR LLOYD CAHILL

Fifteen hundred Australian civilians were captured by the Japanese during World War II. Many were children. Sheila Bruhn was just seventeen when she arrived in the dying city of Singapore and as she spoke of her memories all the passion and observation of that adolescent returned.

When we got to Singapore and found Singapore had been badly bombed, we couldn't believe our eyes . . . just where you expect to see a nice clean city, all you were seeing was dead bodies, buildings being torn down. Sirens going, air-raid wardens telling you to get out of the way, take shelter. Ambulances about, crying people, crying children, terrified . . . but there was nowhere else to go . . .

. . . Towards the end there was panic, everybody was running around trying to get away somehow or other, even trying to get a little boat, a little sampan for themselves. There was a lot of thieving going on because people were trying to get tins of food to store up for emergencies. It was just chaos. Absolute chaos. Sometimes when you would go out on the street there was nobody around, just dead bodies, people were too scared to come out. And then there would be an influx of people running around. Businesses were still trying to keep going. Absolute chaos, no order whatsoever, you just had to manage the best way you can. Try and get food whenever you can, wherever you can. Shelter wherever you can, when you hear the alert go, and heave a sigh of relief when you hear the all clear, and dust yourself off and look around and try and think what's the next step, not being able to find really what the next step is to take.

I was only seventeen, I didn't know much about these things. My life until then had been serene and peaceful and now it was all jagged and disruptive, and I probably didn't take much notice of what was going on except trying to keep myself alive . . . as a matter of fact, I thought it was the end of the world, I didn't think anybody would survive the way it was going. It was too terrifying to think. For me, I didn't think there was any future.

. . . When we heard the news [that Singapore had fallen] and that night when everything was so quiet, I am not sure whether any of us got much sleep because it seemed so strange not to hear all of the sirens and the bombing going. It was unreal in a way. And the next day my father went into town to find out what was happening and he was told we all have to register ourselves because we would all be prisoners . . . finally we were told that we would be taken to Changi . . .

We had people telling us what we should do, we were given chores, we were only going to be there for ten days. We were told to pack enough for ten days so some of us did pack a few things – a bit of food and stuff like that. Because of having kept a diary right through, I had my six exercise books with me, my father's English dictionary, a book of Shakespeare and a book of poems. And on the 8th of March we were told that we were going to Changi prison, so we marched there. Eight miles in the hot sun and when we arrived there we were pretty tired and dusty. Some of the locals cheered and some of the locals jeered and threw things at us. We had dogs following us, and if we didn't walk we got prodded with the butt of a rifle.

The Japanese looked fearsome even in their uniforms, and they were making a lot of noise and came down in a file raising their hands up with their guns and shoving and prodding people out of the way with their bayonets. I just wondered, I had heard stories of them killing and raping women at Nanking. We were told about that, and so I was terrified again. I wasn't sure what they were going to do, and being a young person that was my first thought, 'I am a young person, what is going to happen to me?' In those days 'rape' wasn't a word that I knew, I didn't know anything about that. In fact, I knew nothing of that even when I went into camp. So as far as I was concerned I thought I was going to be killed, and of course when we went out and I saw these heads on poles, as a warning, if we did anything we would be beheaded and have our heads put on a pole. I was quite sure that we were all going to be beheaded, because from stories I had heard the Japanese hated the British and I was considered to be a British subject and in fact it didn't matter, because they did that to the locals too . . . they sort of just bayoneted them, punched them, kicked on them, jumped on them, I couldn't believe a human being could be so cruel, and then seeing a baby be thrown into the air and letting it fall on the point of his blade. That really upset me. That was when all of my nightmares started, every time a baby cried I would see that, even now.

SHEILA BRUHN

•

No matter where you were taken prisoner, your personal circumstances at the time you were captured could influence every day of the rest of your imprisonment. Your physical fitness mattered, the state of your mental health, even whether or not your last letter from home contained good or bad news, for you carried that feeling with you until escape, release – or death. Worst of all was to be captured when wounded, for medical care could be and was, deliberately withheld in an attempt to gain information. This was particularly so in the Korean War. On 25 May 1953, Lieutenant Charlie Yacopetti was leading his patrol near a landmark called Hill 355.

We went out to set an ambush for the enemy coming down a ridge . . . and what none of us knew was that the enemy had beaten us out there and they set an ambush for *us*, just a little further up the same ridge . . . That's when somebody said, 'Skipper, I think I hear some movement over there', in a pretty hushed voice, but yeah, I heard it. And just then a grenade was thrown and landed just behind me, I heard it land and I got up to get out of the way and it went off. And that's when the problem started because I was pretty knocked, you know. When an explosion like that occurs the breath gets sucked out of your lungs. I was a little bit put out by the incident. I heard the explosion, didn't feel the pain straight away, you just feel like something burning into your buttock and then you can just feel the blood flowing on your legs. Then you start to feel a bit sick and queasy and you realise that you've copped it.

    I had this other fellow, Alec Weaver . . . he came with me on this patrol to get some experience. And when somebody said, 'The Skipper's hit!' apparently he took control and he said, 'Okay, we're going to get out'. I got up and started to follow them and that's when I got a couple of bursts of machine-gun fire – one hit me on this ankle and another one hit me across here. And I went down and my Bren gunner, Bert White, picked me up and said, 'C'mon, I'll carry you out, Skipper.' Things were going hazy and I could see that as far as I was concerned I'd had it, this was it: 'Charles Yacopetti, *this* is your day'. So I said to Bert, 'Drop me, you need to fight the patrol out.' He was the Bren gunner, he's got the bulk of the firepower the patrol had. So he obeyed, he dropped me. And if you read the official history, I was left in a weapon pit there with my bayonet fixed on my Owen gun facing them, which is bullshit, I passed out.

    It's not as bad as you think; the terror is in thinking it's going to happen. Once it's happened, 'Oh, it's happened'. There's nothing you can do about it. And when that realisation hits you it's not as bad . . . spin and blank, the mind goes blank and you're feeling really woozy and you just collapse.

    . . . I came to and I was being dragged across the earth by this wounded arm, it was really painful . . . I gathered by that stage that I'd been searched, binoculars had gone . . . weapon had disappeared, what else had disappeared? Compass had gone, wristwatch had gone, that's when I came to. I woke up face down with a Chinaman sitting on my back. How long after I don't know. I wondered, 'What the hell's going on?' And then there's this weight on your back and then there's a few grunts, he's obviously saying, 'Hey he's coming to', or I presume, I don't know.

. . . After that there were a few grunts and somebody came over and talked to him and I got grabbed by the wounded arm and got dragged on my side up the valley. Oh it hurt like mad, I screamed like mad and obviously that didn't please them because you could still hear the battle going on up there, there was shelling and mortars falling, not near us, but falling around. I don't know whether they thought that my scream might alert them to where I was and they might get mortared but I got a swift boot in the back – I think it was probably a rifle butt I got hit with as I was laying on the ground. 'Shut up!' Oh that shut me up all right.

. . . Then it got a bit woolly. I was dragged along for, I would say, the best part of half a kilometre or more from then on. I don't know why I was dragged, they could have easily picked me up, but anyway that's the way it happened and I finished up in a hootchie [a rough cabin] . . . half a kilometre from their front line. Probably no more than a kilometre from ours. And there they came in, undressed me, took my boots, maybe they thought I was going to run away with my legs the way they were. Washed my wounds with hot, salty water I think . . . And I was left there until the following midday, maybe later; somebody came in with some rice and soup, that's all I got that day. And the following morning in came some military officer, not very high level I would say, certainly not very intelligent, by the questions he was asking with an interpreter. And then the interrogation started.

CHARLES YACOPETTI, MC, MID

Some men were finally taken into prison camps only after evading capture for quite a time. This was often true for pilots and aircrew who were shot down over land or sea and remained undiscovered until their attempts to return home finally brought them face to face with their enemy. Their solo journeys through hostile lands can sound like the most amazing tales of 'boys' own adventures'. Except that they're true.

In January 1942, Clarence 'Spud' Spurgeon was flying a Hudson bomber on what they called a 'milk run', a routine flight, along the east coast of Malaya. He wasn't expecting trouble from the Japanese.

We were on our way home and the first word I got was a scream from the back, a fighter was way up me arse shooting, and the next my starboard engine was on fire. He made one pass and, regrettably, my gunner and my wireless operator were both killed, rounds came through over my shoulder, I know the wireless operator was lying there with his head through the doorway on my right-hand side so he was as dead as a maggot, and the gunner had only got two lots of rounds away, and then we were dead quiet so I knew then that, if he wasn't dead, he was pretty sick anyway. But the wireless operator confirmed that he was killed, shot through the head.

. . . The airplane was on fire. I had no alternative but to put it on the water . . . The moment it hit it tore the whole guts out of it, all the bomb doors were torn off and probably a good part of the underbelly of the airplane was damaged and I can remember the water being up to about the top of the wings on either side, it wasn't completely submerged but it sank very, very soon after we got out of it.

I had to drag the second pilot out . . . I had to drag him out without his Mae West [lifejacket] and put it on when we got him in the water and it was then I realised that he wasn't all that good, he'd been hit somewhere else. I never found out what it was because he, quite quickly, I don't know whether he fainted or what, fortunately, I got his Mae West blown up so he was water-borne . . . I was okay, I had my Mae West on and I had kicked my shoes off. So the sea was flat, there was just a little bit of a ripple in it, I don't know what our position was . . . but we were in the sea for all that day and all that night. He, regrettably, succumbed about midnight, he hung on as best he could, but he was a goner.

I suppose in animal terms, one's thoughts immediately turn to one's own survival. I think that is probably the easiest way to explain it, but I can remember even thinking about whether I ought to call on the Almighty and I thought, 'Well, there's not a bloody lot he can do right now', and I'm not an Almighty caller, anyway.

. . . The first thing I remember was, it must have been early in the morning, when whatever moon was left made itself known, and I can remember seeing the silhouette of this hilltop, which is probably no more than 150 feet above sea level. The dawn is very brief in the tropics and it's almost as if somebody had turned the light on and I realised that I was within swimming distance of the coast. It didn't look very habitable; it didn't look like it had a nice sandy beach to land on, it was all jagged rock . . . so I got in there and the next thing the first wave chucked me up on the rocks and the ruddy coral tore my feet to pieces when I tried to stand up . . . so it was simply a question of pulling myself up. I don't even remember how I did that, I remember I had a couple of cuts on my knees from trying to crawl . . .

CLARENCE 'SPUD' SPURGEON, CBE, DFC

Spud Spurgeon could easily be the bomber pilot from central casting. Still tall, dark-haired and handsome, he related his story with all the nonchalance of a man musing on tomorrow's weather. But his courage and stubbornness to get back into the fight were remarkable. He spent a couple of days searching the island, trying to find a way off. Eventually, he encountered some locals and, after a lot of 'persuasion', he convinced them to give him a leaky canoe, which he proceeded to paddle to the main island of Singapore.

I started to walk to Singapore with my feet tied up in old socks and things that they had given me. And I got as far as Mersing, and I had avoided two Japanese patrols on the way down, and when I got to Mersing there was only one way to cross the river and that was you've got to swim it. And, of course, the noise I made swimming across the river must have alerted them and I was just walking across the road, when two Nips on pushbikes came up alongside me. And I think they thought I was some wayward boong trying to cross the road until I turned around and, of course, they realised who I was.

. . . They were a bit unpleasant, they presented me with a bayoneted rifle, which is not the most reassuring sentiment of friendship, and I just stood there until finally they yabbered at each other. And, fortunately for me, I heard the noise of a car coming and there was a major in the car and immediately he took charge of the situation, and I was strapped onto the outside of the car and carted up to Endau standing on the running board. I had my hands inside, you know, where the doorpost is, and they tied me on, seemed like a lump of pork, but, yeah, that was about 15 kilometres, I suppose.

. . . They made up their minds to put me inside one of the little cottages on the side of the road. It was about half-past five in the afternoon and when I got inside I was buggered, I was absolutely buggered, I just flopped on the floor. And over in the other corner, it was quite dark inside the room, I heard a movement over on the other side and I said, 'Is there anybody there?' And this small voice from the other side of the room said, 'Well, what the fuck are you doing here?' It was a Kiwi gunner and wireless operator who had been shot down . . . Kelly was his name. We very quickly introduced each other and that, surprisingly, was as good a medicine as I could have had.

CLARENCE 'SPUD' SPURGEON, CBE, DFC

REX AUSTIN

ALEXANDER BARNETT

BERT BEECHAM

FRANCIS BINSTEAD

SHEILA BRUHN

LLOYD CAHILL

Spud Spurgeon would spend the rest of his war on the island of Formosa and down a Japanese coalmine. He was fortunate in one sense – that he crash-landed close to shore. It was a different matter for sailors in a blue water navy. A month after Spud went down, HMAS *Perth*, with 680 men aboard, was involved in one of the most dramatic naval battles of the war. The ship had already survived the Battle of the Java Sea, but the very next day ran headlong into the entire Japanese fleet assembled for the invasion of Java. Half of the men on *Perth* would die that night. Gavin Campbell was a 21-year-old lieutenant. He was also one of those who made it into the water.

The Japanese were trying to put searchlights onto us, so every time the lights came across, our forward guns would fire, so it was bedlam . . . The flash of the guns were so bright. The heat and the gun flash were blinding.

It was then the torpedo hit forward and the ship just seemed to lift out of the water. Water and oil just rained down on us. Then the second torpedo hit. The captain then ordered abandon ship . . . I could hear people running around. I said to my offsider, 'Well, this is it.' . . . The ship at this stage had become stationary and started to develop a list. The crowd down below had started to put rafts over the side. I went down and as I went down I inflated my Mae West. I gave them a hand with the rafts and put them overboard. I took off my tin hat and for some reason or another, I don't know what possessed me to do it, I laid it on the quarter deck by Y-turret . . . and I went to the port side to jump overboard.

I looked down and I saw the propeller still turning and I thought, 'This isn't for me.' So I went further forward and straddled the guardrail ready to jump, and a torpedo hit on the port side, forward of me . . . It was then that I had a falling sensation. Up in the air and floating through the air. For how long, I don't know. I remember when I came to I was in the water and fortunately my Mae West kept me afloat. There were rafts and driftwood on the water and I decided I'd swim over to one of the rafts. It was then I started to kick my leg to swim and had a stab of pain on my left side. I thought, 'What's happened?' So I very gingerly reached down my leg and it wobbled. I'd broken my leg . . . So I thought, 'What do I do? I'm in the water. I'll make my way across to a raft.'

. . . There were other people on it, of course. So I thought, 'I've got to get on it somehow.' I hauled myself up on this still with my leg wobbling around and a bloke came along swimming and said, 'Are you all right?' And I said, 'No

I've broken my leg.' He said, 'What do you reckon we can do?' I said, 'The only thing we can do is cut some splints.' I had on overalls and so I said, 'Cut the leg off the overalls and then cut it into strips and we'll use those as ties around the splint.' He said, 'Okay, I've got my seaman's knife, I'll go and get some driftwood.' By this time there's broken cases from the Japanese ships drifting around. So he picked up a couple of pieces and split these down for splints. Brought them over and cut the leg off my overalls and put them on. That kept the leg steady.

GAVIN CAMPBELL

Petty Officer Ray Parkin was steering the *Perth* when the second torpedo hit. Despite knowing that the ship was doomed, the captain, Hec Waller, called down the tube to Ray, 'Leave both engines half-speed ahead, I don't want the old girl to take anyone with her.' His intention was that the *Perth* should keep moving forwards so that when the sailors went over the side of the ship, they wouldn't be drawn down by suction. Ray set the speed, then he too went into the water.

There were a lot of men still being killed in the water by shellfire but then we suddenly found ourselves faced with another problem, and that was oil fuel. The ships being torpedoed had bled all this oil fuel out onto the water and where we were there was about 3 inches of it on top of the water. This black, treacly mess, and we had to swing amongst it and when you're swimming, your head's pretty close to the water and if the water's disturbed, well, there was enough activity in the movements of ships and that around us. That was causing the surface of this to be little dollops, you know, got around in waves and slopped up, and if they slopped in your face and you got them into your mouth or nose and happened to inhale a bit, well you'd start coughing and you'd get out of control and you'd probably get more in, and it was a sure way of drowning in a most painful way.

Of course it was getting into our eyes, which were burning, we couldn't prevent that, but there were a lot of people I heard, you could hear it, you know, around you, blokes, and you'd hear this horrible coughing and gurgling and then a bloke'd just go. There was no way.

And then a couple of Japanese destroyers came in and they'd stopped their engines and drifted amongst us and we could see, they were all lit up now, illuminated, there were these chaps on board all in beautiful white suits, you know, and looking so healthy and everything and here were we in the water, looking up like mendicants, beggars and so forth. Oh we had one bloke and he screamed out, 'Help, help, save me!' and all the rest of it and we said, 'Shut up, you bastard!' And then a clear voice came from the bridge of this destroyer and he said, 'Ahh, we good boys now, eh Aussie?' Just like that. It took my breath away. This bloke had obviously lived in Australia, but his voice was so clear and we knew then how much they had us tapped you know, we'd walked right into a trap.

. . . It's a bit unreal. When you see your home going, something you've lived in for three and a half years . . . it was one of those things that you couldn't sum up, it was just a bit unreal, you couldn't believe she was going and yet I savoured the finish, I did see it and I was looking at it very critically. As she was steaming away she did several little things, she was just turning slightly to starboard, just in a gentle swing and as she was doing so, she was going down by the head and in doing that she exposed her propellers. It's got four propellers you see, and one of them was still turning so I said to meself, 'Both engines, half speed ahead.' This propeller was actually turning and then she just gently dipped and down she went, under the water and the blokes that saw it they said she didn't sink, she steamed out.

RAY PARKIN

Most of the survivors from the *Perth* landed at various points on nearby islands. Slowly and inevitably, they were gathered up by the Japanese to begin three years of captivity, some to slavery in Japan, others to the horrors of the Thai–Burma Railway.

We just begged our way for food until we came to a town we found out was called Labuan. It was the first time we had heard English spoken. This woman came out and said, 'Are you from the *Perth*?' We said yes. And she said, 'Your friends are here.' Eventually this other crowd, which had left before us had found their way to Labuan and the chief of the village had stopped them and said, 'You can't go any further. The Japanese have ordered us to keep you people here, or any white people here.' That was it. They tried to clean us up a bit because the oil fuel by this time had dried and it was peeling off our skin as well. So we just stayed at this village chief's house until the day the Japanese arrived.

The front line Japanese soldier is not a very handsome creature. This partic-ular bloke came in, I suppose he had on a fortnight's growth. He had a submachine gun and he brought this up to the ready. We thought this was it. He started to shout at us and we could tell by the tone of his voice that he didn't like us. He was followed by another soldier with a rifle, and it was then I saw my first rifle butt being used on people.

GAVIN CAMPBELL

•

The Germans loved to say, 'For you, the war is over', when they took prisoners, rubbing the salt of defeat into the humiliation of capture. But many men, at that moment, could not be made to feel any worse by their enemy than they already did. Capture brought with it instant depression, a sense of utter failure and the prospect of a bleak and useless future. Lloyd Moule and his unit were desperately defending a fort in Libya when Rommel's tanks overwhelmed them.

It was a terrible feeling; we had a flag flying at the fort which we could see from our gun position back in the distance. We could see the German flag, not the swastika one, the red, yellow and black one go up and ours came down. It was a terrible feeling of almost hopelessness, you felt sad, you felt angry, and all these mixed emotions were taking over of, 'What's happening?' Suddenly you have an enemy with no means of attacking or defending . . . it's a terrible feeling to find that you are a prisoner of war. You don't know what the consequences are . . .

We were herded up and I had this terrible feeling of derogation, and some of our fellows were saying, 'They will probably counter-attack and get us out of this.' We would have waited about two and a half years, I think, before they counter-attacked up in that part of the world.

LLOYD MOULE

It may be 60 years and more since the day they were captured, but some moments in life burn in a heart forever. Alexander Barnett cannot, will not, forget.

It was just sort of unanimous, the order was to surrender, put your hands up but I don't know if they had a flag or what. I do remember putting my hands up. But it's a horrible feeling . . . you feel you've done something wrong, but if you look at it in hindsight you've been wronged, it's a very difficult question, very hard to comprehend. And you think, 'What else could we have done?' And then I had an experience after I came home, I was pretty toey when I came home and my wife had a cousin who had real tabs on himself and he was a real shiny bum if ever I'd seen one, and at a party I was at he happened to say that nobody should ever be a prisoner. My wife intervened; I'd have cut his throat.

ALEXANDER BARNETT

'For you, the war is over.' Perhaps. Or perhaps it was just that one kind of war was over and another had begun. For these newly imprisoned men and women were about to endure an intensely personal war that would test their strength, their self-reliance and their deepest reserves of courage, in the months and years to come.

2

'We learned how to cook rice, didn't we?'

Most soldiers become prisoners of war in the midst of battle-field chaos, such as the headlong retreats on Greece and Crete in World War II, or the bewildering confusion of Singapore's last days. Rarely does capture occur in anything approaching a regimented, orderly fashion. The tumult and disorder that accompany imprisonment, where previously there had been military discipline and certainty, leave many ex-prisoners of war with jagged feelings about their first few days behind the wire.

In particular, their interviews make clear that they care deeply about whether they were *captured* or *surrendered*. To be captured, they say, implies that they fought to the last, honouring their code and their duty; while surrendering means that they either gave up, or worse, that their commanders surrendered on their behalf. Australian soldiers find this last fact particularly offensive and many blamed their officers for their plight. They believed they were the victims of yet another 'top brass' fiasco, and some, bitterly disappointed, maintained they were actually delighted to be prisoners so that at least now, they 'couldn't be buggered round any more'.

Reg Worthington had left the family farm in Murwillumbah in New South Wales, and volunteered to be a driver in the AIF. He'd nursed his big Chevvy truck across North Africa, but when they

were sent to Greece, he and his mates all knew that the end would
be bloody.

I don't think I had any thoughts other than, 'We're not going to win this one.'
We knew that. We knew that right from the day before we left Alexandria
Harbour; we knew we weren't going to win this one. But we still went ahead
with it because we were soldiers and that's what we were told to do . . . we
realised that the establishment had let us down. Even while we were still
retreating we knew the establishment had let us down . . . We were not prepared
at all . . . there were no authorities. We had a few officers around from other
units, but we weren't told anything. We were just told to obey. Now, if you want
to avoid trouble, obey. Some of us did and some of us didn't.

    . . . There was great resentment. You can understand perhaps, it was the
officers we were depending on and troops need to be lead and the officers
have to do the job and our bloke failed us. All he was interested in was saving
his own skin. No, I could never forgive him for that. He was no good. I won't
mention his name, I know it very clearly. And there is no one else that can name
him now because I am the sole survivor.

REG WORTHINGTON

The men's mood wasn't helped by the physical conditions into
which they were thrown, for there was a complete lack of readiness
on the part of their captors. The German forces in Greece and on
Crete were simply unprepared for the size of their catch and at a
loss as to how to deal with them. They gathered the Allied prisoners
together in hastily assembled enclosures, or used existing barracks
and hospitals as temporary prisons. The facilities were either
inadequate or nonexistent and there was initially no food, no
medical supplies and no clean water. Dead bodies littered the
landscape and disease was quick to spread. According to Reg
Worthington the worst experience of all, at least in the beginning,
was the lice.

One of the greatest things in that camp was lice. Body lice. Everybody had
lice. I don't give a bugger who he was, he had lice. If he was in Corinth Camp,
he had lice. You couldn't control them. So then at one stage the medical mob
decided something had to be done with these lice, because they're very
debilitating, lice. They're living off your body.

So the Germans marched us down to the foreshore, long, gradual area where the water is only this deep and then a hundred yards on, it may be that deep. Not a lot of depth to it. So strip off, hold your hands out and go through the Germans and they sprayed you. 'Right oh, go and have a swim.' So you start walking off. 'Jeez they're biting a bit.' By the time you get to the water you're just about fast enough to go into orbit. Because this stuff, whatever it was, the bite, the burn the sting! Oh God it was terrific! We had this swim and wash this stuff off you, come back and put your same old clothes on again. Hopeless. That happened a couple of times. Hopeless. You're putting the same clothes back on again. I hate lice.

REG WORTHINGTON

In a doomed attempt to combine both humour and learning, and perhaps even to try and take the men's minds off their woes, one prisoner in that first camp, who had some scientific knowledge, gave the men a dissertation on the various members of the lice family – the genus *pediculus*. There was the *pediculus capitus* he informed them – the head louse; *pediculus corporis* – the body louse; and *pediculus pubus* – the crutch louse. The reaction to his lecture was not recorded.

•

Apart from the organisational nightmare that the flood of unexpected prisoners represented for Germany, there was also the cost – a toll it could not afford. Since the end of World War I, the country had been constantly shaken by political and social upheaval. The Great Depression had taken it, along with the rest of the Western world, to the brink of collapse, and debilitating labour strikes and grinding poverty had become commonplace. Then, when economic recovery had finally begun, the Nazi regime placed all available funds on a one-way channel directly into the military. There was no money for POWs. Still, as the war progressed, Germany ultimately honoured the Geneva Convention, the international agreement that governs the treatment of prisoners. For the most part, anyway.

The Japanese permitted no such niceties. They refused to sign the Convention and, from the first day of their POW camps to the last, they exhibited a deliberate and pitiless disregard for prisoner welfare and wellbeing.

Bill Coventry and Thomas Smith were part of the Australian garrison called Sparrow Force which landed on Timor just days after the Japanese attack on Pearl Harbor. They were there to defend the island and its all important airfield. It was obvious to Australian command that Japanese invasion of Timor was imminent, but air attacks prevented reinforcements from arriving on the island and Sparrow Force was abandoned to its fate. For four days they fought courageously against a far superior enemy, but short of ammunition, food and water and with 84 dead and 132 badly wounded, 1124 men were forced to surrender on 23 February 1941. Now they faced a far more lethal war. More than twice the number of those killed in that first battle would die in captivity under the Japanese. And the deaths started early.

The Japs formed us up and marched us back towards this Oesapa Besar place, and we got a realisation of war because as we came to little spots there were heaps of native bodies and Jap bodies on a funeral pyre, burning, and the smell was something terrible. And it started to rain and boy when it rains, you know, tropical rain. And they put us all together, all sitting together in a little rise of ground and as the rain came down we just sat there all night, and it rained and rained and we just sat in the rain, no food or anything else, just waiting to see what happened by the morning. By the time the morning came the whole thing was surrounded with water, we are on this little hill, and then they moved us on the next morning.

At the place called Oesapa Besar they formed a prison camp because we had made wire emplacements around it in case the Japs had landed; our boys had put a barbed wire circle around this particular bay, so they put us in behind our own barbed wire.

BILL COVENTRY

There was only a dirty lagoon there, and . . . most of the chaps that drank it got dysentery and diarrhoea and that out of it, because it was polluted water, until they got latrines dug. Except the latrines were right next to the lagoon. Which wasn't very nice. They had these thunderboxes, as we called them. Luckily we had the beach, the sea, right near us, which we could go in. But the thunderboxes got invaded with maggots. You sat on the box and you got them all over you and you had to race to the water to clean off again . . . It was pretty disorganised. Then they made us build our own huts, and bunks and all that, out of bamboo. Everything was made out of bamboo and atap, what they called atap, the thin, palm leaves. That was our quarters, then, for six months.

THOMAS SMITH

Nearly 1000 kilometres away from Timor, across the Sunda Strait, many of the men from HMAS *Perth* were taken to the town of Serang, on the island of Java. Six hundred prisoners were confined in the cinema there, sleeping on the bare floors and breaking up the seats to use as cooking fuel. They had no water for washing and no toilets. The only clothes they possessed were loincloths, leaving them completely exposed to malaria-carrying mosquitoes, and the only treatment they had for the dysentery and diarrhoea that ripped through them till it reached epidemic status . . . was charcoal.

Able Seaman Fred Skeels was twenty years old. He'd already survived the sinking of his ship, near-starvation, dehydration and exposure to the sun causing his oil-covered skin to bubble in the heat before he finally arrived at the Serang cinema.

Up above the stage of the theatre there was a balcony, and the Japs had got a couple of machine guns mounted up there and, of course, you had soldiers marching around with their rifles, all around. We were lying facing the screen, as it were, facing the stage, and the orders had been given by the Japs – no man was to lie down during the day, you had to sit up, and you sat in rows, you weren't supposed to speak to one another, but they couldn't stop you talking. You had seats to sit on, and you just sat there with your knees up as best you could. That's how you were supposed to stay.

Well after a few days you sort of couldn't do that, and you'd stretch out and now and again a nasty Jap would come along and stick his rifle butt into your chest or your back and tell you to sit up . . . I was there for four weeks.

. . . But that was the standing rule, during the day when you got off the floor, you had to sit up. And often they would enforce it, just out of sheer thuggery, they'd do it for the fun of it, you know? They'd just go around and bash everyone that they could reach, and beyond that sometimes, just to get what they wanted you to do. And their method of bashing you was either a slap in the face, across the head, a rifle butt on your back or your chest or your stomach, a boot, anywhere they could reach you with their boot they'd use that. And so you realised what they were going to do and what they can do and what they could do, and so you lived within those boundaries, to save yourself any suffering. You never sort of bowed to their will, but you never broke your spirit, you just kept quiet and kept out of the way of the swines, and that was it.

FRED SKEELS

Along with nine other men, Fred was finally moved from the cinema down the road to the Serang Jail, where he expected conditions would be better. They weren't.

At the jail in Serang I immediately went into a cell, it was only about 15 feet long, had two concrete platforms with an aisle down the middle, the platforms were about 6 foot long with a metre between them and there was 27 men in there when I got there, and up on the door it said, 'This cell is for six occupants.' There were 27 of us shoved in there.

. . . Every morning there was a bucket pushed in there that we used as a latrine, all of us, and then when the meal came around, they brought another bucket and put that next to the latrine bucket, and that was our rice that we had for the day. And the rice often was as dark as your pants, you know, it was dirty all the time. It was cooked by the other Javanese prisoners that were in the jail elsewhere, but it was a filthy situation there . . . I never imagined that I would have been able to live through it, thinking about it later on, you wondered how the hell you did.

FRED SKEELS

All across South-East Asia, thousands of captive men and women were wondering the same thing.

•

So, they were alive – imprisoned, but alive. No small thing in the middle of a war. But there was no time for relief, or even serious consideration of their future. The immediate need, the fundamental rule of survival that would become a daily obsession for them all, was food. How to get it and how to keep on getting it. It is a terrible thing to be so hungry they all say, to be so hungry that everything else pales into irrelevancy and you're left like an animal, expending your life's energy on simply staying alive. In today's world, where concerns over obesity are the stuff of daily headlines, it's irresistible to wonder how we'd manage. If we managed at all.

We were put in groups of 100 with our own drum cut in half, that was our cookhouse. I don't recall where we got the wood from but one of our blokes, he was the cook, and supplies were given to us in bulk and it wasn't very much, and he'd cook them and do this with it and help make the best of it. I know at one stage a little fox terrier dog came into the area. I think he was a foxie. Small, a dog similar to the size of a foxie. We all chased him and our bloke caught him. He tasted pretty good in the stew. Poor little dog. But survival is very strong.

We were sent off into different work parties after the Germans had organised us. I was one that was lucky enough to get sent off into a work party frequently and you got extra rations, you might get half a biscuit or something like that. Half a biscuit to an ordinary person is nothing. But to us it was important. It was worth going and doing a bit of work to get half a biscuit.

REG WORTHINGTON

There were new manners to learn, a kind of survivor's etiquette. The division and sharing of food became all-important.

They had nothing on Salonika to give us much to eat but a bit of watery cabbage soup in the morning. And you used to get a small round flat loaf of bread that had to go to eight prisoners, so you got a little wedge. That in itself, if it wasn't serious, it was comical, because you'd select one to cut it and all the eyes'd be on it so that they didn't get any more than the next one, and then you'd draw cards to have your pick, and I can tell you I doubt if there wouldn't have been a sliver of stuff more on one cut than another. And that's all you got all day.

KEN DREW

If they were not to fall prey to the anarchy of self-preservation, then rigid rules had to develop. There was only a certain amount of food and it would never be enough for them all so cooperation was critical. 'Share and share alike' had never had such poignant meaning as it did in the camps, for men like Bob Simonson. Shot down over Germany in April 1940, Bob, just twenty years old, was only a couple of operations short of a full tour. The next year would change his view of what mattered in his world.

As far as the soup was concerned, we used to determine in the hut, there might be 50 guys in the hut, and they used to have a roster for who was serving out and where you came in the queue to get your meal because it was very important as to, if you're early in it, you get the watery soup. If you got down the end where the stuff had dropped down, even though they tried to stir it all up, but anyway the stuff always went down the bottom and so it was pretty important that if you were at the end of the queue rather more than the beginning of the queue you got maybe some sauerkraut stuff, which wasn't good but it was better than water, and some chunks of bony meat stuff. And all those sort of things were very rigidly observed. The idea was to try and give nobody an advantage over anyone else and particularly not to cause any antagonism between people. You didn't like the thought that somebody was getting any advantage.

 . . . It was rather funny how things were important . . . we used to sit around and eat and take as long as you possibly could to eat it, of course, and there'd always be one guy who could always take longer to eat than the rest of us and we always used to get upset about him because we've all finished and he's got a little bit more to eat and, 'Why don't you finish when we finish?' He had this ability to make it last longer, and the same way with the bread. We had this chunk of bread and you could cut it about that thick and if you had a sharp enough knife, you could cut it into really fine thin bits and you'd eat a thin bit and you'd come back a bit later on and eat a bit more. So this was an ability you had to make it last longer. It was very important; you had nothing else to do . . . it was your big thing in life. So that's what we did, imagine how crummy an attitude you could have.

 . . . Nothing, absolutely nothing was wasted. People used to get to peel the potatoes. I think you even used to get volunteers for peeling potatoes, but you peeled a potato and you didn't waste anything. They were pretty terrible potatoes, they had holes and black things . . . and we found that actually there was an advantage in that if the rubbish didn't get too messed up you could go and get some of the potato peelings and if you had a sharp enough knife or a razor blade, you could get some more, even though we reckon there's nothing left on it, you could actually get a little bit more off it . . .

 That's where we were, pretty mercenary, pretty minor but it wasn't so minor then.

BOB SIMONSON

Sauerkraut was not a common food in Australia in the 1940s but at least it was recognisable as food to the men imprisoned in Germany. The prisoners of the Japanese were generally treated far worse than their countrymen in captivity in Europe. The food in Japanese camps was always inadequate, usually bad and, in the beginning at least, regarded by the men as a bad joke.

Somebody told the Japs that we had no food, what [was] he was going to do about food, and the Jap informed that person that there was plenty of food there at the entrance to the camp, and they found three bags of rice. Well, being Australians, we don't know anything about rice in the thirties. The only thing my mother used to make, a rice pudding sometimes with eggs and bread or something, and custard sort of thing, boiled rice in that way, we didn't know how to cook it, Australia didn't know how to cook rice in the thirties and forties, not like we do today.

So they asked all the fellows to supply their dixies, which is our eating dixie, and we dug several long trenches, gathered up burnable material and made long fires and put the rice – I mean, they knew that you boiled rice. So you put a dixie of rice, and you put some water in it and put it in the fires and, of course, as the water boiled the rice came over the top of the dixies and put the fire out and then it didn't cook and everything. Oh, so we found out – but slowly, as time went by we learned how to cook rice, didn't we?

BILL COVENTRY

Most of the rice the Japanese issued to their prisoners was of the worst quality, so inferior that they would never eat it themselves. It was often contaminated with rat droppings and worms, or made up of whatever grains could be gathered from the harvesting floors. Right across South-East Asia and into the Far East, wherever the new Japanese empire extended, rice was the staple food of prisoners everywhere and simultaneously loathed and desired.

In China, thousands of civilians had been caught up by the Japanese when they invaded the country after Pearl Harbor. Howard Walker, the son of missionary parents was taken as a fourteen-year-old boy into the POW camp in the ancient walled city of Yangzhou.

There were three meals. As I recall it, breakfast was a sort of rice congee, but it was really pretty awful rice, it was probably condemned rice from somewhere.

And the bakery baked a little, what would be a sort of smallest bread roll for every person, every day. So we got this bread roll and this rice congee for breakfast. Lunch was usually some sort of stew, it had to be stew because that's the only ingredients they got was stuff they could put into stew. In the evenings there was again stew and if we were lucky we used to get some meat sometimes, probably a bit of buffalo, little bit of pork, stringy stuff.

And not only was it pretty awful it was completely inadequate . . . I was a growing lad and should have been putting on weight then but they weighed us and in the first twelve months I lost 8 kilograms at fourteen years old. So that was the food problem.

HOWARD WALKER

Howard Walker would have been considered fortunate by many – he had meat 'sometimes'. The endless, numbing monotony of a rice diet turned many a group of imprisoned men into fantasists, dreaming up meals and remembering past feasts which they described in loving detail to each other at night. The cooks, once they had learned how to actually prepare the stuff, did everything they could to vary it or season it, using vegetable dyes to change its colour. They even attempted to flavour it with grasses and grease from shoe polish. But rice it remained. Howard remembered a camp poet in Yangzhou who translated their miseries into verse.

At the prison camps in China, conditions were not so nice.
And we fed on a diet that was wholly, solely rice,
Not rice as mother knew it, nor done as she used to do it.
Not baked rice, nor flaked rice, with sugar and with milk rice,
And all as smooth as silk, no, we got glued rice,

Half stewed rice, stone cold rice, grown old rice,
Unfit for even dogs, the sort they threw to hogs.
We got broken rice, outspoken rice, that argued with your plate,
Unpolished rice, some polished rice, some few years out of date.
We got burned rice that wasn't rice, like bits of festered cinders,
We got boiled rice, quite spoiled rice
And kerosene drum oiled rice that no one could call rice.

We got baked rice and caked rice that weevils made their bed in,
We got bad rice, sad rice that fills you with its sorrow,

We got podgy rice, stodgy rice that meant tummy pains tomorrow.
We got limed rice, grimed rice and ought to have been crimed rice.
Disrupted rice, corrupted rice, undischarged rice, bankrupted rice,
We got sloshed rice and squashed rice, but never any washed rice.

Half-cast rice, half-mast rice; we got lots of jungle grass rice,
We brewed rice, we chewed rice, the lucky ones they spewed rice,
We starved on but we lived on, in spite of everlasting rice.

ANONYMOUS

The radical change in their diet immediately showed in the prisoners' health. At first, constipation overtook most of them, resulting in many a terrified soldier consulting the regimental doctor about his inability to go to the toilet for anything up to two weeks. Very quickly afterwards though, they would remember that time with longing as the chronic diarrhoea of dysentery and frequent urination overwhelmed them. They had to find other sources of food and, like prisoners everywhere, they began to find ways to trade. In the European camps, this was a little easier as the prisoners of war were permitted some contact with the locals.

We were taken out on wood parties which was marvellous. I was a non-smoker. We got ten cigarettes. It was frowned on very much if you exchanged those with a smoker for his food, but outside they were wonderful. You could get a loaf of bread for two cigarettes. You could get a dozen eggs for four cigarettes, so it was trading with the Germans that you would meet outside, basically farming communities nearby. And while there you were collecting your wood to bring back, a marvellous source of extra food for people. The guards allowed it because they were hard put to feed us.

JOHN MATHEWS

Three boys, friends of Howard Walker in China, simply took matters into their own hands with all the carefree daring of adolescents.

One of them was called George Courtney, his brother Eddy and another fellow whose name I've forgotten. George and Eddie were a little bit older than me, two or three years and they were fitness fanatics, bodybuilders, and they kept this up to some extent, exercising and so on. I think they felt the lack of food probably more than most of us. And they began to get the wild idea of climbing over the wall and leaving camp at night to get some food to eat and coming back again. They observed the guards when they did their rounds and felt that they could do this. And I mean it wasn't razor wire or anything like that on the walls. And with two or three of them they could handle getting over the walls okay. They wouldn't allow me to be involved, I was too young fortunately.

And so one night they tried it, one dark night they got over the wall and walked to the nearest Chinese village, which wasn't very far away. The Chinese of course were delighted to see them, hated the Japanese, and welcomed them. And they had a great meal at a little restaurant there and came back and climbed back into camp and oh it was great. And they thought, 'Oh what a wonderful thing to do!'

But of course that was going to be a once-off, but as time passed they again began saying, 'Well gee you know, that wasn't difficult was it?' Or, you know, 'Why shouldn't we do that again?' And eventually they went over again. No problem, great meal, came back. And so they started doing this a number of times. And inevitably they got caught. Very fortunately, they got caught climbing back in not climbing out, otherwise they most certainly would have been executed escapees.

But the three of them were caught and taken up to the guards' room, which was just below our room above. And I'm sure there was nothing in the Japanese guards' manual to tell them what to do with people climbing *back* into camps. So this was a puzzle with how to punish these people; they'd done something very serious and they had to be punished. So they did the obvious thing and they sort of tied them up and they beat them. They beat them and beat them, all night we heard them thumping them. And it went on the next day and the next night, and the next day they let them out. Fortunately they were fit fellows and young and well fed at this stage and they survived and they didn't go over the wall again, they put up with the food.

HOWARD WALKER

Hunger bred larceny. Men who would never have considered stealing so much as a comb in civilian life became experts at theft, bribery and fraud. Perhaps it was an ingenuity born of a hard, pioneer life, or the recidivism that convict ancestry bequeathed us as a nation, but Australian soldiers rapidly became far and away the finest thieves in the camps. They were nicknamed 'hydraulics' because they could lift anything. In Timor, Bill Coventry and the men of Sparrow Force were model exponents of the five-fingered discount.

We were unloading these ships and carrying heavy boxes and things up to these little houses and stacking them, and we found out that there was some food in some of these boxes. So we took our turn, drop off to single file, dive into one of these things, get into the boxes, open up the food and have a bit of a feed and then come back, and then it is your turn and it is your turn, you know.

Well, I'd had my turn and I am back on the work party and Bill Rainbow, he is in there . . . opened up the tin and he is eating away whatever was in the tin, and a Jap came in. And the Jap lined him up and spoke roughly to him in Japanese and Bill just said, 'Oh go and get a woolly dog!' you know. And with that the Jap hit him, and Bill just opened up his eyes and said, 'What the so-and-so . . .' you can imagine his language, '. . . do you think you are doing!' So, *whoo!*, in one blow Bill knocked the Jap clean off his feet and he knocked him out.

He realised what he had done and he said, 'Oh, things are pretty tough.' So he came out, shut the door and everything else, and said, 'Don't go in there,' he said, 'I just flattened a Jap!' Well within a few hours we were all lined up and this poor little Jap with his face all swollen up like . . . going along trying to pick out who hit him, but he never ever found Rainbow. You don't hit Bill Rainbow I tell you, *whomp!* . . . We called him Bollocky Bill, Bollocky Bill from the Bush.

. . . Then there was another time, we were all pinching stuff and the Japanese captain came on and lined us, we all had to line up on the side of the street. And he called out, Captain Campbell I think it was, and he lined him up and he told Campbell that the Australian men are '. . . very bad soldiers, steal everything, terrible. Japanese soldiers very honourable, do not do that.' 'Ah no,' said Campbell. 'No, no, no. Australian soldiers just as honourable as Japanese soldiers, never do anything wrong, all fine men,' and everything else, and the Jap is getting cross with him.

All of a sudden the Jap hit Campbell across the face, knocked his cap off and three tubes of toothpaste fell out. Well, all hell broke loose, he screamed and roared for a bit. Then machine guns were up on top and we thought, 'Gee, this is going to be nasty.' And they had the machine guns on top of the edge of the buildings. So they got a big army tent fly, big canvas thing, put it down on the ground and said, 'Everybody go round it.'

And you should have seen what was in that tent fly by the time it was finished; everybody had to empty out their pockets . . . but we will never forget this officer saying how wonderful we were . . . boom, cap fell off and out the . . . oh dear, oh dear.

BILL COVENTRY

Survival was all about making the best of whatever food came your way, regardless of how you might have felt about it before the war. Ron Zwar was a 21-year-old farmer from South Australia who was used to a plentiful supply of food, even during the Depression. But from the moment he entered Stalag IVB in Germany, his major concern, and that of the 16 000 other men there, was the food.

You'd get three little spuds cooked in their jackets, no five little spuds. I said three because there would only be three edible, the other two were riddled and you couldn't eat them, and one little round of brown bread made of a lot of *ersatz* [imitation] materials and there was a lot of timber sawdust mixed in with it. You could get a loaf of bread and hold it and just rub the bottom and after a while you had a handful of very fine sawdust. And that bread, if I'd brought a loaf home it would be as good today as it was then, just moisten it a bit. It had no goodness in it, just roughage. It was edible but sourish. Had no goodness to it but it just kept the body and soul together.

And you'd get a little bit of margarine, and if you heated it up . . . it would turn to water. Not even oil, it was mainly water and it was made of black coal. The coffee was made of acorns, roasted acorns. The soup we got was mainly grass and would have little bits of a huge big turnip, you see them in the market here, like a brownish turnip. They were called *mangelwurzels* – in peacetime they fed them to the animals. They would chop these up and throw some of that in the water and that would be a soup with grass and whatever else chopped up. Now and again there would be a little bit of meat in it.

RON ZWAR

The prisoners in Germany also had a little extra fortune when the Germans, abiding by the Geneva Convention, agreed to allow them access to their Red Cross parcels on a regular basis. The parcels saved many lives.

There were New Zealand food parcels, Australian, British, Canadian and American; five different types. And now and again we would get Argentine bulk food in, so you might get a large cheese or something and that would be meticulously hacked up amongst however many it was needed for. A food parcel could contain, firstly there were 40 cigarettes, a little slab of chocolate, there would be a little packet of dried fruit, maybe raisins or prunes or something like that, a little tin of condensed milk, a little tin of coffee, a little tin of margarine and the Canadians usually had a bit of fish in with theirs. And, oh yes, also a small packet of biscuits, usually hard, fairly hard, a bit like Sao biscuits but hard and they served a good purpose later. And that roughly was a Red Cross parcel. In the very good times you might get a parcel a week.

. . . So it was the Red Cross food parcels that kept us alive and brought us home. And we've pointed this out to the government, that it wasn't the Australian government that paid for our maintenance over there, it wasn't the English government; it was our own people back in Australia contributing to the Red Cross.

RON ZWAR

In the Japanese camps, however, the Red Cross parcels were almost always deliberately held back as a punishment, or pilfered by the Japanese soldiers who were themselves on a close to starvation diet. It meant that the prisoners had to obtain protein wherever they could find it.

The rice was pretty unpolished stuff, it was pretty dirty stuff. Later, our doctors wouldn't let them wash it because they had grubs and grub nests in them, and if you washed them out, you've washed all the vitamins out. So when you're eating your rice, you'd see little brown heads looking at you.

It's surprising what you can make out of a bowl of rice. When you've been on it for so long, you can think of roast dinners and . . . you can really imagine a nice roast dinner and roast potatoes . . . but you come back to the real world, after a while.

THOMAS SMITH

In Changi, food supplies were a little better than the far-flung camps, due to its closeness to the port of Singapore. But even there, Sheila Bruhn, desperately trying to keep some flesh on her teenage frame, resorted to eating food she would previously never have dreamt of.

First of all I found a worm. It was such a nice fat worm, and so I thought, 'I wonder what it will taste like?' And then I found another worm, and then I found a clot of soil with lots of worms, and so I gathered them all up and I cooked it, of course being worms when you cook it there is nothing left but skinny bits. But a little bit of salt on it and it was quite tasty.

Then I found a nest of baby mice, and once again hunger overrides everything and I looked at it, they were only that big, tiny little things. Nice and pink, and I thought, 'I wonder what that tastes like?' And before I knew it, I had opened my mouth and swallowed the thing. I was very disgusted with myself, I will admit, and I tried to make myself sick but I couldn't do anything about it. I was ashamed of myself too, to think that I had gone down that low, to eat a poor little mouse. I apologise to the worms that I see these days, but not to the mice though.

SHEILA BRUHN

In Germany the origins of some food became seriously questionable.

One day someone sang out, 'Eh!' He said, 'I've got a bit of meat!' Just a morsel floating in his container, and then someone else let out an oath and I said, 'What's the matter?' He found a human tooth in the bottom of his dixie. Now how did that tooth get in there and what was it from? It was a human tooth. We like to think that it was somebody in the cookhouse . . . must've felt hungry and had a bite and lost a tooth without knowing it, and threw the lot back in the pot before he was caught, before he was noticed. That's what we like to think happened; we don't like to think it was anything else.

RON ZWAR

It's not hard to sympathise with Ron's desire to reject the notion of an alternative source of the tooth in the soup. The experience of John Mathews, however, a radio operator from Bomber Command, placed the origins of his food beyond doubt.

We had large cauldrons of soup, rich in flesh and it was very sweet, and I actually didn't like it and I thought it was making me ill. They came up with teeth with gold fillings in them and someone identified what were bones of a hand. There had been a hefty air raid 24 hours before. 'Well, three of the bodies make a soup of them.' And we had been cannibals. It was once, and it was once too often.

They were German civilians. We understand it had happened elsewhere too. It saved the massive number of graves that could be encountered but the flesh actually offended me. Maybe . . . I don't know why but it offended me. The other prisoners were often violently ill. The reaction was to just throw the whole pot out . . . I'd got down from 10 stone to round about 6 stone, with the three days on the toilet and I was still trying to come to grips with eating anything. The weight just went. You could almost see it go.

JOHN MATHEWS

The average age of the Australian men imprisoned by the Japanese was a little over twenty. Few of them were strangers to hard work, and the deprivations of the Depression had toughened many of them to the point where their expectations of what life could or would offer were almost embarrassingly low. But even they were reduced to almost caveman-like acts of survival by their captors.

I got taken on the wharf in Singapore in late July, before the war ended, and I walked away, I had done my share of digging, we were digging holes, square holes, metre square holes or something, half a metre deep on the wharf. And I walked away and I walked about oh, 10 or 12 yards away, because at the side of the piece of timbers that were stacked there I could see a little bit of green, grassy stuff growing. We were very bad with scurvy, and if you could get a piece of green grass and bear to put it in your mouth, the sting was something terrible, but it relieved the scurvy for a while.

So I went over to pick this little bunch . . . and the Nip from over there saw me move away from the party, he must have thought I was going to break through from the camp away from the fellas. And, of course, I got me little bunch of greens that I was going to share with the blokes around me, coming back to the work party, and he came down and got me, and he gave me a belting with his fists and all that sort of thing for a while, and I was very, very groggy.

And when he finished he went back to his post and I sat down in the hole with my feet in the hole on the edge . . . see there would be two men or three men, one shovel. So you could only work alternating about each turn, and it wasn't my turn to work anyway, so I sat down to get rid of this groggy feeling and he went over there and saw me sitting down, so he came back with a pick handle, he got stuck into me with a pick handle.

Now if the war hadn't finished I would have been gone, because your system was so bad that if you got a hiding like that you didn't live through it, but I was lucky the war finished a couple of months later and I got away with it. But my story is not sad, you want to hear some of the boys, get up the Burma Railway and things like that.

BILL COVENTRY

As bad as it sounds, Bill Coventry is right. Conditions on the
Thai–Burma Railway, where many of the men had been sent, were
inhuman.

We were getting sicker and weaker, and more malnourished, because your
food, you didn't get any niceties in your rice, like a bit of cucumber or whatever
they called it, which you did in Java, and you got a little bit of that in Singapore
when we were there. But we never got anything like that in Burma. You might,
if you're lucky, see a few fish eyes floating around in the rice, or you might get
a little bit of vegetable which became known as cucumber or radish, whatever
you like to call it.

    . . . Now and again you'd get a little bit of fish brought into the camp in big
boxes. Most of it had to be thrown out before they could use it, because it had
gone rotten, and now and again we had meat in the camp, but the cattle used
to always be driven up to the camps by road, you know, on hoof, and they were
in a very, very malnourished condition when they left wherever they came from,
there was nothing left of them but skin and bone when they got to us, and by
the time the Japs had taken their share of the meat, there was very little left for
the troops. But you might find a little bit of something floating around in your
rice, didn't matter what it was, you ate it because that's all you had.

    . . . If you didn't go to work you didn't get fed, if you stayed back in camp
your rations were cut down so you had to share – you got what was given to
you as a sick patient, which was never always as much even as a working man.
So if you got sick you were not as well off, it meant you didn't work but it didn't
mean you were going to survive any quicker, it was no good being sick.

FRED SKEELS

The prisoners of war of the Japanese were deliberately forced onto
a starvation diet. It was the principal reason why so many of the
men died. They were starved to death. There was no greater
atrocity committed by the soldiers of the Emperor than this.
The survivors have never forgotten. When Bert Beecham spoke
of the Japanese attitude, his arms became tightly folded, his
face implacable.

Conditions were so filthy. It was mud and it was faeces, there was no clothes,
there was no self respect, they were less than animals and they breathed and
they worked. That's what they're s'posed to do. They weren't even fed. So how

the hell could you have respect for a thing like that? You had anger, you had pity but you had bugger all else. Used to make you very, very angry to see men working with faeces running down their legs. Legs swollen up twice their size, their testicles swollen like footballs, going out to work. Could you have respect for that? Hatred, yeah, I still got it. I still hate them for what they did to my mates. But no respect, no. Respect for the dying. Does that answer your question?

. . . It made me angry, very angry that people could do such things to other people and not worry or care what they're doing. I mean, the treatment of the POWs workin' on the railway line was absolutely horrendous. Not only in the way they were treated, the way they were fed, the way they were beaten, the way they were abused, the way they had no clothing. Some of 'em were working in bare feet and a piece of rag tied 'round their waist. That was their gear, they worked in that and they slept in it, ate in it. That was all the clothing they had. They might have had a blanket back at camp but that was wet.

The food was disgusting if you got it at all, sometimes twice a day, at one stage there we got it once a day and people were dying like flies. We had cholera, we had malaria, we had dysentery, we had scrub typhus, we had beri-beri. What else did we have? Well that's a few to get on with it. And people were dying like flies. We were burning up to 30 bodies a day. You can't imagine, you'd be talking to your mate in the morning and tomorrow morning he'd be dead. Twenty-four hours of getting cholera and then he's gone. And this happened for nearly three months of the time we were away.

. . . That's the sort of people you were dealing with, they were animals. Animals wouldn't treat their young like that. But I get very angry, there's a lot of hatred in me with the Japanese.

BERT BEECHAM

LAWRENCE CALDER

GAVIN CAMPBELL

RALPH CHURCHES

RAPHAEL CORBETT

GEOFF CORNISH

BILL COVENTRY

3

'There was some good officers, but there were a hell of a lot that weren't'

In any locality where there may be prisoners of war, they shall be authorized to appoint representatives to represent them before the military authorities . . .

FROM ARTICLE 43, THE GENEVA CONVENTION, 1929

We are an orderly people, we Australians; generally known as a polite, decent mob. Despite our long-cherished belief that at heart we are rugged individualists, a nation of nonconformists who rebel against rules and authority, in fact we're remarkably well behaved. We operate well in queues, for example, frowning upon clowns who try to jump the line and responding to requests from those in charge with mostly good-humoured obedience. Civil insurrection is virtually unknown in this country and, if alcohol was taken out of the equation, half of our police forces could stay at home on the weekends, so compliant would we be.

When Australians entered POW camps, they carried these character traits with them. They each had a long, personal history of obedience to authority. They'd learned it at home from their parents, from their teachers at school, from the law as young adults and then from the most authoritarian body of all – the military. They were trained, disciplined men and women and their commanders expected them to continue that way.

But this was not an ordinary situation. In their other life, they could always get free time from whichever authority figure controlled their days, whether it was home leave away from the service, or the simple privacy of the pub, or one's own room. You could always score a breather from the boss. Not any more. Prison was permanent – there was no relief. And the first place their thoughts turned was to those they believed had caused them to be imprisoned. Especially after a debacle like Singapore in World War II.

I think they were all ashamed of themselves, and not being given a go and it was stupid of the government to send them there, knowing full well that the place was already fallen, virtually. They never got onto the mainland, they landed on Singapore Island, and they never got off the island. They fought there for two or three weeks, and then they had to capitulate with the rest. They were very frustrated and they were very disappointed in . . . the whole army, right down to the prime minister, I suppose . . . they realised it was just a waste of time, the skills that they'd learned for four years or three years, had not been utilised anywhere, you know?

. . . Even in little debating groups they'd tackle their officers on it: 'Why us, and why did we get sent?' The officers couldn't answer.

FRED SKEELS

The officers commanding the men captured in Singapore faced a unique problem – they had thousands of soldiers imprisoned, still in the configuration of the platoons, companies and battalions in which they had fought. On the one hand, this military structure should give them the advantage of unity and loyalty, but would it hold up under these new pressures, would order and obedience stick?

For the first few days in Changi Gaol, an overwhelming numbness robbed everyone of initiative. The Japanese left them pretty much alone, even to the extent of not constructing a perimeter fence – that would come a little later. And it didn't matter anyway – where could they go? Why should they bother? They considered themselves failures, and, in general, thought the same of their officers. Their first battle had also been their last, and excuse and blame sat heavily in the crowded air of the jail.

Then the long-standing habits, the strength of training, kicked in. Units were assembled; officers and noncommissioned officers

(NCOs) began issuing orders. The food supply was inadequate and that had to be quickly corrected. Latrines had to be dug, washing facilities constructed and buildings adapted to their new uses. The men responded in the correct manner, though it must be said that, initially at least, they quite properly refused to build the requested officers' mess.

Inactivity was seen by the commanders as the men's worst enemy and so they marched them and paraded them till the quadrangle was blue with complaint. But the discipline kept them focused and active and although they hated it, they hated it together.

Elsewhere, surrender did not bring such cohesion. Around 1100 Australian soldiers had landed on what is now the Indonesian island of Ambon, in December 1941. They were designated as Gull Force by Army Headquarters, and their task was to join with Netherlands East Indies troops to defend the strategically important airfields on the island. But, as so often happened in the early months of that war, they were inadequately prepared, ill-equipped and hopelessly outnumbered. Almost 800 Australians survived the inevitable Japanese attack and went into captivity. They were given a rude introduction to their new circumstances by their commander, Lieutenant Colonel W.R.J. Scott.

Discipline was going to rags, it was disintegrating fast until Colonel Scott took a very strong stand and said on parade that anybody that queried an order from an Australian officer would be handed over to the Japanese for punishment, and that was the final straw. The men lined up on the road and he strolled up and down with the cane going whack, whack, whack, and we hated him from that point.

I can't explain to you the mental attitude or feelings of people in that situation. I couldn't believe some of the things that I felt then, based on what I was before I went into the army. It is impossible to put people who have never been in that traumatic situation, so far from anything you have ever experienced in your whole life, to suddenly be thrown in and to have to make decisions which are virtually life and death and which are going to colour your thinking for the rest of your life, no matter how short it might be.

WALTER HICKS

The Australians captured by the Italians and the Germans in World War II did not enter imprisonment as whole units or squadrons and would mostly find themselves 'in the bag' with soldiers and airmen from Britain, Canada, South Africa and the United States. The combination of nationalities made for a very different, disciplinary structure. The British outnumbered all the others and their officers, at least, were still seen by the troops from the dominions as the overlords, the commanders of the empire. The dominance of British numbers meant that control and command generally fell to them in the guise of the camp leader, called the Senior British Officer (SBO).

We had eight in a room and we finished up with eighteen, six three-tier bunks in exactly the same space. And the feeling of being hemmed in by people was huge. You wanted to bust a chap's nose in just because he was there and he was too close to you. As they say, 'invading your space' is the term now. You knew it was no good losing your temper or picking a fight or something like that because you had to live with him 24 hours a day.

Okay, there were some minor scuffles in the first week or so. But people soon learnt to control their temper and to control their attitude and to be more thoughtful of others. In that way it was wonderful discipline, you had to pull together as a unit and you did. It was treated as an RAF station. There was a Senior British Officer; the most senior ranking from our side was in charge of the camp. Although we didn't have to obey him, we would do what he suggested.

GEOFF CORNISH

The SBO was responsible for basic discipline inside the camp. Within limits, he had power to punish the men under his command but he was also expected to fight for their interests with their captors. It was a no-win juggling act – stand up to the Germans and earn plaudits from the men, or keep a tight rein on punishment and control and so gain respect, and therefore possible concessions from the camp commandant. Some SBOs were more successful than others.

Group Captain McDonald, our Senior British Officer, was only late twenties, early thirties, and he, in his welcome speech, turned round and said, 'In this camp discipline is going to be stronger, you will experience more than you probably will on a RAF base back home, but when we're playing sport or anything like that I'm McDonald not Sir, you don't turn round and say, 'Excuse me, Sir, would you pass the ball,' you say, 'Pass the bloody ball McDonald!' And that's exactly what we did when the senior officers played the junior officers or the senior NCOs at soccer, there'd be a bunch of blokes standing alongside the field and every time the poor old group captain got near the ball you'd hear the bunch of voices go, 'Pass the f . . . ing ball McDonald!' And he'd grin like mad, he reckoned that was great.

REX AUSTIN

It has been said that being a POW is a great leveller for all kinds of men; that once you enter captivity it doesn't matter which service you come from, which unit you had been a part of or what your task had been. But officers *were* treated differently to other ranks (ORs). The international law known as the Geneva Convention, which governed the treatment of prisoners of war, was originally drawn up by men from the privileged classes and its clauses continued that very same privilege to officers. Men of rank did not have to work and received greater amounts of pay for work from their captors than the ordinary soldier. And both of those apparently straightforward facts could mean survival rather than a wretched death in some of the hellholes they endured. Even punishment was meted out in a prejudicial fashion.

The Italians had a peculiar system, they had two systems of punishment – 'rigorous punishment' and 'simple punishment' – and that varied depending on your rank. If you were a private, you copped the lot, if you were a sergeant you were a little bit better off, and if you were a warrant officer you were better off still . . . in other words, warrant officers got no period in irons, sergeants got two hours of irons per day for the first ten days, or something like that. Corporals and privates got five extra days, they got a month instead of 25 days, and they had four hours in irons per day for the first ten days, all for the same offence. I asked one of my Italian patients 40 years later how this was and he, being an old Italian naval bloke he said, 'They punished the privates for being silly enough to follow the sergeants.' Whether he was being facetious . . . ?

THOMAS CANNING

The old world of class and privilege came under enormous pressure during World War II, so much so that by the end of hostilities it lay disrespected and undermined. And nowhere was that pressure greater than in the camps controlled by the Japanese. The 'we're all gentlemen' myth of World War I and the assumed superiority and rights of the officer class were held up for brutal examination in South-East Asia, and when they were, many officers would fail the test miserably.

They were so filled up with their own importance, being in charge of all these prisoners, you know, and they never did very much, for our prisoners, the officers, they weren't a very trust . . . well not trustworthy, shouldn't say they were distrustful, but you had no faith in them, you know? No respect nor faith, it wasn't always their fault, because they weren't allowed to work, the Japs wouldn't let them work, but the old British officer's principles are a cane under the arm and swagger sticks and polish your boots and all these sort of things, you know? It was a good thing for discipline, but if you had no boots to polish, and no polish to put on your boots, you couldn't very well look very presentable, and we never ever looked presentable whilst I was a prisoner, as such.

Fred Skeels

In the beginning, the relationships between officers and men in the camps were similar to those they knew from regular service life and the agreed disciplinary code between the ranks held up. The greatest difficulty for the POWs in Europe at that time – was boredom.

Some of the guys suffered from psychological problems, 'barbed-wire fever' as they used to call it. Blokes just didn't behave the way you would expect them to behave but you'd become very tolerant behind the wire and that was one thing that Group Captain McDonald in his welcome speech at Sagan said to us: 'Whilst you're behind the wire you will be required to rub shoulders with guys who under normal circumstances you wouldn't be bothered with.' And that is very true.

You learned to swallow the words if you were going to go crook about something, you learned to turn around and shrug your shoulders and sort of say, 'So what?' . . . If you're going to punch up every bloke who disagrees with you, you're going to be in trouble. So you learn to roll with the punches, if I can put it that way.

We had one guy commit suicide. One young Canadian fellow at night-time climbed out of his room and climbed up on the roof and attempted to jump over the wire from the roof. He was shot in so doing and everybody sort of said, 'Dickie did it deliberately'. I understand he had a major domestic problem back home and that's the worst manifestation of it; the other is just the fact that guys tend to forget what they're doing.

REX AUSTIN

It was food that changed everything. Or rather, the lack of it. When hunger, and then starvation, became the all-consuming passion for each and every prisoner, some simply could not manage and they discarded any veneer of honour and discipline. They took sustenance wherever they could find it, regardless of what that theft might mean.

Reg and I . . . we bought a loaf of bread. Black bread, bought it from the senior NCOs' camp which was opposite us, and we had it by the side of our beds and it was stolen, and we reported the stealing of it. Group Captain McDonald threw a complete parade of all the people in that compound, announced that Tyce and Austin had had a loaf of bread stolen and turned round and gave them an hour or two hours, I forget which now, for the loaf of bread to get returned, and if it wasn't returned then if the culprit was found he would be court-martialled . . .

When the next lot of bread came up, the first loaf of bread would go to Austin and Tyce he said, and then the remainder would be cut up on behalf of everybody else, and that's exactly what happened. No culprit was ever found and the next time bread was issued and it wasn't issued you every day, it was issued every few days, Reg and I were given a loaf of bread, then they calculated what the ration would be for everybody else. And that's the way it went.

REX AUSTIN

The crunch question for all prisoners was how far would you go to keep yourself alive? How much risk would you take? In their enclosed world, where civilisation and brotherhood clung to existence by a fingernail, the line between what was outright thievery and what was simply self-preservation, was razor-blade thin. But to cross it, and then be detected, meant enduring the permanent judgment and loathing of men who had stood by your side from training through to battle. It broke men, that purgatory of exclusion and punishment by their mates, and it presented both officers and NCOs with harsh choices.

Lawrence 'Jack' Calder had survived the siege of Tobruk, carrying out with him a wound and a decoration. Then he'd fought at El Alamein before being captured. He'd seen hard days he could never have envisaged as a boilermaker back in Melbourne. Now though, as the company sergeant in charge of a prison camp in Sicily, he had to make decisions for which the army could not prepare him.

We were in this particular camp and we found that one of the cooks, who was an Australian fellow, was having more than his share of food. We substantiated that without much trouble and we asked the Italian authorities if they would do something about disciplining him and they said, 'No, this is one of your internal matters. You do what you want with him.'

So we tied him to a tree and another fellow and I gave specific orders that he was not to be touched, physically, that he could stay on that tree. You could spit on him, abuse him, do what you like as long as you don't physically touch him. We left him there for two days. Let him off. Nobody would talk to him.

He never stole again. Neither did anybody else in the camp. That was our way of penalising a thief. If we had marked him in any way we could have been in trouble later.

. . . He became more or less a hermit type. Eventually when we got to Italy I don't know. Because he was never in the same camp as me. So I don't know what happened. He got back home here, to Australia, the same fellow. We heard that he was living in such and such a place. We wrote to him and told him that there would be reunions and that, but never heard a word.

LAWRENCE CALDER

As conditions deteriorated and the supply of food reached near-starvation levels, the officers and NCOs kept a tenuous hold on discipline, mostly by staying aware of every undercurrent and intervening only when the threats of violence became all too real.

There was one case which we had to stop in our hut. A couple of chaps had a hatchet ready to cut a fellow's hand off because he was caught stealing some bread, and that was very far fetched, but usually it would amount to beating a chap up. These things would happen somewhere else and they'd be just between individuals. Nothing was ever sanctioned from a hut point of view . . . whatever retribution took place was always on a personal private level . . . we were basically responsible for discipline within the hut, so you would watch certain things and maybe if two fellows were squaring up maybe step between them and say, 'Calm it down boys.' That sort of thing. Because, as I say, when stomachs were empty and people had a lot of time on their hands, then arguments and so on could develop fairly easily.

ALEXANDER KERR

In training camps back in Australia, sergeants and warrant officers had occasionally allowed the men to sort out an offender from within their ranks in their own, mostly violent way. Armies have always done this. It was particularly the case if a man was caught, say, stealing from his mates in the barracks. No doubt it was rough justice, and sometimes highly dangerous, particularly if the punishment went too far; during World War II one thief was dropped out of a second-storey window in a camp in New South Wales; another 'accidentally' fell overboard from a troopship after he was found taking money from his mates' kitbags. He was never seen again. Even so, the NCOs found turning a blind eye a useful tool to bond the men together and make the power of the unit stronger than any individual, a quality they would desperately need in battle.

On Hainan Island, though, while under Japanese control, Australian soldiers became vigilantes – but only after the officers approved.

We only had two cases of people stealing food and instead of handing them over to the Japs, the boys got permission to have their own punishment. So they bared their backsides and put them across a table and gave them a few good whacks with a bit of cane and from then on we never had any more, that we know about anyway. That stopped that. It only happened the once and sort of everybody got together and decided to form a vigilante committee, as they called it, but they had to ask permission of the head officers, could they have it, and they gave them permission on condition that they tell them what they were going to do first. So it was all passed legal and everything. And they weren't getting hidings like they would get off the Japs, they were just given something they would remember and it brought them into line, that's all.

ATHOL 'TOM' PLEDGER

•

It's a truism to say that the ultimate purpose of all military training is effectiveness in battle. But the discipline that brings that about, that makes an efficient soldier is, of necessity, composed of one part blind obedience and one part compulsion. Without it, how could a man possibly go forwards under fire? Yet there was just a shell of that discipline left in the camps. Theoretically, of course, every one of them was bound by army, air force or navy regulations, but any fool of an officer who insisted on that and that alone would be rejected by his men or simply be either ignored or sabotaged. Moral authority was what counted behind the wire, plus clear perception and unyielding conviction that won men's hearts. And above all, courage.

We had some very, very good officers and we had a few weak officers. In fact we had one officer who, when he went into action, he couldn't get out of the foxhole, he sat there and cried. The corporal had to take over the platoon. I won't mention any names, the poor man is dead now but he was a leading light in legal history.

The average bloke who came from out in the bush turned out to be good officers; the ones they picked up from around the city some of them were a little bit dubious. Most of them had all seen army service in the friendly battalions like the 30th Battalion and the one that was formed around Bathurst, the 2/10th, they were nearly all local officers from there, but they did dig up a few people around the city area who got in for different reasons. We had some very, very good corporals, excellent corporals, and they made things very, very easy for some of the officers.

DES MULCAHY

Des Mulcahy himself, was clearly a natural leader. He went into action in Singapore as a corporal, was made a platoon sergeant when the losses became too great and within 24 hours after that, he was the company sergeant major. In Kobe, in Japan, where they worked as slave labour in the coalmines, he was promoted to warrant officer. Des understood his men.

The crux of the whole matter fell on your shoulders. You were responsible for all the men. They eventually took all the officers away and left one officer, from 8th Div Sigs, and the lieutenant with him, but they were more or less just to keep the numbers in order and to make sure the rations were drawn and things were done in camp. When it came to the work party everything fell on me, so I was responsible to take the work party out and responsible to bring the work party home. Any troubles with the work party it was my trouble, not theirs.

The only power I had was my own power over the men, that was all. Actually, I couldn't do anything as far as power was concerned, I couldn't dock the men, I couldn't say, 'I'll put you on a charge sheet.' Because we had no law with us, you just had to look after the men and do the right thing by them and hope they would do the right thing by you. That is what it amounted to.

. . . You had the odd rascal. You had the odd bloke who would try and beat you on a point or two but you wore him down eventually. It was just a

Des Mulcahy and members of the 2/19th Battalion after the war had ended

case of just battling on and keeping things churning over and they got into a routine, a certain routine worked out in the camp and the men got to work in it, and there was no trouble at all . . . You couldn't let frustration take over. If you had a collapse and let frustration take over you would have men running in all directions doing mad things. You had to keep them under control all the time.

The discipline they got in the army helped a great deal in the prisoner of war camp. They knew what discipline was and they were prepared to accept it. The only trouble was we had a lot of the young boys that came over there and they had only been in the army for about a month. Some of them couldn't even fire a rifle when they got there because they went straight into prisoner of war camp. Some of those were a bit hard, but they soon learnt.

Some of the old boys got them by the neck and scruffed them around and they soon learnt the trade and got back into line. We didn't have to do that very often. It was something you more or less tried to do by experience and show them how to go about things and tell them, 'That is how you do it. You don't do it this way, you do it that way.' They soon caught on. They realised they were prisoners of war and we were old hands at the game and we were doing all right, so they fell into line. They came around fairly quickly, fairly well. Some of them were only fifteen or sixteen years of age.

DES MULCAHY

Talking to ex-prisoners of war about their officers is a little like being caught in an endless rerun of the great Akira Kurosawa film, *Rashomon*, in which a crime is witnessed by four individuals but, later, each one describes what happened in mutually contradictory ways. If you name any of the prominent prisoner officers, particularly from the South-East Asian camps, an argument will immediately begin that perhaps owes more to individual reactions to the officer in question than fact. But these were harrowing times, in which every accepted understanding of human behaviour and humanity was either brutally crushed or rendered bitterly laughable. The mundane and the ordinary could not survive.

Six months after the Allied surrender in Singapore, the Japanese removed all officers above the rank of full colonel from Changi and sent them to camps in Manchuria. Most would survive the war there. Left behind was the new AIF commander, Lieutenant Colonel F.G. Galleghan, better known to his men as 'Black Jack', as much for his manner as his dark complexion and hard, brown eyes. Galleghan was 45 years old when he was taken prisoner. He'd been a sergeant on the Western Front during World War I, wounded twice, but denied a commission, something he neither forgot nor forgave. He rose through the ranks of the Militia between the wars till, as a lieutenant colonel, he was given command of the 2/30th Battalion, 8th Division, and sent to Singapore.

Black Jack Galleghan was old-school, a passionate believer from the 'Church of Holy Obedience' whose main conviction was that discipline not only controlled the men but sustained and promoted their morale. Some of his junior officers said years later that they were more frightened of him than the Japanese. He was inflexible, obstinate, a stickler for rules and regulations, and undoubtedly saved many men's lives because of his refusal to give up or give in. He hated the very idea of his men thinking of themselves as 'prisoners' and, after the war, refused to associate with any prisoner of war organisations. 'You are not going home as prisoners,' he told his men. 'You will march down Australian streets as soldiers.' The young, regimental medical officer, Lloyd Cahill, looked upon him with humorous affection.

Changi, with old Black Jack Galleghan in command, he still ran it as though it was just the first day in the army. You had to behave yourself all the time and he was a first-class commander. He was the man of the day. I always remember after we had been in about three months, some smart-arse, a few of them decided they would take him on and they grew a beard, started to grow a beard, and he heard about this and had them paraded to him.

These three coves came and fronted to old B.J. and he said, 'What do you fellows think you're doing?' And they said, 'We're growing beards, Sir.' And he said, 'Don't you know you're not allowed to do that?' And they said, 'Oh well, we haven't got razors, Sir. We can't do anything about that.' He said, 'How are you getting on, are you able to eat all right?' And they said, 'Oh yes, we're okay.' 'What do you use for that?' They said, 'We've got a knife and a fork.' He said, 'Get that bloody knife and go and get it sharpened and you'll have no beard when you come to see me in three days' time!'

Everybody then shaved every day, and that's the way he ran the camp.

LLOYD CAHILL

If the martinet ways of an officer like Black Jack Galleghan saved some of his men, the fiercely protective attitude of the medical officers did even more. While it may seem absurd to use a word like 'lucky' where POWs are concerned, there is no other way to describe the good fortune the Australians had with their doctors and medical orderlies.

Over 100 doctors, all volunteers, had entered captivity in Singapore. Thirty-six would go with the men into the horrors of Thailand and Burma and many, many men walked out of those camps again only because the doctors had been there. Every prisoner of war from Thai–Burma knows for an incontrovertible fact that *his* doctor was the only doctor worth talking about and while he's sure that the others did a good job, only *his* medico deserved the ultimate honorific of 'a good bloke'. It feels tribal, this loyalty between the men and their doctors, a ferocious devotion born out of unimaginable hardship and displays of courage that left them all linked to each other in profound and unspoken ways.

The doctors seemed to have no doubts about their role. There was a kind of moral righteousness about their work and, coupled with the extraordinary medical challenges they confronted, dealing with diseases they'd never seen and with little or no resources, it may have forged a steel-like obstinacy in them; for in the face of entrenched Japanese cruelty, they just would not retreat from care for their men. As their reward, they suffered abuse, torture and cowardly beatings, always the beatings. Lloyd Cahill remembers two of the more extraordinary medicos: Bruce Hunt and Edward 'Weary' Dunlop.

Bruce Hunt, yes. Well, he's an extraordinary man . . . it was just natural for him to be arrogant but he didn't mean to be arrogant. I thought, 'Well, I know you pretty well and I know you're a very able cove.' It wasn't until I read his obituary that I realised that he had hidden a lot of his achievements or I didn't know about them. He didn't talk about them at all. He was a most able man and a ruthless fellow.

When he came up there, to that camp, he came in and took over immediately. He took over from the medical people and they were very happy to let him do it. So then he called the fellows up and just said, 'Now this is what you're presented with.' And laid it out to them. 'Now you've just got to pull together and get together if you want to live. Your only chance of getting back to Australia is if you do what I tell you.' Bang. 'The first thing that you'll do is get all this earth off this ground here and we'll get this camp going.' So then he said, 'Who can do this? Who can do that and do the other?' And then he had the whole thing organised and that's the way he went on the whole time.

Then he'd be fighting the Japs. Even the Japs respected him. They'd call for, 'Hunt Tai, Hunt Tai', Major Hunt. He'd argue with them and up on the railway line, when he was marching up, he got into an argument with some Japs, little Nips, and he wouldn't give way to them so one of them had a No. 5 iron, golf iron, and he just bashed him with that and fractured his hands. Bruce had his metacarpals broken. And he was just fearless of them. He didn't care. He just talked down at them.

Weary Dunlop was the same, I'm sure. I saw Weary when we passed through and when he was talking to me a little Jap came up and started screaming at him and Weary didn't take any notice because Weary was a very tall fellow, Hunt was sort of tall too, so the little Jap ran off and came back with the bamboo and screamed at him again and he still talked as though he didn't notice him. And he started belting Weary around the legs and Weary just kept on talking as though he wasn't there. This chap gave up eventually. Now Hunt was the same as that. You see, he got beaten up with the No. 5 iron and took no notice and just went on.

The troops just admired him. He was a tough man but whatever Hunt said, they'd do. If he said, 'Go and disappear over the lake there, I don't want you any longer,' they'd go. An amazing fellow. And he was tireless, he'd just go on, and even when he was asleep he seemed to be thinking and planning what he was going to do next day. Sometimes he was right, sometimes he was wrong. If he made a mistake, well, that's just bad luck. It didn't worry him in the least.

He had become a very successful physician in a short time and of course then he enlisted and went away. He had been in the army. You know, he just missed out on the 14–18 war. He was one of those fellows, he was worried about the fact that he just didn't get away and he was into this one and he'd better get into it properly, which he did, of course, and with a great deal of distinction . . .

I don't know how he would get on these days. I just don't know how Bruce Hunt could exist. Authority was nothing to him, he hated it. *He* was the only authority. Wonderful man.

LLOYD CAHILL

In every camp there was never enough food, vitamins, drugs or medical supplies. The officers became a target for many of the doctors who would demand some of their money for a fund to buy supplies on the black market. Most officers gave willingly, but some had to be badgered and the doctors were not backwards at informing them of their responsibilities. Tom Uren, later to become a federal minister, was only 21 years old when he saw just how effectively this system could work under a leader like 'Weary' Dunlop.

Weary's leadership wasn't pronounced or boasted about or loud-mouthed in any way. He was a very kind, quietly spoken human being. He led by example. And I didn't realise until after I read his diaries how tough it was for him to get the officers to contribute their money into the central fund.

Under a sham, under the Geneva Convention, the Japanese paid our officers a medical allowance and Weary was able to convince them to put the majority of that into a central fund. The men that went out to work were paid a small wage and they did likewise. They put the bulk of their money into the central fund. And Weary would use that money to send people out and trade on the black market, dealing with Chinese and Thai traders . . . and he was using this, what he could get, for the drugs and the food to look after the sick and the needy. And in our camp, under Weary, the strong were looking after the weak. The young were looking after the old. The fit were looking after the sick. And there was this collective philosophy.

Just before the wet season set in . . . about 400 British came in. And for temporary arrangements they had tents. The officers took the best tents. Senior NCOs took the next best and the men got the dregs. There was this British tradition. Within about six weeks, only about 50 of those men marched out. They'd either died of dysentery or cholera . . . they did very little work but they suffered greatly. And only a little stream, a little small stream divided both of us. On one side, the law of the jungle prevailed and on the other side, was this collective spirit under Weary.

TOM UREN

But as the months and then years went by, the differences between the officers and the men became more and more noticeable. There was simply no question – the officers had the better of a bad situation and some made the most of their luck.

The officers never had to work, they had to go out on the line and supervise the troops. Now that put them in a pretty onerous position; although they didn't have to work they had to be the contact point between the men and the Japs . . . and we had a lot of our officers bashed in trying to stand up for the men, trying to get the Japs to accept the men's point of view.

But not all officers were the same and some officers were far better than others at doing that. And some didn't quite make the same stand as others but a lot of the officers put themselves into extremely onerous positions. I wouldn't have liked to have been in their position. You were far better off down the line working your guts out hoping for the best, rather than be up there facing the Japs all the time.

COLIN HAMLEY

On the Thai–Burma Railway the contrast between those officers who wholeheartedly stood up for their men and those who refused was stark.

People were disgruntled and whatnot and they'd disagree with some of the officers' attitudes and instructions and whatnot. 'We're POWs now, you've got nothing to do with us.' But that only happened amongst a few of them, generally speaking it was okay and personally speaking I'm pleased that we stayed in our own system rather than go to the *Kempei-tai*, the Japanese Military Police. It would have been disaster.

I think most of us saw that maintaining our own structure was important, and it was. Yes we had some rules; some of it was a little bit over the top, but generally speaking it was the best thing to do and I'm grateful for it anyhow . . . that way we had an approach, an official approach back to the Japanese and somebody to argue our cause when things weren't going as well as they should – so yes, they did a lot of good.

IAN WALL

There was one thing in common between the officers and the men – they all wanted to survive, to get home. To achieve this, self-preservation was everything; it was above duty, responsibility, sometimes even mateship. And only a rare man could withstand that elemental desire. The officers were better placed to receive any small privileges than the enlisted men and this produced envy and hatred in equal measure. It's hard to think well of your leaders when they're clearly better fed and clothed, and when they don't have to slave in the way you do. Rarely did it occur to any of the men that had they been in the same positions as their officers, they may well have behaved in an identical fashion. Once the mob 'got it in for a bloke', whether he be sergeant, captain or lieutenant, it stayed that way. In fact, that mindset still exists. There are prisoner of war officers who have never been to a reunion, never marched on Anzac Day, never contacted or have been contacted by any of the men with whom they shared so much deprivation and loss. Some feelings go to the grave.

Some artist or sketcher, he had sketched a sketch about that big, and pinned it to one of the palm trees, and I saw it there myself, it only lasted a day. I'm sorry I didn't snitch it; it would be worth a fortune today. On it was a troopship, sailing up the Thames, and all these officers are lined along the rail of the ship, and there's Churchill on the wharf and it shows the voice projection, and he says, 'But where are all the men?' And the voice comes back from the officers, 'They died that we may live.' I tell you what, there was a lot of officers in that camp who didn't laugh. They tried to find out who did it. They never found out who did it, but they would have court-martialled him.

THOMAS SMITH

Cyril Gilbert, the son of a cane cutter, had watched for every year of his childhood his father walk the length and breadth of Brisbane, looking for work when the cane season ended. Welfare and want were the two constants of his growing years and now, in a prisoner of war camp, he was not a man inclined to accept laziness and selfishness in another, regardless of rank.

We also reckoned we had the AJA, the Australian Japanese Army, our officers, some of the officers. One officer told a Japanese, 'I enlisted to fight the Germans, I didn't enlist to fight the Japanese. I have no trouble with you; I enlisted to fight the Germans.' Some of the officers, if you speak, well, I don't know, our majority of POWs would tell you there was some good officers but there were a hell of a lot that weren't good. To save their own souls, they couldn't give any consideration for the troops. So we classed them as the AJA.

. . . They had the food, they had the money, they got paid much more than we got paid by the Japs. See the Japs'd pay you, say, ten cents or fifteen cents a day, if you were out on a working party, with Japanese money. But the officers used to get about, oh, they'd get 40 or 50 cents a day and they didn't work, half of 'em. They never went to work, a lot of them never worked on the railways or never worked on the working parties at all. And if the Jap said he wanted them to do something like that, he'd say, 'Righto boys, you do that.' Some of them wouldn't argue with the Japs, whatever the Japs said they'd do it. We didn't have a very high opinion of some of them, I can tell you that much.

. . . Our CO, he died not so long ago down at New South Wales. He wasn't so good in action, but as a POW officer he was all right. He would only keep the same amount of money that the private got, the rest he would distribute amongst his men. When we were in the jail in the end of '44, he said to me, he said, 'How many of our unit is still in there?' And I let him know how many we had there so he give me five dollars for every man that was in there for Christmas you know, for them to buy extra things from the canteen and everything like that. Some of them were like that, others fought for their men, stood up for their men . . .

We had some ORs the same way. We had a cove . . . he was from our own unit, and even over in Borneo, they used to call him 'the White Jap'. He used to curry favour with the Japs and I think that's what saved his life because the Japs said, 'You better go, because otherwise you're not gonna live. You better escape. If you stop here, you're gonna die.' So he got out of it, but well, in my opinion he was a mongrel.

CYRIL GILBERT

Put men, any men, *in extremis* and distressing tales of betrayal, injustice and incompetence will always follow. It was ever thus. But perhaps the saddest of all leadership failures in our prisoner of war history arose from the troops who were captured on Ambon.

There *were* strong and efficient men among the officers in the POW camp on Ambon, but a series of misadventures robbed the unit of their best hopes. An Allied bombing raid killed two of the finest and most of the rest were transferred to Hainan Island, off China, in 1943. They were to suffer their own tragedy, but most of the enlisted men left behind on Ambon, under the care and command of the last of their officers, would die of overwork, malnutrition and disease brought about by one of the most brutal regimes of the war. A total of 582 men stayed behind – 405 died. And they were not helped by their leaders.

The officers had their own quarters and their own mess in this prison camp. They tried to live as best they could, as officers were entitled to live in the army.

They developed quite a sizeable vegetable patch where the bomb crater was, which was adjacent to their hut. And because they didn't go out on work parties, they wouldn't go out on work parties, they had all day long to establish and man their gardens.

Not surprisingly, they became rather attractive to us. Now I was never able to do this but occasionally there'd be fellows who would 'bandicoot' their crop . . . Do you know that phrase, bandicooting? They'd go under the ground, dig down under the ground and take what was growing under the ground.

. . . It's a matter of survival, the officers kept the fruits of their labour; they didn't share it with the rest of the camp, oh no, it went to the officers' mess. So it was pretty understandable, you'd agree, that when they got the chance at night-time, somebody would go and bandicoot.

Well the officers didn't like this, naturally enough, and as their task was to maintain discipline in the camp the CO got permission from the Japs to erect a barbed-wire cage inside the camp . . . It was, say, four corner posts and posts linking them at the top and then barbed wire rolled out between the posts to make a cage. The roof was all barbed wire and the walls were barbed wire. No shelter of any sort, a barbed-wire cage with a gate on it. And the reason why the CO got that built was to punish people who were caught bandicooting in their vegetable garden.

And as you might imagine, that did not endear the officers to the men. In fact, I blame in part the CO for hastening the death of one of my mates, Jack Morrow, because he was one of the ones that was caught and he was put in that cage, exposed to all the elements, had to spend several nights in that cage and then go out on a work party. But that was how our CO in the Ambon camp, one of the ways he maintained discipline.

. . . The CO said, 'I'm not going to have my officers humiliated in that way,' and thereafter made sure that there was an NCO in charge of a work party. So we had really little contact with our officers, didn't see much of them at all . . .

There was never, as far as I'm aware, no open hostility towards them, no physical abuse or anything like that but we just came to hold them in very low esteem. Mind you, there were exceptions, a few exceptions, but I think my view, my feeling when I came home, was shared by most of them, and there weren't many, but in the main we had a pretty low opinion of the officers. The CO especially, it was often remarked on and it's been remarked on since too, we rarely saw him; it was as though he was frightened of the Japanese and was content to let his front man, the adjutant, be the go-between between us and the Japanese interpreter.

. . . Very few of them ever bothered to come to a reunion but those that did were people that we had regard for, as it happens.

MARIC GILBERT

For the Gull Force men transferred to Hainan, events would become even more bizarre. At 53, Lieutenant Colonel Scott was one of the oldest commanders in the Second AIF. He had served with distinction in World War I on both Gallipoli and the Western Front, was twice Mentioned In Despatches, was awarded the DSO (Distinguished Service Order), and had reached the rank of major by the war's end. A more than admirable military career.

But between the wars he became deeply enmeshed in Australia with an organisation called the Old Guard – a mostly rural, secret army who had sworn to defend 'law and order' as they saw it, in the face of 'socialist revolution'. It might seem a curious artefact now, but there were 30 000 men under Scott's command in that army during the 1920s, and they came perilously close to violent action against other Australians.

Even stranger, during the 1930s, Scott had become publicly enthusiastic about Japan and the Japanese, spruiking the worth of their foreign policies and their national intentions. He had visited Japan at their invitation and lobbied on their behalf with the Australian government. Now, he was their prisoner.

Physically unfit and very much the wrong man in the wrong place, by the time he commanded Gull Force, Scott was incompetent and wrong-headed and his junior officers had completely lost whatever confidence they may have held in his command. On Hainan Island he became progressively more fragile, perhaps even mentally unstable, until, in possibly the most appalling act committed by an Australian officer in the camps, he handed over one of his own men to the Japanese for punishment. The men who were there have never forgotten that day.

Poor old Jitter Roy. He was a woodcutter . . . he came from just over the Murray and he was a hell of a nice bloke, much older than most of us. He had beri-beri, which we all did, and some sort of sores or something on his legs . . . and he had been in the hospital for some time and the doctor said he was all right to go, but he was to bath his legs at all times, it didn't matter, as many times as he could.

Now up there we used to have a bathhouse with a big concrete trough in it and you could go in there and you had dippers to wash yourself, this sort of thing. They had certain hours which were for officers only and anyway, the doctor had told Jitter to bath and Jitter just took him at his word.

He was down there this morning bathing his sores and one of the officers, no names no pack drill, went in and said, 'What are you doing here?' And he said, 'I'm bathing me bloody legs!' 'Well,' he said, 'This is the officers' bathing hours.' And he said, 'But I've been told . . .' And he said, 'You are not supposed to be here and I will have to report you.' and he reported him to the colonel and the colonel reported him to the Japs and they took him over and strung him up on the horizontal bar and beat him 'til he was carried back to the hut unconscious.

And the doctor heard about it and I was in the hut, we were all in the hut. It was late in the afternoon I remember that, and Bill Aitken the doctor, I could hear him, 'You bloody bastards!' And he was racing up the bloody alleyway between the beds and I think he was going to kill the bloody colonel . . .

There was nothing we could do about it and I think everyone was so horrified that that had happened. I'm not saying that in some cases, I mean if even then, if you had a bloke that was against the government all the bloody time you know and you just refused to obey an officer, I suppose he was entitled to some sort of punishment. In this particular case, to hand a bloke over to the enemy for punishment knowing the type of punishment that they could possibly . . . I just I don't think any of us could accept it at all.

And poor old Jitter, he came through, he got home, and we were over just down here . . . at an army barracks and we were going through there on dental parade and he dropped dead. So he got all the way home and I would say that would have started him on the way – he wasn't a young man at all.

Ross McDonald

It was very close to a riot. Everybody was so taken back by it. From that day on they had no faith in Scott. Well he did some good things after – helped organise parties to get medicines and food and that into camp from outside and things like that. But that finished him as far as the troops were concerned.

Athol 'Tom' Pledger

It did indeed finish him. He remained despised by the men . . . and still is. Scott never attended a battalion reunion and would have been rejected if he had.

PAT DARLING

KEN DREW

TERRY FAIRBAIRN

JOHN FITZHARDINGE

BILL FORDYCE

CYRIL GILBERT

4

'It's amazing what talent there was'

'While respecting the individual preferences of every prisoner, the Detaining Power shall encourage the practice of intellectual, educational, and recreational pursuits, sports and games amongst prisoners, and shall take the measures necessary to ensure the exercise thereof by providing them with adequate premises and necessary equipment.'

ARTICLE 38, GENEVA CONVENTION, 1929

Understandably, a prisoner's first priority was food and water; for all else paled beside daily survival. But when regular sources of food, however meagre, were stabilised, the numbing routines of prison life became glaringly apparent and morale started to slide. Hope was in short supply, boredom plentiful.

That's one of the things as a prisoner; you develop fairly firm habits in terms of what you do with your time. The Germans had us on rollcall, every morning you were there at nine o'clock, every morning you stood there till the Germans finished counting you all and that could take an hour or more, a couple of hours at times, more than that at others. In the afternoon you had exactly the same thing; lights went out at a given time so you knew what you could do from one time to the next and that's what prison camp is really about. It's very, very monotonous. There's nothing that really excites you.

REX AUSTIN

You got up at typical six o'clock, army time, and you'd mooch around until it came to breakfast time, you'd go out and join the queue at the cookhouse and line up for your tucker. Morning breakfast usually consisted of what we used to call 'pap', and it was just boiled rice, instead of being steamed – it used to get boiled up into a mash, like a porridge, and in Java while we were there they used to also sprinkle a tablespoon full of sugar over it, because they had sugar in the camp. And so, that was your breakfast.

You'd have nothing to do then until the working parties that you might be in took off, and you'd just line up down the pathway there in front of the guard-house and they'd count you, and you'd get out into a truck outside or wherever you were going, and you'd go off to wherever you were working. Out there you wouldn't get fed during the midday meal on your working party, usually the Japs made no effort to feed you, and then you'd come back in the late afternoon, get counted again and just go back to your camp.

FRED SKEELS

In the end, they had only one place to go for any kind of intellectual stimulation or diversity – each other. And so they began the 'barbed-wire universities', the clubs, the concerts and the workshops, in a bloody-minded refusal to surrender the more civilised aspects of their remembered lives.

Stalag Luft III, in Poland, was a permanent camp for airmen; a camp that would later become famous for what was called 'The Great Escape'. Captain Geoff Cornish, an Australian pilot shot down over Holland, was an occupant of that camp and took part in the escape. But he remembers how lifting the men's spirits was, initially, the most critical matter.

The sheer boredom did drive some of the guys a bit stir-happy, a bit crazy. But to combat that the senior officers in the camp used to organise classes, and there were always elementary German classes, middle German classes or advanced German classes. Or French. It didn't matter what you wanted to do, there was somebody in that camp. Remembering there were about two and a half thousand people who had either finished their tertiary education, or were into it before they joined up.

If you wanted to learn photography, if you wanted to learn to make wine or distil spirits, there was somebody who would do it for you. If you wanted to learn Mandarin Chinese, Squadron Leader Murray had been in Hong Kong, in the Far East, for twelve years and he spoke fluent Chinese. You could learn Japanese. Russian was a very popular choice. A lot of people learned French while they were there. I mean, I had the science master from Edinburgh University giving me one-on-one tutorials in chemistry and physics! He was delighted, it kept him interested and occupied and it was great tuition for me.

GEOFF CORNISH

Small, oblong cardboard boxes weighing about 4.5 kilograms made it possible for these classes to catch and hold as a regular activity in the European camps. The boxes might contain cheese, biscuits, milk, sausages, margarine, bacon, tinned meat and fruit, marmite, chocolate . . . and the solve-all-troubles drink of the British Empire – tea.

The packages came, of course, from the Red Cross, and saved the lives, and the minds, of thousands of men. Along with regular mail, replacement uniforms and boots, they put strength into the prisoners and what had once seemed irrelevant or simply too hard to contemplate now became important as symbols of hope and life. POW education flourished.

I attempted to do some studies whilst I was behind the wire and you could not have had a better opportunity to study . . . There were guys there, RAF officers, Canadian officers, Australian officers and so on, who were highly qualified in every conceivable profession that you can think of . . . we had plenty of solicitors there, we had engineers there, we had one guy, a Canadian, who had been a lecturer in economics at a university in Canada. Now if you wanted to study economics, what better than to have a guy like that who would take all the time in the world because you've got it, you've got a full daytime to study and these guys could help you out?

. . . The classes were loosely organised, of course. It was a case of someone turning round and saying, 'Oh, what would you like to do, do you want to do law, company law, what do you want to do?' And the guy who was going to run that class would make himself known . . .

There was a bloke by the name of Percy Northropp who was an RAF flight sergeant. Percy Northropp was the middleweight amateur champion in boxing for the Northern Counties in the UK – he took boxing lessons. Wing Commander Stanford Tuck who was an RAF fighter pilot of great note during the early stages of World War II, he had a qualification in fencing, so he taught fencing and I think he had been an Olympic representative . . . there was even a professional golfer there who took golf lessons! Now you didn't have a golf ball or anything like this but you had golf sticks and you had woollen balls and he could teach you how to swing a golf club properly. If I had only been that interested in golf at the time; I regret now that I didn't go to his lessons.

There were exams run through the Swiss Red Cross. The university could set examinations and they would be done through the Red Cross and they would be monitored by a monitor in camp, so yes, people could do examinations. I don't think they could have done medicine or dentistry or those sort of subjects, but certainly, with economics, commerce, law, yes, they could do that.

REX AUSTIN

In South-East Asia, Red Cross parcels were often deliberately and criminally withheld from the prisoners by the Japanese. But even on their near-starvation rations, the desire for intellectual stimulation was never completely quenched. It was a matter of concocting it from whatever sources they could find.

Dr Rowley Richards had been sent with a group of men designated by the Japanese as A Force, from Changi to the Burma Peninsula, near a town called Tavoy. They were ordered to construct airfields for the Japanese, and, in this relatively calm period before the horrors of the Burma Railway began, they unearthed a small treasure.

There was a large British community in Tavoy itself, with the result that there was quite a large library with books in English in it and we conned the Japs into allowing us to get those books for toilet paper, to relieve sore backsides. You know, palm leaves get a bit rough after a while, and so we got these large numbers of books and we distributed them among the men, three or four each, or whatever they were.

Now they were everything from encyclopaedias to books of verse, philosophy – you name it. I don't know whether you know Will Durant, one of these American philosophers, well I first read him up there.

Now what happened was that it didn't take long for *Lady Chatterley's Lover* and a couple of others similar, to lose their appeal you know, that wasn't on, and *Golden Treasury of Verse* et cetera were the things that appealed most and the encyclopaedias – they used to pore over these things and look at all sorts of, the Seven Wonders of the World, or how tall is the Leaning Tower of Pisa and all sorts of stuff, and this captured their imagination, and as a result of these books we were able to run these quizzes as it were, going all the time and then at night, after lights out, they'd have a quiz and once a fortnight or once a month or whatever, if we were given a day off, they'd have a proper quiz session, a concert and a quiz session. So that blokes kept their minds pretty active.

CHARLES 'ROWLEY' RICHARDS

Captivity, hunger, beatings and despair. Nothing it seemed, could prevent their minds wandering across whatever topic took their fancy. Food, of course, dominated.

They were constantly interested and obsessed with food or the lack of it and some of them had the most amazing collection of recipes, obviously Dutch to start off with, and then with the British, you'd get all sorts of recipes from Gloucestershire or from Worcestershire or Yorkshire or wherever, whichever were their traditional dishes and so forth, and some of them had really an amazing variety of dishes.

There were others who designed houses, designed their dream house and I was very fortunate in that I was in a little group, my closest friend was John Shaw, he was an engineer, he finished up as Commissioner of Main Roads in New South Wales, and one of the group was a Tasmanian, Stuart Handerside, who was an architect. He'd started life as a builder and then did architecture. So he understood building from a practical point of view and also the aesthetic point of view, and I designed my house. I lost the design, of course, but this went on for weeks, refining this thing. The engineer would bend his mind to it and make various suggestions, and then the builder would look at it and make his suggestions and the architect would look at it from the aesthetic point of view and so it went on.

CHARLES 'ROWLEY' RICHARDS

In the absence of books the mind of a man could suffice, as long as he had something worthwhile to share. After HMAS *Perth* went down, Fred Skeels was thrown into an overcrowded cell in the infamous Serang Jail. Already in there was an escapee from Singapore by the name of Rohan Rivett. He had been the one who had broadcast to the world that Japanese forces had landed on the island. To Fred, who had not left Western Australia till he joined the navy, Rivett was a walking, talking encyclopaedia.

The cell I was in was occupied before I got there by a chap who had escaped from Singapore, spent about three weeks creeping down the islands in a boat with three or four other chaps . . . he was a journalist in Singapore . . .

But there were men there who were fairly, well, let's say educated blokes, and we used to have a lot of conversations with one another, which probably kept your mind off your own troubles, you know? As a journalist, he'd travelled all over the world, he worked for the BBC in Singapore, and if the Japs had known who he was at the time, they would have probably killed him, but he was under an assumed name from the time he was taken prisoner.

. . . He started a lot of debates amongst us all about different subjects and different places, and some of the others had been in other parts of the world. All I could talk about was Inglewood [in Western Australia], so that was all I sort of could join in. But I was interested in discussions on sport, cricket in particular was still then a very popular sport amongst we old blokes, AFL football didn't exist, sort of thing, and so we talked about the cricket matches between Australia and England, and we'd spend hours just talking about that, and comparing one batsman against another, or a bowler against another – you did anything to kill time.

But you were starving all the time, you were very hungry, and so you talked about food a hell of a lot, and some of the meals that you remembered your mother making, or what he'd had over in the Parisian restaurants or Budapest somewhere or other else, you know? All those things were interesting to me. I found it so, and he probably saved the sanity of most of us. None of us wanted to go crazy but we were all still sane enough to try and retain what we had.

FRED SKEELS

Sometimes the capacity of one man to pass on his knowledge to another would reach a level of intensity and complexity difficult to conceive of outside the wire. The claustrophobic conditions that oppressed some could provide a hothouse of learning for others. Geoff Cornish, who was to make a postwar journey from bomber pilot to doctor, found his mentor in an English medico called Norman Montennuis.

I can't remember our first contact, probably I reported to sick bay with a sore hand or something like that. But he was always interested in everybody in the camp – as a doctor should be, we were his patients and he was very professional – in who we were, what we were doing, what our interests were. I probably confided in him that I one day wanted to be a doctor too.

And then he would come in and just sit down at a table with me and he had been trained at the Middlesex Hospital in London and he had been through his exams about three years when he joined the army and got posted to France and got caught at Dunkirk . . . so he was not that much older than we were.

And, as I say, because nobody else in the camp wanted to talk medicine we gravitated together, because I just loved hour after hour of medical talk, where I was picking up and I was learning – well, private lectures instead of being in a class of a hundred, it was one-on-one with a wonderful teacher. So it fostered and we became very, very good friends.

. . . He started to teach me as much as he could, doing things like how to bandage properly, what ointments to use, what simple stitching, how to put in a local anaesthetic. How to work with simple aseptic techniques so that you didn't contaminate anything with your fingers. The same treatment you would get in a casualty department, virtually identical . . . It was the opportunity I had been asking for. To be able to do medicine, that's why I joined the air force in the first place, the end picture that I never lost sight of. And here was a huge step forward closer towards it, actually being as close to a real medical school as I could get. And I learnt a tremendous amount in that year with him. A tremendous amount.

GEOFF CORNISH

In the civilian camps, children were often incarcerated along with their parents, and once the routines of the camp had been established, it was clear that the adults would have to find a way to continue, or even begin, the children's education.

In China, many of the civilian prisoners remained in the same camp for much of the war and this helped them to cobble together all kinds of schools, despite the loud protests of their kids. Schooling was a constant challenge for the adult prisoners who acted as teachers to provide what was needed, but their inventiveness, and their success in terms of the outside world, were extraordinary. In Pu Dong Camp, the fifteen-year-old Howard Walker was one of the children who benefited from the adults' efforts.

Cambridge University had an external studies, I think it was called, department, which set the syllabus for . . . primary and secondary schools for British colonies, any part of the British Empire, the Commonwealth, if they wanted to use it, and it was used throughout China in the British schools there. And at the end of the secondary schooling you sat for what was called a Cambridge School Certificate which would be equivalent to the Leaving Certificate here in Australia. And if you achieved a particular level in that, you were granted matriculation into university.

Now those who started teaching in Pu Dong Camp of course had no access to the current syllabus, the Cambridge syllabus. So what they did was to create for each year a new syllabus and teach to that, with the different levels of students that were in the camp. That was enormously time consuming and kept them very busy, which they probably were pleased about. And that kept us schoolchildren busy too, which we weren't so pleased about, but we were pleased about it later.

And we had to study, we were still under extreme difficulties because there was no paper supplied, or pencils or pens, and we had to sort of gather these from everyone who could let us have them. We used to use toilet paper if there was any to spare and jam tin labels from people who got parcels and every bit of paper they could possibly use was given to the school. And the whole thing was taken very seriously and I received a few years of very good schooling there.

. . . To complete that story, in 1945 when I was sixteen, I reached the stage where I was ready to take the School Certificate at the end of secondary school. Again, they didn't have the Cambridge examination for that year, so these people set an examination as precisely as they could, to replicate what would have been a Cambridge School Certificate examination – questions and essays and so on. And we sat for it under examination conditions and first they marked the papers and awarded, for those who achieved that, a Pu Dong School Certificate – and I've got a beautifully scripted, drawn-up, Pu Dong School Certificate – which they hoped that after the war would be accepted in the countries which we'd be returning to. They also sealed the papers and, immediately the war was over, they sent them to Cambridge University with a letter explaining what they'd done, hoping that Cambridge would come to the party, which they did. And Cambridge then sent out School Certificates to those that they thought were worthy of it.

HOWARD WALKER

In the segregated women's camps under Japanese control, keeping hearts and minds alive was a more complex and difficult task. The Japanese were uncomfortable with women displaying any form of independence and the women learned to use subtler methods to

get the very small concessions they did gain from their captors. Pat
Darling and the other Australian nurses did not take long to get
organised and working.

We had 24 people in our house . . . seventeen of whom were nurses, and we
elected a British camp commandant and the Dutch elected a Dutch camp
commandant and they dealt directly with the Japanese so that we had no need
to have any contact with them. The guards of course marched up and down
and back and around, and you were supposed to bow to them as you passed
them. There were a few incidents of face slapping, but not a lot.

It was in this camp . . . that they also started a series of talks in the evenings
because the moonlight gets very bright and different people gave different talks
on things that had happened in their lives, and they were all very interesting
and that was good. And we formed a library. People who had books took them
along and it was as civilised as you could be in camp.

. . . One of the nuns offered to give drawing lessons, so I went along to
them and found that I could draw quite nicely . . . and we made cards from
a photograph . . . and they were quite good to play. I had found a bottle of
black ink which had been thrown out of the window when people were
escaping, and the nun only gave lessons for about three weeks and she
became ill. Well, you know, with the cloistered lives they lead it must have
been terribly difficult for them.

PAT DARLING

According to the Geneva Convention, medical personnel and
members of the clergy who fall into enemy hands are not to be taken
as prisoners of war. Rarely, though, were they ever released in World
War II, not by the Germans, and certainly not by the Japanese.
Their captivity presented particular challenges. For Sister Berenice
Twohill and the other 350 missionary fathers, brothers and nuns
captured by the Japanese when Rabaul fell in 1941, the problem
was less one of education and more that of keeping the faith.

We had our religious duties to perform; it does take up some time . . . if we
couldn't do it at such-and-such time, we'd do it another time. That's one thing
that the Japanese did not interfere with us in that way, they never did. Although
towards the end they told the natives, 'We are losing because you are praying
too much! You Christians, you praying too much, we are losing the war!'

. . . We had mass every day. We made a meditation every day. We had Adoration every day . . . Adoration is the Blessed Sacrament, and that's part of our duty. Then we have a spiritual reading every day, from a book of spirituality. Then we just have community prayers where we just pray for something special – special prayers that are composed for our community alone. It is what we enter for and what our aim is, to make the Sacred Heart that Jesus is, everywhere known. That is our motto.

. . . We had the Blessed Sacrament even in the trenches. We made a little niche in the mountains and this was where it was kept. We kept a little light that we had made out of coconut oil, and that was there all the time while we were in the trenches. We had mass in the trenches.

SISTER BERENICE TWOHILL

Sister Twohill was to be imprisoned for three and a half years on Rabaul. Her accommodation slowly degenerated from the

Sister Twohill (right) and the tunnels at Ramele

Vunapope mission buildings to native huts surrounded by barbed wire, and finally, to muddy trenches at the bottom of a ravine in the jungle.

•

The English author George Orwell could have been talking about Australians when he said, 'Serious sport is war minus the shooting.' And while it's facile to compare them, sport and war share some of the qualities we associate with that ephemeral idea of 'being Australian' – courage and teamwork, physical ability and mateship. The Australians who went to war did not leave behind their love of the game and they carried it into the prison camps as well. Like the classes, it beat back the tension and the boredom for a while.

There used to be volleyball competitions. The Yanks had a big court over in their area, and we had one in front of the camp, the barracks where I was. And they used to have quite ding-dong volleyball fights between the two nations,

Ken Drew and other POWs playing volleyball

and they used to get quite heated at times. And I suppose there was a lot of gambling went on too, amongst the blokes that had a bit of money or something. You know, might be a packet of cigarettes the Aussies win today, or something like that.

FRED SKEELS

Wherever they were imprisoned, and while their bodies held up, Australian servicemen found a way to play sport. If they didn't have the equipment, they constructed it, if they couldn't play their usual games, they adopted the local ones. And there was no better coincidence in the entire war than that alongside them in some camps was the old sporting enemy – England.

At one stage we had an oval which was big enough to play cricket and there was a cricket match, the Aussies versus the Poms of course, as you would expect, and the captain of the Australian team returned to Australia and played with New South Wales for a while – Keith Carmody was his name and he was captain of Western Australia.

REX AUSTIN

Raphael Corbett in high jump at Blechhammer Athletics, 1943

In civilian life, Keith Hooper had begun his career in journalism the old-fashioned way – by selling newspapers in South Yarra. By the time volunteers were called for the 2nd AIF he was a copy boy on the *Herald and Weekly Times*. His immediate enlistment meant that his ambitions to be a reporter would have to wait till the war ended. How curious then, that the strange combination of sport and prison was to set him on the path again.

I was involved with the camp newspaper, *Time,* which we used to get published once a month down in Regensburg. Alfheimmer, this camp commander, he was a great man. He used to let our editor, a chap named Dave Lewis of *Cavalcade Magazine*, London, go down to Regensburg with a German guard and get the paper printed down in a printery in Regensburg. In addition we used to have our camp newspapers, the *Australian Journal*, and there were a couple of others like that. And I'd be writing for some of these things or editing some of these things.

. . . We had a test cricket series there, where we played the English. We had rugby there, where we played the English and the South Africans. The sport was interesting. The cricket we could play. We played every summer except that summer of 1940, the winter except 1944 – 1944 became a bad time. That's when we were going in to the Battle of the Bulge and so on, but 1942 and 1943 mainly . . . we had two series of cricket matches. And we had a couple of good players there too, who had actually played state cricket.

. . . For the football series we made our own shirts. Old T-shirts and just dyed them, you know. One team had green shirts, one team had red shirts, one team had blue shirts. You could make the dye up quite easily out of various things. It's amazing the number of men we had there.

. . . I used to send sports results back home to the Australian newspapers, believe it or not, by bribing the censor with a tin of Players cigarettes and sent it to London, to the *Melbourne Herald* cable service, and they'd send it back to the *Sun News, Victorian Herald* in Melbourne. It was used there and also used in the *Courier Mail* in Brisbane, the *Advertiser* in Adelaide and the *Western Australian*. Mostly stories about sport, you know. One of my stories about the test cricket was published in the *London Daily Express* . . . because I thought, 'Oh well, we're playing the Englishmen, maybe I can sell this thing in England.'

When I got to England I went around to the *Melbourne Herald* cable office and there were two things there for me – one was a letter from Sir Keith Murdoch, my original boss, Rupert's father, congratulating me on being out of the prisoner

Rugby team at Blechhammer

of war camp, and I got a cheque from Trevor Smith, the London manager, for £100 which was a lot of money then. 'The boss asked me to give you a cheque for £100,' he said.

KEITH HOOPER

In Stalag Luft III, escape became a religion and every possible means was used to support the various tunnels that were constantly being dug. Sport was a useful tool for the escape committee in their efforts to outwit the Germans. Geoff Cornish was on that committee.

There was a plan hatched to escape in daylight, by cutting your way through the wire with a pair of wire-cutters which we had made ourselves, with material in the camp. But to do that we had to have a big diversion.

So, many people in the camp were told to take up some sport and there were homemade javelins flying in every direction across our open ground, guys doing shot-put and discus, sprinting, hop, step and jump, high jumps and this feverish athletic activity. And then we invited the commandant and his officers to come and see us put on a miniature Olympic Games amongst ourselves.

And when the commandant looked up the date that we were going to have it, it was on the day that our Swiss protecting power was supposed to be coming in to see that the Germans were doing the right thing. Well, if the protecting power could see that they had allowed us to have a sports day they would get great big marks. And they giggled to themselves behind our back, 'Oh, they boo-booed this time, they don't know!' Of course we knew.

So there was this feverish physical activity of sport going on for many hours during the day and the days were really good. I mean Laurence Reavell-Carter, who lived in the room that I was in; he was the British 1936 shot-put and discus representative at the Berlin Olympic Games, just three years previously, so if you wanted tuition in those sports he gave it to you. And the standard of ability got very high indeed.

But then you would get a directive from the escape committee, 'While you're training you have got to fall over and hurt yourself. No mucking around, it has got to be quite a bad fall, a sprained knee or twisted ankle or something that was quite obvious and not just put on.' Which meant then that you had to go to the sick parade and get attention, until there were so many people off limping around the place that the Senior British Officer called off the games.

The Germans were horrified, of course, 'What is the matter?' 'Well, particularly, what you call the sports field is so rough that we can't train on it accurately.' But also the running track, which was inside the barbed wire, a rectangle about a mile around, that was rough too. So we said, 'We want a good running track . . .'

We hinted, why didn't they put some smooth sand on it? They didn't have grass so there was no way of turfing it, so we just said, 'Look, ordinary yellow sand.' Because though it was black sand on the surface, the ground was bright yellow underneath and disguising it was one of our major horrors of tunnelling. So we said, 'Just put three metres of yellow sand around and we can keep that smooth and train on that.'

Well, they thought that was a good idea. So then we could disperse all of our sand on that and people would never know that it was building up . . . And that's how we successfully and unobtrusively got rid of most of our sand . . . and the Germans fell for it completely and absolutely.

GEOFF CORNISH

There is no more iconic prisoner of war film than *The Great Escape*. Something about its ever so English, 'what-ho, old boy' antics satisfies the audience's sense of the plucky underdog, and many of the mythical stories about POW life sprang from it. Hollywood took many liberties in the film, but the one thing they did get right was the vaulting horse tunnel. It was probably the most cunning use of sports equipment in the whole war.

There was a thing called the wooden horse and people did actually escape using the wooden horse, the vaulting horse where you jump from a springboard and get onto the horse. Well that, of course, is hollow inside, so we asked the Germans for timber to build a vaulting horse so that we could do gymnastics on the sports field, and they gave us the timber and we made it.

So after rollcall and breakfast in the morning we would bring this horse out, but it was always placed very carefully in the same spot, not too far from the outside wire. But in absolute open territory. It took about four to six guys to lift the horse out because, being Germans, it was pretty heavy timber and they just made light of it and picked it up and put it down in place and started their vaulting . . .

But when they carried the vaulting horse out, there were two guys curled up inside it, and when they put it down on the same place and started vaulting over it, the guys inside just pushed the sand away, there was a wooden trap buried underneath and when they lifted that out there was the start of a tunnel. And so they went down and deepened and lengthened the tunnel and put sand back up into racks within this horse, and then at the end of the gym session, they lifted up the vaulting horse up with the two diggers and all of the sand and took it back into the barracks.

And then we were able to dispose of the sand inside the barracks, and there is no evidence left, it is all covered over, and the Germans didn't notice, of course, because different guards on every shift and probably most days of the week. So there is nobody to say, 'Why are they always putting it on the same spot?' But to the Germans that would be logical. That was the place that it went and it should go there. So there was no suspicion over it at all.

GEOFF CORNISH

•

It's always been an ironic joke in Australia that bushmen and farmers can fix anything with a piece of No. 8 fencing wire. And like all jokes about the national character, there is some truth in it. The 2nd AIF was fortunate to have many of those same farmers and bushies in its ranks and they, too, went into the prison camps of the Germans and the Japanese.

'The true creator is necessity, who is the mother of our invention', said Plato, around 350 years before the birth of Christ. He might just as well have painted it on the wall of the hut in Stalag

IVB in Germany, where a farmer from the Barossa Valley, Ron Zwar, was holed up with his mate, Jim Simpson. They had an unusual problem . . . and found an unusual solution.

We needed knitting needles and . . . we had a canteen in the camp and with the International Convention of the Red Cross, all camps had to have a canteen but the canteen was useless, there was nothing in it worth having. So you couldn't go along and buy a set of No. 12 knitting needles or whatever. So the Germans used to ride little light motorbikes, little Excelsiors, they were, that was the name of them and . . . they had spokes. Some that long and some that long and so on.

A mate of mine who was the knitter, he had a pair of pliers. So we got the guard who rode his bike up to the hut and he came in, he knew if he'd come in, he'd get a cigarette. We got him talking and we gave him a couple more cigarettes and asked him whether he'd like to think about buying some soap off us and things like that, just to keep him involved while Jim Simpson, Jim was out there with his pliers nipping spokes out of his bike.

He got about sixteen spokes out of it – some out of the front wheel and some out the back. And he said to me later, 'Hell,' he said, 'I hope he doesn't strike a pothole on the way out or the whole thing will collapse on him!' And that's how we got most of the knitting needles. Some of them we got from the handles of dixies, they were just a bit thicker and we straightened those out and sharpened the points. So we had ample knitting needles. And not only did we knit, when I say 'we', he did 95 per cent of it, he allowed me to do some of the blue outside stuff, the sea as he called it, and we knitted a couple of tennis jumpers – one with a V-neck and it had a blue band around it – and they looked quite good.

We got the wool from the white flying jumpers that all the aircrew were issued with. Mine was taken off me when I got into camp, how some of the chaps managed to keep theirs I don't know, but the Poms, they were not very meditative in using things. The jumpers got ragged, so in the warm weather they just threw them out in the rubbish heap. And Jim would go along and wash them and then unravel the best parts of them . . . He didn't have to do it, it was just something he did and back in Kosciuszko he was a rough-and-ready old bushwhacker. He's still alive, he's about 89 now, living back on an old homestead that his parents had. Yeah.

RON ZWAR

Australian prisoners became brilliant improvisers, feverishly collecting and hiding any bits of glass, metal, string or wood that they came across or could steal. Anything that might, with skill and imagination, be transformed into a tool of some kind, or a medical instrument perhaps. Every plant, every local herb, every living thing was examined, tested, tasted, and, if possible, utilised in the constant struggle to survive. And nowhere was that more desperate than in the camps of the Japanese. As a medical orderly, Bert Beecham saw at first-hand how invention and imagination could save lives.

Without the old bamboo we'd have been nowhere. It was a very handy piece of wood, bamboo. You burn it, you sleep on it, make furniture out of it . . . and you eat it. Bamboo, yep. The shoots, bamboo shoots. We'd always start with the flower up the top . . . that is a delicacy in the tropics. So it's quite a very handy piece of equipment, the old bamboo. Don't knock it.

I'd never seen bamboo like it. Used to grow up about 80 feet and I've seen it that big in diameter with spikes on it about 6 inches long. Like 6-inch nails, they were. And they used to cut the real big ones down and split them, roll them out, and make platforms to sleep on. They used to make boxes out of it, make beds for patients.

In the army we had hundreds of very educated and highly skilled trades-people, even engineers and professors. So you've got an abundance of handy people around you if you're lucky, that are gonna do and make these things. They had workshops and they used to make artificial limbs and they used to make musical instruments, they'd wind their own strings for guitar. Very clever men, very clever men. They used to make blade razors out of files and they used to grind 'em down. You couldn't tell it from a Bengal razor, the old cut-throat . . . But they were incredible blokes, they could make anything.

They used to make vitamins and they had a grass factory going. They used to make yeast for vitamin B for the sick blokes, used to pump it into them with the old beri-beri. They were very, very clever men. They used to get the peelings off the fruit and the vegetables and a bit of sugar. We very seldom saw a sugar ration, we didn't mind that, but that went towards the hospital, towards the making of yeast and stuff for the hospital . . .

. . . A lot of vehicles had been bombed and blown about and bashed up, so they used to strip them down to everything but the chassis and the steering assembly and they'd leave the brakes on it and they'd have wires or a pole and they'd get a limbless bloke, a bloke with no legs, they'd put him in the seat.

He'd steer it and eight to ten blokes would pull this chassis down to the beach with 44-gallon drums on it. There'd be about eight drums on it, maybe more, full of salt water, and they'd bring 'em back to the camp and they'd use it in the cooking, so we had salt. Smart cookies, weren't they? The limbey used to go, he was the jockey.

BERT BEECHAM

In some places, the camp workshops would collaborate in the making of goods, not for their own use, but to earn money from whomever they could sell them to – the guards perhaps, or locals with cash. The money the prisoners obtained could then be used to buy medicine. And medicine could buy life. Pat Darling began a cottage industry of her own.

And to earn money, of course, we made hats from the straw bags that they used to put the rice in. We made toy kangaroos from a bit of cloth and a bit of dried grass stuffing and sold those. All sorts of things we did, and a Chinese woman asked Pat Blake to mind her little boy in the mornings so that she could do her household chores and Pat was paid for that, and she also knitted for him and I also made clothes for him and she wanted a hat made for him. So I had to make a real Akubra-style hat. I couldn't make a coolie hat for him because his father was a very wealthy Englishman and she was a wealthy woman in her own right, anyway.

We did all sorts of things like that to make money, and every now and then we'd have a sale of goods for people who wanted money and had goods for sale and I'd usually put in two small drawings . . . we had other ways of sort of earning money as best we could.

PAT DARLING

Perhaps, though, the most devious and crafty inventions were created and manufactured in the European camps, where the possibility of escape was always tempting. Clothing, forged documents, compasses, maps, weapons and medals, any artefact that would help to disguise an escaped prisoner was turned out of those clandestine tool rooms in the camps.

We used to make our own solder. In those days every cigarette packet had silver paper lining it. We used to take that out, crumple it up and we would put it in a little tin – those tins of fishpaste and things that you use for spreading on sandwiches. We would take the top off with a tin opener and we would put a piece of wire around the top rim, twist it into a long handle and push it down so there was a spout on one side, pushed all of the cigarette paper crumpled up inside of that and we had made a tiny little forge where, with bright bits of coal dust, we could get the temperature up very high and we could actually melt that silver paper and get it like solder.

And then we would take a piece of cardboard with corrugations and we would split the corrugation open a little bit . . . and we would just pour the molten solder down into there and it would cool and solidify as it went down and then you would just break it open, because it would be charred, and you were left with thin sticks of solder to be used for metalwork.

. . . There was a use for everything, usually in an escape plan somewhere. I mean, cardboard cartons, okay, from the food parcels – you couldn't hope to use those. But then when the American Red Cross came in, most of their food-stuffs came in, those big plywood cubes. And they made perfect theatre chairs . . . and we turned one room into a small theatre, made our own seats and everything. Some of the best actors on the British stage and in early tele-vision were guys who learnt their trade in acting in our camp. *Macbeth*, live Shakespeare, comedies, mysteries, everything. You would have a full cast with

The Blechhammer Follies

a director and a producer, lots and lots of rehearsals and then put on a very credible show. Say you had a magician, you had singers, we had our own band, and they were a very good band, too.

GEOFF CORNISH

•

On just the second day of captivity inside Changi Gaol, an Australian concert party gathered together and began rehearsals for a show. Anyone who wanted to could get up and perform and they busied themselves looting potential props and costumes from the empty houses of Singapore, sneaking out when the Japanese weren't looking. That first concert was the beginning of what were probably the most surprising and unique theatrical productions that had ever taken place, anywhere. In camp after camp, there seemed to always be at least one person who had the necessary drive and ability to utter that legendary theatrical line: 'Let's put on a show!' And put one on they did. Right across Asia.

They started to organise concert parties in Batavia, and with that number of people to call upon, they had quite a lot of skilful artists there, singers and musicians, and the Yanks had brought all their music with them, guitars and banjos and whatever else, trumpets and whatever, and we had some – well while I was there anyway, I went to three concerts, I think, and they gradually got better and better, each one, and they were really worth seeing, the things that the boys put on, you know? Dressing up as girls and playing the part of women in these things that they put on. It was very, very good – very clever.

. . . There was satire, particularly against the politicians of the day, and against the Japs always, even when the Japs were attending the concert, there were things said that you know, went over their heads, thank goodness, that they got away with. But a lot of the acts that they put on were very skilful in the way they did their work.

. . . Some of the paintings and drawings that the blokes turned out of nothing and made a stage set up for a play, and the plays were quite in-depth plays in some respects, you know . . . I know one of the *Perth* survivors, he was very clever with a knife, and he made a model, I suppose you'd call it, of the *Perth*, in wood, that he carved out with a pocket knife, gone into the finest detail that he could work, with virtually nothing.

And in one of the concerts that they had there . . . someone who had the skill, we had electric light there, they somehow or other blew this thing up with the use of lighting you know, which directed the light onto a big screen, the screen was probably only made out of matting of some sort, or towels tied together or something, but it was sufficient for this to be – he probably had the boat over here on a bit of something or other, and over here with a bit of string – and they dragged this across this screen, and you would have sworn that it was the *Perth*.

FRED SKEELS

Even after so many of the men were moved from Changi to the Thai–Burma Railway in late 1942, the concerts continued. In fact, the prisoners performed a new show every two weeks till the end of the war. And the complexity and professionalism of the productions grew and grew. On one of their expeditions around the city they 'liberated' a piano from the British submarine base, while other instruments were smuggled back into the jail by men on working parties. One group even managed to dismantle a drum kit they'd located somewhere, and, piece by painful piece, smuggled it back in under their G-strings. The piano, a Morrison upright, not only made it to the end of the war, but was brought back to Australia by the men, where it survives to this day.

The men in Changi had the advantage of stability that remaining in one place provided. They could scrounge a sewing machine to make costumes and know they could, once they got it safely into camp, keep it. In camps such as Ambon, the very idea of a concert was tough enough, let alone acquiring the paraphernalia needed for it. But still they persisted. Marc Gilbert had been a storeman in civilian life, but now, in Ambon, he discovered unforeseen talent.

A fellow who must have been a born entrepreneur made it known that he wanted to get concert parties going. And he spread the word around: 'If you can sing I want to hear from you, or if you can act or do anything that will make us laugh, let me know.' Now he got together a small group of people and I put my hand up. Why I put my hand up was this, before the war I had memorised a few of the monologues that a well-known actor-comedian, Stanley Holloway, had recorded, and you used to hear it on the wireless quite often. And I sort of loved these, probably because of my part-English background. I got used to his pseudo accent from Lancashire. So I put my hand up and said, 'I can deliver a couple of monologues, I know them by heart.'

So I helped to form part of a concert party . . . one of the fellows, I think it was a journalist from Melbourne, Bunny Porter his name was, he wrote a series of scripts based loosely on the *Dad & Dave* theme sort of, and there was characters in it like Dad and Dave and the heroine was Mabel. And somehow or other they persuaded me to play the female lead. Well, of course, the first obstacle to overcome is the matter of boobs. Well, what better than getting hold of a coconut shell and cutting it in half and I must say, that did the job fine. But then there was the problem of a dress. Now don't ask me how this happened, how I did this, but somehow, somebody got hold of a dress from the Dutch women in the compound adjacent to the camp. And as for hair, well, I put a handkerchief over my head. And there I was playing the role of Mabel. That was my first debut, really, on the stage. Anyway it was all good fun and I like to think that it all helped, we all helped to break the boredom and improve morale a little as well . . .

Some of the guards came and watched us but they probably didn't have a clue really, what we were on about, because there was satire and nonsense that would only be understood by fellows like ourselves.

. . . The concerts had to be before dark because there was no electricity in the camp at all of any sort. So we had a day off once a week, possibly even the Sunday, and that's when the concerts would have been, during, say, the afternoon sometime. But we eventually persuaded the Japs to let us have the use of a hut which wasn't being used for anything, to turn it into what you might grandly call a concert hall.

And enough people got together and we got material to make a stage and a curtain, now this has special meaning for me, because talk about a work of art! Again, don't ask me where we got the material from, but being scroungers from way back, we got material. And it was all black for this curtain and I was one who helped to sew on that, to make up, out of coloured material, and sew on it, replicas of the unit badges of all the units represented in the camp, apart from the battalion, the ambulance and the engineers and several other units, on this grand curtain. And we had an opening night and somebody had managed to collect enough cigarettes and as each person arrived for the concert they were given a cigarette, oh, big deal!

. . . We tried to hold those concerts and did hold those every week for quite a few months throughout most of 1942. They really started to peter out when the Japanese started to make demands for men on work parties which of course inhibited us considerably. We either didn't have the time to rehearse things or we were just too tired anyway . . .

Then the bomb dump blew up. The whole thing was destroyed when the bomb dump was hit and the whole place went up in flames and we lost all that. That was the end of the concert parties, very sad.

MARIC GILBERT

On the island of Sumatra, in a women's camp, a musical group developed among the prisoners that would have been remarkable at any time, but was extraordinary given the circumstances. In the camp were Australian nurses, Dutchwomen who had been living in the East Indies, Englishwomen from Malaya, missionaries and Catholic nuns, and women from other countries who had been swept up by the Japanese advance. It was a diverse group of people, with apparently little in common.

By September 1943 though, when they were in the camp at Palembang, hard times and deprivation had removed the differences between them. Their needs had coalesced into the same desires – food, medicine and hope. The lack of food and medicine would get worse, but hope came from an unlikely source. Margaret Dryburgh, a missionary with an astonishing memory for music, and Norah Chambers, a trained violinist, would together create something beautiful in a place made ugly by cruelty – a vocal orchestra. Pat Darling was in that camp.

It was started quite early in the piece and Miss Dryburgh and Mrs Chambers, Norah Chambers, was a graduate of the Royal Academy of Music and she was very talented, and Miss Dryburgh was the most amazing person. She was the senior missionary . . . and she was working in Singapore with her group of missionaries when Singapore fell and she was quite an amazing person. She used to play the piano for church services and things like that.

. . . They trained them very assiduously . . . we were allowed to have gatherings in the evenings and people would give various talks and things like that and it was basically from that that the vocal orchestra started because they realised that they had quite a lot of people who were very interested in music and were prepared to perform, because they asked people to come forward who wanted to be in it and who felt that they could hold a tune and it was quite amazing what they produced, it was absolutely marvellous.

PAT DARLING

Margaret Dryburgh, using her copious memory, wrote down the music, the scores, to about 30 classical orchestral pieces, a miraculous feat. Chambers copied them out and together they arranged the pieces for women's voices, substituting their singing for the instruments of the orchestra. They sang sounds, not words, and the effect was beautiful, transforming.

We all loved it and it was a great relief from the tedium of the days which consisted always of carrying water for at least two hours a day . . . it took us into another world. It's a bit like now, if you just go to one of the concerts, it's a lovely feeling when you walk out, you know, if you go to a really good show or a concert at the Opera House you walk out more or less floating on air 'cause it's such a lovely experience.

Apparently, we were the only camp that had it and we realised how lucky we were. They gave their first public performance, probably Christmas '43 I think, and women weren't allowed to gather in groups, so they used to wait till the evening came and they would go behind where the kitchens were, and obviously the Jap guards must've heard them but they obviously felt the same about it. It was so lovely they wouldn't stop them and they didn't see them.

PAT DARLING

From the very first concert the orchestra gave, after initially trying to stop it, the Japanese too, surrendered to the beauty that the women produced in their performances. So much so, that perhaps through wounded pride, racial as well as male, they struck back with a performance of their own. For Pat Darling, it was a surprising event.

The Japs, honestly, they said that *they* were having a concert. Obviously they had appreciated the fact that this particular camp had created the vocal orchestra. So we were very snooty about it and we said, 'We need food for the body, not for the soul.' . . . You see, all requests in all the camps for better food and more medicine, they just fell on deaf ears, and so they put on this concert for us.

. . . A few of us were lying down in a hut that I was in and we had determined not to go and the guard came along screaming and shouting so we thought we'd better go and as we walked up the slight rise to where they were, the music from *Poet and Peasant* [operetta overture] came floating through the air. We said, 'This is really good, this is lovely.' So we went there and sat. It was actually quite beautiful . . . there they were, an immaculately turned out band and they stood strictly to attention, even the tenor who was very, very good. The only thing that moved about him was his head and that went up and down, so we sat there and it was a lovely experience. It had a marvellous feeling.

The rubber trees were in their full glory with their autumn toned leaves and the grass on the ground was very beautifully green, so altogether, it was quite a beautiful experience and the Dutch women of course, joined in. They played mostly German music, well they were allies, and the Dutch women joined in the singing with the various pieces. It was really quite uplifting. For the first time I realised what a pretty area this camp was in, which I hadn't before, and they had the most beautiful dragonflies and you'd put a finger like that and one would settle on it. They were absolutely beautiful.

PAT DARLING

Music, dance, theatre and sport, they all passed the time and helped to dispel, for a while at least, the crushing boredom for many prisoners. When the performances were good, and that was surprisingly often, they had the power to make the camp disappear, to allow the men and women imprisoned there to imagine, if only for a moment, that one day this would all pass and normal life would resume. For the children, this was especially important. Sheila Bruhn remembered the delights of the performances in astonishing detail.

Concerts usually consisted of a variety of items. There would be a singer, a comedy act, a couple of dancing acts, a sort of a fashion parade, chorus singing, chorus dancing, acrobatics. We even put on a circus, which was quite extraordinary, considering that we didn't have much in the way of costumes. The things they did – a fat lady and a boxing kangaroo, a performing seal, a trapeze artist. It is quite amazing what talent there was when you started looking around.

Then you would have a singing competition and an acting competition. Writing competition. We would have a sports competition. There was a ladies' bridge party, card games. You name it, we did it. It is extraordinary how we managed to find things to do. Of course there was a craft section and language classes. And we would occasionally get men from next door to give us lectures. Mainly their experiences before the war. Someone who had been in Algeria or some other country, mainly experiences of what they have done. And even the women also had lectures on their experiences before the war, where they had been . . . we had an old gramophone, dancing classes.

. . . We had poetry reading, Shakespeare reading, people taking part. It was pretty widespread for a lot of things. Rehearsal sometimes would be in the morning or the afternoon. Usually the concert would be given some time in the early evening unless we were giving the concert to the men, and then it would be in the day, in the courtyard. Men would give us concerts too, but being so close we could always hear them practising and hear them singing.

SHEILA BRUHN

Sheila kept a secret diary during her time in Changi. This excerpt, from early in her imprisonment, gives an evocative sense of the mood the concerts could produce.

Wednesday, the 25th of November 1942. The Men's Concert. We were allowed to see the men's concert – permission given by Nakajima and Mr Chuchitana. The concert was held in the courtyard with sentries keeping an eye on proceedings!

Took our places in the main courtyard at 7.15 pm. Stage looked great though somewhat small. The actors were all out in the yard (other prisoners were behind the grilles – saw Dad and waved to him). At 7.45 pm the show started with a march, *Under Freedom's Flag*. Sat on some stone tiles, which rocked perilously to and fro as I kept time to the music.

The Camp Orchestra was well and truly appreciated by all. The last on the programme was the Camp Choir and we marvel at those marvellous voices and we all sang *God Save Our King* – after which Dr Hopkins called out for, 'Three cheers for our men!' – we cheered as loudly as our lungs and voices would allow! It was a lovely evening and we do appreciate what the men have done for us. Hope there'll be another one before long – God bless the men.

SHEILA BRUHN

The women in Changi Gaol were another diverse group – British wives of officials, teachers, medical staff and missionaries. There were some Eurasian children of white fathers, like Sheila, and women from the Netherlands, Australia, New Zealand, Canada, and the United States. They were responsible for their own administration, discipline and order and the physical maintenance of the camp but many of those who had previously seen themselves as 'upper class', felt it was beneath their dignity to clean drains or queue for food. For a time, the camp was a very unhappy, fractured environment until loss and deprivation levelled out the whingers and the lazy. Ultimately though, they were able to produce, by working as individuals and then joining that work together, three pieces of art that I regard as the most beautiful and touching symbols of hope and love to come from the POW camps of that war. Sheila tells the story.

We had sewing classes. A lot of the women had brought in some of their work baskets with them that they had been probably working on before the war. Some of them had tapestry; some of them were doing crocheting and knitting, embroidery. So we had a lot of threads and oddments and patterns and things, and we had sewing classes to sew a few things, to make things that we could barter with.

. . . Elizabeth Ennis, she was a Scottish lady in the British Army, and she was the only military person who was interned with us. There were no army nurses, all went on the *Vyner Brooke* and all got interned elsewhere, so we only had civilian nurses and she was the only military one. Her husband was a pathologist and he was a prisoner of war, he was in the army too. And she had been in Guiding all of her young life and she decided that she would start a Girl Guide group.

She got about twenty girls between the ages of eight and thirteen and taught them as much as possible about Guiding and the girls decided, when it was her birthday, to give her the gift of a special quilt that they made, with the name of each girl in a little square that they had created. And Mrs Mulvaney, when she saw the quilt, it gave her the idea that perhaps the women might like to do the same thing. Not only to occupy their time, but also, if they could request the Japanese officials that it could be sent over to the military camp. Because quite a few of the women had husbands in the military and when we surrendered their husbands were taken away from them without having the chance to say goodbye, them being in the army, and they wouldn't have known what had happened to their women folk. The women knew where they were, but the husbands didn't.

So they felt this way they could let them know they were in Changi Prison and that they were still alive and reasonably well. So it was done in the first three or four months of our internment. I had mine dated the 1st of May. Most of it, I think, would be finished by June, and they were all collected, and she suggested that they make one for the British soldiers from the British women, one for the Australian soldiers. Of course there weren't that many Australian women in camp, but at least it was a way of letting the Aussies know that we were thinking of them.

And she suggested another one for the Japanese, which wasn't very well received at first. Quite a lot of women didn't want to contribute to that, but as Mulvaney explained, if we only did it for the British and Australians it wouldn't get past, because they would query all of the messages on the squares, they would wonder if they were secret codes.

And so, reluctantly, they agreed and they did one. And of course I always think, I would like to think, that's my personal opinion of course, that Mrs Mulvaney would have presented the Japanese quilt to them first. And it *is* a very beautiful quilt, beautifully done. And the Japanese do appreciate beautiful things, because they have some beautiful silk paintings and things like that.

Well, they did accept it, and then she would say perhaps they would like to deliver these others to the military camps. They probably wouldn't have even thought of looking at it, probably think it is more or less the same as theirs and pass it over.

. . . We were given an eight inch square, all of us, especially cut out from the sacking that had the rice flour and sugar, so that was unpicked and washed and carefully cut out and given to each of us that were interested in having

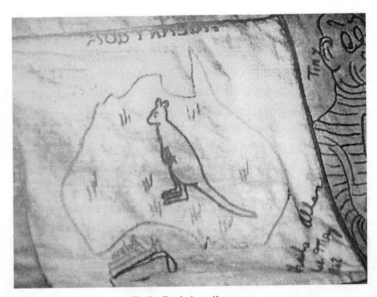

Sheila Bruhn's quilt square

one. I did a map of Australia with a kangaroo in the centre, an aeroplane at the top and a sailing boat on the bottom to signify that I was going to get to Australia by hook or by crook, somehow or other. But unfortunately I forgot the island of Tasmania which I didn't know existed, my father never told me anything about Tasmania, he only told me about Australia. So that is something that I still have to apologise for.

. . . Another one of them was a cheerful Tommy [British] soldier with the thumbs up sign. And another famous one, of course, was three dwarves with two menus saying, 'There will always be tomorrow.' Of course some of the more national ones would be, 'There will always be an England as long as Scotland stands.' . . . there was one there with two bunny rabbits, the mother rabbit, and the baby rabbit had a blue ribbon around its neck to indicate that they had a son. There was another with two sheep, and the baby lamb had a pink ribbon around its neck to indicate that they had a baby girl.

. . . Freddy Bloom did a clock with wings on it to indicate that she wished time would fly. Elizabeth Ennis did a ship called *Homeward Bound* with the hope that one day she would be sailing home with her husband. And of course the very famous one I would think, was by Iris Parfitt, our cartoonist, a square of a lonely figure in a cell saying, 'How long, oh Lord? How long?'

There were other bits and pieces, funny bits. Dr Margaret Smallwood had her cell decorated with underwear and called it 'the room with a view'. And one who had a humorous one, had a sketch of just a plain brick wall and called 'Changi Holiday Home'.

Anything that would bring the men perhaps a bit of laughter, or a smile to their faces. To know that in a way, the women are keeping their end up.

SHEILA BRUHN

The Australian and the Japanese quilts are in the Australian War Memorial, in Canberra. Go see them.

MARIC GILBERT

PHIL GREVILLE

COLIN HAMLEY

ALLAN HERD

WALTER HICKS

KEITH HOOPER

5

'To kill a person . . . was no different to killing an animal'

*All forms of punishment, confinement in premises not lit by daylight
and in general, all forms of cruelty whatsoever are prohibited.
Collective penalties for individual acts are also prohibited.*

FROM ARTICLE 46, GENEVA CONVENTION, 1929

In 1859 a very bloody battle was fought in a small town called Solferino in Italy. On one side were the armies of France and Sardinia and on the other, the Austrian Army. The fundamental cause of the battle was the desire of Italians to become one country. Around 200 000 men hurled their bodies at each other to determine the outcome. In just nine hours of fighting 5500 men were killed and over 22 000 wounded and the dying and the wounded from both sides were mercilessly shot or bayoneted as they lay on the ground.

The French and Sardinian allies were victorious, if such a word can be used to describe that day, but what eventually resulted from the battle was of far greater magnitude than simply another military success. Jean-Henri Dunant, a Swiss businessman, witnessed the horror, and, appalled by the carnage, he began a campaign for change that ultimately resulted in the establishment of the Red Cross and the international agreements we call the Geneva Conventions.

The conventions are four treaties that basically set the standards for the treatment of noncombatants and prisoners in times of war, and over the years leading up to World War II, they became the accepted rules of conduct for nations engaged in conflict. Accepted, that is, if a) you had signed and ratified the treaties, and b) you were prepared to abide by them. After all, the Geneva Conventions had been drawn up by optimistic statesmen in peaceful times, but war could so easily make a mockery of both hope and morality.

Ken Drew had enlisted, underage, as a boot repairer in the infantry, but the lottery of war sent him into battle in North Africa and then Greece, where he was captured. He would not see Australia again for five and a half years. Like all the men in his company he would be forced to learn the first law of POW life – helplessness.

Outside the wire enclosure there was a Greek girl, about twelve, I suppose. Threw half a loaf of bread over the fence. One of these German guards seen her, and knocked her down and bull-whipped her on the ground. We can't do a thing about it.

Then when we were marching to the trains to go to Germany. It was like semi-Anzac Day. People came out on the streets, were saying goodbye and all this. This woman, I would say, mid-twenties, my estimate at that time was that she'd be about eight months pregnant. She stepped out and gave one of the prisoners – I didn't know him – a piece of bread. And these guards seen her, hit her with a rifle butt, kicked her, she lost everything. She was starting to lose everything as we marched off. They were mongrels in themselves.

KEN DREW

From the moment of surrender, the prisoner of war is at the mercy of the military force that captured him. From that moment on, he or she must abide by its rules, its discipline, its principles, its culture, and particularly the demands and orders of its individual representatives. The prisoner is vulnerable and weapon-less, unprotected by agreements made in more civilised times and, for a time at least, unknown and unseen by the rest of the world. The temptation for the captors to indulge in punishment and humiliation can often be too hard to resist.

We all had to be deloused, of course, which I'll tell you about. You leave all your clothes in a certain area and you'd hang 'em up and they'd delouse them.

And you walked into this barrack, naked, about twelve or fourteen at a time. Seats down the middle, they had German soldiers in overalls, one sitting facing this way and one sitting that way. And you'd line up in front of 'em and they'd shave every hair off your body, that's bad I know, and then the next moment, you had to stand there raw naked, not a hair on your body.

Then they brought in the first lot of Polish conscript workers, all women, all in their twenties or thirties, stark naked, make 'em stand in front of ya, while they coat every hair of their body [with delousing solution]. That then was done to try and break your willpower down. That's what I put it down to. That's when I had this feeling. I thought, 'If they could do that, what's in line for us now?'

And then when they done that we had to go through into another room. There was a huge barrel, oh, probably about as big as this room. The women would come up one side, we came up the other and there'd be about 25 or 30, body to body, because you couldn't move. And when they said 'duck', you'd duck, cause it would kill all the eggs and lice and that was just to demoralise you, but it failed. Because of the fact that, you get starving people, a naked body didn't mean a thing to you.

KEN DREW

In one of those diplomatic two-steps that allow nations to weasel out from under moral imperatives, Japan had signed but not 'ratified' the Geneva Conventions of 1929. This meant that many a prison camp commander in the years ahead could justify the brutal treatment meted out to the men and women under his control.

The very concept of a 'prisoner of war' was rejected by the Japanese military. The aggressive militarism that had produced their zealous nationalism demanded complete obedience to the Emperor and did not allow for the idea of surrender to one's enemy. To do so meant abject failure. So the people captured by their conquering troops were seen by them simply as 'captives' rather than combatants. They were possessions of the Emperor and, as such, they could be dealt with in any way a commander determined. Often, this could mean taking no captives at all. As they claimed victory after victory in South-East Asia, the Japanese committed murder on a grand scale, massacring noncombatants and surrendered soldiers alike.

The first Australian troops to be murdered by the Japanese were at Parit Sulong, a small village on the west coast of Malaya. On

22 January 1942, 110 Australian and 40 Indian troops, wounded men who had to be left behind after the Battle of Muar, were captured by the Japanese Imperial Guards Division. The Japanese beat them, deprived them of food, water and medical treatment, then shot them and burnt the bodies with petrol. Somehow, two men escaped the massacre. One, Ben Hackney, would astonishingly then survive Changi and the Thai–Burma Railway to later bear witness to the atrocity.

Less than a month later, in Muntok, the Australian nurses who had escaped the sinking ship, the *Vyner Brooke*, had an unexpected and very welcome arrival into their prison camp. An Australian nurse, Vivien Bullwinkel, along with 21 other nurses and a large group of men, women, and children had made it ashore nearby, at a place called Banka Island. They were joined the next day by about 100 British soldiers. With no water or food, they decided to surrender to the Japanese. As Pat Darling tells, it was a fatal decision.

About a week later Viv Bullwinkel came in and she had been in the boat, in the lifeboat that I put Cath into and they had landed on the beach about five o'clock and they lit fires as beacons for us to make our way to, because we couldn't get there.

Anyway, next day a group of Japanese came and ordered them to stay where they were but the women with small children with the heat, of course they had to find somewhere for their children, so they went into a small village and the nurses decided to stay with the wounded men. There were quite a few men who had been wounded and were on the boat.

Then another Japanese patrol came along and they took the men away and came back wiping their bayonets, ordered the nurses into the sea and Viv Bullwinkel walked into the sea, with Cath actually, and when they got to a certain depth they machine-gunned them and of course, Viv for a while thought, you know, she had to be dead, because she'd been shot.

When she realised she was alive she came ashore and met a badly wounded English soldier. He was in the Australian Army but he was an Englishman and he had feigned death after the bayoneting and for a while the native people supplied them with food but understandably, they were terrified of being caught by the Japs, they would be very badly treated by them, so she came in.

She was able to tell us that there were 21 of the girls who were dead, who'd been shot, and she was the only survivor, so that made us 32 altogether, out of 65.

PAT DARLING

There were more and even worse murders in those first weeks – 130 soldiers who had surrendered at the Tol Plantation on Rabaul; and 300 unarmed Australian soldiers were slaughtered by the Japanese at the Laha airfield, on the island of Ambon. Laha was to earn a dreadful reputation as the site of the largest of the atrocities committed against captured Allied troops during 1942.

In the end, it was probably sheer numbers that saved other lives. There were simply too many captives. The Japanese, like the Germans after Greece and Crete, were overwhelmed by the tens of thousands of prisoners they had suddenly amassed and had to hurriedly put into place the necessary resources and administration to contain them. It would not take them long, however, to realise that the prisoners were themselves a resource – as slave labour.

And even if the number of captives had not been so high, the prison camps of both Europe and Asia were always going to be doubtful propositions as humane or even efficient institutions. The problem lay in the most fundamental of facts – that the military, an organisation designed for the aggression and destruction of war, was now assuming a double role as jailer and carer, a very difficult ask. The administration of the camps would require commanders of the highest calibre and they were being used elsewhere. Any halfway decent officer was inevitably utilised by the conquering armies to prosecute the war and those who had been overlooked for promotion or were incompetent or second-rate took over as the commandants of the prison camps. The noncommissioned officers (NCOs) and guards, the men with whom the POWs had the most contact, were often even worse. The lack of preparation and strong leadership produced ill discipline, the rule of the rifle butt, and appalling punishments for whatever capricious reasons the captors could conjure up.

Lieutenant Terry Fairbairn had been captured in Crete and taken to a POW camp in Germany. During an interrogation he made a provocative comment about Hitler. A comment he was to pay for.

I was belted and belted and belted. I had fingers stuck up into my anus. I was shaved, all my body, eyelashes were pulled out, eyebrows gone. Every hair in my body went, with a blade razor. I was told to get dressed, which I did, and when my boots were on, my boots were wired round my ankles, trousers were wired around my ankles and the trousers were wired around my waist and I was given a great big mug of castor oil and belted a few times from here up to here, front and back. The door was locked and that was at eight o'clock in the morning and the same thing happened at four and it happened for twelve days, every day . . .

They gave me a boiled potato, which I couldn't eat. I just simply couldn't eat anything. One boiled potato, a little small one, but I couldn't eat it, I just couldn't. I made a lot of mess. There was nothing you could do. There was no toilet, there was no bucket, no nothing. Besides, I couldn't get my clothes off. I might have been crazy, I don't know, but I certainly was very angry with them, not with me, with them.

You think of people at home and you think of what would they do about this if they knew about it, which they didn't, they never did know about it. I only wrote it. The last thing I wrote was two or three years ago, the first time I wrote that, and I wrote it only just trying to get rid of the damn thing, but I haven't got rid of it and no, there was no sense in telling people about it and they wouldn't even think that I was being treated like that and so on. I was the only one in that camp that I know of that was treated like that, because I'd criticised Hitler. Quite astounding.

TERRY FAIRBAIRN

Lieutenant Fairbairn escaped from the Germans in the last year of the war and fought alongside the advancing Americans. He has never forgotten: 'I've never set foot in Germany ever since. I've been in Europe seven times, but I've never set foot in Germany and I never speak to a German if I can avoid it.'

Bashings, deliberate humiliation, even torture could and did take place in German and Italian prison camps, but it was never as widespread or as systematic as it was for the men under Japanese rule. There were no 'good' Japanese camps, just degrees of awfulness. Each day brought the terrifying instability of never knowing from which guard or officer the next bashing might come, or for what reason. Bill Coventry, a POW in Java, puts it as well as anyone.

We were white men, they were Japanese, the superior race. There is no logic in the Jap, you can't work out what he is doing and what he is thinking, they would give you a hiding for something you wouldn't know what you have done. They would just pick on you, pick on me, just because I was taller than he was or something and find an excuse to give you a hiding, but we all got very bad ringing ears and all that sort of thing, bloody faces and so forth.

BILL COVENTRY

After surviving the sinking of HMAS *Perth*, Fred Skeels was imprisoned and worked to exhaustion in Batavia, Singapore, Burma, Thailand, Saigon and finally, Japan. His odds of surviving must have been lengthening by then but it was over the most seemingly inconsequential of matters that he came closest to death. Only the whims of his guards kept him alive.

They didn't agree with stealing very much, that was one of their finer points, if you like to put it. Stealing was foreign to them, if it was within their own circle of mates. They could steal off us as prisoners if they wanted to, because they could do that. But if we were caught stealing something of theirs, you know, pinching some rice, stealing a bag of rice or something like that, or if you were insulting to them, where they lost face in front of their mates, they would get very cruel in their punishment that they meted out. You learned all these things about them, and so you avoided the Japs in doing those things to them. But unfortunately some people didn't, and they were caught, and they were literally beaten to death . . .

I got caught, I'd been crook with dysentery and I'd been off – hadn't been down the mine, I was on what they call light duties . . . and the commandant lived in a house behind the camp, the commandant of the camp, and he had a family of a wife and couple of kids there, and we had to walk through his vegetable garden to go to where we were working – we were digging a hole in the side of the mountain, which was just behind his house. I think we were digging our own grave if the Allies had landed, quite frankly, but we were digging this as an air-raid shelter for his family.

And on the way back on this particular day, walking through his vegetable paddock, I pulled up a handful of spring onions and shoved them in my shirt or whatever I had on, and got into camp and then I was stupid enough to be cutting up the onions with a blade of my knife that I had, and I was doing it on the windowsill of the little room that we had in our camp – there was ten men to our room, Japanese-style houses, bamboo mats and bamboo walls and sliding doors and all that. But I was stupid enough to use this sill of the window as something to cut the spring onion up, I was going to have it on my rice, spread it out amongst my mates in the room for the rice, it was going to be sweet, dessert you know, spring onion.

And the bloody, excuse me, the Jap guard came past and he saw me and he came over to see what I was doing. And, of course, he saw what I was doing and probably knew where I got the spring onions from, so I got hauled out in front of the guardhouse and each guard in the guardhouse had a go at me for a few minutes, bashed me across the face, you know, on both sides of my face – they'd swing an arm out and bash you, nearly knock your teeth out and nearly knock your head off each time, and it nearly makes you fall over often. But you've got to keep on your feet, otherwise you get the boots, you know? So I put up with that from them for probably ten minutes while the guards that were not out on duty had their go at me.

And then the next lot of guards changed over their shift, the new ones came on and they probably got told what I'd done, I was still standing to attention in front of the guardhouse, and they came over, several of them or one at a time, came over and had their turn at me, and instead of bashing me, they started to practise their jujitsu on me, you know, and they'd grab me by the arm and heave me, or come behind me and trip me and throw me down. And they were laughing amongst themselves while they were trying all these little tricks that they thought they knew about jujitsu and all this stuff. I had to put up with that for about another ten or fifteen minutes from this little group of change of the guard.

After they'd finished I had to stand to attention again, and I stood to attention all that night in front of the guardhouse, and every now and again one of them would take it into his mind to come over and slap me. So I put up with that all one night and half of the afternoon, just for pinching a little bunch of onions. When the morning came, for some strange reason they just sent me back to the hut and it was all over.

That was the worst beating I took from any Jap, apart from individual little smacks with a stick when you were working, and you didn't work hard enough or something. It was a bashing but not to the point where they were killing me. But if it had been in the minds of the sergeant of the guard to be nastier, they could have done it until I dropped down and didn't get up. But that was that.

Other blokes weren't as lucky as that, they got beaten until they actually didn't get up, beaten unconscious, ultimately were left on the ground to die.

FRED SKEELS

Stealing a few spring onions could result in that kind of punishment, but far worse treatment awaited those who attempted escape. Alex Barnett had been put to work in a sugar factory in Germany for twelve hours a day, on meagre rations. Sent to a nearby hospital for treatment on a wound, he saw his chance on the return journey.

I was returned to the sugar factory, the guard was a young bloke and was standing on Breslau station, you know, they've got three or four platforms with trains coming in and out and they were steam locomotives and the guard started chatting up a couple of sheilas and the train pulled in and I thought, 'That bludger's not looking!' and I just, on impulse, jumped into the train and took off, so I escaped. And I thought, 'Oh God, what am I going to do? I got no tucker, no nothing!' This was not real good so I thought, 'Now I know these Huns – the moment the guard looks around and finds me, I'm gone. They'll know what train went out and they'll have them waiting.'

So I decided to get out at the next station and I'd catch another coming back, that's what I thought I'd do. By this time we were in British clothing which we got from the Red Cross, and it's the same sort of clothing that the French and the Belgians and all the rest of them were wearing so I wasn't too conspicuous.

So I picked a train that went through about four or five ruddy stations, more than that, and by the time it stopped, there was the Gestapo and oh, you had no chance – they just came in both ends of the carriage and you just have to give up again. So they made me crawl on my hands and knees down the carriage, getting booted all the way down. Pigs! And they were telling the people I was a 'pig dog English', not an Australian, always English, and they took me in their car and it makes that horrible noise, not like our sirens, and I got taken to the police station where I was interrogated.

They stripped me off and then they mocked me, they reckoned I was a Jew, an American Jew, then I was a British Jew, even though I had my tags on. And they put some electrodes on my genitals and gave me a couple of charges and that's not ruddy funny, and up on the table with lights like that and you can't see them and they're yelling at you, and belting you, all sort of things and you become confused, and they want to know what plane you're from, where did I escape from, or jump off and all the rest of it. Then they said I was a Jew and I was going to the concentration camps with the Jews, they were going to do this and do that.

They kept me, I think it was about 24 or 48 hours. It's very hard to judge time and then the lights go out and you don't know where you are and you are on the table and still starkers and it's cold. And then finally they decided that I was what I said I was, so to punish me, they put me down on the floor and they got a very fine [metal] punch and they punched the roots of my teeth, which I haven't got anymore. They were quite adept at it, they had done it before, it's quite excruciating, I can tell you that. I was picked up by some guards from the sugar factory, taken back, and I got my job back.

ALEXANDER BARNETT

Australian prisoners of war seem to have been more capable than most at irritating their jailers. They surprise them with their refusal to submit to rules, their extraordinary capacity for theft and, at those times when a prisoner is least expected to strike out, their impulsive risking of the lot in one brave if foolhardy moment. Robert Parker found this out the hard way when he was recaptured after escaping in Korea.

So they took us back, and they caught all of the others. They put us in what they call a sweat box, for a month; 30 days in this little place about the size of those tiles there and there was about 30-something of us in there and we used to have to sit all day, from four o'clock in the morning until eleven o'clock at night, we had to sit with our backs up against the wall and our skinny backsides on this knobbly pine floor, and we had to sit with our knees up under our chin and our hands on them like this. All day from four o'clock in the morning until eleven o'clock at night . . . We could stop for lunch and we only had one meal a day, sometimes it was a handful of soya beans, sometimes it was millet, rotated, it was only once a day.

Sometimes they would let you out to the toilet and other times they wouldn't; they wouldn't let me out one day. We had these little caps by then, called 'the people's caps' . . . just an ordinary, light material cap. So I did my business in the cap, and then I called the guard and he stuck his head, looking through the grille and I went *splat!* with the hat.

ROBERT HOOPER

ALEXANDER KERR

MALCOLM KESHAN

ARTHUR LEGGETT

JAMES LING

JOHN MATHEWS

I shouldn't have done that, they came in and they belted the hell out of me. I had to kneel on the edge of this platform, kneel on it like that with my hands on my head until I collapsed, out to it. And they did that to other people, too.

And then they would come in and belt you with clubs and pistol butts. And they had this stick, they put this hole through the mud wall, they stuck this stick through it and it had a pointy end and you had to kneel in this little passageway between the door and the ramp we were lying and sitting on, and you had to kneel with the stick in your mouth and the guard would walk past outside and all of a sudden he would go *bang!*, sometimes that way and sometimes sideways, and it cut you in the mouth.

Later on I wrote down that it didn't happen to me but it did. I didn't want my mother to read about it and upset her, but they're all gone now so it doesn't matter . . . that went on for a month like that, they finally let us out.

ROBERT PARKER

That same stubborn refusal to be ground down often led to Australian NCOs and officers being on the receiving end of vicious bashings from the Japanese, particularly if they were perceived to be responsible for their men's rule breaking. Many of the men recall instances where an officer or NCO, in an astonishing display of courage, deliberately chose to take the blame in order to deflect punishment from the soldiers under their command. Des Mulcahy was the warrant officer in charge of his camp in Japan.

We had a lot of trouble with our food and we had a little smart Japanese bloke and he was pinching our Red Cross parcels – not many, just one now and again – and taking them out and selling them on the Japanese open market, and also some of the rice was disappearing. We had a Captain Patterson there with us, but he wasn't interested, just let it be.

This particular day I was called up to the officer and they said, 'Mulcahy!' See they used to bypass the officer because I was in charge of the men in the camp – I was in charge, not the captain, he was in charge of the camp, I was in charge of the men. They called me up and they said, 'Mulcahy-san, we want everybody to write a letter of 100 words of what they think of the treatment they have received by the Japanese since they have been a prisoner of war.'

When I took the papers down and gave them to the NCOs, I said, 'Now look, tell the boys not to be silly, put in anything at all but don't put in anything that is derogatory that will cause trouble, just write a little bit of a note, and I will write the main letter and put it in, I will take the blame for the camp.'

I sat down and I complained about the pilfering of our parcels, the selling of some of our rice, the lack of meat, which we were supposed to get every ten days, the lack of fish, which we were supposed to get every three days, which we weren't getting – all the items of as far as food was concerned that we weren't getting. All to do with the health of the troops.

I took the letters in and nothing happened for two or three days, and we came back this day from work and there was great activity. There were strange Japs running around everywhere, there was a stage built on the parade ground and all the rest of it. This little 'Morimotum' we called him, Morimoto, after one of the pigs that won the prize at the show that year, that was the nickname we gave him, he was in charge of the camps from Osaka and this was in his area. He got up and he gave a great talk with the Japanese interpreter. It all boiled down to the fact that whatever you think of the Japanese you mustn't write it down because someone else can read it and could find out.

So that was all right and he called me up and said, 'Break off the parade.' so I broke off the parade and he said, 'Now I want you and you, come here.' The other bloke was Horrie Pauley. I don't know what Horrie had put in his letter, because we all had numbers on. He took us around the back where no one could see us and got the interpreter out and had a bit of a talk with Horrie and gave Horrie a hit under the ear and told him to get back to the hut. So Horrie just got one hit under the ear and away he went.

He came over to me then, the interpreter said, 'Mr Sukiama doesn't think you understood what you had to write about.' I said, 'Oh yes I did, I knew what I had to write about. I had to tell all the troops what to write about.' 'You are sure you knew what you had to write about?' I said, 'Oh yes, I am quite sure.' I said. 'Right,' he said.

He called three of his Japanese guards with bayonets on. They got one either side of me with a bayonet underneath the armpit and one on the back with a bayonet in my spinal column and he got into me.

He turned out to be the champion boxer of the Japanese Army this bloke, heavyweight boxer, I didn't know that. He belted me about eight times but couldn't knock me down or knock me out and he lost face, because the troops were all there to see this bloke knock hell out of this Aussie and he couldn't knock me down, so he lost face straightaway.

So he walked away disgusted and the little ration sergeant came up then and he was done up like a little toff, brand new suit and everything was lovely and flashy. He came up and he went *whoosh!* This time my mouth was full of blood and when he hit my jaws the blood spat out all over him. He was blood from the top of the head to the boot. He looked at his uniform and he couldn't get away quick enough from me.

Another little medical orderly was lined up next to give me a hit and he wasn't game to hit me at all. He just swore at me and told me to get back to the camp.

So I went back down to the hut and I said to one of the boys, 'Go and get the Dutch doctor.' They came back and said, 'No, he can't, he won't come down. The little Jap has already been down there and he said if he comes down to treat you he will get the same as what you have got.' I said, 'Okay then.' With that over came this great big old Dutchman, Von Zonda, from the kitchen. He said, 'Give me a look at your mouth.' I think he had done a bit of first-aid work on the ships. He had a look at my mouth, he said, 'You have both jaws broken and two teeth knocked out but don't let anybody touch it until I get back.' I said, 'All right.'

So he went away and he came back a bit later on and he had this big crepe bandage in his hand and he had a glass full of soya bean sauce. He said, 'Here, rinse your mouth out with this soya bean sauce, it is not an antiseptic but the salt in it will kill germs and heal it up a bit quicker.'

So he did that and he said, 'I am going to put my hand in your jaw and put those two teeth back in the hole. There is a hole in each side and if I can put the teeth back in, they are still hanging by a bit of the skin. I will poke them back in and close your jaw, they might grow back in.' I said, 'All right.' So he got his great big hand, it was as big as a foot, and got it in and he got these two teeth and put them back in the holes, bound my jaw up.

Next morning, of course, I had a head like this, and went on parade, and as soon as I went on parade this Japanese bloke came over and he pulled the bandage off my head and threw it on the ground and said, 'Now run around the parade ground.' The first step you took, your jaw went down and broke again. Some of the boys, as they went out of the camp would pick this bandage up and pass it up the line to me and put it back on my head as best I could. Anyhow, the jaw healed up and the teeth – one lasted fifteen years and one lasted twenty-odd years.

DES MULCAHY

Sacrifice is an odd word to use these days, it's as though it's an out-of-date idea, a concept that belongs to old-time religion perhaps, or the study of anthropology. But there is no other word that can describe the actions of Sergeant Nicky Hallam on the Thai–Burma Railway.

I remember one time a party come back off the railway and they were one short when they got back to camp, and the Jap said, 'Right, you stand there until the other one turns up.' See, if a bloke gets crook on the way back, he'd fall by the wayside. And after an hour or so he would come good and come back to camp somehow.

This day they got back, it was pretty dark when they got back, but one short. And the Jap said, 'You stop there until the man gets the right number.' A little Tasmanian chap named Nicky Hallam, he had dysentery and malaria and all that, and he is lying in hospital and he was a sergeant. He thought he would keep it up and he takes this bloke's place to make up the party and they saw him, and they said, 'You are not on party, you are hospital!'

They grabbed him – threw him backwards and bashed hell out of him for about ten minutes, quarter of an hour, and then they started to throw him into a fire that they'd built. And all our chaps are there and they can't do anything about it because even if they'd attacked them, they'd call out and there would be somebody, and they'd call our chaps off.

They chucked little Nicky Hallam backwards and forwards into the fire for about half an hour until he was unconscious. He died two days later. But he gave his life because this mob had to stand there until they got the total. That is what went on, absolutely shocking.

FRANCIS BINSTEAD

The POW veterans of the Japanese all say that the further your camp was from Singapore, the further it was from being overseen by Japanese command and consequently, the more brutal the treatment would be. Ambon was a long way from Singapore.

To start with, some of the Dutchmen, I've forgotten the exact number . . . we weren't allowed to fraternise with them but they were in the same compound, they were caught trying to send letters to their wives who would have been in this other compound and the Japs took a dim view of that and grabbed a number of them and started flogging them.

They took them up to headquarters and an event which we came to call 'The Dutch Garden Party' occurred on one afternoon, where they flogged these blokes with pick handles, mostly with pick handles and anything they could get their hands on. That showed us very clearly that the Japs didn't mess about. If they were angered at any sort of behaviour they would take quite severe, what we thought were severe methods to get the message across they didn't like it. As I say, that gave us a bit of an idea of what might happen if we were caught doing something we shouldn't do.

Well it so happened a little while after that, it might have been only a few weeks again, the actual period fades a bit, but not long after that it seems that some of our fellows had been managing to get under the wire and go down to a local village to get food and get back again without being observed. I didn't know this was going on, just a very small little group of fellows. Of course it had to be kept secret, well they kept it secret, so I don't know how long that went on, but one night, well, the Japs woke up that something was going on and they must have found where they were getting out and they waited there one night and they apprehended three or four fellows as they came back into camp.

Well the Japs were pretty sure that there were more than four involved, those four were taken up to Japanese headquarters. So the next day the Japs, through their interpreter, had everybody in the camp except those that were bed-ridden in hospital, line up in the open area of the camp and they brought the Ambonese from this village where these fellows had actually gone, brought them and told them they were to identify anybody that they recognised in the line-up as people who had been going down to their village.

Now it mightn't sound much, but that line-up was one of the most terrifying and nerve-wracking experiences we ever had, because I'm sure everybody was thinking what I was thinking: 'God, I hope I don't look like one of those fellows!' As it happened, they picked out a number of men; I think another eleven, who had in fact been the so-called 'guilty' ones.

They took those away up to Japanese headquarters in the grounds which over-looked the camp, the Japanese headquarters, and they were flogged, I think, for at least a week. We couldn't actually see the floggings going on but we could hear the beltings and the screams and the groans, and it was just horrible.

Then they took them away and cut their heads off, executed them, buried them in a mass grave. There's a photo of that in my scrapbook, that grave, with their names on it which somebody in our camp managed to erect and carve the names on.

So that's what the Japs meant by severe punishment. Like they said, if you own up – there must have been a few that owned up – if you own up in this instance you'll get light punishment, if you don't you'll get severe punishment, words to that affect . . . that was the way things were in Ambon, late 1942.

MARIC GILBERT

•

To Australian eyes, ears and hearts, the Japanese were nearly incomprehensible, both as an enemy and as a people. Language alone was a formidable barrier. Most camps did not have an interpreter and although it was common for there to be someone among the prisoners who could speak or understand a little Japanese, misunderstandings were frequent and the subsequent punishments inevitable. Making sense of Japanese motivation and inexplicable cruelty was virtually impossible.

Every excuse that they could they would turn it into something vicious – you know, hanging fellows up by their thumbs for hours on end. And why the human body will take so much punishment is beyond my comprehension, the human body takes a hell of a lot of punishment. Fellows left in the sun for hours and hours, between your elbows across your back with a pole and your arms stretched back like . . . and you try, for two minutes, it hurts more than anything. Fellows with poles at the back of their knees and told to kneel on the pole, let alone what your knees do to what the rest of your body . . . it is those sort of things.

And then I have seen them line up Dutch girls – the Dutch were very prominent in Java – and there was a camp further along with a lot of womenfolk with their daughters, and they used to wave to the boys inside, and this was at this hospital at Marta de la Rosa. They lined up four or five little girls one time and stripped 'em, and they went along with their cigarettes burning them. Just deliberately callous, nasty fellows.

BILL COVENTRY

At the end of World War II, when retribution and judgment turned from desire to reality, close contact with the Japanese allowed some Australians to form more complex, subtler opinions of their enemy. Captain Athol Moffitt had been sent to Borneo as part of the 9th Division military government when his superiors, aware that he had been admitted to the bar just before the war began, seconded him to the army's legal department, where he would take up a role as Australia's prosecutor in the war crimes trials.

So far as the prisoners were concerned, Japanese culture was such that they felt they had no duty to people who were foreigners, and strangers who were in occupied country. This was revealed by some writings of a Japanese professor after the war. The Japanese culture is based on a sense of duty – it's a very fine thing, their duty to different groups. And if you have a duty to a group it's very wonderful, and we do too. But if you had a higher duty to another group, the duty to the other one didn't exist. So if you had a person who was just a friend in your house you had some kind of duty to him. But if you had some higher duty such as to the Emperor, that duty to the stranger in your house ceased to exist.

And for those who are complete strangers, like in occupied territory, there was no duty, and in the Japanese culture, the Japanese writer, Professor Doi, explained that the Christian–Judaic culture of right and wrong hadn't ever got through to the Japanese. They had no sense of something being right and wrong, and to kill a person to whom you had no duty was no different to killing an animal. That's how it was.

ATHOL MOFFITT

One place where Japanese belief in duty deliberately ignored humanity was the Thai–Burma Railway. A railway line already existed between Bangkok and the Malayan peninsula, but the Japanese wanted to continue it from Bangkok to Burma. A railway through there would enable them to supply their troops already in Burma and open a route to China and India, a critical part of their expansionist goals.

The line was not a new idea. A British company had investigated extending the line in the years before the war but rejected it on the grounds that the terrain was too dangerous and they would lose too many workers to disease. The Japanese had no such compunctions, especially the engineers who were responsible for the construction schedule.

They wouldn't recognise frailness. They were fanatical about keeping up to their goals – they had certain goals these engineers, and they were fanatical about it. So much so, these people are still – they go to the shrine each year in Japan. They think that they've achieved a great achievement. They don't look at the sins and crimes that they committed in building the railway line.

. . . They just forced the position that they would keep to schedule. And keeping to schedule – if you marched sick people out that could hardly, you know, are very weak and frail, and make them walk six kilometres out to a job, in wet weather, slipping down, sliding down. Then having to work all day and then having to come home at night – no wonder so many of them died. If you've ever been to Kanchanaburi Cemetery, walk through that cemetery and you'll notice the age of the people that died. They were mostly young, and also, the period in which they died. They died in the second half of 1943 and that was the cause of it. It was kind of a slave position.

Tom Uren

After the war it was estimated that the effort to construct the railway involved building 4 million cubic metres of earthworks, moving 3 million cubic metres of rock, and building 14 kilometres of bridgeworks – all over a period of about ten months and by workers using tools that would not have been out of place in the Middle Ages. There were 300 000 people working as slave labourers on the railway, 61 000 of them POWs. A total 12 399 prisoners would die, 2646 of them Australians. The indigenous labourers suffered the worst – 90 000 would lose their lives.

Yet in some respects, the Japanese Army was treating the prisoners no differently from the way they treated their own troops. The hierarchy of rank was rigidly observed and maintained, and any diversion from instant obedience to an order would result in immediate physical punishment. From the Emperor on down, each level of rank abused and humiliated the one below, and at the very bottom of the pile were the Korean soldiers. Colonised and exploited, they were forced to prove their worth by being even more vicious than their Japanese masters.

This is the thing about Japanese discipline. There were three classes of privates: first, second and third class. If something went wrong, the first-class private would take it out on the second-class private and then he would pass it down to the third-class private. So the third-class private would take it out on the Koreans. What happened to the POWs? The Koreans would take it out on the POWs. We were last on the line.

. . . Colonel Williams, our CO, was made to stand outside the guardhouse for two days at attention. Now, it's bad enough standing to attention for ten minutes, these are the things they would do. Just sheer bastardry. People were made to kneel on rough surfaces and this is a whim of a third-class Japanese private.

And no matter how you protested or your commanding officer protested, it didn't carry any weight at all. This was what they wanted to do so you had to do it.

GAVIN CAMPBELL

Even after they had lost the war, at a time when one could reasonably have expected some degree of fellow compassion and mateship to show itself, the Japanese held fast to their ruthless discipline. Athol Moffitt spoke to an Australian sergeant who had been responsible for bringing defeated Japanese back out of the jungle to a prison camp.

He said, 'The conduct the Japs showed, they were really only animals. Officers, when they had the sick parade in the morning,' – this was on this march after they had surrendered – 'would give their own men who could not stand up a mighty kick. Or who could not hold up their head, a hit across the face. No man would help another who fell down or was too sick to walk.'

They had to be ordered to help each other, the Aussies made them carry three or four who couldn't walk, and when the Australians were round a bend out of sight, the others would beat them to make them walk. Once, one was missing. The Japs said he died and the Australian sergeant went back and found him hanged on a tree. As he said, 'You have no friends in the Japanese Army.' Another, the Japs beat to death.

When they arrived at Lawas, now this is my own account, when they were at Lawas, only one was being carried . . . his spirit was such that he refused to die. He was thin and his leg looked paralysed. The Japs beat him over the head to kill him but still he lived. I saw his face which hardly looked like a face any more. His head was battered; his cheeks were swollen up to the eyes, a bluish mass of pulp. I can understand now all that is said about the brutality of the Japs to our people when this is what they did to their own people.

ATHOL MOFFITT

In this fanatical atmosphere of institutionalised cruelty there were inevitably some Japanese guards who relished the terrible freedoms they were allowed. The men remember them well. Ian Wall had joined the army at the age of sixteen, telling the recruiters he was 21. As he said, 'I had more front than Myers.' He was just eighteen years old when he was confronted by the malevolence that could be found in the human race. The guard was called 'The Storm Trooper'.

The Storm Trooper – he was a big man, he was about six foot three, enormous brute – he was vicious. He'd walk through the hospital, and if you were in hospital as a POW you were really sick . . . He'd have those that were sick and dying stand up to attention while he walked through and all this sort of thing, and some of them couldn't and those that couldn't he'd belt them. These are people within days of their death.

That's the sort of people they were . . . terrible, terrible people . . . he didn't have to bash them too hard and they were completely flattened. And somebody'd have to pick them up and put them back in bed. Some of them within days of dying. It was pointless, absolutely pointless what they were doing. It was showing power. I think that they were probably peasants themselves in true life and they were relishing in their position as a guard . . .

That Storm Trooper he would even kick and keep on kicking you. You couldn't retaliate – if you did you were dead. It was as simple as that. You'd never ever get out of it. Three or four of them would get stuck into you and beat you within an inch of your life. What were you to do? So yeah, that was the way it was.

IAN WALL

Some prisons attracted the sadistic and the evil. The Japanese reserved a particular place for 'special' punishment – Outram Road Gaol, in Singapore. Built in 1837 as a civilian prison, it was a decaying hulk of a building, a place of starvation and torture where many prisoners would lose their sanity or their lives before the war's end. Bill Young was taken there after he had the temerity to attempt to escape from captivity in Sandakan, in Borneo. A Japanese court sentenced him to four years' hard labour and his first days were emblematic of the endurance he would need to survive Outram Road.

It was about 38 days, suddenly the door was opened, and we were told 'Cuchi coy!' – come out. We came outside and there's the eight of us that come over from Kuching and they marched us outside and there was the greatest shock we ever got in our lives. I've never forgotten it. We thought we were thin and we thought we were badly off. We were introduced to the inmates. They brought them out for an hour in the sun. They were all squatted in a line on the concrete outside. And they were so thin and they were all full of sores, scabs an' that. Apparently it was scabies that was the trouble. I knew, I was itching myself. And they had pellagra, vitamin deficiency – their eyes were all running with pellagra, pus was running.

Over on the side from them there was this big hipbath. If you had it today it would be worth a fortune. Because wherever they got if from, I don't know, but it was a beautifully built hipbath which, ingrained into it, embossed into it, was all these Egyptian hieroglyphics round it, you know. It was a work of art. They'd scrounged it from somewhere and they used it.

. . . We're wondering what the hell is going on. You're not allowed to talk or anything like that. And you're sitting down and you're wondering, holy, and the smell of it, these blokes, and the guard holds up a Swan ink bottle, Swan ink. Remember? Do they still have Swan ink? Well this is a good advertisement for Swan ink. But it was full of disinfectant. And he'd hold it up and quite a ceremony, and he'd 'Ahh!' pour it in and he had a big stick and he'd swirl it around . . .

Now this poor skinny fellow that I'm sitting next to, and I never met him before, didn't know who he was. Everyone, after a while you got used to it, you talk without using your lips, I can't do it now. In those days I could talk like that and not move at all, you know. He says, 'Where're you in from,, what battalion?' Obviously an Aussie, his name's Kenny Bird. I said, 'What's going on there?' He said, 'That's the scabies bath.' He says, 'Now, when he says "ush", his nibs say "ush",' he says, 'for God's sake get in quick,' he says, 'because three of the Indians have got syphilis.'

That was a lovely introduction, an' I said, 'What!' Then all of a sudden the Jap guard says 'Ush!' and everyone, the Aussies and the British, and they're all diving to get in front. Blow me down if I didn't miss out and I'm behind the Indians and I'm wondering which one of them's got syphilis. Well when it's my turn to get in the water, the water's just filthy, scabs and all that sort of, and you've gotta get in! There's no beg your pardon. Well that was the scabies bath.

BILL YOUNG

At Outram Road the guards tortured the prisoners through deprivation, starvation and beatings of the worst kind. Within the walls was a world of almost unimaginable viciousness, where individual Japanese soldiers played sadistic games on helpless men.

I just sat in the cell. I could stretch my arms out like that and that was the width of the cell. It was 12 feet long; there was a light globe that burnt all night long. It was 100 years old, of course, the building, it'd been condemned. It was full of cracks and vermin. Ah, insects of all description – scorpions, you name it – it was there. It was all wet with humidity, green, discoloured, had been painted over dozens of times, with lime wash, whitewash, and it was all flaking off and then the walls were cracked and things like that.

Now, that was the atmosphere. It was a concrete floor, there was three boards and a wooden block with a little curve in it for your neck. I never ever used it myself, I slept without a pillow, and there was a little bit of a cotton blanket that you had. And you had a pair of shorts, Japanese shorts, on and a shirt with your number, mine was 510. The cell door was in front, you sat cross-legged with your hands on your knees and you looked at the cell door. The door was a thick wooden door, about 3 inches thick, with steel ribbing across. And there was a slot in the middle, where they pass you your bowl, a little bowl of rice. There was a little peephole as well, swivel. The Japanese guard could swivel and look through the little peephole at you . . .

An' there was one guard in particular we used to call 'The Postman', he was very, very particular about it. He'd open the door and come and bash you if you weren't sitting properly . . . some of the guards you knew were lazy or indifferent and you could get away with standing up, resting your legs out, reading the graffiti, Morse code. And there's some guards you would never send a message or anything like that, you'd never read graffiti and you'd never not sit cross-legged, and the worst one was the bloke we called 'The Postman'.

And sometimes, I know on one particular time, probably one of the first times I was caught by him. I didn't realise he was on duty. I'm sitting back, with my back on the wall with my legs stretched and I'm shaking them and one thing and another, relaxing, and I heard the knock and that was the signal, only one knock, *bang!*, just one knock like that. There was about two or three minutes, which seemed to be hours in time, and you knew he was outside, you knew.

Now after that you'd hear the key'd go in the lock, now it wouldn't turn, you'd hear the key go in the lock, and then for another two or three minutes there'd be silence, but you'd know he was outside there, and then he'd turn the lock and you'd hear it turned and there'd be nothing else. Two, couple of minutes.

And then all of a sudden, *bang!* the door'd be slammed back. Frighten the life out of you. And there would be The Postman. And they all had swords. But it was an old-fashioned jail and the locks were old-fashioned and the keys were great old-fashioned things. And he'd come in . . . and you'd be looking up and you'd be at attention, as if you were like that all the time, you're willing your hair to grow a bit thicker because you know what's coming.

And he'd stand just a little bit behind you on the side. Not much room between you but he'd get there, wasn't a very big bloke actually, and then he'd be giving you a lecture or something like that an' all of a sudden, while he's doin' this, he's raising this flamin' great big key and then *bang!* down it comes. And oh, God, flamin' lump or a cut, sometimes blood'd come down, and you couldn't do anything and you're sittin' there and the tears'd come into your eyes because when you've lost all your weight, your food, your muscles go down, it's not only mentally, everything goes down too. Your resistance goes down. Your resistance to pain, your resistance to everything. So consequently the build-up to that was tremendous, it was gigantic. From the moment of that knock on the door, so as a consequence, you did your best.

. . . An' you're sitting there all day, and I tell you, there's a lot more hours in those days than there are hours in these days. There was a window barred, right up the top, you couldn't see it or anything and to restrict it, further out from the window was a steel shelf so you couldn't see the sky or anything like that. So for over two years we didn't see the sky, didn't see the night, didn't see the stars . . . And there's a steel ventilator at the bottom, and that's the door I looked at for two years and one month.

BILL YOUNG

Athol Moffitt was given a small glimpse inside the mind of the commandant of Sandakan prison camp, Captain Susumi Hoshijima, when he was on trial for his life, accused of the murder of hundreds of men. Moffitt was the prosecutor.

When it came to the final addresses, the Japanese defending officer did very well; he made a very able address, as well as could be in the circumstances, although the evidence was so against Hoshijima at the end. So Hoshijima asked for permission to address the court himself. And he addressed it then in English, and he talked for a day and a half, on and on and on it went. Everything that had ever happened. He never did a wrong thing in his life.

. . . And then when they eventually retired, and there was a long time, and they came back and they found him guilty and sentenced him to death by hanging. And I thought at this stage, recorded it there, Hoshijima stood up, still with his shiny boots, leggings up here, immaculate, saluted, clicked his heels and marched out.

And that was Hoshijima, who these prisoners had to put up with. He had said, 'You are cowards'. He said this to the prisoners when they got there. 'You are cowards, you surrendered. You don't deserve it but the Emperor preserved your life and now you'll work for the Emperor from dawning till dark. Until your souls rot under the jungle sun.' This was his introduction to the prisoners in Sandakan. That's the kind of man he was. And that's the man that we still saw, fighting to the end.

And then they, I wasn't present, but they talked of his execution. As he ascended to be hanged, a man who called out you know, 'This is for all the Aussies you killed at Sandakan!' And then he yelled out, 'Banzai! Banzai!' as he dropped. That's the story I did hear.

ATHOL MOFFITT

•

It wasn't only captive soldiers who suffered under the systematic brutality of the Japanese. Many more civilians, particularly the people of the conquered countries in South-East Asia received far worse treatment. In their racial division of the world, the Japanese considered the Chinese, Malays and others to be beneath any kind of consideration.

When Sonkurai was divided into two, and Bruce Hunt took the sick up to Burma then the Japs said, 'Well, there's only half of you there now, so you'll have to have only half the camp.' And they filled the other half up with these poor unfortunate natives who almost 100 per cent had cholera, and they died like flies. Had babies. It was an appalling sight. One of the worst sights I've ever seen or anything I've ever had to deal with, when newly born babies looking for their mother, they knew their mother but they had no one to feed them, and we couldn't look after them. It was really appalling.

And the Japs at that stage, they had no compunction about it at all. They wouldn't do anything. They just didn't want us to go near them and they wouldn't feed them and they didn't feed them. The further it got away from Singapore the worse it became, and the further you got up on that railway line the worse it became. It was just an appalling business there.

You can't understand them at times, I don't know, an occasional Japanese would do his block completely and just bash and kill somebody he didn't like, a native, but then, the whole thing was, nobody cared about it all. It was no good going to the sergeant who was usually in charge of the camp. He couldn't

Hospital on Cholera Hill, Shemu Sonkurai camp

care less. You know, you could never forgive them really, as a race, when that kind of thing went on . . . Nobody would know how many really died on that railway line. They said once, 'one death per sleeper'. Maybe that's right.

LLOYD CAHILL

It was the casualness of the violence and the killing that shocked the prisoners. Life wasn't just cheap; in some cases it held no worth to the Japanese at all. In the first few weeks after the surrender in Singapore, Bill Young witnessed an incident that has never left him.

We were sitting down on some bags of rice. It was lunchtime and we had our little, whatever we were eating, rice and stuff, and the gate at the side, there was a Jap guard and he was looking. Every truck that came in he'd look at their papers and things and he would let them go by.

There was a truck pulled up and he was looking, he was on the other side of the truck, the guard, and he was looking at the driver's credentials. And a Chinese fellow came, pulling a rickshaw. He didn't see the guard, and he came through this side, and he went into the compound.

Well the guard saw him out the side of his eyes, and the next thing he shouts . . . he rushed over to the Chinaman and he smashed the rickshaw to pieces, and also the poor old Chinaman lay dead. He smashed him up, just like that. This is a peaceful scene; we're having our lunch, all's well with the world, lovely view. The water, the waterfront, all the activities, people going about their business . . . He's quite innocent, he just went through, an' then the next minute everything's smashed up.

And then the Jap went back over there as if it was nothing and continued with his work.

BILL YOUNG

While the Germans for the most part adhered to the rules of the Geneva Conventions regarding the Allied POWs, they behaved appallingly towards their Russian prisoners. Russia had not signed the conventions but that was not the only reason that the Germans deliberately mistreated them. There was a kind of intense hatred between the two nations that reduced thousands of Russian prisoners to abject, starving beings. They were often confined in compounds alongside the Allied prison camps and the inmates, recipients of Red Cross kindness, could only watch in horror.

They took tremendous numbers of Russian prisoners, hundreds of thousands of them, and they just marched them east, and if they dropped they shot them. They had ruthless disregard for Russian prisoners' lives . . . and the dislike, the hatred came in one episode where the Russians were so hungry, because they didn't get any Red Cross food, that at night they used to break into our camp, climbing over the wire. They would be shot on the way in. But they would break in at night and get into the bread store, a small wooden hut which held the bread stores for the next day.

They would get inside there and stuff themselves with bread, and they would stuff loaves under their uniforms. And then crawl on their hands and knees under searchlights and machine guns to get out and back to their own camp. And although the Germans shot quite a few of them it got to the point where they got sick of shooting them, and one day when the Russians were in there they just locked them in.

And then in the morning they brought in about three or four Alsatian dogs whom they had starved for a few days and then they opened the bread stores and let the dogs in. Well, the yells and the screams and the fight, they locked them in. It went on for quite a long time. Then the Germans, if you can have a cross between glee and grimness, they opened and told the Russians to come out, thinking a lot of them would be wounded, or the dogs had ripped into them.

The Russians came out with broad smiles. As soon as the dogs arrived they set about them and they killed them and they skinned them and they ate them.

And they made the typical Russian headgear out of the skins of the Alsatian dogs . . .

We admired the Russians so much for that and, too, we thought it was a very cowardly and filthy thing for the Germans to do.

GEOFF CORNISH

•

Again and again in these interviews with Australia's prisoners of war, I encountered a remarkable moment. It didn't matter whether the person had been imprisoned in Germany or Burma, Korea or Thailand; the moment was essentially the same. It always came without warning or preamble, there were no deep breaths or obvious gathering of courage; and it was made all the more remarkable because of that. The moment was the straightforward, factual description of a time of endurance and pain that seems almost inconceivable. But it *did* happen. Listen for a moment. This is Robert Parker in Korea.

We were doing up to 25 miles a night and by this time we had started to go some places cross-country just straight up these mountains. No track or anything, and by this time Slim Madden was pretty crook, he started to go down and he started to get crook.

One time we were halfway up this mountain and we were going up and slipping back, up a bit more and slipping back. And Slim started to slip quite a lot and the guard would just come up and belt him in the lower back with the butt of the rifle. 'Get up there!' And he finally made it up, I gave him a helping hand, he finally got up the top but from then on he degenerated a bit and we got back down onto the lower road again and started marching again and a couple more days and I suddenly went.

And I was just lying down on the road, there had already been a lot pulled out, mainly Koreans, and I started to get a bit weak and then this one American, one of the American Negroes, he went over and couldn't get up. And what had been happening, some of the Koreans that went off, if you couldn't get back in the line, you just got shot. One of the guards would go out and they just shot them.

And so when this American Negro, Siggy, when he fell over and couldn't get up, the blokes and myself we carried him. Don't know how we did it, but one of his arms around our neck each and we sort of lifted him up. And dragged his feet along, we dragged him and dragged him and finally he come good a little bit and could walk a little bit, and that wasn't so bad, so we carried along and Slim tried to help, but he was too crook to help.

And then suddenly I fell over and couldn't move. It must have been four or five days after we had been captured and we had only had, no water and two meals of what do they call them? Soya beans. A couple of handfuls each time. And only half cooked, they weren't cooked like our baked beans or anything. We used to call them 'mystery beans' later on, because no matter how you chewed them they still came out the same way.

Okay so I am lying there and, 'What am I going to do now?' Just lying there like a foetus all curled up on my side, and, 'Oh, they can shoot me.' Then I suddenly remember, just before we went across to Korea, when we were in Japan, we went out on this place called Haramura Training Area, to watch a final little bit of a firing display, and from there back into our main camp was about 25 mile and we started marching back. The original idea was for the trucks to come and meet us and take us back, and Colonel Green, his orders were no, he sent the trucks back. 'They can walk.' And our commanding officer at the time was a chap called Lieutenant Mackenzie, and he was leading us on the march back and I was already carrying two rifles, mine and one of the other boys that had just about had it. And this Lieutenant Mackenzie's feet were just a mess of sores and that and, 'You better get a lift back, Sir.' 'No, it will be all right,' he says. 'Bat on,' he says. 'Carry on, bat on.' And he walked the whole distance and everyone admired him for that, he was always called 'Bat on'. Anyway, I am lying down there and I can hear this voice, 'Bat on'. So I got up. I don't know how I did it, but I got up and away I went.

ROBERT PARKER

Captain Phil Greville was taken prisoner in Korea while leading a work party repairing minefield fences. One of his men was killed and six were wounded. He was the highest ranking Australian officer captured during that war.

I was shoved in a wooden box . . . It had been a crate surrounding something like a domestic refrigerator. It was 4 foot 6 long and it was about 2 foot 6 wide and 3 foot 6 high. You couldn't stretch out in it. You couldn't stand up. You could barely sit up without hitting your head on the top and I'd been very comfortable in this for nearly three weeks. There was a stream, tiny little stream just above the box and they let me out to wash once a day and I was able to keep myself clean . . . and I thought, 'Well, you know, I can hang out here.' But I didn't realise that I would be under such intense interrogation day-in and day-out for the next 21 days.

The interrogation was mainly about military matters on the front line and that was easy just to keep on saying number, name and rank and that was it. They offered me tea. I didn't drink tea. They offered me cigarettes. I didn't need cigarettes, and these were little wins for me. They couldn't give me anything, couldn't sweeten me up in any way and I was able to sort of say, 'No I don't want this'.

. . . It's very difficult to explain to people what solitary confinement is like. The only way that I can do it is to say there are 60 seconds in a minute and there are 60 minutes in an hour and 24 hours in a day, seven days a week, and if you think of 90 days of nothingness, that has to have some effect upon you. Fortunately in my case, it was broken up into sort of 30-day periods and in between I managed to be in a group of people in which I could talk to people again. The other thing about those 90 days, I suppose, from suppressing this business of non-involvement, it has probably made me – it changed my personality, I suppose, from an outward-going one to an inward-going one. It hasn't affected me so much as my family.

. . . Anyway, after about 21 days they shoved an ROK soldier, Republic of Korea soldier, a South Korean soldier, who had been captured, in with me in this little box . . . We couldn't converse very much, you know, 'number one', 'number ten', were about the limits of our joint experience, nevertheless I was quite comfortable with him in the sense that he could sit opposite me and my feet and his upper body sort of fitted the box reasonably well.

But a few days later they put in a civilian who was incredibly dirty. His clothes were filthy. His nails were filthy and his manners were appalling, but the poor fellow had a rope around his neck which was tied to his feet and it was very difficult for us to let him sit in any way that gave him comfort. The ROK soldier was immaculately clean except that he'd been wounded in the chest and he had gangrene. The Korean, the civilian, when they brought in food, they brought it in a common bowl and he just stuck his hands in and grabbed what he could out of it, and in a couple of days I was starting to get pretty sick and I decided that rather than get terribly weak, I'd get out of there.

About the third night after he'd been in there, the civilian managed to get some slack in the ropes and he pushed his feet in such a way that the rope around his neck was strangling him. It was possible that he was a spy or accused of spying or something of that nature, but anyway he was dead keen to kill himself this night and all I can remember was waking up from a fitful sleep with this face about that far from me and spew and spit and everything coming out of him and I just pushed him back as a reaction and the guards came running and everything like that and he was taken out and made to sit outside for the night.

That was one of the incidents I think which made me decide that I was going to get out of the box as soon as I could. I didn't think I would survive too long with the three of us in there.

Phil Greville

Charlie Parrott worked as a slave labourer in a coalmine in Poland, and saw firsthand the shocking lengths to which men would go to try and avoid one more day of misery.

In the coalmines, people got so distressed that they couldn't get out of it. It was from four o'clock in the morning till eight o'clock at night in the mine, that was a day. You had to do twenty days straight and you got one day off, which, with the food we was getting, was pretty disastrous, I can tell you. I've seen chaps put their hand at the end of the table and get a mate with a stick to smash all their fingers to get time off. Chaps scratched their arm, put salt in the hair in it and tied it up to make it go septic.

The worst one I seen was a chap scratched his arm and another bloke had a boil and squeezed the core out of it and laid it on his arm and tied it up and he was really, really sick he was. I don't know whether he lived. One of these South Africans, to get a day off, he put his foot in a bucket with his boot and sock on and got his mate to fill it with boiling water. He had a really bad foot. When he took his sock off the skin and everything came off.

Charlie Parrott

Ian Wall survived the Burma Railway.

One of the Japanese favourites was kneeling on a piece of wood and usually, not so much sharpened, but they have an edge on the wood and you'd kneel on that just under the knees and hold up a heavy log above your head and you just had to stay like that for hours, and every time you weakened you got a belting. And some people, I'm not talking about five minutes or ten minutes, I'm talking about days in some cases, and people have just collapsed because they just couldn't stand it anymore, understandably.

And there was water treatment, where they'd just keep filling you up with water in your mouth and you'd just expand, and expand, and expand . . . they were full of those tricks. There was a case where 'Spit' Easton was tied up like a dog and water put just out of his reach for days and days on end and made him crawl round like a dog and things of this nature. And they'd bury you and sometimes put food close by you to bring the ants. So the ants would worry you, you know you couldn't, your arms were buried.

IAN WALL

•

Against all of this, the prisoners developed a kind of stoic fatalism, a muted acceptance that this was their lot and they just had to cop it. For some, though, the hardest thing to do, particularly for an Australian it seemed, was to not react to the simple injustice of the punishments, to strike back against the whole damned unfairness of it all. Doing so was obviously a brave action to take, but it could also be foolish in the extreme.

When a guard was trying to swing their punch to hit you, you'd ease back like that, they'd miss you every time and then you'd have to bend over like that so they could reach up and whack you across your face. Oh, your blood'd boil up inside you, you know – feel like whacking them. But of course if you whacked them that'd be the end of you, kind of business.

One of our chaps did in Borneo, in Sandakan, he was working in the kitchen there and he whacked the Jap. The Jap used to come up and wash his dirty handkerchiefs or clothes in the blooming clean water this chap had dragged up from the creek. So he threatened him about three or four times and he didn't do it, so he just hauled off and whacked him, broke the Jap's jaw.

Well they got him and they broke both his arms, set them back to front so he'd never hit another Nippon soldier, tied him up with barbed wire during the night. It was only our officer got out and gave him a morphine injection that carried him through. They tried him and sent him to Outram Road Gaol, which most probably saved his life too. Because had he stopped there he would've died there.

Len Darlington was his name, from New South Wales; he came back. He won the heavyweight championship on the *Queen Mary* going over, as a boxer, and he had a fight in the ring when he got home too, down in Sydney, after all that.

So those are the things, that if you did hit back, well you could be shot, you could be executed yourself, you didn't know what to do. So, life is sweet, you had to cop a lot and just swallow it down like that. But it was hard, I can tell you.

CYRIL GILBERT

Some prisoners did get a kind of revenge, but it was often unsatisfactory. By the end of the war, the prisoners of war were too tired, too empty and too desperate to find anything that remotely approached normal life, to want to burden their souls with any more death. No matter how great the justification.

After Stalingrad the Russians moved right down through, right down into Poland, they got very close to our camp. Within one night we could hear the guns firing, before they put us on foot and started to march across Germany. These parties were marching all over Germany from different stalags, different camps. The Germans were insistent on us easing away to the west slowly, day by day, by day, by day.

And we saw Jews being shot in the snow as we were marching along the roads, terrible things that you could see. They just, you know, I can still see those eyes looking at me, they'd be lying on their sides imploring, but you couldn't do anything because we were under guard. Not very pleasant, some of the things I can't talk about . . . They were buggered, just lying there waiting to be shot.

And one guard, one of our own guards, shot one of our own fellows, one of us, out of camp E3. His name was Arthur Russell. He was just a little slow getting up, you know, we had a rest every hour, roughly. And he was just a bit slow getting up and this stupid young guard, I could see his face even today, he just turned his rifle around and shot him straight through the chest. And there was bloody near a riot, but we were all so low in spirit and weakness that we couldn't do anything, because we had a full complement of guards either side . . . we buried him that night in the village, little village there, and we couldn't do anything about it. So we waited and we waited and we finally got the guard in the finish.

. . . The day we were liberated . . . the great American Sherman tank pushed down the gate to my compound in Munich. And the Yanks hopped out, and we could see the Germans running for their lives, being sprayed with bullets by other tanks in the distance, running across a green field and valley. And I said to myself, 'Serves you bloody lot right!'

. . . And the little guard, the idiot who shot Arthur Russell on the march, one of our blokes, they handed him over to the Americans, and they summarily shot him, just down behind the compound. They said, 'Would you like to?' They offered a friend of mine the gun, and they said, 'Would you?' And he said, 'No, I couldn't shoot him.' So the Yanks shot him, 'cause he was guilty of murder – heinous, heinous murder. Arthur Russell was a nice guy, he was one of the elder ones, probably married, I don't know whether he had children, but he'd be about 30-something, quiet guy, never any trouble to anybody, and this idiot just shot him because he was a bit slow getting up that day in the village somewhere in Czechoslovakia.

. . . When you're released, you don't take revenge, everything drops away from you, like a wet cloak. Anyway, the Yanks heard the case and summarily executed him.

RAPHAEL CORBETT

Sometimes there is no sense, no apparent logic; no way to fully understand what being a prisoner of war was actually like. Only those who were there can properly speak of it.

Being a prisoner of war changed me definitely, because I was just a young sister. I saw life at its best and its worst. I saw what human beings could do to each other, what hatred could do and yet what faith could do and what kindness could do. That's what we are here for, to help one another. I saw how useless all this is, when people go on hating one another and killing one another. How someone lives with that I don't know, lives with themselves, I mean.

When you have just massacred a whole lot of people, how would you feel? I don't know. We are all born with animal instincts in all of us. War brings it out in so many. In war it makes some men, men; but others . . . it just makes them animals.

SISTER BERENICE TWOHILL

6

'They were human beings – and a little like us'

Prisoner of war camps were small islands of isolation and necessary self-centredness; almost complete little worlds where customary civilised rules and ordinary human behaviour were notable more for their absence than their presence. Nonetheless, life inside the camps did reflect one critical characteristic of life outside: it was never simple. The usual complexities of our existence were there in abundance, not the least of which was that despite the understandable need to do so, the prisoners could not lump all their captors into the one basket of dislike and hatred. Fred Skeels found at least one man who exhibited some humanity.

Only once in one camp I was in there was a Jap, he was a Jap guard, he was a soldier, he was an engineer, his name was Hirushi, and he told us that he was a Christian, and he acted as one, you know, he was as good as he could be without losing face amongst his cobbers, he treated us with whatever he could in the two camps that I spent with him.

He moved up and down the line apparently, because other camps knew of this Hirushi bloke. But he was the only one that I came across that would show you any sort of decency or respect, this bloke. He was only a little Jap soldier but he reckoned he was a Christian and he did act as such, he tried to help you when he could, without being found out by his fellow guards, who would probably have given him a bashing or something else, you know?

FRED SKEELS

Even in a hellhole like Ambon, the smallest display of humanity shown by a guard, just a reluctance to bash perhaps for no reason, would leave the men with a long-remembered gratitude. They'd learned through brutal experience to have very low expectations of any kind of decency.

Were there any decent ones amongst them? I only really remember two, they really stood out and I don't think they were marine guards, or marine people, I think they were part of the air force. Why I think that, they both wore air force boots, what the pilots or crew wear – boots that come up the leg.

So, not surprisingly, we called the first one 'Boots'. I don't think he ever beat anybody. He was as near to humane as could be. And then shortly he had a mate helping him, of course we had to call him 'Saddles', didn't we? Boots and Saddles. But they were the only two that I can remember that showed in any way at all that they had any humanity.

But see, they'd been infiltrated with a hatred of the white man, not surprising really when you really reflect on it, reflect on what the white man had done to Asian races. Here they were for the first time lording it over the white man and the humblest coolie on a truck or something had their permission to give you a belting if he felt like it.

Maric Gilbert

War can make for curious bedfellows and the prisoner world was no exception. After the hideousness of the Thai–Burma Railway, Lloyd Cahill and the men he doctored had every right to regard the Japanese as inhumane and barbaric. Yet in the aftermath of the railway, as the survivors were being transported back to Singapore, they encountered some momentary truths aboard a decrepit and rusty cargo ship.

The Japs who were on this ship were Jap soldiers who had been fighting in Manchuria and they were the best Japs that I saw, that we ran into anywhere. They were very good. The first thing they said when we got in there and talking, one of the old sergeants, Gunsa, said to me, 'These Koreans, bad men.' I said, 'Yeah, bad men.' And he'd say, 'Which one bad men?' And he'd always wait for them and if they didn't salute him, he'd give them a good old bash.

The troops christened him George Robey, who was a famous comedian in British films in those days, old George . . . and he thought George Robey was a marvellous name, so the troops would go and salute old George any time and have a yarn with him.

We had an extraordinary trip down on that thing. They only had frozen Australian beef on this little old ship from Singapore, cold storage. They used to turn this on for the troops and they got some decent food, and not only that, he then made these Koreans wash whatever we were eating out of, and they had to do the washing-up!

Another extraordinary thing was there was a little Japanese lieutenant who could speak very good English and we used to talk to him a bit – I don't know how long, it might have been ten days or a fortnight or something getting down – and he became very interesting and he told me he had been a professional baseball player and he had been in Manchuria fighting and so forth and so on, and he had no doubt that they were going to lose the war. This was in '43.

And one night he said, 'I speak with you tomorrow night under the captain's bridge.' The bridge was a rickety old thing. You wouldn't give tuppence for it. It was like a hen coop. And I used to go and I used to talk to him there at night and one night he said to me, 'When this war is over what will happen to you?' I said, 'I don't know, but if I survive I'll go back to my country.' He said, 'Back to your country?' And I said, 'Yes.' He said, 'Oh I cannot understand that.' I said, 'Why?' He said, 'Oh we cannot do that.' I said, 'What will happen to you when the war is over, won't you go back to your own country?' He said, 'Oh no, I don't think I can go back. Maybe, maybe.' And I said, 'That's interesting. I don't understand that either.'

He stopped then for a while and he said, 'You see that star up there?' And I said, 'Yes.' He said, 'That's your God and that's my God.' That's about as near as I ever got to the Japanese. Very interesting little bloke.

LLOYD CAHILL

Sometimes, somehow, men reached across the gap that their cultures and the war had placed between them. Bill Coventry encountered more than his fair share of brutality, yet he too, remembers one, bright moment.

There was a protective point of land, and there was supposed to be 9 acres of ground there, and we got there and it was jungle. And with the Australian Army shovels that the Japs had been able to scrounge, we cleared that away and dug it up and turned it into a big vegetable garden, we had irrigation channels running through it and everything . . .

And when the boys used to take malaria attacks and so forth, we grew cucumbers on long sticks, and underneath the cucumbers we used to put the fellows that were sick, and they would lay underneath there all day until they got over the malaria, and the Japs couldn't see them.

But I later became the water sergeant and I walked up and down the water channels with a shovel on my shoulder and I let the water out to all the different places. And there came a new little guard, a Korean guard, and he is up on his Korean tower that they built so they could look over, and he saw this long slab of a skinny Australian walking up and down with a shovel on his shoulder doing nothing, so he comes down out of his tower and lines me up and he is going to give me the biggest hiding he had ever gave anybody.

And he stands me down in the trench so as he could reach me and he started to hoe into me, and so forth, I didn't know what for but I realised later it's because I was walking up and down the water channel. I wasn't working, was I? I wasn't digging.

. . . And he into me and so forth, and the next minute, coming from behind me a bicycle. *Ptcheoo!* Goes right past me and a figure flying through the air lands full bore onto this Korean, and it was a Japanese sergeant that was in charge of taking us out to the farm. And he and I, if you can say it in a way, had something in common, he was a sergeant, I was a sergeant, and he always walked at the back of the crowd when we went back to camp at night-time, a sergeant's place is at the back of the unit, he always marches in the rear. So I was the sergeant, I walked in the rear and the Jap sergeant rode his bicycle alongside me, and we did converse a little bit and so forth, and he helped me get a lot of boys out of a bit of trouble.

But this squirt of a Korean was belting me, and somebody told him, and he came around on his pushbike and so forth, and he let his bike go – I knew it was his bike when I saw the thing – and he flew through the air, and he into this Korean, by gee. And he took out his pack of cigarettes and handed me the packet and told me to go and sit under the big pine tree. So I nearly got a hiding then.

I have never known any other Japanese to have any tendency to converse with us or be anything, he was a proper Japanese soldier, he would be a professional, he had been in the army a long time, he would be in his mid-twenties and so forth. And I lost him after that, I saw him once in Singapore, but he was an absolute soldier, perfectly dressed all the time.

BILL COVENTRY

Curious shards of memory remain with many of the POWs. They are often small moments which, if they had occurred at other times in their lives, would barely rate a mention, let alone be clung to as a brief shaft of light in a gloomy place.

If you were fortunate enough to be in a camp where there was an Austrian guard, he would do everything to give you little comforts. You could ask him to get extra cigarettes if you produced money to do it, or something that he could exchange for cigarettes.

Some of the Austrian guards would come into your compound at night and play a musical instrument. There was one particular fellow who played a zither. He was in a band playing the zither prior to the war. He'd been forced into the German Army, onto the Russian Front, was frostbitten on the Russian Front, lost most of his toes, brought back to Germany and was given the job of a guard on a POW camp. He used to come and play his zither of a night-time. For nothing. Just to play. If he had have been a German, that wouldn't have happened.

LAWRENCE CALDER

Music mattered to these men and women. It was so at odds with the harshness of the world they endured that its appearance became a weapon against inhumanity, denying the apparent soullessness of life. It was a gift, treasured in the receiving and the giving. Sister Twohill, supported by her faith, saw humanity even in the face of her enemy.

In front of us they put the wounded Japanese soldiers, their hospital. Those poor creatures, we used to feel so sorry for them. There were just no sanitary conditions, nothing. How we lived through it, I don't know. How we didn't get all the diseases; anyway, we lived through it.

The piano, we had it on the little veranda out the front, it was just near the barbed wire, not far from the barbed wire. These poor little creatures would come along and they would listen, and when you finished they'd clap their hands. 'More, more, more!' You felt so sorry for them. After a while they brought their nurses, their own nurses out . . . they were beautiful girls, their spotless white uniforms and they would come over to these fellows. They tried to give them injections, they chased them miles around the place, they thought they could catch them. We got a lot of laughs out of it; really, it was so serious, but still.

They would line up at our fence and watch everything we were doing. Anything we did they would sort of imitate; they'd try and imitate us. A lot of them were just little teenage boys, they were just dressed up as soldiers, they were dragged in from the country.

. . . While we were still there, because we had machines, we had bought in our machines with us and we would be sewing, and so forth. After a little while some of them, we didn't know the Japanese and they would ask, they had torn trousers, torn shirt or something else, we would understand what they wanted. We said, 'If you give us Atebrin or quinine.' There was long grass between us and they would leave their little bundle of stuff there and walk away and they would put the Atebrin or quinine in there.

That was our little secret. I never let that out before, nobody, even their officers, none of them ever knew. The poor little creatures, what are you supposed to do?

Sister Berenice Twohill

The prisoners and their guards were forced by their circumstances to agree to a compulsory relationship, one which they certainly would not have maintained otherwise. Over time, depending on the characters involved, rigidity was sometimes relaxed and more personal feelings displayed. The relationship brought them into an unwelcome intimacy, a bizarrely arranged marriage where one side always had the upper hand. But, like a too-long-together couple who have arrived at the point where they wish each other mortal harm, each side did come to know a great deal about the other.

As an ambulance man, Ray Norman had cared for wounded Australian soldiers all through the battles of Benghazi, Bardia, Tobruk and Greece. Despite being taken prisoner, he had managed to hang on to his sense of humour, but it was now combined with a bloody-minded stubbornness in the face of fools, particularly German fools.

Our first guard was a farm lad that knew nothing else but farming. So he used to have us up at half-past bloody five in the morning, and I kid you not, if we didn't stand in the same position each morning, he'd thought some bugger had escaped, that's how dumb he was. You've seen *Hogan's Heroes*? This bloke was dumb, I kid you not . . .

Anyway, he went, we got the bloke we called 'Mickey the Mouse'. Him and I didn't hit it off right from the word go. He was one of these little blokes that liked to throw his weight around. We worked six days a week, and on the Sabbath was our cleaning day, and we used to take it in turn to do the billets out. The billets by the way were cow stalls, above the cowsheds, in the grounds . . . and it was the winter of '41. It was the coldest winter Europe had had in 91 years, and there was an inch of ice on the inside of our bloody windows while we were sleeping in that . . .

Come my turn to scrub the billets out. I thought, 'I won't get on my hands and knees; I'll get a stick and put it on the scrubbing brush.' Mickey the Mouse didn't want that, he wanted me down on my hands and knees and I wouldn't get on my hands and knees, so he locked the door and he went and got the sergeant in charge of the area . . . and looking back, it was like a B-grade movie, you know, when the door suddenly flies open and there's the Huns there with a bloody revolver and the barrel looked about that big.

And he says, 'Which one's Norman?' The other eight blokes step back and I'm left in the middle . . . and I don't blame them for that, don't get me wrong,

Ray Norman and mates in 1942

I would have probably done the same thing. 'Bugger him, he's stupid enough to do this, it's his bloody problem!'

He started, 'Why won't you take orders?' I said, 'He's a private, I'm a corporal.' He says, 'But you're a prisoner!' We argued for a while, and finally he quietened down . . . I said, 'Righto, I'll be good.' . . . But I've always had a big mouth.

So anyway, he was there for a while, and then we got Franz. Well, he was good. His wife was the one that used to have Communist classes in Vienna. He brought her out to the camp at one stage; she stayed there for a while. That was only after he'd been on with every single sheila and some married ones too, in the village. He was a beauty, was our Franz. He had every little sheila in the village on the go, but he was a good bloke. He had been a waiter in Vienna . . . and while he couldn't speak much English, he had mixed with different countries and he knew that Hitler wasn't the be-all and end-all.

But he was a funny bloke. He only knew one English song, one that he used to sing every time that he got drunk. 'Get Along Little Doggie' . . . I don't know the bloody words. Where did he pick up the words for that? I don't know. It could be the same way that I picked up words to a German song, the only German song that I ever knew, and I can still remember the words to that . . . but he was great.

Rick got a note from him before he come home, in the camp that he was in, saying that they had finally caught up with him; they had put him in a unit at the first opportunity to give himself up and he was acting as a batman to a Yankee major or some bloody thing. I believe him too, because he was a real con artist, but a likeable bloke, he was a good guardian. We had no problem with Franz. Only the village maidens had a problem with Franz and I don't think they stayed maidens long with Franz either.

RAY NORMAN

In some of the German camps the prisoners ran an organised and perceptive campaign utilised against the guards. They tended to be the camps where escape was thought of as paramount and the guards were regarded as a means to an end. There was little sentimentality or shared humanity in this view – it was manipulate or perish.

Deep down, of course, they were white and very like, more like us probably than the French were. They often used to say, 'You should be on our side fighting against the Russians!' A point of view which we never shared. But that was quite frequently said to us over the years. Because of that similarity you're able to think like they thought, but you know the subtle differences between the way we as British thought and spoke and they spoke and thought, we were able to utilise that as well.

   . . . That was really our aim, always to keep the guards within bounds as much as we could within our very limited ability. But they came to respect our attitudes as well. And I am sure if we hadn't done anything we would have been bullied and smashed around, if they knew they could get away with it they would have done it, but they knew they couldn't and they didn't try. Outsmarting was the best thing. If we could do it without losing our temper or shouting or anything like that, then we did it. Because as soon as you did raise your voice or retaliate, the Germans would just point a rifle at you and you had to back right off. So we quickly learned that that wasn't the way to achieve our aims. And we adapted very early on.

   . . . I mean, you soon realised that they were human beings and a little like us, but essentially different . . . first and foremost I would say, no sense of humour. No lateral thinking. An order is an order. *Befehl.* That's a command. *'Befehl* is *befehl.'* A command is a command, an order is an order and they would carry it out and then stop. Whereas our side is, 'Well, I don't think that order is very good. I can vary it a bit and get a better effect.' And you would, and I think that's a typical Australian attitude and I think that's why Australian armed forces are very good. Because they tend to think for themselves and act logically and well. As opposed to senselessly and just because you're blindly following instructions.

GEOFF CORNISH

The Italians were frightened of us 'cause they are small. And the boys – an Australian is arrogant and if you are yelling in a foreign language he'll tell you what to do and it doesn't matter if you've got a gun or not. The Hun knows how to shut you up but the Italian was frightened, and you had to be careful because he'd use a bullet when he didn't need to. An Italian would shoot when he didn't have to, he's so frightened; you have to be careful of frightened people.

   A Hun, you know, is tough and you treat him that way and you can goad him to a point, you become psychiatrists and psychologists, you learn how to do things but you had to be very careful with an Italian because we towered over them, generally speaking, and they were frightened of us, and you know, because the boys were raucous, they told them to get the hell out, and half the time they did. It's absolutely stupid when you think about it in hindsight. Telling your captor what to do.

ALEXANDER BARNETT

Without wishing to diminish the deprivations and punishments they suffered, it's occasionally inescapable to feel that some of the European POWs were caught up in 'the great game', a kind of 'boys' own adventure' of the sort that became so popular during World War II. Or perhaps it was simply that they *were* continuing to wage war in the only way they could. Whatever the motivation, they were playing a good game of chess, but against an inferior opponent. Geoff Cornish's analysis of their qualities is penetrating and accurate.

The difference between the prisoners and the guards was that the quality of the guards, on a scale of A to Z, they were Z. Because anybody with any intelligence or ability was at the fighting front. And the guards that were too old or too stupid but were in the services, were sent to be guards to us. That suited us fine because to be in aircrew your education level had to be high indeed. And we had 24 hours a day, seven days a week doing nothing but plot how we would get out of it. And how we would outwit the Germans psychologically, physically, in every possible way, bluff, whatever.

They had what they called ferrets, each of the huts was raised about 70 or 80 centimetres from the ground on wooden pillars. They are wood with wooden floors, but of course we had to start our tunnels from the ground level, so the Germans had these ferrets as they called them, which was quite descriptive – funny little men who would go disappearing, trying to find holes to disappear down. And it was their job, with a long steel prodder, to try and find a weak spot and say, 'Oh well, that's where they have a tunnel, they have hidden it, put sand over it and a wooden trap.'

So Charlie was the first ferret. Then there was a keen type who was always terribly conscientious and trying to find it. Charlie couldn't have given a damn; he just filled his day in. He was easy meat, give him a cigarette and a cup of tea and he was quite happy.

. . . in charge was a man called Glemnitz who was an East Prussian and a professional soldier before the war, and he was the equivalent of a warrant officer. He was absolutely unbribable. But he was fair. We would say, 'Sit down, Glemnitz, have a cigarette and a cup of coffee.' 'Oh, okay, thank you.' So he would sit down and have a cup of coffee. 'Have another cup?' 'No, trying to find a tunnel, you want to keep me here.' And he would walk out. Some of the guys would sit down and have three or four cigarettes and three cups of coffee. We knew which ones would stay and so which clandestine activities we could safely work while they were in the room.

GEOFF CORNISH

Rarely did the relationship between the Australian prisoners of war and the Japanese and Korean guards reach that level of subtlety. Cruder matters were on display in all those camps; baser, more evil displays of human behaviour. Still, Australians being incorrigibly insubordinate, they found other ways to strike back.

Well, they all had nicknames, all the Jap soldiers that were guards for us. Most of them by this time were not Japanese, they were Koreans. The Koreans that the Japs had taken over, they brought a lot of their Korean troops in under their army banner, and they became our guards right from the days in Java, and they worked all the way through with us . . .

Generally speaking the Koreans were worse than the Japanese, because they were a lower element in nature's things according to the Japs, they were the lowest thing on earth, the Koreans. They've always been enemies, you know, like the Chows [Chinese] and the Japs have always been enemies . . .

But the Koreans were worse; they looked the same as the Japs, they were as ugly as the Japs were as a whole. And they all used to get names for the different ways in which they looked, or the different things that they did, or the different punishments that they meted out, or how lousy or bastardy they were, you know?

We had camps with Japs in them. Mickey Mouse, he was a little runt of a Jap, about the size of this chair, he got nicknamed Mickey Mouse of course. But there were other blokes that were called 'Boofhead'; a bloke called 'Stalin', a bloke called 'The Boy Bastard', there was the 'BBC' – the Boy Bastard's Cobber – all these sort of nicknames. And they were all known by them, we never knew their names, but in the camps, from one camp to another, you talk about the BBCs and the Dillingers and the BC [Bastard's Cobber] and Stalin, they all knew them, from being in their camp at some stage. And they were real ugly so-and-sos, the Korean guards, they seemed to take more pleasure out of punishing you than the Japs. But they all had these nicknames and so they were all treated by us with contempt.

FRED SKEELS

I've got a list in my scrapbook of the names of some of them, or the nicknames that we gave some of the more notorious ones so that we could refer to them without them knowing that they were being talked about. For instance there was one we called 'Black Bastard', and then we'd come across another one who was just as bad so he was called 'Black Bastard Number Two'. There was one called 'Creeping Jesus'. I don't know why he was called that, but one of the ones that was kinder was called 'Charcoal Charlie' and he was in charge of a work party where we burned material to make charcoal, I don't know what they used it for, I've forgotten now. There was another one we called 'Frill Neck'. he must have had a neck that suggested that. These nicknames were handy for us to talk about them. We coined a word, what's the word, generic word? To refer to all Japanese as 'Noggies'. I don't know who dreamed it up, but they became Noggies. We used the word Noggie when they didn't know what we were talking about.

MARIC GILBERT

As part of the testimony he gathered for the war crimes trials, Athol Moffitt collected all the nicknames for the guards that the men had told him over time. It's quite a list.

These were the names the Australians had for the various guards: 'Black Panther', 'King', 'Ming the Merciless, Intercourse', 'Intercourse Henry', 'The Ghost', 'Flannel Foot', 'The Weirdo', 'Weasel', 'Junior Ball Kicker', 'Little Marmite', 'Scarface', 'Red Eyes', 'Gold Tooth', 'Joe-Louis', 'Fish Face', 'Goldfish', 'Silent', 'The Big Cook', 'Frenchy', 'Wrestler', 'Tick', 'Quick Quack', 'Big Annie', 'Whispering Bear', 'Big Marmite', 'Lecarse Annie', 'Warthog', 'Stuttering Sam', 'Sword Swallower', 'Black Bone', 'Pig Boy', 'Rastus', 'Village Blacksmith', 'Little Gentleman', 'Pimples', 'Pockface', 'The Bear', 'Banjo Bill', 'King Kong', 'Pig', 'Bunny Lynch', 'Little Pig', 'Roman Nose', 'Parker Nose', 'Jalan Jalan', 'Mulligatawny'. I'll just read a few more: 'Moon Face', 'Woman Beater', 'Myrna Loy', 'Doll', 'Shito', 'Piano Legs', 'Clark Gable', 'Papaya Legs', 'Mackanwalla', 'Machan Basher', 'Little General', 'Little Colonel', 'Moon Rat', 'Bushey' and so it goes on and on – 'Mr Middleton Jnr', 'Bullfrog', 'Maggots' and 'Ball Kicker'.

ATHOL MOFFITT

Bastard instead of Bluey, Scarface instead of Shorty, Shito instead of Simmo. Nicknaming is a long-held Australian tradition that the prisoners got right when they not only carried it on, but twisted it to fit the men they were up against. Humour shines all the brighter when it's hardest to express.

'The Boy Bastard' and 'Louvre Lips' and 'Mucken'; he was a real bad one. 'The Duck Shooter', he used to walk around with his rifle under his arm like a duck shooter. 'Dillinger', named after Johnny Dillinger the American criminal. We never had an Al Capone, but he was a mate of Al Capone's.

All the Japs, and particularly the Koreans, had these names and the word would go around that Mucken or Johnny Dillinger was on the rampage, the word would go around camp quickly, and everybody would duck for cover and get out of the road and make sure they weren't there when he came into their end of the hut. Duck around the other end of the hut and come in the other end.

And they were forever searching our possessions and anything that they figured that we shouldn't have. And some of the things that they figured that we shouldn't have were books and things like that. We needed books for cigarette paper. We used to use the books for cigarette paper and we got very adept at splitting paper down the centre and opening it up and making it nice and thin for the cigarette paper.

In fact my mate had a New Testament, and I worked on him for months and months and months to smoke his New Testament. And in the end he gave in and he said, 'Well, you can smoke it but you have to read every page before you smoke it.' And it was nice, thin paper, really good stuff. We finished up reading the whole of the New Testament and smoked it in pretty quick time. That's what life was like, it was pretty cruel and it was very bad but at times we had lots of laughs. And we would laugh about lots of things and tried to laugh as much as we could, and make jokes of things rather than take them too seriously.

COLIN HAMLEY

Not taking things too seriously. Now there's a challenge in the midst of the inhumane excesses of a Japanese prisoner of war camp. Yet, as Colin Hamley says, they *did* achieve it, often enough for those memories to be the ones they chose to share with each other in the years afterwards. Lloyd Cahill, a genial, good-natured man whose joking manner fails to disguise his compassionate heart, was able to take the mickey out of a Japanese commander, even as he treated the diseased and dying men who surrounded him.

He was in the camp and he came to me, he was a new arrival and a nasty little bit of work. He had about three whiskers and he was very proud of this beard. He used to talk about it all the time. However, he came in for various things and one day he came in to me and he had a piece of paper, and he had drawn his trouble and he was going, 'Ohhhh . . . !' And I looked at this thing and all I could see was a hole here and a hole down here, and then it dawned on me that he had a bellyache. This was his mouth and this was his backside and oh, he was going on about how bad this was.

So anyway I said okay, he had been paying me cigarettes every time he came to see me so I said, 'I'll do something for you.' And I had a pharmacist in the camp with me, and we got down and we told him about it and I said, 'We'll make up the most vile stuff we can think of.'

So he went up to the Jap orderly room and they pinched some red ink from the Japs and we got some of this foul water from some place round the camp and then they got some wild ginger and they had quinine, we had some quinine which, that alone is bitter enough, so that we put in there and then some stuff called acidphetedine, now that's one of the worst-smelling stuff. It used to be in the British Pharmacopoeia. I don't know what they used it for, but it's the vilest thing I've ever tasted or smelled.

So we mixed up this terrible mixture with the red ink in it. It looked absolutely fantastic. So I got Loki-san and said, 'Well now, here you go.' I don't know how much it was. 'You've got to take it three times a day, eight o'clock in the morning, twelve o'clock and six o'clock at night.' Because we knew he was on duty in these hours. I said, 'You've got to come up here to the sick bay where I am and we'll give it to you, it's too precious.'

He came up and I gave him a cupful of this stuff and he would drink it down and he would go, 'Ohhh!!' And he would go on with this and eventually the troops heard about this and they would come to see Loki's performance. It went on for days; it went on for a couple of weeks.

LLOYD CAHILL

Every prisoner of war camp had its own black market, whether it was confined inside the wire or encompassed the local area as well, and the Australians were masters at scrounging and trading. In Europe, many of the prisoners were taken outside the camps on work parties, which made it easier for them to interact with the locals. The people had goods to offer and the POWs had the great good luck to have something to trade – their Red Cross parcels.

Charlie Parrott had survived everything the Italians and Germans had thrown at him from North Africa to Greece and Crete. Now he needed different skills, more like smuggling than soldiering.

I used to run the black market in Munich, for our camp, when I was working at the railway workshops. A little 2-ounce packet of tea was worth 7 kilos of bread.

In another place in Munich, where I wasn't at, but I know the boys were, in the heart of Munich, a 2-ounce packet of tea, they'd go to a brothel. Have a beer, what they went for, and 5 marks change for a 2-ounce packet of tea! That's only when you were in the heart of Munich . . .

At Freimann, with the black market, I used to get sticks of German sausage, which was very hard to get. The German guards, they'd let me in with bread, but if they caught me with a lump of sausage they'd take that. They'd have that for themselves.

I didn't like losing this sausage, so we had a lot of parachute cord that we brought. Everybody brought parachute cord from Crete. I used to do that macramé work with making belts and everything from parachute cord. So I made myself a belt and I made a couple of little things to drop down the inside of my leg. When I got the sausage I used to hook it onto the inside of my leg and I'd walk into camp, they'd search me, go through everything else. I'd get into the camp, I had my sausage. That was the hardest thing to bring into camp. Bread they could get plenty of.

Mainly most of my black market dealing was women that worked in the canteens at the jobs. They was the ones that wanted tea or coffee or chocolate. We didn't have a lot of it. We were supposed to get a Red Cross parcel once a week. I'd say we averaged, during my time as a prisoner, if I averaged a parcel every six weeks I'd be pretty lucky. Because it's one of the things that the Germans used as punishment . . .

There was no profit to it; you do it for the boys. You'd have to get people to help you. I used to get eggs. Down the coalmine we used to get the carbide lamps that we used down the mine. At the end of your shift you'd ship all the dead carbide out and you could fit two eggs in that hole. Close your lamp up and come into camp with two eggs in it. If I got a dozen eggs I'd have to get another five blokes to carry eggs for me.

They're the worst enemy, your own blokes. One fellow I trusted to bring them up and he gets into camp and, 'Oh, the silly bugger didn't know I had eggs in this.' And it opened up. So next thing we know, every lamp was inspected before you come into camp. Your own people do stupid things . . . it was really annoying, your own blokes' stupidity. It wasn't laughable in those days, because it meant a bit better than what you were getting. I found our own blokes; you had to be very, very careful of what you did with some of the blokes. They didn't mean to do it, just stupidity.

CHARLIE PARROTT

Like Charlie, Ralph Churches had grown up on a small farm in Australia, living hand-to-mouth during the Depression and learning how to make-do in any situation. In the camp, Ralph could see that it was a simple equation – on the one hand the prisoners had a surplus of unwanted goods from the Red Cross parcels; on the other, outside the wire was a deprived population, hungry for these supplies. All he had to do was bring them together.

In those Red Cross parcels there was always one packet of tea and one packet of coffee. Now what Britisher, whether Australian, Kiwi or Pom, is going to drink coffee when he can drink tea? At that stage it was ridiculous. The message was, black market. The central Germans, they're addicted to coffee. You just couldn't get proper coffee in Germany. What you could get was roasted barley, ground down. *Ersatz* [imitation coffee]. Yeah, *kaffee ersatz*.

With that coffee there was chocolate, lovely toilet soap as against the grotty, little, grubby, weekly thing that the German ration scale allowed. Cigarettes. Oh yes, we got 100 cigarettes a week. The non-smokers, righto, their smokes went into the magazine, into the pantry – good black-marketing stuff, cigarettes.

And under the Geneva Convention prisoners of war must have sport or exercise other than work one day a week. Well, they weren't going to supply us with a football ground or a basketball court or anything like that. I just suggested, 'You could always take us for a walk in the country on a nice Sunday afternoon?'

Well, you see, we'd have a guard – you'd be amazed. It didn't matter how Nazi the guard was, he couldn't resist the temptation to be able to make himself a cup of coffee. So, 'Righto, Charlie, get it straight. This is yours when we come back from the walk. If you just keep your back turned.' So, we just black-marketed. We were able to get fresh vegetables, all sorts of goodies from the farmers. All manner of things. So we lived very well indeed.

RALPH CHURCHES

Their focus wasn't all on improving their living conditions. Escape was always on the minds of most of the men and once the escape committees were functioning properly, the black-market goods became the primary means by which the prisoners ensnared the guards into criminal behaviour on their behalf. They wove marvellously complex webs of threat and blackmail around the very men who were supposed to be controlling them.

So it was decided by the X-organisation, the escape organisation, that the way to do it was to bribe German guards. Now, in my room we had one of the members of the escape organisation and his job was to get certain things from a certain guard. This guard used to walk through the hut exactly at, I think twelve o'clock every day.

We were given by the escape organisation a lot of coffee. Now coffee was very hard to get in the camp. But we were given a big container of it and as soon as we knew this guard was going to walk down there we would have coffee brewing and, of course, the Germans could never get coffee in Germany. We'd have the coffee brewing. We'd have the door open. Blokes'd be swilling coffee as he walked past. And we'd say, 'Oh come in, come in have coffee.' '*Nein nein.*' They wouldn't do that.

But as the winter drew near and it got colder, one day we managed to convince this guard to come in and have coffee. So for about a week every day he came in and had a good cup of genuine coffee, and then one day one of the men who had this big container of coffee, dropped it on the floor purposely. And he sort of said, 'Oh bugger that', and kicked the coffee about and the guard was absolutely horrified. He got down on his knees and was getting every grain up so as not to waste it. So this escape man said to him, 'What, do you want some coffee? You know, we've got plenty. Just say if you want it.' So this German guard went away with a reasonable size container of Nescafé.

And once he'd done that, we used to get chocolate in clothing parcels. We'd give him chocolate which, of course, was . . . worth a lot of money in the camp to us. So to them it must have been incredible, the value of it. So we'd ultimately get to the stage where he was going out of our room with coffee and with chocolate and with various other things that we felt he'd want.

And then one day the escape organisation man said to him, 'By the way, we want you to get some film.' Such and such a size for this camera. And the German was horrified. He said, 'I can't do that. I couldn't possibly get you a film for your camera!' And the Englishman said, 'Listen, me boy, you'd better. It's bloody cold on the Russian Front.' Because if he'd been found with anything like that he'd have been sent straight to Russia.

Now they had a good time in Stalagluft 3, the guards. With food and safety, but if they went to Russia they'd be dead. So this man then would give us films.

BILL FORDYCE

When one of your guards was going on leave, if you were in the bribery department, you would say to him, 'Look, we're not all terror flyers.' *Terror fliegen* they used to call us. Terror flyers, the Luft Gangsters, the Americans they called 'Air Gangsters'. 'We're not that at all, here is some soap for your wife and some chocolate for your kids and some cigarettes for you, have a good leave.'

When they came back they had had a wonderful leave and perhaps six months later they would be going on leave, and they would just say to you, 'I am going on leave next week', and expect to be given all of these things, see? And we might give them to them the second time, too. But on the third occasion, might be a year later, we worked very patiently, we would say, 'No, they are in short supply.'

Well, straightaway he knew the children would be whining and whingeing, and his wife would be the same and he wouldn't have any cigarettes to smoke either, so we could say, 'We do have a few on the condition that you could bring back this or that.' 'Couldn't possibly, no, I would never do that.' 'Please yourself.'

But I remember saying to one guy, 'You know I am studying science here?' And he said, 'Yes.' And I said, 'I need a magnet because I am studying magnetism and electricity.' Well, that made sense to him, he knew it wasn't true but it was enough logic that he could say, 'Well, he told me that and so . . .' So I said, 'Give me a small magnet, it doesn't have to be anything.' Of course that was used for making a compass.

And you knew from one of the Germans who were already in your bribery which town he lived in and what suburb of it. So you would say to the guard who was already in your pay, 'We want you to go into the hardware store and buy a magnet. Throw it away, do anything you like with it but keep the receipt, that's all I want.' And when he came back and gave you the receipt you would give him some contraband for his trouble. And then when the little German came in sweating and fearful with the magnet that *he* had smuggled through and he was shaking with fear that he might be found out and gave to you, you would thank him very much and all was well. But then when you asked him for something much bigger, like a radio valve the next time, he went, 'Oh, I will not do that!' You would say, 'Well, you have bought us a magnet.' 'You can't prove it.' 'Can't we? You went into such and such a hardware store, you bought the magnet there.' And you could see it was rocking home because that was exactly where he bought it . . . So then we would say, 'So, we will get the radio valve, won't we?'

. . . We had all of those techniques and we really used them well. And it was fun using them. It was very satisfying to be able to put one over the Germans like that, time after time. There were times, if somebody had been shot at, or a few times when people were actually shot and killed there was, of course, a tremendous freeze for a long time. But that got you nowhere, there would be no communication, and you were cutting off your nose to spite your face, sort of thing. In other words, you had to have the means and the access to get the things that you wanted to go into different escape activities. So we did our best to keep it on an even keel so that we could do that.

Geoff Cornish

We weren't nice people, I can assure you, as POWs. Matter of fact, if I was a guard I'd have shot every damn POW I came across for peace of mind, for everybody.

Ronald Wall

In some camps in Germany, relationships between the guards and the inmates became so relaxed that the prisoners traded anything that could be bought, sold, or exchanged. Even sex.

One guard used to hold the wire apart of a night-time and there was one occasion he let about twenty guys out, they used to go and visit their girlfriends at the *dorflager*, which was just up the road. It was full of Russian and Ukrainian women, who used to, they were so big and strong these women, they were huskies, they used to unload truckloads of cement.

Anyway, these guys got out a couple of nights running and all of a sudden, I think it was the third night, the alarms went. And everybody, we had to all race out and get on parade, stand in the snow and ice and whatever on the football ground, to get counted.

And apparently what happened was, the commandant was a wake-up to this guard, he used to let them out between his shift, say, between seven and eight of a night-time, let them out, and then they'd come back when he was on again, say, between three and four in the morning. But on the third night, the commandant was waiting there with other armed guards and captured them, put them in the cooler, and do you know what he did next morning at the general parade, just before we all were sent out to work? He congratulated the British troops for keeping their word like gentlemen, because they'd promised the guard that they'd come back, and they all came back. If one had not come back, they'd probably all have been in big trouble.

He stood up there on that bank, in front of the whole assembled 800-odd, and thanked them for all coming back, and for keeping their word like British gentlemen, would you believe it! See, Germans are funny people, but they are great sticklers for discipline, or they were, they're probably all gone by now.

Raphael Corbett

In the end, however, the jokes and the trickery, the conniving and the humour could only sustain the prisoners for a while. A gritty, ruthless stubbornness was needed when the laughter stopped. And in the Japanese camps, it stopped often.

It was so humiliating to have to bow and scrape and all that. It was really humiliating, all the way through, and it bugged us so much. We had to bow and scrape and I still don't like that. We'd bring it on ourselves a lot.

Driving these piles for the bridges, they'd have to put it up in a frame; we'd have to build the framework. We had four poles, all wired together, twitched with wire, maybe 50 feet high and they'd put the pole up through it, into the centre, and then have a big long steel rod on top of that with a big iron monkey. And on the top of the frame there would be a pulley. We had ropes coming each side of it, and on the end of each rope there was like a cat o' nine tails, another lot of ropes, so you'd put a person on the end of each rope. This big steel block, it was heavy, and we'd pull it up and then that would be the pile-driver.

We used to sing a tune to it. What we started with was, 'Itchy knees and savvv', [*Ichi, ni, san, shi*] that was 'one, two, three, four'. So after we got sick of that we'd sing, 'You little yellow bastards! You little yellow bastards!' Until someone put them wise to what we were saying. Then we'd all get done over. But it was worth it. We'd vent our spleen out with words like that.

. . . And, of course, going to work and that, we'd pull the same stunt. Going to work you would be pretty downhearted, and one guard would be going along beside you, 'Nippon, okay?' 'Nippon okay . . . you little yellow bastard!'

. . . In the bad times as well as the good, we had a bit of fun and the good times would boost our morale a bit. But things were very, very . . . it was like a black tunnel, we can laugh about it now, but it was so depressing, this dark tunnel and there was no light at the end of it. We had no news. Day after day we lived on our nerves. We didn't know whether we would be alive tomorrow, or the next day or the next day. Because they shoot you for nothing, or belt you for nothing, so we were living on our nerves day by day. This was the darker side of it. I mean, I can laugh about it now, but it was very depressing and very humiliating.

THOMAS SMITH

And that, after all, was the truth of it for the men and women imprisoned in South-East Asia. The overwhelming memories they have of their guards are dark and almost unremittingly abhorrent. When they single them out individually, it is generally to illustrate the unbelievable savagery with which these men tormented their prisoners.

We had guards there that were just sadistic. I saw one guard, 'Mucken' we called him, he was mad. 'Mucken' with food – he was always eating, and he was mad as a rat and he'd belt everyone. I saw him make one of the chaps who had dysentery, make him get down and lick it up again. He couldn't hold it in. All that sort of thing . . . rather nasty. The nasty parts. We don't like to remember them too much, but that's what they did.

If you came out on the sick parade, when they brought the sick ones out on the line, the interpreter would come along. 'What's wrong?' 'Dysentery.' *Bang!* In the tummy. 'Ulcers.' With a cane he would whack them across the ulcers. That sort of thing. Sadistic. Really nasty. A lot of that went on, which is pretty cruel.

They were this way, one could give you a cigarette, he would start talking to you and give you a cigarette, all right, and then he'd go away and then the orders would be that there was a bashing blitz on, and then he'd come back and belt you for nothing. It wouldn't faze him out. After giving you a cigarette, he could come back and give you a belting and walk off as if nothing had happened.

They would boil up big drums of water for their bath, the Japs, and they would have other big tubs and they would have these blokes pouring the water over them, while they were having a bath in this tub. And some of our blokes would volunteer to do it because they would get a bit of food and a smoke and all that sort of thing. There was only a certain few that would do it. We hated them that much that we wouldn't go near them. But there was those who were, 'Well, I'll get a free feed out of this, a bit better food. I will do it.' I don't think they had very high characters. They would do anything to sort of get out of work. But to wash them, that was . . . no, no. That was . . . shudder. But some of them would, they'd have half a dozen there that would do it.

THOMAS SMITH

They are not logical. They want something done, get an order from up above, and they want men, 'All men do this, all men do something else!' you know. And the way they would line 200 men up or any number of men, they would go along and they couldn't count. We would line up in fives, we would line up in ten, and they couldn't count 30 men, they were just peasants, and so we had to count ourselves.

That Sonei bloke, one night in Bicycle Camp, every man in the hospital or anything, no matter how sick you were, dying or anything else, had to get out on parade, and the whole camp had to be counted. Well I reckon it was dawn – the sun had come up before they got the count. And we had counted ourselves and gave them the numbers and everything else, they *still* couldn't get the count!

And Sonei, at the end of that, as the dawn came – he got on the table, which he was famous at doing, he stood on the table and he wanted a '*light-oo*', a *light-oo* above his head. And the electricians had to come and hang the globe above his head and he wanted every man in the camp to walk past him, like that, so as he could look. And if your hair was too long he gave you a kick in the head as you went past, because if your hair was longer than that, you could get a hiding, you had to have your head shaved all the time

BILL COVENTRY

It's over 60 years since the end of World War II, but the passage of years has not blunted or softened the passion the prisoners of the Japanese still feel about their captors.

They thought of us as barbarians with no culture, no skills, no training at all, and I thought, 'Will I set out to show them that I am a person of sensitivity, of intelligence?' And I wrestled with it in my mind and talked it over with some of my friends, Ross Milburn and others, and they said, 'Go for it, Hicks.'

I was treading a very fine line between cooperation with the Japanese and trying to inculcate in their minds, particularly with the apprehensions that were there, that we were *people*, that we had the same sort of feelings and attitudes to life. I found when I could talk to them that they shared many of it but some of them were incredibly cruel – you were beating your brains on a concrete path to engender any feelings of sympathy, liking or understanding within some of them. They were out to kill as many as they could.

WALTER HICKS

They were harassing us day and night in the camp, and when you look back, if we had taken them prisoners, we might have been the same to them, but when you really look at what they were doing, I guess they were trying to get on top of us to make sure that we knew who was the boss. And they continually walked around the camp harassing people, standing them up, making them bow to them which was a bloody awful experience, having to bow to a bloody Jap.

And even these days when I see somebody bowing to a Jap, by jeez it makes my blood boil. But it was something we never ever did. And bowing was a form of inferiority and you were just made to feel inferior by doing it as far as we were concerned. But to them it was the normal thing to do, to bow to each other. They made us bow to them instead of saluting and that was very hard to take.

COLIN HAMLEY

Even now, it seems inexplicable to men like Bill Coventry, that as much as he and his mates may not have understood the Japanese, the Japanese did not, in turn, make any attempt to understand them.

If they had said and told us, even in broken English that we understood, that 'we want to take the side out of that hill', or they want to build a railway from so and so . . . If they had said, 'We want to do job (a) to (b), we want you to work with us and you are working with us', and so forth, it would have been done. Our boys could have built the Burma Railway and built it properly, but they had to kill half the bloomin' population to do it, so their cynical madness is obviously there. And you speak to anybody in business here in this country that has been associated with Japanese, they will tell you stories that just about curl your hair – what they will do to con people in, to do things in business, they are ruthless, and they are just made that way. And I don't wish to hate anyone, I don't hate the Japanese, I can't stand them, what they do, but if you hate you get sick inside. I won't hate anybody, but I don't trust them.

BILL COVENTRY

Suspicion of Japanese motives, distrust of what they see as the national character and an almost visceral dislike of them as a race, live on in the hearts and minds of many POWs. And why should it not? We, who were not there, can only travel so far in our desire to understand the cause of their emotions. But the very existence of those emotions and their longevity are, at the very least, to be respected.

See, you have got to always remember that the Japanese started our war in the '20s and they started 100 years of advancement of the Japanese nation, and it isn't till 2020 that the first 100 years finish. They started in 1920 to train their soldiers, went into Manchuria and did barbaric things, they bombed Pearl Harbor in 1940, and they got us fellows and they treated heck out of us . . .

You people want to think how much the Japanese own, because we will never beat them, because they are sadistic. They are still playing with the white man to this day and we don't realise it, we are too complacent, we are too genuine. But underneath all that, this is what the Japanese go on with, they are the superior race, they really believe that, and ultimately they will do anything. See they own Hawaii, they own a lot of the western part of America, they own what they want in Australia, and people say, 'Oh they will never get it.' Oh won't they?

BILL COVENTRY

One day several years ago, Bonnie and I used to play golf with our son, we used to go out here to Karrinyup Golf Course, and we were in the room where you collect your clubs and pay your fee and all that sort of thing, and the golf master or whatever they call him was there and he said, 'Would you like to have someone come with you?' And I said, 'Oh yes, we don't mind that.' He said, 'Well that gentleman over there . . .' and it was a little flaming Jap, so I just said to the bloke, 'I'm sorry,' I said, 'no, I'm not taking him with me.' So that was that.

On that same day that we were coming down the fairway, we just got off the putting green and moving across to the next fairway, and somebody behind us had hit their ball and it'd gone into the trees and there must have been a bunch of Jap golfers under the tree there, and as soon as the golf ball hit the tree, they went out of it like that, like little rabbits. And I laughed like hell, you know, because they got a scare, these Japs. And I was happy that they'd got a scare. Simple blasted thing, but there we are, that's your mentality, I suppose, towards them.

I mean I don't – I can't say I hate the Japs now, but I could never trust them, I wouldn't want to talk to a Jap who was of my age, and could have been in the services, I wouldn't want to talk to him even. But the Jap civilian of today, you know, it's not their fault that their fathers went to war and did these things, and you can't hold them responsible, but I still wouldn't – don't have much respect for them as a race, couldn't trust them.

FRED SKEELS

Prisoners of war were able to form relationships with people other than their jailers – locals, allies, workmates and women all played their part in the lives of Australian POWs. Some of the relationships began through circumstance and some through choice, while others were forced upon them. At the beginning of their imprisonment, the 'welcome' from the locals could occasionally be worse than being captured in the first place.

We had the big trip finally, up to Tripoli, taken up by truck. It's hard now to put an exact number on the days . . . I suppose three or four days, it's just hard to remember. There was a lot of dysentery at that time and there were shocking conditions. I don't know whether to repeat this, about the Australian triumphal entry into Tripoli. The Americans had a triumphal entry into Tripoli. Our triumphal entry, because of the dysentery, they pulled the inners out of their tin hats and the poor fellows had to use that in the truck; others put themselves over the side and held on, because dysentery is a terrible thing and you've got no control.

We were going into Tripoli and it was a Sunday and there were these local inhabitants in all their good Sunday gear and they were standing on the road and giving us heaps . . . and one fellow said, 'I've had enough of this'. And you can image the putrid stuff that would have been in the tin hat and he said, 'Here, split this up amongst yourselves!' and he threw it at them . . .

I thought that everyone of us was going to be killed because they stormed the side. But to the guards' credit – we had Italian guards in the truck – to their credit they kept them at bay; they were bumping their fingers when they were trying to get into the truck.

It's a terrible thing to do, here you are in your Sunday good clothes and all this putrid stuff gets thrown over you, but the men were down to a pretty low there, you couldn't stand any more of that cheering so they gave it to them. The convoy speeded up a little bit and got through and we survived that.

LLOYD MOULE

Relations between the Allies were often scratchy and uneasy. When they were fighting side by side, the different ways of the various armies meant that they were inevitably critical of each other's prowess and personal habits, and eagerly invested entire nations with specific characteristics, none of them attractive. But at least in that situation they were heartened by the knowledge that they were fighting for approximately the same cause.

In the camps, however, these national prejudices and bigotry were given free rein, and in South-East Asia, it was the Dutch who became the recipients of everyone else's dislike.

The Dutch went right through to Burma with us . . . you'd have to line up in the camp, and this Dutch officer . . . sometimes they'd give us a bit of melon, pig melon we'd called it, like watermelon. There was nothing in it. Anyway, if he could find anything in it, 'One for you and one for me', as he went past. He made sure he got plenty.

Anyway, one of them caught him doing it and they kicked him out of it. One of the Australians said, 'If you don't stop doing it, we'll get you anyway'. He didn't do it anymore, but that is what they were like.

One fellow, he was the banker fellow, he said, 'I've got to get back to Java.' He said, 'Java can't run without me!' The Japs were running it all right then without him. But that was their attitude, though. They didn't want anything to happen with Java, because they were going to be able to take over again when it was all over. And we knew jolly well that the natives were going to have a go. They said straight out, not only once, but time and time again, 'This war finished? We start another one with the Dutch.' They were fair dinkum, too.

But their attitude was they had to live, regardless . . . if their lower ranks died, well, that was too bad. So that's why we didn't like them. They were dirty to us. Offal-eaters, as we called them. We struck a lot of good ones, mind you. I don't brand the whole lot of them like that. It sounds awful, but there were a few that made it bad for the rest of them. A lot of them were nice people, very nice people. You couldn't wish for nicer people. But I suppose you strike that with ours, too. There were some very nasty Australians. They would do anything to survive. And you couldn't blame us, the whole lot, for what a few did. I suppose I was a little bit out of line saying most . . . most of them on the whole were pretty good.

THOMAS SMITH

We didn't get on with the Dutch mostly, I am sorry to say. They would put you in as soon as look at you to the Japanese. They wouldn't tell a lie to get out of anything; they would rather put you in than tell a lie about it. They were the cause of quite a few of our chaps getting beltings. There was a couple of quite nice blokes, I got to know a couple of them.

I can tell you an instance: we got back here in Melbourne, there was one of our chaps, Rocky O'Donnell, and Rocky was on the tramline going out to St Kilda, and Rocky got a few aboard this day and was going along next to the tramline and he ran into one of the Dutchmen who was in with us. Well, he done his block and he punched this Dutchman and he had him down on the tramline and he has got his head across the rail and he is trying to get the tram driver to run over him. Just because they were a little different, I don't know.

They never did things to me but I know a few things. I know that after they capitulated a couple of them led the Japs to where we were and those sorts of things . . . I thought they would be all for us and do anything for us. I think that a lot of them, how they came to be out there, were misfits at home. Came out to the island, got a bit of, what's the word . . . status, and I think it went to their head a bit and I think that might have had a bit to do with it. Because when we went to Ambon they were dead against us talking to the natives. 'Mustn't talk to the natives.' Of course, the first thing we did was sit down and talk to the kids, give them chocolates and this sort of thing. They didn't like that at all. They had got them, colonised them, and they were under their power, see?

ATHOL 'TOM' PLEDGER

What used to irk us was to see a lot of the Dutch people walking around the streets with swastika armbands on, you know, which really got under our skin. But what we found in Java, the Dutch women, I think they had more guts than their men did. They were the ones that really gave us a lot of support when we were in working parties.

They would throw food into our, you know, they couldn't come and give it to us, but they threw it on the sidewalks in amongst the troops and we had a lot of time for them. As for the Dutchmen, we had no time for them at all, no time, the Dutch Army troops.

COLIN HAMLEY

The Dutch were difficult and I'm going to tell a story now. To the Brits the Dutch were always the F- Dutch, 'fucking Dutch'. Now one day, a Sunday morning, I remember they said, 'Oh God, have you seen the notice up there in the Dutch lines?' And I said, 'No.' 'Go and have a look at it.' They had a great big blackboard and on it was written in chalk, on it, 'We are your allies, not the fucking Dutch!' They just couldn't get on with anybody.

LLOYD CAHILL

Globalisation was, of course, an undreamed-of concept in World War II and nations were far more singular and unique than they are today. The cross-cultural monsters of television, satellites and the internet had not yet arrived to smooth out some of our national differences into a kind of beige conformity, and strangers were exactly that – strange. As well, Australians then as now believed they lived in 'Godzone country' and were clearly better than the rest.

I think the ones who survived the most and the best were the Australians, in my experience with people that I was in camps with. The Yanks were probably the next best. The British weren't that good, and the Dutch were deplorable . . .

The Dutch were a lazy race, the white Dutch were a lazy race by virtue of their having been in control of this country for 200 years and always been the master of the country, and they always had all the affluent people and always had servants to look after them, and so they couldn't look after themselves very well when they became prisoners; they didn't have servants, so they didn't know how to bring themselves up . . . the white Dutch died because they were too damned lazy to get off their backsides, and didn't know how to get off their backsides anyway.

. . . The Poms were – their hygiene was not as good as ours, I don't know why it should have been so, but I think as we all, Australians, have made a joke of things over the years, you've probably heard it, we shower every day, and the Poms only do it once a week, they have a shower once a week and that's adequate, as far as they're concerned. The whole family has a bath on Saturday night and probably use the same bath, you know, and it's not because that's all they have, they would have showers no doubt now, and going back 50 years maybe they didn't always all have showers, but they would have had some sort of ablution facilities in most towns in England, I would think. But generally speaking the Poms were not as hygienic as the Australians, and so they suffered as a result through sickness.

And they too were subject to a lot stricter discipline within their army, and they'd been brought up with that discipline, and if they didn't have an officer to guide them they couldn't stand up on their own two feet as easily. That's again my opinion, but from what I've heard, what I've seen and what I've read, that's the opinion I've formed, the ones that I've lived with.

And the Yanks were about on a par with the Australians I would say, although there were times when you could see quite clearly that the Yanks were a bit more spoilt than what the Australian soldier was, or sailor, you know the American Navy had ice-cream in their battleships and their ships of war, Australia didn't. Little things like that that you know where you differ from the other country or race in the way you live . . . The Australian I think has the ability to stand on his own two feet and use his own initiative a lot better than the other ones I've spoken of. His officers are of a similar ilk and therefore you didn't have to lean on your officer to get guidance, you did it yourself, or you didn't wait to be told to do something, you did it because it had to be done.

FRED SKEELS

Few Australians had been able to travel at that time and one of the greatest shocks for Australian prisoners was to be plunged into the life and culture of the enemy nation. This took place mostly in Europe, where the men were sent out on working parties. Those who left the camps to live and work on farms became more involved with the locals than any other prisoners, even if the experiences were not always happy.

They took us to a place called Hollstadt . . . and then they brought in a herd of farmers from the town, there was fourteen of them. They came in and they were allotted a POW each, that had to go and work for them. Well I drew a live lulu, oh, he and I really we didn't click from the time we met, but some collected the good blokes, they were well looked after but the bloke I went to . . . a bloke by the name of Irvin Reinhardt and old Irvin was a First World War returning soldier, a German bloke. And as I say, Australians meant nothing to them, we were British you know, and British really stuck in his craw and he couldn't take British and he made me suffer for that.

    . . . It wasn't like modern German is today; where we were, we were in the backblocks of Germany. Even the German population detested what they call *bauer* which is poor farmers, you know, really hillbilly type of farmers. And the culture shock was unbelievable, even for rough tough blokes like we'd become.

    The next morning I went to work and the old Irvin spouse, she got stuck into me first, God knows what she was talking about. I wouldn't have a clue but I can just visualise her yelling and screaming under my face and too, no teeth in her damn head and a big thick skirt on and she's laying down the law to me, and I'm just standing there. And anyway she moved away and – yeah I'll say it – when she went and walked away the old devil had a wee while she was yapping at me. And I couldn't understand how the hell she'd had a wee but she had a wee right there, there was a great big pool of water where she had been standing!

    . . . They thought they'd get the prisoner to load up the wagon and the *frau* and the *fraulein* got on either side of a bag of spuds and threw it onto my shoulders and of course I collapsed under the damn thing and they had to lift the bag of spuds off me so I could get up again. So I wasn't much use to them.

He and I we just did not get on. He tried to lord it over me and I wouldn't take it and I fought with him for I don't know, three years I suppose. In the finish I got jack, oh he had me charged for everything, sabotage and God knows what, everything. But in the finish I got fed up and I blew through, two sergeants and myself took off.

We went up into the wild, we didn't last long, we had nowhere to go, I was right in the bang centre, in the middle of Germany. I got away for a while and when they caught me they slapped me in the boob, in a place called Neustadt an der Saale and I was in there for a few days and they sent me back to work for this Irvin Reinhardt and I told them I wasn't going to and they said, 'You *are* going to.' I woke up that I had to at that stage. So I said, 'Oh well, if he behaves himself.' And this German officer said, 'Well, we've told him he's got to be better to you.' It lasted for a little while but he just hated the British that much that we didn't get on.

FRANK ROY

Others experienced a more comforting humanity from their farmer masters and remember them not just with affection, but gratitude.

We went down to the train and went 25 kilometres north back over the old Austrian border. And we got off at a little railway station at a little town called Ehrenhausen and there waiting for us was a big, jovial sort of man with a great, big, handlebar moustache.

. . . And waiting for us there were the surrounding farmers or peasants . . . there were ten of us. And I think half a dozen farmers there . . . So the farmers' leader he grabbed two for himself. Then another bloke, he grabbed a couple. Another couple, that was six. Then there were two singles. And that left the other little engineer mate and me.

So a young peasant came up and he nabbed my mate and it left me. Well, I was nobody's pick. I didn't blame them. But I did feel awfully, 'nobody loved me, nobody cared'. I was wondering whether – but there was this charming old gentleman with a drooping moustache and a kind look on his face, and I'm sure he took me out of sympathy. He asked me, 'Well, would you like to come and work for me?' And I said more or less, 'My oath I would.' I wasn't fit to work. I wasn't fit for anything . . . So he marched us off. So there we were.

And I found out there was this big two storey house – that's where the lord of the manor lived, only it wasn't a lord. It was a very old lady in a wheelchair who was looked after by two spinster daughters. I established that. My bloke, Meinhardt, he was the senior peasant. His cottage more or less was just a vehicle track separating him from the manor house. There we were and that's where I was to work.

. . . Our meals were pretty homely. Meat probably still is a luxury in that part of the world. You might get a meat dish twice a week. They'd starve without potato . . . Adjoining the house was a bit of a lean to where they kept some light farm machinery and so forth. There was no motors or anything like that. But that's where they put their scythes and hoes and all their agricultural implements and so forth. I think there was a single furrow plough there. But I noticed a set of scales, platform scales. I thought, 'This'll be interesting.' Because my enlistment weight was nine stone seven. I got on those scales and weighed myself and I was seven stone five. No wonder I felt a little bit weak.

I forget what they had me doing, but they worked a lot. There was the father, there was the mother, there was the crippled daughter and a not-crippled daughter who was already being chased by a neighbouring young man. The menfolk, there was the eldest son, who was only about 98 cents in the dollar, but he did a service for me. Then there was about 16-, 17-year Ferdinand and there was a young school goer – I think about ten year old – Fritzl – Frederick or Freddy. Anyway I settled in.

But I think the second afternoon, we were out raking up hay – they'd been out scything the grass for hay. You see, for the winter they've got to have a loft full of fodder. Because their working beasts were two huge oxen. They were kept in stalls. And you have to have your fodder in for when the winter comes. That's what we were doing. And I just collapsed. Fell over in a heap. Passed out. The next thing I knew – I was that miserable that when I recovered consciousness there was a voice, 'Iss zere somesings I can do to help you perhaps?' This was one of the spinster daughters, who could speak quite good English. Now I'm lying on a heap of straw up in the hayloft. She climbed up the steps and got to me. Anyway she had some quinine and for days and days after that she doped me up with quinine and I begged her, I said, 'Madam, please don't let them send me back to Stalag. I am sick, but I will recover. I've a strong constitution, I will recover. But I won't if you send me back to Stalag.' She says, 'Yes.'

. . . Mind you, the family which I was with, these Meinhardts, they were very sturdy Roman Catholics and very Christian in their outlook. It's a bit of a tangled skein, but they were very kind to me.

. . . Come the winter the pigs would be slaughtered and cured into bacon. They hadn't thought of cholesterol I don't think, because all these pigs would be solid fat. They put fat on everything. Breakfast was invariably maize meal made up into a – not a porridge, but a malleable loaf sort of thing. A big platter in the middle. And pig fat, bacon fat melted and strewn all over it. And everyone dipping their spoon into it you see. They were experts. They had good suction. They could suck a mouthful but I don't think I tried very hard. I made a mess of it. So they got into the habit of serving me separately with my own serve. But I soon got the hang of it.

They looked after me very well. Indeed with the rather fatty food they were feeding me I was putting on weight very quickly. I discovered of course they grew all their own food. Beans and beans and beans and beans. Spuds and spuds and spuds and spuds. Root vegetables and so forth. It was a big garden. But their cash crop was wine. Grape vines. That was where I first found riesling.

. . . Anyway there came a day of great, big, dark, slatey, grey cloud blew over the horizon and in no time flat, little flecks of moisture. White things were falling on my hand. Bloody snow! I'd never seen it before. And we got used to snow falling but virtually that was the end of it because it was the winter coming on. It was early November. No more work for us. So it was a rather sad goodbye. Because I realised that they had restored me to health. I was all right. I'd put on weight. In fact, I certainly got back to my nine stone seven anyway. They were a very kindly Christian people and I remember them with a great deal of affection

RALPH CHURCHES

Escape did not always mean capture, even in a hostile country where the expectation was that the local people could, and would, turn a prisoner in. Australian escapees from prison camps in Italy were often aided and guided by villagers who risked their lives to do so. The escapees were helped particularly by the partisans, the Italian resistance movement which fought against the occupying Germans and the Italian fascists.

We was billeted at a place called Collobiano and we was given a shovel each and diggin' the banks up to hold the water, like from last year's crop the banks were fallin' away a bit, so we were diggin' the banks up and in the meantime the war had started down below in Italy, and these young sentries, they weren't keen, they weren't too tough sort of business, like what they were, they were arrogant buggers. They weren't so tough.

So there was five of us and we said, 'There's a river down there where we got the water from for the rice.' I said, 'Let's get down there one day and have a little bo peep.' So we worked our way a little closer and we seen this boat there on the river and we said, 'All right, tomorrow we go.'

We got on this boat and pushed it away from shore and away we went. Then the next time we hit shore it was a little village, not so far away, called Oldenico. Of course we were hungry then, something to eat. I went into the first place, I knocked on the door, explained we were Australian prisoners of war escaped and all this sort of business, would you have any food available? This fella came to the door, his name was Giuseppe Bosco, he was a wonderful man. He took us around to a place where there was a kind of river flowing. In the middle was a kind of island, you could walk across the water onto the island. He made some accommodation for us like, branches of trees and all that sort of business, and a blanket, if he could afford one.

Anyway, we were there for a week and all of a sudden there was a fella come past, we were outside there and a fella come past, he was chasing hares. And of course when we told Giuseppe, when he come down with a bit of tucker that night, 'Oh, oh.' he said, 'Him!' Evidently he was an informant of the Germans. So rather than get Giuseppe into bother, we decided to leave, all bar one.

One fella fell in love with a local girl . . . Andy, how he met this sheila I do not know, I do not know to this day how he met this sheila . . . he was a ginger-headed boy he was, head of my battalion too. He stopped, he said, 'I am going to stop here.' I said, 'All right, mate, it's your pigeon, lay in it.'

So anyhow the four of us moved off. Giuseppe told us how to get up to these partisans, the best way to go. Of course we had to travel by night which was very awkward, but anyhow we got up the rise to this big tin shed and it was all quiet there, and all of a sudden out they come like you know, they all had guns and firing them in the bloody air, and it was crazy . . . We got to them and said, 'We are trying to get into Switzerland.' And they said, 'All right, I'll take you up, four o'clock in the afternoon. Took us up further up the mountain, the top there and pointed, 'Switzerland is over there.

ERNIE GRANLAND

It is either a series of events that come close to forming a miracle – or merely a reinforcement of that old truism: 'Love will find a way', but the number of romances, affairs and assignations enjoyed by Australian POWs with local women in Europe is simply astonishing. Ken Drew was one of them.

There was a big line of apartment buildings. They were an L shape . . . and my job was pulling nails out of the boards for future use, and I tell you what, I would have been dead in a week, I was frozen.

On about the third day I was there I was doing this and all of a sudden there was a plunk on the side and I looked around and there was a brown paper parcel about that long, that wide. I didn't know what it was. When I looked up there was a woman standing on the corner, and when the guard wasn't there she pointed to me, and pointed to the parcel. I kicked it around behind a stack of bricks.

When I opened it up it had woollen long johns, a woollen singlet, pair of earmuffs and a pair of socks. I never had much to strip off there, but I stripped off in the snow and all that coldness and I put them on and when I wanted to wash 'em in the barracks I washed them and stood them in front of the potbelly stove and I'd stay there for about three hours to stop anybody pinching them.

Well, she walked off and I saw her then, occasionally. She used to walk out in the street and go to the shops. Occasionally she'd drop a little parcel off with some food, half a chicken or something. I used to share that with two or three of my mates. Then, when the summertime come, by this time you've got a little bit more confidence in yourself, you get a little bit that way that you can sum up the guards and when they're out of action you do certain things.

We used to go over to a hut which was behind the big building, to have lunch; they used to bring your lunch out in a big can. It was only a very thick soup kind of thing. They'd be in there; you'd have about an hour. I used to leave that and go back to the building, because occasionally she'd walk past and I then got to talk to her and there was no guards. She told me her father was a member of the opposition party when Hitler came into power and he went to a concentration camp. He died there. She had no love for the Nazi Party whatsoever. She was a woman, 35, and she had a son who was eleven and she lived with her mother. So we got a lot of occasions to talk there. I'd learnt German, so by this time I could speak fairly good.

Then, when next winter came along we couldn't work on the building job, we couldn't mix concrete or anything. So we were put into cellars, convert the cellars into air raid shelters, reinforce them. We'd meet in there and have a talk when the guard wasn't around. Then I got out on four occasions at night time and joined her. I don't know whether that should go into the history or not, but it's good really . . .

On this particular night, she left me, this is at about quarter to five in the morning, it was still dark. I walked down the road and as I turned the corner to go into the street to cross over to the building, I run into two policemen and they were walking down just talking. And for what reason I don't know, but I was that close to them that they parted and I walked between the two of them.

My heart was pounding, but they must have thought I was a worker going to work, so they didn't even challenge me, so that was all right.

. . . It was a passionate relationship in the finish . . . she done everything for me. Without her I wouldn't have survived . . . I was only nineteen by this time, just right about to turn to twenty.

This particular day, at the lunch hour when I went across to the building to see her, we got caught by a civilian worker, a little fellow he was. And he grabbed us. He went to grab her and I hooked him and knocked him down and she went up the steps and took off. He got up and dusted himself off, he wasn't worried about that. But we used to get the Red Cross parcels and in the parcels at that time you used to get two ounce packets of tea, and he wanted six packets of tea, otherwise he'd report us. So I did have one back there and he wanted one the next day and he wanted six in the week. But you couldn't, because you only got a parcel once every month.

So when I went back, I spoke to the Australian sergeant who was in charge at the camp, fellow from Sydney, and I told him. He said, 'We'll fix him.' . . . So he arrived and I gave him his one packet of tea and he said, 'I want five more.' I said, 'No, that's the last one you'll get.' 'Oh,' he said, 'I'll get the guard.' But by this time the sergeant had arrived with the guard up the alleyway. I said, 'If that's a fact we'll call him now, there's one there.' With that he panicked. I called the guard, he pushed the packet of tea back, he didn't want it, I never seen him any more. 'Cause he was in trouble if he was accepting food from POWs . . .

So that was that, so after that we never met down in the cellar 'cause it was too dangerous. She wouldn't even go out and shop for weeks. Her sister used to do her shopping . . . we were lucky to get away with that incident, so we stopped meeting at lunch time. But it was not long after that we were moved. When the first lot of Russian prisoners were brought in, they moved us across town to a place called Wolframsdorf. It was right opposite the cemetery and then she couldn't contact me over there. Then I spent about five months over at the other camp when they moved us up into Poland. She went really about three years without finding out what had happened to me or where we'd gone.

KEN DREW

Where Ken had gone was into a camp in Poland from which he not only escaped but met another girl, fell in love, and brought her home to Australia as a war bride. But that's another story. It is though, uplifting, to hear of how women like Fanny, who looked after Ken, would risk everything for what love there was to be found.

Some, as Charlie Parrott discovered, would do the same for simple friendship.

When I was in Munich I used to get a little bit of meat. A girl helped me. Her father had a butcher shop. She used to ride a bike. I didn't know who she was or anything. She was only a girl of 16. She was a very nice looking girl and she seemed to be very friendly towards the Brits. Whenever we walked around she'd be on a pushbike and walk alongside us. I had a theory that if I let the guards think I was a little bit crackers I could get away with a lot more. This girl used to ride the bike along the footpath and I'd say 'Isn't she lovely?' Always making nice comments.

One day we're walking through the workshop, the new railway workshops and we did the beautification like the rose gardens. I'm walking through the workshop and this German bloke he beckons me. He was scared stiff somebody was going to see him and he was looking all directions and beckons me over. He was a lathe operator. I went over to this fellow and he handed me a note written in English. When I say English it was not good English, but you could understand it.

I went out and read it and it's this girl. She's learning English at school. Her father owned the butcher shop that we used to walk past all the time. A sentence that she wrote I'll always remember, 'When you will a sausage, tell me now.' So if I wanted any sausage, I had to let her know. But the way she put it, 'When you will a sausage, tell me now.'

She used to send me in meat ration tickets . . . there was an Italian bloke working there who I got quite friendly with. He used to take these ration tickets out to the butcher shop because he could go where he liked and they'd give him the meat for me. I used to get little bits of beef – enough for my brother and I. She knew I had a brother in there with me. I used to drop a note back to her and give it to this bloke.

It came Christmas 1942 and she'd told me that she was giving me a bottle of wine and some meat ration tickets for Christmas in a little note she sent me. So I didn't hear anything from her for about three weeks, into the New Year I hadn't heard anything from her. This particular morning we're going . . . and the chap in the front of our column, a German, walked along the street and said, 'For Charlie,' and give it to this bloke in the front of the column. So when we got into the workplace he knew who it was for, he come and give it to me. It was from this girl.

This Italian bloke that was one of my mates outside, his son was in the German Navy, he came home on leave and he must have found out that he was taking notes to me, and he told his father he was going to report him to the Gestapo. So the old man hung himself in the bedroom. He drank the bottle of wine first and he destroyed all the evidence that he had. This girl and his wife went through everything to make sure there was nothing in it to incriminate the girl or the wife. It's a shocking thing that they did over there. Everybody was so scared . . .

It was great to think there was somebody. Her father must have been all our way too. It was great to think that we had some people that was friendly towards us. You couldn't boast about it. You couldn't let any Germans know, because she would have been in. She was brave that girl; there's no doubt about that. She was brave. The penalty she would have suffered if she was caught!

CHARLIE PARROTT

Arthur Leggett had already had a pretty tough war – Bardia, Tobruk, Derna, Benghazi, Greece, the Brallos Pass, Crete and the Battle of Retimo before he was finally captured in 1941. Eventually he ended up in Munich and was sent to an asphalt works where he got a job on the wagons, delivering bitumen to the road gangs. For a POW, he found his way into unusual access to a city and its people.

The people of Munich are remarkable people; they're the finest people I met in all my life, actually. They really took to us. The day that we were taken to this place, the Germans just looked at us, and we thought, 'Yeah, we're bloody British, you're German, all right.' But the next day they came in and they brought in food off their ration cards, because they never realised men could look so bloody awful. We thought it was hostility, but it wasn't, it was just shock.

We grew quite well. And of course, as we got our Red Cross parcels on a regular basis, which was one parcel a fortnight, well you would muck in with someone else so the two of you would have a parcel between you every week. We would whack out a few things to these Germans and we become quite matey, actually.

. . . The offsider, he worked out where the house of ill-fame was, he must have had an instinct for this sort of thing, I don't know. And we bribed the tractor driver to have a breakdown outside this place. Now it was wintertime in Munich, and snow every-damn-where . . . we had warm winter clothing, we had a battle-dress, we had thick woollen socks, we had English Army boots, even had overcoats. So from that point of view, we did all right.

Anyway, when we were out on the wagon we had blue overalls on, as well, over our battledress. So we bribed this tractor driver, he breaks down simply by turning the gas bottles off. He climbs under his tractor with a spanner and bangs away, gives us the nod.

Well, we get out of our wagons and see two big doors. And there was a big lounge room. And just inside the door was a counter, I suppose there was a till there in the early days, I don't know. And over the far side, there is half a dozen blokes from the German Army Afrika Korps talking to half a dozen of the women. I said to my mate, 'Let's get out of here. I thought they would all be in the front line!' 'No,' he said, 'Hang in.'

So we stood by this counter, near the door, to get out in a hurry, and two of these blokes come over and they looked us up and down. We had been in Munich about eighteen months now and we could speak the language a bit. They looked us up and down. 'You're not German?' 'No, we're not German.' 'And you're not Dutch?' 'No.' 'Well, what are you?' Now that starts a fight in any brothel, I can tell you. 'We're bloody Australians!' 'Oh, Australians!' And here they are – 'Now, have you been in Tobruk?' 'We took Tobruk, mate. We took Tobruk from the Italians.' 'Oh, the Italians!' . . . And then we started discussing the virtue of the Italian soldier, as a mate.

It's hard, but here we were, there's the Germans and us blokes discussing this in a German house of ill-fame. Finally he says, 'You want women?' 'Well, that's what we come in for, more or less, mate.' He said, 'A blonde or brunette?' Well, my mate laughed. This German said, 'What's funny?' He said, 'Jesus mate, we haven't seen a women for two years. We don't give a damn what colour they are!'

They put their thumb up for one, and that's two. Two of these girls come over – I won't go into all the details. Later on coming down the stairs, these two blokes over there, 'Good?' 'Yes, thank you.' My mate said, 'Well, what did you give her?' I said, 'I gave her tea, two ounces of tea, and got five marks change.' He said, 'Yeah, so did I.' So we got back in our little wagons and off we go. But that was Munich for you.

ARTHUR LEGGETT

Arthur and his mates spent around eighteen months working in Munich. Long enough it seems, for very, very strong relationships to form between the prisoners and the people.

It didn't last forever. But gradually over a period, I got to establish contact with a German girl, who was a charming girl, and in due course we were going to be moved across to Poland to work in the coalmines. The chap who used to go down to our camp at lunchtime, to get a billy can of soup for our lunch, he said, 'They're packing up, they're moving. Everyone's leaving.'I said, 'Oh, bulldust.' He said, 'No, they're all going. We're going tomorrow.'

'Cripes,' I thought, 'How am I going to tell this girl?' I knew where she lived, it was just in a block of flats . . . So I shot through. I scrambled over the fence and hid in a forest nearby a bowling green; they had indoor bowling, and waited until everyone had gone.

Of course there was a lot of fun and games amongst the boys in the counting, moving around, trying to confuse the guards, but eventually it was realised that I had escaped and this was bad business. They were marched back to the camp; I saw them go through the forest.

I stood then on the corner where I knew this lass came home, and it was snowing like hell, and there was this little old lady looking at me through the window. I thought, 'I can't stand here all day. I must have missed her; I'll go and knock on the door.' One of our chaps had been planning an escape but of course this move frustrated that, so he lent me his Tyrolean hat to wear a disguise this afternoon around the town, while I was trying to find this lass.

So I go and knock on the door when I worked out where she lived, and her mother opened the door, a short dumpy woman, and I asked her if Ellen was home. Well, Ellen suddenly appears, 'Oh, it's my Australian! Come on in!' She puts her arms around me and mum puts her arms around me and they take me into the kitchen, sit me down, open up a bottle, a small bottle of beer, and here I am yapping away with these two women.

And after awhile there is a sound at the front door, and her mum flies out of the kitchen. I said to Ellen, 'Who is this?' 'Oh, that's Dad.' 'Oh cripes, I thought he would be up the Russian Front!' In comes dad, a big bloke and shakes me hand. 'Oh, sit down. This war is bloody awful.'

Here I am with this family until about nine o'clock at night, I had a meal with them, we're yarning over every damn thing. Well, I've got to go back to camp anyway. I bid them all farewell, and mum hands me back my little Tyrolean hat. And I tramp back to the camp.

And inside the camp there's all the guards going around and around the camp shining all these torches on the shuttered up windows and all the doors. The German guard barracks were inside the compound, inside the barbed wire. I couldn't get in the place; I didn't know what to do. So I finished up shaking the gate, and the German sergeant major came out and said, 'Yes?' I had blue overalls on and the Tyrolean hat. I said, 'I'm one of the prisoners of war, I'm just coming home. Can I get bed and breakfast in there?' And he opens the gate and bows and says, 'Welcome home. Into the guardhouse.'

Well, they take me into the guardhouse, into the commandant's office, and our British interpreter is there, too. 'You're back?' 'Yes, I'm back.' 'Name and number?' I give them my name and number and he opens a drawer and I think, 'Oh this is it, rubber truncheons.' He drags out a bit of paper and scrapes it off. 'Right. Take him away.'

So on the way back I said to our English chap, 'What's going to happen to me, do you reckon?' 'Oh nothing.' I said, 'Come on, there is bound to be some reprisal for this.' He said, 'No, there was about fifteen of you love birds shot through during the afternoon, and the commandant has been worried, should he call out the police, the Gestapo, to round you all up. But I convinced him that you would all be back by morning.'

So he wrote out a list of who was missing and he said that if we weren't all back he was going to tell the Gestapo that our sergeant major had assisted in the mass escape and he would probably be shot.

There was only one bloke missing. By the time I got back all the rest had come in, there was still one bloke missing and they knew where he was, so they sent a couple of guards down to get him. And that was the end of that episode. Nothing ever came of it.

. . . Anyway, we were taken to a railway siding, which was elevated above the common level, placed in carriages, which was much nicer than we had been used to, they were sit up carriages.

And you won't believe this, but around that station area there would be about two to three hundred Germans come to see us off.

ARTHUR LEGGETT

For all the apparent fun and games, Arthur, like all his mates, was not really free – just pretending for as long as possible. He could not ever forget that despite the commonalities he shared with his German workmates and new friends, they were still at war with each other, and for now, only he was a prisoner.

We were locked up. We were in a prison camp. You can't overcome that, it's not a nice thing at all. So as we started to pick up in our health and our attitudes and our spirits, so you would look around a bit. You're in a German city and you get the hang of the Germans and you don't exactly hate them like you did, because they're no different to us, you begin to realise this, and they respond to your friendship. I know, in this fitting shop where I was, I got a message the night before, in a letter, that my father had passed away.

Well, the next day I was down in the dumps and the German asked me, 'Mate? What's wrong?' I told him. They all came over to me, 'What happened?' I said, 'He just died.' They said, 'How old was he?' 'Fifty-three.' 'That's not old.' 'No, he was gassed in the First War on the German front.'

And one of them just walked away and he swore in German something terrible, and then he came back and he put his arm around me, I've never forgotten this, he put his arm around me, and, in German you can understand, he said, 'Arthur, I am so sorry for you.'

Well, you just think, 'Well, what the hell's it all about?' In fact, there were several Germans there said to me, 'What the hell are we fighting each other for? You and I are getting along all right. We're not scrapping. We're working in harmony with each other.' But what can you say? You can't say, 'Look, mate. There's this bastard Hitler' because they weren't allowed to say that themselves.

People don't realise the power that that man had, because no one could argue with him, he was a dictator, his word was law, and if you went against it, he had the blokes that would back him, and they'd just destroy you. So you had to bow to it all the way. I couldn't very well say to him, 'There's this Treaty of Versailles, mate,' and carry on from there.

ARTHUR LEGGETT

ROSS McDONALD

ATHOL MOFFITT

LLOYD MOULE

DES MULCAHY

RAY NORMAN

ROBERT PARKER

7

'The good men stood up, and came through okay'

'The good men stood up, and came through okay'

O ver the years since World War II, Australia's prisoners of war have become one of the most well-known groups in our veteran community, especially the prisoners of the Japanese. And even though those who were imprisoned by the Germans, or the Italians, or the Chinese, can rightfully feel that they have been over-looked from time to time. The reaction that arises when a veteran identifies him or herself to a civilian as any sort of POW is often slightly reverential, as if their experiences somehow remove them from the rest of us mortals.

Consequently, it often startles people to see a group of ex-prisoners of war roaring with laughter. It feels inconsistent with what we know of their lives. Yet humour is now, as it was then, a kind of healing detachment; a necessary survival strategy in the face of memories and experiences that are simply too painful to continue to confront. In the camps, laughter was seized upon eagerly, whenever and wherever it could be found.

There was always somebody telling lies or they'd be telling dirty stories or some damn thing. But wherever you go there's always one bloke who makes you laugh. Yeah. There was one bloke there called Harry Smith. He came from a circus family and he used to tell us the things they used to do in the circuses, like the dancing duck. And this duck always dances on top of a kerosene tin, see. And the reason why he dances is 'cause they've got a candle burning underneath the kerosene tin. And it gets hot so the duck lifts his legs up and down. Things like that.

Then they'd start arguments about, is the front of a car pushed or pulled? – or is the axis of a dray pushed or pulled? And just to get the blokes thinking and get 'em a bit cranky, you know. They used to argue with each other, get 'em going, take their mind off of the day, the daily drag of being a prisoner of war.

BERT BEECHAM

And it was a daily drag. Malcolm Keshan, imprisoned in Germany, dreaded the beginning of each day, knowing that men would get up and say the same thing they had said the day before and the day before that and all the days stretching back. The repetition and emptiness produced boredom and despair and so men invented their own unique ways of coping. Sometimes, an attractive diversion, like a positive virus, could infect entire groups of prisoners. Malcolm remembers how it happened in his camp.

In Stalag 383 you were looking for something to do all the time. Something to occupy you. You had to be occupied . . . Educated blokes used to walk around the camp and talk to themselves. There was one bloke that used to walk around and around the camp, talking to himself, reciting Shakespeare. He could tell you anything you wanted to know about Shakespeare. He went nutty in the finish. Couldn't help it.

The only one who survived was that McInty. We had a big pool, what they called a fire pool. It was filled with water in case of fire. After a while it used to get very murky. McInty used to sit on the side of that with a stick and a piece of cotton and he used to fish in it. He'd sit there for hours. Blokes would come along and they'd look at him. He survived. It's different ways of surviving.

The huts along the bottom of the camp alongside the fence, for some reason the bloke in the first hut got the idea of building and painting his hut like an Indian [locomotive]. He painted it up to look just like an Indian going along. It sort of took off. The blokes next-door thought, 'That's a good idea.' So they painted theirs to look like a carriage, and it went down the line. There was about four carriages.

In the finish, the Germans were amazed, they couldn't figure it out at all; you could see a bloke walking down the street driving a car and a bloke walking behind him carrying a bag. He'd say, 'Where are you going?' 'I'm going down to catch a train. It leaves at one o'clock.' 'Right-o.' Away he'd go. He'd go down

Malcom Keshan (front, middle) and mates in Stalag 383

and get in one of the huts with his bag. It finished up there was a stream of blokes used to go down to catch a train and see it off. They used to blow a whistle and the train would take off and the German guards, you could see them on the side looking. 'God, what's wrong with them?' It was a real regular occurrence. That was just for something to do . . . It was just funny. Anything that was funny was good.

. . . You've got no idea what a letter meant. Just to make the contact. It was really, really something. You used to get real uptight if you didn't get a letter. The letters came around and there's another funny incident. Each block had a postman. That's how big the blocks were. They used to come round and just read out the names and dish out the letters. This day, the post came round and he went into a hut, he read out the names, and he read out the name 'Bluey Einshaw'. There was an Englishman in the hut, he called him over. He says, 'Do you think you'd mind reading this letter out to him? He's not very well educated and he can't read. He'd really appreciate it if someone read it for him.' 'Yeah, sure. No trouble. I'll read it.' So he gives him the letter. Out he goes.

The Englishman opens up the letter and he starts reading it. His wife's left him, his girlfriend's pregnant and he's reading all this out. He said, 'I can't go any further!' Everyone burst out laughing. It was a letter that had been written out especially for him to read. That's the sort of jokes they used to play on each other.

They also used to go on holidays. If you got sick of everyone in your hut you'd pack up and go round, find a hut with a vacancy in it and you were in there. That was a holiday. You could come back if you wanted to. They used to do that often.

MALCOLM KESHAN

Best of all from the prisoners' point of view anyway, was to be able to laugh at their captors. These days, political correctness prevents the public expression of humour based on racial or national characteristics. Fortunately for their wellbeing, POWs were under no such restraints.

In Korea, the stolid literality of the Communists gave Charlie Yacopetti and his mates a decent laugh and a momentary respite from prison life.

Lice reminds me of an amusing anecdote, in that when two or three of the soldiers said, 'Look, Sir, there's . . . I'm pretty sure this is lice, so we best . . .' Yeah there was lice, in the diggers, in their hair. Which is surprising because having cyanide in the water, surely that would have killed all the lice, but anyway.

So I requested a meeting with the camp commandant and I pointed out there was lice in the camp and this could get quite serious and I would like some assistance in the way of whatever medication they had to treat the lice. Anyway, he said he would give it his greatest consideration.

The following day I was summoned in my crutches again up to the commandant's office where a staff member met me and told me, I think it was one of the interpreters, told me that he'd given it his serious consideration and he agreed we should not have lice in the camp and therefore I was to put a sign outside of each hut, 'Out of Bounds to Lice'.

CHARLES YACOPETTI

Some jokes were deliberately perpetrated on their enemy while others came about naturally, as the different cultures banged up against each other. The Australians were never slow to grab a laugh at someone else's expense, particularly if it was as a result of what they saw as another nation's curious behaviour.

Alex Barnett had been captured by the Germans at Derna, in Libya, and in company with a couple of hundred other Australians, he was handed over to the Italians for safekeeping. It didn't take long for the differences to show.

We arrived in Naples and I might have mentioned that it smelt and possibly that we attributed to it Mount Vesuvius. They had us down in the holds and that was the first time we came up, when we got into Naples, and we were very scruffy and scraggy. We had beards – well, some of us had beards, I've got a Chinese beard, there's one curl, that's it – and one of the boys had wheedled a pair of nail scissors from the guard. During the night he had trimmed his beard and moustache, and his name was Noel . . . and Noel was quite a fastidious sort of chap and overnight he had trimmed his beard and his twiddly little moustache and even his hair and he had, not red hair, but a tinge of red, very Titian I think.

So we were lined up on the top deck and they had a big gangplank for us to go down . . . and down below, waiting for us like a Roman holiday, were all the inhabitants of Naples – the military, the brass, you name it. Generals with medals that rattled all over the place, and we were going down in two, threes or fours, and the mob was booing and hissing and whatnot and my first thoughts when I saw them was, 'Here we go for another Roman exhibition'. You know how the Romans used to take the slaves into Rome and walk them around?

And as we went down and I was ahead, I saw one of the waiting generals sort of genuflect and kneel. And the whole mob did, and then I looked behind and here comes Noel with his goatee and twisted beard and for all the world he looked like a Titian Jesu Christi, and they said, 'Jesu Christi!' and ever after that we called him JC.

ALEXANDER BARNETT

Sometimes the enemy's habits or cultural conditioning were used against them, though never without a degree of risk.

I should tell you the story of 'Thommo' Thompson. We were still way back in Timor, and we are getting a few cold nights, and some of the boys with malaria were shivering, no blankets or anything like that. The Japs were great at sort of no clothes on, just a G-string type thing, 'cause they seemed to have plenty of weight on them, a lot of them – rice makes them fairly round. And they were laying in the sun or they had been sleeping it up before in this hut, it was just outside our gate, it was supposed to be their guardroom.

And they had taken the blankets, which were Australian blankets, and they had hung them across the barbed-wire fence to dry and warm in the sun, or something like that. And this fellow Thompson, he said, 'I think I want a blanket.' And I said, 'Oh yeah, we all want a blanket.' He said, 'I am going to get a blanket.' 'What do you mean?' He said, 'Well look, see that blanket there that has got the grey strip down the middle of it, different to all . . .' There was an odd army blanket that had been made out of different coloured wools, and there was a light coloured grey with a dark grey strip down the middle and the strip was about half a metre wide. And Tommo said, 'I am going to get that blanket.' And I said, 'You are mad!'

So with that, he takes off, and we are all watching him. And he goes up to the guard on the gate and puts his hands clear to his side, bows to the guard and says, '*Ush.*' The guard just takes no notice. And he walks around, goes around to where all these blankets are on the line, goes to the first one, shakes it all, puts it back on again, goes along, shakes it all, and all these Japs are laying in the sun and nobody is watching him, nobody; they must have thought he was being a servant or something, he is shaking all these blankets.

And he comes to this grey one and gives it a shake, folds it up very carefully . . . puts it under his arm and quietly walks around to the gate and bows – with the blanket under his arm still – bows to the Jap on the gate, comes back inside again.

And then we said to him, 'Now you got the blinkin' thing home, you idiot, what are you going to do with it?' He said, 'I am going to put it on me bed.' I said, 'You put it on your bed, they will bloomin' do an inspection, they will see it surely!' He said, 'They won't even know it is there.' Sure enough, they didn't know.

Now the guts that it took that man to do that is indescribable, because if they had caught him, his guts would have still been hanging on the barbed-wire fence, I'm telling you.

BILL COVENTRY

If one man's meat can make another man seriously ill, then one nation's humour can bring another completely undone. Arthur Leggett was working as a slave labourer in a coalmine in Poland when a simple joke by an Australian POW resulted in joy for the entire camp.

There was one fellow who brought up a kilo of sugar into the camp, smuggled it into the camp. You did that by simply having it in your dixie and when they give you a body search, you held your arms out. They never thought to look in the dixie. And he puts a note on this, 'One spoonful per cup, or else you will become a victim of The Claw.' And he drew a horrible bloody claw.

Well, then, someone else wrote a note to his mate, 'Don't do this, or that, or you become a victim of The Claw.' Well, it got down underground and on one of the cement walls one of the blokes with his lamp wrote, 'Twenty wagons per man today or you will become a victim of The Claw.'

Well, the Poles got onto this. 'There is a secret society springing up amongst the prisoners. Oh, it's terrible!' Reported it to the Germans. And we were all lined up on our day off, and in came a German colonel with an interpreter, and he made a brilliant speech. 'We're all soldiers. We mustn't lose our sense of pride in what we are doing . . .' etc, etc. 'And we've found out there is a secret society sprung up amongst you. Now step forward all those who are victims of The Claw.'

We had been locked up for four years, and the whole parade dissolves in laughter, and he could never work out what the joke was.

ARTHUR LEGGETT

And in Italy, it was language that worked for Lloyd Moule.

There was a fellow by the name of Albert Farrow and he was World War I and he had a magnificent voice. He said he used to sing with Dame Nellie Melba and we found out later that everything he told us was true, and he had this magnificent voice. Of course he'd sing and the Italians heard him singing, and of course he knew everything in Italian, he could speak a little bit. The officers invited him down to their mess in Prato all'Isarco to sing for them and he said it was all right and they plied him with wine.

. . . Bert Farrow decided on having a concert and he got some of the fellows that were handy to make with tins a sort of a light, and the stage there that lent itself to having a concert. He said, 'We will do well out of this and we will invite the Italians into our concert.' He looked for a choir and said, 'You blokes will do, all you have got to do is sing *Funiculi Funicula*', and we said, 'We will try that, Bert.'

He gave us a few run-throughs and said, 'I think you are better at physical stuff than you are at singing but you will do.' He said, 'This will give me a break because when I want a break between songs,' he said, 'I will just walk out and raise my head to look around and you will know to come on so I can have my break.' We ran through the song but we had other thoughts.

So Bert came out and he rendered this beautifully, all the Italian officers were up the front and we did our bit, we sang,

Muso [Mussolini], *muso, muso won the war;*

Muso, muso, muso won the war;

Pig's ass he did, pig's ass he did;

Pig's ass he did, pig's ass he did;

Pig's ass he did, pig's ass he won the war!

Poor old Bert went the colour of ash, and he froze and said, 'What have they done to me!' And the Italians turned around and went, 'Bravo, bravo, bravo!' We got the praise and old Bert got the fright. That's the sort of thing about the typical Aussie. He called us in and said, 'You bastards, what did you do to me?' We said, 'Well Bert, you didn't get shot, did you? You are still alive.' They thought it was good, they didn't understand a word of it, of course.

LLOYD MOULE

By far the most enjoyable humour of all for prisoners, though, was any incident, whether premeditated or not, that caused embarrassment or humiliation to the enemy. Rarely did this occur in the Japanese camps, because there, any loss of face would inevitably be followed by terrible bashings and the possibility of death. But in the camps of the mostly po-faced, disciplined Germans, the larrikin nature of Australian humour occasionally proved to be too much.

Budapest was where they were going to march us through as an exhibition, to show the soldiers that they'd captured Australian soldiers and everything in Egypt. They took us up in the train and they pulled up outside Budapest and they unloaded us. Then they started to march us through the town. With that, we started singing. The Germans were screaming to shut up. So they shut up. Then a team down the other end would start singing. Then the guards had rushed down the other end to stop them from singing there. They were singing 'Roll out the Barrel' and 'Hang Out Your Washing on the Siegfried Line'. When they'd rush down the back, the ones up the front would start singing. They stopped the ones down the back and the front would be singing. This went up and down the line for about quarter of an hour and then they decided they wouldn't march us through the city because they couldn't shut us up.

MALCOLM KESHAN

We 500 Australians used to terrorise a German officer who had [to] look after this *appel* [rollcall]. The whole 4000 had to line up and be counted to be sure nobody was missing. This German fellow, he had bifocal glasses, obviously he'd been kept out of the war in Russia. He wouldn't have done much. He was a captain but he was a funny little man. He had some funny expressions. We used to annoy him so much, keep the parade waiting, and he'd get more and more angry.

On one occasion he pulled out his rifle and he said, 'Look you Australia, you get into line or I will shit myself!' Another time he said, 'I am being told about you Australia. You think you know fuck all, but you know fuck nothing!' Anyway that time from then on we obeyed him because he spoke our language.

KEITH HOOPER

We always knew when someone important was coming to inspect the camp, because the day before they'd send in the rubbish cart and empty all the rubbish dumps in the camp. On this occasion the Germans were in a tizz for days. They emptied the rubbish dumps a couple of times. They even repainted the white post along the *Lager Strasse*. Then we heard the reason for all this panic. The visitor they were expecting was the general in charge of all prisoner of war camps, in Germany. He was an *oberst* [topmost] general, colonel-general. So he was very big time indeed.

The great day dawned and we went on parade as usual at nine o'clock, and as far as we were concerned that was it for the day. So we weren't at all pleased when the on-parade bugle went again at about eleven o'clock. We took great exception to these parades in the middle of the day. They always went on for hours, so as usual we took absolutely no notice at all. Well, as usual, they turned out the guard company and we were periwinkled out on parade. You know how you get the periwinkle out of its shell with a pin, when the guard company came in with bayonets and prodded us out on parade, we used to refer to the operation as periwinkling.

Eventually, knowing we were going to be there for ages, we always made sure we had plenty to smoke and something to read. Some people took stools, something to sit on. One group not far from us took a blanket and a pack of cards so they could sit down and play bridge. Eventually we got on parade and the officer of the day was a captain. I don't know his name, but we always called him 'Quack-Quack', because whenever he said anything, it always sounded like 'quack-quack'. We were always amused whenever Quack-Quack had anything to say. According to one of the interpreters he came from some remote Bavarian mountain village and he said, 'They all speak like that there'.

Well, Quack-Quack came down and counted us. Surprise, surprise, there was exactly the same number of us as there was a couple of hours before. Then absolutely nothing happened. I suppose we'd been standing there for an hour and a half and eventually the general, with an enormous entourage, came in through the main gates. His entourage included the Senior British Officer, so our parade was commanded by the deputy SBO, a major from the Welsh Guards.

Anyhow, the general had a look in Block One and in Block Two. Then he went over and inspected the camp kitchen. Visiting generals always have to inspect the kitchen. He went and had a look at the hospital, and then down to the lower part of the camp, and had a look at a couple of blocks there. I suppose we'd been standing there for two and a half to three hours by the time the general headed towards the parade ground. Well, to say the least of it, our ranks had got a bit ragged by that time and the clouds of smoke were going up, and the good buzz of conversation.

As the general got close, Quack-Quack was getting quite excited and when the general was nearly on the parade ground, Quack-Quack decided that his moment of glory had come, so he filled his lungs, and he shouted, 'Quack, quack! Quack, quack!' Well we were always amused when Quack-Quack had anything to say but to hear Quack-Quack shouting was really priceless and we all roared with laughter. He obviously wasn't getting the message through, whatever the message was, so he tried again and that was even funnier. We roared with laughter!

Well by this time the general was right on the parade ground. We were drawn up in a hollow square and the general would come in one corner. What he could see was a German officer in the middle shouting orders and 2000 British officers laughing at him. Well, that's not the sort of thing you expect to see in a well-run army and the general could see it was up to him as the senior officer on parade to do something about it. So there was a great shout from the general, 'Halpmann, come here!'

So Quack-Quack marched across to the general and the general said, 'What's going on?' Quack-Quack said, 'I have called the British officers to attention and they just laugh at me.' The general said, 'That's a jolly poor show.' He said to one of the interpreters, 'Fetch the British officer in charge of the parade.' So James Mortimer was sent for and he came across, and speaking through an interpreter the general said, 'Halpmann here has called the parade to attention and the British officers just laugh at him.' James Mortimer replied, 'Ohhhh, is that was he was saying! Of course, he was speaking German. British officers don't speak German. British officers speak English.'

Well the general thought about that for a while and he thought, 'That's a pretty sensible answer.' He turned on Quack Quack and he said, 'You fool! You were giving orders to the British officers in German. Don't you know British officers don't speak German? British officers speak English!' He went on at some length then and wondering how anybody as stupid as Quack-Quack had managed to reach the rank of captain.

Anyhow, when the general had run out of breath, James Mortimer said, 'Would you care to inspect the parade, Sir?' The general said yes he would. So James Mortimer marched back to the centre of the parade ground and he called, 'Brigade', and called us to attention. We couldn't hear what was going on but we had a jolly good idea and had been taking a keen interest in the whole thing. By the time James Mortimer got back to the centre of the parade ground we'd shuffled back into line and people had put out their cigarettes, and the people who were playing cards gathered up their blanket, and when he called us to attention we were ready, and *bang*, up we came. James Mortimer marched back to the general and said, 'The parade is now ready for inspection, Sir!' The general said, 'Please ask the British officers to stand at ease.' So *bang*, down we came.

Well, he went right around the parade, right round the square and as he came to each company, the company was called to attention and he was absolutely delighted. The old boy was beaming from ear to ear and he was saluting and bowing. He obviously thought it was an absolutely tremendous show. When he'd been right round the whole parade he finished up and he made a little speech. He said he would like to congratulate the British officers on their discipline and their steadiness on parade, and he went on to say, 'There are some German officers who would do well to heed the example that has been set for them today by the British officers on parade!' Well, Quack-Quack never forgave us for that.

WILTON EADY

Just to ensure fairness, Australian POWs made certain that their Allies too, received the full blessings of their laughter and mockery.

Where the Dutch were, they didn't use toilet paper when they went to the toilet. What they had was a channel running about that wide, and about that deep, and they had cubicles like this, and the channel came underneath the whole lot, and they had a big cistern up this end. So every two minutes – they would have it timed – about every two minutes a flush of water would come and take the lot out. But they used to use water to wash their bottoms, they never used toilet paper. We didn't have toilet paper, anyway. We did have plenty of newspaper.

So this bloke said, 'I'll get them Dutchies.' So he piles a great pile of paper down next to the cistern, you see. He waited until there was a whole heap of Dutchmen there, squatting over the channels, and just before it was set to go off, he lit it. And you can imagine the screams that went up as the paper went through, alight, because a big flush of water would take it through in a hurry. The bloke cleared off pretty quick.

THOMAS SMITH

But the officers, the Poms were rushing around saluting the officers . . . we got to this camp at Sabratha and there was heaps and heaps of Poms, and officers. Look, you've never seen so many officers in your life and the rotten sods are walking around all dressed up like chocolate soldiers. They had their mess kits with them, some even had tartan trews [a kind of knee breeches] on. They're swaggering around the joint and the stupid Poms are saluting them.

Well Australians don't salute very much. If the Australian salutes you he respects you and it's not this, 'I'm not saluting you, Sir, I'm saluting the uniform'. But these officers . . . they're all dressed up as though they were on parade and we heard, walking in the compound, one of the sycophants called out, 'Stand fast, soldier!' Of course, you sort of look around. 'Don't you salute?' And we look around. 'Don't you know who we are?' And the bloke near me said, 'Yes. You're the stupid bastards who got us into this.'

ALEXANDER BARNETT

Bad days, good moments, strange happenings and bizarre events. Humour was definitely located in the particular funny bone of each beholder and, as a result, certain individuals, human and otherwise, and the things they did have lived long in the memories of Australian prisoners of war.

There's a tall skinny bloke down in one of the rooms, Kelly said, 'Come down and I'll show you something.' So we went down, and he was a tall skinny Welshman, one of the Welsh Guards. And they said, 'We'll bet you two cigarettes this bloke can fart when he wants to.' I said, 'Oh bull, he can't just.'

So they pulled him down from the top bed, and bent him over the table, which usually sat over the middle of the room. And he did, and they lit it with a cigarette lighter, and it came out like a stream of blue flame, that's what potatoes do to you. Kelly can vouch for it, that's one of his stories; he tells it much better than me, I'm a bit shy.

RAPHAEL CORBETT

There was a funny old pair of Englishmen in Changi – Darto, Major Dart, and Preston, Colonel Preston – two old Indian Army types and they were just incredibly beyond everything. They were just floating along. And Darto had a little dog and he used to give half his food, his rotten issue of food to this little dog. The little dog became very famous.

At one stage there, it was when I had dysentery and I had just woken up, it was when an Indian ship came in and it left a lot of food including eggs and so forth and so on, and they said, 'Well, these eggs are good, obviously we'll have to do something ourselves.' And they managed somehow, these chooks appeared and one of the officers . . . started this little farm, a chook farm and they produced eggs and gradually more eggs and more chooks and he got a farm going.

This was very famous this farm, but the egg production started to come down and this was a disaster because that meant that not so many eggs coming to the sick people and then a terrible accusation was made that Darto's dog was eating the eggs, and this nearly precipitated a war between the Brits and the Australians and it got to Black Jack Galleghan and the English commander about this thing and they thought the only way to solve this was to set the watch and catch the culprit.

So they arranged to go back before dawn about five o'clock one morning and they let the dog out and they had hidden themselves, Black Jack and the lot of them, behind various things, to see what the dog did, and they let him go. And he got into the compound, in among the chooks and he walked round until he found the eggs and he sniffed on them but he just sniffed again and then he lifted his back leg and peed all over them, and Darto said, 'I told you so, I told you so. That's what he thinks of your bloody eggs!'

LLOYD CAHILL

We had a fellow in our truck, on the cattle truck, by the name of Dick Beale. Now Dicky Beale, his parents used to own a piano place in Bourke Street in Melbourne, Beale Pianos, and Dick had lived pretty comfortably all his life, his young life. He was a little, thin, weedy little bloke but he lived very comfortably. And he was lying in this truck, this carriage and he's moaning and groaning and he said, 'Oh God, if I don't get something to eat I'll think I'll die!'

Anyway, there was a big raw-boned, Western Australian bloke down the other end of the carriage and he jumped up and he said, 'You little bugger, you die, I'll eat you!' And he waved this knife under Dick's nose and they reckon it was the only thing that kept him alive. Every time he got a hunger pain he used to look at this engineer bloke.

FRANK ROY

Atkins was a real dumb Tasmanian, I used to have to take him on sick parade in the morning, every time in the morning after rollcall and breakfast you called sick parade, and you line the blokes up who are going up to the doctor to be sick. And we had a Doctor Brown, a nice young fellow just out of university. But poor old Doc Brown used to sta-st-sta-st-stutter terribly, oh, he had a terrible stutter, and Atkins would line up every morning to go on sick parade.

And Doctor Brown said to me once, 'S-s-sergeant, t-take this m-m-man out of my sight, he b-b-bloody well (excuse me) drives me nuts, and I'm sick and tired . . . and I d-don't want any . . .' And he stuttered like that, and he started to swear. And Atkins is standing alongside me, he said, 'Excuse me, Sir, you are an officer, Sir, you are not allowed to swear at me, Sir.' And you can imagine what the Doc said. Atkins is standing there, 'You are not allowed to swear, Sir.'

So anyway, that passed off. Another day we are on sick parade and Atkins is there, so Doc Brown he thinks, 'I will fix this bloke.' So he writes across his sick parade report, 'This man is pregnant'. So he tells Vic he is pregnant, so oh, Vic is a very sick bloke, from then on he is a very sick bloke, he is pregnant.

We are in prison camp taken by the Japs several months later and Vic is laying on his bunk and dear old young Doctor Brown, he was a very young man, about 22 or something like that, he walks into the tents, to the huts and so forth, looking after the men to see if they are all right because they are pretty sick. And he comes across Atkins, and Atkins is laying on his bunk. And he stops, he looks at Atkins, he says, 'Atkins, I am very pleased to see you', but he's st-stuttering, you know like this. He said, 'That problem you had w-w-way back in Noonamah, I can see by looking at you, you haven't got it any more, so you are a good man.'

Vic believed him, he didn't have a clue what pregnant was. So, you know, you have got to meet them, haven't you? Yeah, that was a, that is a real, true story that not many know about, Atkins and his bloomin' . . . But he was a menace this bloomin' Atkins, he was the funniest fellow. He unfortunately died when he came home, yeah.

BILL COVENTRY

For the prisoners under Japanese rule, like Bill Coventry, humour took a curious turn into areas that many people could regard as either disgusting or personally degrading. Yet this *was* their life for those horrendous years – a disgusting and degrading universe. If they could not find humour in it they would have had to succumb to its awfulness, and in succumbing, they would die. The strength of character and stubborn humanity displayed by these men and women in making jokes, in seeing the humour, is, I think, a matter for admiration and wonder. And if those of you who have contemporary sensitivities can sideline them for a moment – it's also bloody funny. Athol Pledger was on Ambon, in the hospital at Tan Tui.

Tinea, now they used to get it in the crotch a lot, and a lot of them weren't circumcised so it would get under the foreskin and a lot of them had to be circumcised. Used to circumcise them and stitch all of the thing to their penis and that would be it, until it would heal. But then during the night they used to get a urine erection and of course the stitches used to go – pain. So we had one little jar of ethyl chloride which is used for spraying, so as soon as we heard, we would race up and *phhst*, and the old boy would go plonk. That was funny.

Another chap he had it bad and they used to have their shower and then they would come up to the regimental aid post and the chap in charge, and we had a box of dusting powder and also the dentist was there and he had a box of plaster of Paris, big, army, wooden boxes.

So they used to come up after the shower, hold it up and dust all around you know, and off they would go. One chap, he turned out a doctor after, marvellous too, but he could get far away and be out of this world. And he was in charge of the RAP [Regimental Aid Post] this day. And a chap by the name of Con Connellan, he was about 6 foot 6 and a big bloke. Timmsey [the medical orderly] dusts him all over and off Connellan goes; they would usually have a lie down after that.

Anyhow, when Con woke up his whole testicles were in a solid mass. Timmsey had put plaster of Paris on instead of the dusting powder and the plaster of Paris had set hard, it was like cement. Poor old Con is all set in this cement; we had him in hospital for about three weeks, chipping little bits off. Oh I could tell you some stories about that hospital. These little funny things that happened.

. . . They used to trade with the Chinese outside, you know, the guard would be away down there and they would trade with someone behind a bush here or a hut there and get something. There was a Dutchman down on a work party and there was nothing around anywhere. Anyhow he traded something in for two pork chops. And they were rolled up in a bit of paper but he couldn't keep them on him while he was working because he only had a pair of shorts on. So he rolled them up in this paper and put them under a shrub.

So then, when they were going to come home he grabbed them and he had put his shirt on by then, and put them in his shirt. Hopped on the truck and he is there and the Jap guard has got his hand on his shoulders and that. What he didn't know was that these pork chops were covered in these great big bull ants. And they started to bite all around his testicles and that. And he couldn't do a thing; he had to put up with it until they drove the 10 kilometres back to camp. We had him in hospital for over a fortnight. He was just, where the ants had taken to him, see sweat and all of that around his groin, they just took to him.

But he said he still had his chops.

ATHOL 'TOM' PLEDGER

We had one particular nasty rash which affected the genital area of the males, 'cause there was no females with us, and they used to become a brilliant red and the skin would peel off . . . and it was very, very painful and sometimes the sores become diphtheric . . . so they'd send them back to the hospital.

But the only treatment we could do to them in the room, the ones that weren't so bad, was to apply a solution of Condy's crystals [potassium permanganate] to the affected area, and it used to be the funniest thing, the funniest sight of a night after they came back from work and have their showers; you'd see all these men with tins and containers squatting down immersing their painful parts in Condy's crystals. It was hilarious, I mean, what was said. I can't tell you what was said but it was quite funny.

GEORGE BEECHAM

It was my eighteenth birthday, 1942, and I wasn't too bad. I was okay to go to work but I didn't go this day and I went on sick parade and I fronted up to Rowley Richards and he was sitting on a bamboo platform with an overhang and he was there with Colonel Anderson and he said 'Yes, Wall'. He had a great memory, he knew everybody's name in the camp, 1000 people.

He said, 'Yes, Wall, what's the matter with you?' I said, 'Nothing, Sir.' I said, 'I was just wondering if I could have a day on light duties because it's my eighteenth birthday.' And he looked astounded at me and he looked at Colonel Anderson who was sitting with him, and Colonel Anderson thought for the moment and he said, 'Give this man light duties for the day.' So we did and away I went. Did my light duties and all the rest of it. Celebrated my eighteenth birthday by doing that.

The very next day I was on sick parade again with my half a blanket that I had, and I'm shivering and shaking and whatnot, rotten with malaria. And I front up to Rowley Richards again and Colonel Anderson wasn't there that day and he said to me, he said, 'Oh, good morning, Wall'. He said, 'Whose birthday is it today, your grandmother's?' So he was always with it.

That was a camp that we all had our first stages of pellagra. Pellagra is a disease where initially your tongue would split – it was like herringbone – and swell up. And also your scrotum would swell up and crack and weep, and it's shocking. And you could see all these blokes, we didn't have much 'eusol' [disinfectant]. I think it was eusol that they used to mix up, a disinfectant type of thing that they used to swab down in hospitals.

And they all had a little bowl and Rowley Richards'd put a bit of eusol in all of these little bowls of water and you'd sponge them with whatever you had and you'd sit down on this drain that was there – one of the hut's drains. And this row of blokes there with all their scrotums all on show bathing them, it was quite humorous to see. It wasn't very funny, but if you had've been there with your camera it would've been marvellous.

IAN WALL

We had one bloke – he was very old, he must have been over 50 – Blackie Kelo. I will never forget him. Poor bugger, he has been dead many years now, but he got back here. We had another bloke in the medical part of it, a fellow called Brian Timms, and he was an orderly . . . I have never forgotten this bloody thing.

He was on duty this day and Blackie Kelo, we used to try to keep him off as many work parties as possible, he was too old but he got pretty crook at times. But any way eventually . . . he used to have an enema every morning . . . He used to go down to the cookhouse and get a cup of tea. One thing we did have. We either bought it from the Chows [Chinese] or something you know, tea leaves or something or other . . . and the cooks used to give him a cup of tea.

This morning he had been down to the cookhouse and he had got his cup of tea and went back to where his bunk was and he just put it down beside the bunk and the next minute Timmsey breezes in and he said, 'You've got to have this bloody enema. Drop your strides.' And anyway, 'Oh, I'm going to have me bloody tea, you'll have to wait.' And, 'I haven't got time for you to have your tea. You will have to have your tea after I'm bloody gone. Come on, quick and lively!' And Blackie grumbling and that sort of thing.

Anyway he gets down and Timmsey's talking away to him and Blackie's talking and he said, 'Well come on now, just a minute, Blackie. Now don't move now.' And the next minute, he said, 'Jesus Timmsey! That's bloody hot you know! Bloody hot!' So Timmsey said, 'Oh shut up you dopey old bastard. You are always moaning about something.' And he said, 'Come pick up your strides on.' And he pulls him up . . . and so he turns around – 'Timmsey, you bastard. That was my tea!'

ROSS MCDONALD

It was during the wet season, of course. A man had a loincloth to wear, and I go to work this day and I got this itch on the rectum, and I thought I better go and see the sick parade when I got back, and when I got back [Weary] Dunlop had a look at my bottom and he said, 'Good lord, it is your haemorrhoid, son!' I said, 'Yes.' He said, 'Well, if I don't take them out and they turn septic, then you are gone.'

So, like all young Australians I had piles from piers and all those sort of things. I never heard what haemorrhoids are really like, so I said, 'If they have got to come out they have got to come out.' 'But,' he said, 'I have got no anaesthetic.' And I said, 'Yes, well, so what?' And he said, 'Well, it is a serious operation in Melbourne, let alone up here.' So I said, 'Go ahead.' 'All right,' he said, 'but it is going to be bad.' He said, 'If I don't take them out, you are gone.' So I said, 'Whiz them out.'

So overnight they built this table out of bamboo in this surgery of his. I went up the next morning and we had Colonel Dunlop, Major Moon, who was a gynaecologist, and Major Corlette, who finished up a specialist in Sydney after the war. And we used to call Corlette 'The Gangster'. He had a very husky, hard voice and we used to reckon he was a gangster, but they were all champion doctors.

So Moon and Dunlop got down the bottom end and Corlette held my head down and he said, 'Have a cigarette, Banjo.' I said, 'I don't smoke, Doc.' And he said, 'You'd better smoke this bastard!' So I had a few puffs of it.

Anyhow, it took him three and a half minutes without anaesthetic and I reckon I conked out just before he finished. That was the hard part of it. All these things have a funny ending, or some of them do.

After a few days Dunlop said to me, 'They are healing up well, Banjo. I will let Corlette handle you from now on.' So The Gangster Corlette, he used to examine me every day for about four or five days. After about the fifth day he said to me, 'I'd know this bloody arsehole anywhere after this.'

FRANCIS 'BANJO' BINSTEAD

These, then, are the stories that they laugh at, again, when they meet at reunions. They are the stories that protect them, that help guard against the long nights that visit them more frequently the older they get. They laugh – but they also never forget.

When you lose your freedom, you lose everything. But you make do with what you have, day by day. Just because we made all our own amusement, our own fun, you're still a prisoner, still not free to come and go. You're allowed to breathe and that's about all. But if someone escaped you'd be hauled out in the middle of the night, and snow and ice, and you could feel the cold coming up through your legs, standing out there, while they're doing a count at one o'clock in the morning, in whatever you're standing up in, when they called the alarm for the check parade. There were days like that. They were black dog days. Churchill called them that, 'black dog'. Bad hair days they call them these days, don't they?

RAPHAEL CORBETT

•

I know why our death rate was less. If ever I hear anyone knocking mateship; they don't know what they are talking about. We would have had 2500 dead too, but fortunately the Australian mateship was there. We consciously, or unconsciously, from the first day onwards, ended up in groups of six or seven mates and if one was in trouble the other five or six looked after him.

I never saw an Australian left to die on his own. Never . . . The British didn't have that mateship to the same extent. They were realistic. Talking to them, they said they were realistic and if a man was going to die within a few hours, often he was made comfortable, as much as they could underneath a bush or something, and they all said goodbye to him and that was it . . . mateship is very alive and well, I think. And it does a wonderful job.

JAMES LING

James Ling (left) and mates

James Ling's view is reinforced by the numbers. On the Thai–Burma Railway, in the worst of the Japanese camps, British prisoners died at twice, sometimes three times the rate of the Australians. Partly that was due to the better health of the Australians at the beginning of the war and partly it was because of their bush skills. But in an environment where men were reduced so quickly to a morally destructive self-preservation, the strength of the Australians as a group saved many that would otherwise have died, and that same strength cared till the end for the others. It may sound a little facile, but they *liked* each other as countrymen.

At night-time, see there was no electricity in the camp, so there was nothing else to do but lie on your bunk and talk and talk and talk. 'Do you remember what won the Melbourne Cup in 1921, George?' And someone would say, 'It was so and so.' 'No it wasn't, it was such and such!' You know, for half an hour it would be an argument about the Melbourne Cup in 1921.

And they would go over and over that sort of thing. We never ever stopped talking about the steak that we'd have when we got home. 'Oh, I'm going to have the biggest steak you can ever imagine.' We talked and talked. I don't know how many steaks we ate in our imagination . . . but we talked, see, we shared, we had an opportunity, you had a lot of opportunity to share about yourself. We talked over and over again about our background, our families and what we did at work and all this sort of thing. And that was a bonding thing, too, when you got to know a person and what they did and what they were feeling.

MARIC GILBERT

We were all in the same boat so there was no difference. We were all POWs. That's the way it was. We were all brothers in arms. There was no conflict or anything there; we were there to help one another as much as we possibly could. And there was a saying, and it's true, that any POW who didn't have a mate had nothing. He had nothing to live for. Every one of us had someone to care for us and we cared for them. It was a relationship more than just friendship, way and above that; mateship is a special circumstance. You lived for one another. They looked after you when you were sick and you looked after them when they were sick.

There were times when certain illnesses like dysentery and things like that, diarrhoea, where you didn't feel like eating and if you didn't eat, even though the meals were not very nutritious and whatnot, you'd force them down. If you got sick you didn't want to eat, so the mate was there to spoon-feed you if necessary and that was very important.

. . . If you threw in the ghost there was just no hope, you just faded away to nothing, you know . . . You sort of overcame all the problems that you had by dismissing them as much as you possibly could and just living your life with all your mates around you and doing what you could there, you know. Eating as much as you could, when you could, which was all very, very little but you had to keep on going. You know, have that urge to keep on going, irrespective.

IAN WALL

In the women's camps the need for each other was no different.

Having somebody you can always depend on, no matter what sort of person you are, they still accept you, it does mean a lot in life. To be able to rely on somebody like that, particularly when it is a matter of life and death. And you know that it didn't matter what you did, you have got somebody there who will help you and try and understand. And you miss that person when they go. Feel as if you have missed somebody, almost like a partner, a part of you, because you have been through the same things and shared feelings and shared some terrible thoughts with each other. Some good thoughts . . . and I have learned to appreciate the word 'mate' and 'mateship'. It is truly Australian.

SHEILA BRUHN

The small markers of a life well-lived, the ones they cherished from the world they had left behind – the birthdays, the passing encouragements, the thoughtful hand when a person felt low – these things took on enormous significance in the camps. Their presence in these men's lives, in those god-awful pits of inhumanity, is breathtaking. It happened in Germany . . .

I had my 21st birthday at Sagan, south-east of Berlin, in January '45, and the boys in my room grabbed me, stripped me naked, took me outside in the snow and they gave me 21 bumps in the snow. They threw me up and caught me twenty times, on the 21st occasion those so-and-sos didn't catch me, with the result I ended up naked in the snow. Then they wouldn't let me get back in the room and, believe you me, I had fears at that stage of the game of my future. I was a little concerned about frostbite. There was a German guard standing there with his alsatian, and that alsatian had eyes on me and I had eyes on him.

They finally let me back in the room and then they turned round and decided that I was wet and cold and that I needed drying. So the buggers put me onto the table and they dried me and you can imagine how they dried me, with towels as hard as they could go, oh dear oh dear, they livened me up no end, and I thought that was the end of it till later on in the afternoon, and remember winter it gets dark about fourish, I was taken for a walk by Reg Tyce, this rear gunner of mine, and Reg turned round to me and said, 'Come on, chum, we'll go a walk'.

So we went for a walk around the perimeter of the camp and when he got back here was these guys from my hut, from my room, lined up each side and down the end of it was a bloke by the name of George Lloyd who was the senior NCO in our room, and George is standing down there with a tray and it was an absolutely magnificent chocolate cake. The blokes had saved up their semolina and everything else over a period of time and they made a chocolate cake which would have been 12 to 15 inches square, and on it was, 'Happy

Birthday To Rex'. And with it they handed me a key, which was also so big, with 21 on it, and it was in fact made out of cardboard with silver paper over it taken from cigarette packets.

Now you know those sort of experiences, gee, you know you really feel it. And they'd alerted other people in the hut as to what was going on, that it was my 21st and the number of other members from that hut and other huts who came over and shook me by the hand and said, 'Happy 21st, I hope you're not here for your 22nd!' It's quite extraordinary, and they're memories which will never leave you, never leave you.

REX AUSTIN

And in Japan . . .

It is a funny thing during the prisoner of war time how it affects some people, other people it didn't. We had one bloke with us I called an uneducated psychologist – Freddie Brown was his name. Freddie had no education at all but he finished up in charge of the garbage can in the Cronulla Shire after the war, before he died. I had to give an oration at his funeral.

But Freddie had a knack with people. If I saw one of the blokes started to get a bit down in the dumps, a bit morose, I would say to Fred, 'Fred, I think so-and-so could do with a half hour of your talk, would you go and have a yarn with him?' Freddie would go down and sit down with this bloke and before you could say Jack Robinson he had him laughing and joking. He would completely change him around altogether.

He didn't do one; he did a dozen blokes, that fellow. He was absolutely fantastic the way he could get these blokes out of their mood, getting them back up on their feet again. He would cheer them up. He had no education whatsoever, it was just his manner. You meet all sorts in the army.

DES MULCAHY

And on the Railway as well.

A sense of humour and guts was all. That mateship is what got us home. If you didn't have a mate, you never got home. I remember in Thailand a mate of mine – he is still alive – he is South Australian. He had dysentery, malaria, the whole lot, he was on his last legs, he was gone, he hadn't eaten for a week.

Coming back from work this day the Nip shot a snake about 10 foot long and he chopped about 2 feet off for himself and went to go away and we said, 'What about us?' So he come back and chopped about three or four pieces about that long and we got one piece, and there was four of us that used to bunk in together, four mates, and we got it back to camp and boiled it up. It was just like fish, white fish. Smelly was dying in hospital and we said, 'Oh, what about old Smell?' . . . they said, 'He wouldn't eat snake!' And I said, 'Why call it snake? Call it fish.'

Anyhow, I went down to Smelly and I said, 'How are you going?' And he said, 'I'm gone, Banjo, gone, on the way out.' I said, 'Do you reckon you could eat some fish?' 'Fish!' he said, 'gee, where did you get the fish from?' I said, 'They blew the river today.' 'gee, I don't think I could get that down.' So I feed him this feed of fish – of snake. He said, 'Gee, can I have some more?' I said, 'Hang on, hang on, you haven't eaten for a fortnight or a week!' I said, 'We will bring some down in the morning.' One of my other mates took some down in the morning for him and he never looked back, he came good.

And he came up to Japan with me, when we finished. In Japan we were having a party the night the war finished. We were all saying, by gee, how lucky we were to be there. A couple of them said, 'Oh Smelly said to me, gee I was lucky,' he said, 'the night Banjo came down with that fish.' He said, 'I never looked back after that, I wouldn't have been here only for that.' And Bob said, 'You wouldn't have bloody well been here if you had known it was snake either!' He said, 'That wasn't snake!' 'That *was* snake,' they said. 'You wouldn't have been here if you hadn't have eaten it.' But that is how things went on.

FRANCIS 'BANJO' BINSTEAD

What took place between these men is not a matter easily understood, or commented on. Few of us will ever reach that place with another human being, where we have seen the best and worst of each other, in the foulest of circumstances . . . and love still remains.

I can remember when I was in hospital with dysentery, the day was long, and one of the things I looked forward to was Eric coming home from a work party and sticking his head through the opening which was a window and saying, 'How are you going, Eddie?' And if for some reason or another he was late, I fretted like mad. That was *so* important to me, just for him to come and stick his head through the window and say, 'How are you going, Eddie?' That moral support that a mate could give, and did give.

. . . Eric got dysentery. He was coping, we were coping, surviving, and only about a month before the war finished he got dysentery, but he was so far emaciated that he couldn't pull out of it and he died after only about a month.

Maric Gilbert (top right) with B company mortar detachment and locals

I forget the exact circumstances when I learned, perhaps I'd been out on a work party. I knew he'd been in hospital with dysentery, I went over to see him and was told that he had died a while ago. I forget the exact circumstances. I know it was devastating when I heard it.

. . . The will to live is very strong. Who said, 'Life is sweet?' I mean, I do know, and I'm satisfied, that those who stopped fighting within themselves were less determined to survive, [and] they didn't. Or if they didn't have the support, the moral support of a mate, and I'm talking about the moral support as much as any food that might be shared, their chances were less, too . . .

MARIC GILBERT

It is also important to record, though, and the veterans themselves are insistent on this, that not all men, not all Australians, met the challenge that mateship presented. The veterans are equally as insistent that it also be recorded that they understand why.

You couldn't grow a garden within the camp, because the fellows who didn't garden would pinch your stuff at night and that is not mateship. I had at one stage decided to grow a pumpkin and I got some burned-out rods from the galley of a destroyer that they had refitted there and I built a cage around the pumpkin and I wired it all the way round and the pumpkin was about that size and I thought, 'Beauty, I am going to have a pumpkin at last!' Because all the others had been pinched.

I woke up one morning and they said, 'For God sakes, Hicksey, your pumpkin is gone!' And I said, 'What do you mean it is gone?' They said, 'It's gone!' I said, 'How could they get it?' Because I had driven the stakes about 2 feet into the ground and wired them up at the top and twisted it, so they cut it out with a knife and took it out in slices and that is what had happened.

The fellow who did it was a sergeant and was a friend of mine; I got on very well with him . . . When they told me who had taken my pumpkin I went to see him and he was dying, I could see that, he died within four or five days and I reproached him, but without any bitterness, I could see that his life was – you could see when people were going to die . . .

WALTER HICKS

I got home from one working party, I got home with two coconuts, not one but two and that was really a prize. Of course, Eric would have had one and I'd have had the other . . . and on this occasion I left them on the end of my bed at night-time.

When I woke up in the morning they'd gone, they'd been stolen by a fellow prisoner. I've written a story about this and I've said in my story, 'I have never ever killed anybody, not even a Japanese did I kill, but murder was in my heart that morning'. If I knew who had done that I would have been tempted to murder him. He had taken my life away. I had my suspicions but I never ever, could never ever be sure who did it. But that took a lot of living down. I was beside myself with rage and anger. I'd lost two coconuts.

. . . I don't think I ever confronted him, no, no. No, I don't think I could ever have brought myself to do that. But that, to me, that was really devastating because at that stage our ration was getting very, very slender and meagre. But I reflected – probably after I came home, I became less judgmental about whoever did that – and I reflected about the strains put on a person's morality in a situation where we were all starving, really literally starving to death and the temptation must have been too much for this person. It wasn't – I suppose the person wouldn't have been a mate so he probably never had any qualms. He's probably long since dead anyway.

MARIC GILBERT

Weary Dunlop once said in an interview that it was a matter of huge pride to him that 'the Australians outworked, outsuffered and outlived every other national group on the Burma–Thailand railway'. He could have added that they out-cared everyone else as well. These men, who had never stolen in their lives, stole remorselessly. They lied, they dissembled, they wheedled and traded and connived – all for their mates. Their generosity is heartbreaking.

I know one chap, and he was a big fellow too, he sold his watch and he said, 'I'm alone. I'm a loner.' He didn't want to share with anyone. So all right, we said, 'You'll need friends.' 'No,' he said, 'I'm on my own.' He had dysentery and he had ulcers. That was all right, he couldn't get off his bunk, he had to get someone to carry him down to the toilets, which was just a bamboo platform with little slots in it, over a great big hole. Which was pretty nosey.

That was all right while he had the money to buy food. But when he ran out, who was going to take him out to the toilet? No one would bother. He was there stuck. Of course muggins, me, carried him down, but that was me, I was soft-hearted, but I couldn't see him stuck. But that was his manner. Most would have let him go, because he wanted to be a loner and share with no one. That was his attitude. I couldn't let him go. But I suppose, then, coming from the country . . . those things, you bypassed a lot.

Anyway, as I say, he was a pretty heavy bloke. When you come home from a day on the railway line and you have to carry him down to the toilet, it wasn't very nice. I don't know what happened to him. He went, I don't know whether he died or what happened.

THOMAS SMITH

Jack Dale, who was a friend of mine, was a bootmaker, and he was in high demand for everybody who had a pair of boots, including the Japs, of course; they had no bootmaker either. They used to use him a lot and Jack used to get handouts from the Japs because he had repaired their boots. Sometimes they would give him a handout, that was very helpful 'cause he would share that amongst his mates as well.

. . . But Jack, he realised that he was in a privileged position because he was working in the camp all day on bootmaking, helping out the boys and the Japs. So at night, he took on the responsibility of taking sick people to the toilet and he did a marvellous job in that wet 1943, carrying people to and fro of a night-time.

And you have got no idea of what the toilet was like. The toilets were just a big hole dug in the ground, they were about 10 feet deep and about 5 foot wide and across the top they just put bamboo poles. And in the wet season, of course, the hole would fill up with water and it was just an open hole. And the maggots would breed like mad and you would go down there at night-time and the bamboo would be covered with maggots and [you] used to have [to] stand there with bare feet while the maggots crawled all over you. And it wasn't that unusual for some poor cow to slip off the slats on the top and finish up in the pit and be dragged out in the middle of the night, to be cleaned. And fortunately, it was raining just about all the time and you stood them out in the rain and it washed them down in the rain under the eaves of the hut. But oh, it was a shocking situation.

He did a marvellous job and he helped so many people. He was one; he should have been decorated for what he did.

COLIN HAMLEY

One of my mates, a fellow by the name of Bill Halliday – I was never really close to him prior to our surrender. He was hit in the leg . . . and that turned, you know, fairly septic with ulcers and everything else. And in the sick bay when he was back in the camp, I would go over to see him. And in the early days when I'd go over to see him and take him something, if I could scrounge something to take to him, he was never very grateful, there was no mateship. He was always kind of whingeing. But again, as the time went on, his hope grew in him and he used to look forward to seeing me and I used to look forward to seeing him.

And I'll never forget, he was so skinny that you could see his backbone through his stomach, lying on that bed. And he had this awful leg. And the stench of the ulcer wards – it's like death itself. It's such a smell you could never ever forget, it really does stick in your lung with the stench. It's just like – I've only smelt it once as bad as that and that was – I saw a woman dying of cancer, that was being eaten away by cancer. But it's like, it's – anyway . . .

. . . The thing about, if I can say this about Bill Halliday, was that even though he was a whinger and a whiner in those early days, in the end, you know, he used to look forward to seeing me and I would look – but his eyes, they shone – beautiful eyes. I could just see them. They shone like beacons in the night. Just, it was so beautiful – you couldn't help but love the guy for it . . . I went on to Singapore and Burma–Thai Railway and he stayed in Java. But, of course, he did get back. And he lived until the late '60s. Yeah, anyway.

. . . It was mateship, really. I had nothing to do with it. Just, he was a mate and I never gave up on him. In the end he was the bloke that made his own decision he was going to live.

TOM UREN

You learn a lot over there, you learn a lot of psychology. What brings out the best in a man, and what the worst in a man is, and how to treat people to get the best out of them, and others, you see the worst that comes out in men too, over there. The worst – well, you see how low a cove can go, thieving off his mates. That happened many times over there.

And the best that it could bring out in a man is that chap I was bashed up with in Singapore, Jack Gilding and I, who went into jail together in Selerang. He went to Japan and I went up on the railway. He was only a corporal in the ammo sub-park from South Australia; he'd been manager of Nestlé's Milk at Broken Hill before the war. He would not get on that mess line. When there's a mess line everybody used to line up to go up, except the officers, they had their own mess line. But we'd all hop in, you'd go up and get your dixie out and get whatever you got in.

He wouldn't get on that line until every one of his section had got on and gone through. So if the food ran out three-quarters of the way through the line, he wouldn't have any. But he wouldn't get on that line until every one of his section did. And there wasn't another man over there that I knew would do that. Even I'd get on the line with everybody else, I wouldn't wait for everybody else to get on the line, but he did.

He went to Japan and they were flying them home, and they were on the airport over there and there's a chap, Stan Edwards from Woodridge. They were standing beside one another, you on one plane, up to you on the other plane. Stan Edwards got home; Jackie Gilding's plane went down in the drink on the way home, between Japan and Okinawa.

When I found out that, it soured me on life. For him, he would have been about the wisest man I knew. He was the best man I knew for his men and everything like that. And for him to go through everything like that, finish the war and on his way home, had to go down in the water and die. I felt there's no justice in this world. I wouldn't have the blooming local clergyman come in that front door there, I shunted them all away. I wouldn't have anything to do with them all and yet I was very religious before I went away . . . I felt there's no justice in this world. If there's a God, he must have been asleep, half the time.

CYRIL GILBERT

Coming home was often the most difficult thing of all, because it meant separation from each other. Families and friends could not compete for the hearts of the men for a while and many ex-POWs felt lost and lonely without their mates. There were other duties as well.

The worst experience I had after I come back, the whole family – my sister had a place, renting a place down in Southport – and we all went down there for a weekend. And this afternoon we all went for a walk. And when we come back to the house here is a little old grey-haired man sitting on the front veranda. Excuse me if I get a bit churned up at times, it will come good.

And he said, 'Are you Tom Pledger?' And I said, 'Yes.' And he said, 'Did you know Jack Smith?' He was my particular friend and I knew he had been beheaded at Laha. We had been right through the whole show together. And I said, 'Yes. You're Mr Smith?' He said, 'Yes, can you tell me what has happened to Jack?' And I said, 'Look, all I can tell you, Mr Smith, Jack won't be coming home.'

I couldn't, it's the only thing that broke me up. It still does. Because Jack and me was tent mates right through. They selected him to go to Laha and there he was beheaded. And they found a skeleton with his name tags still on so he was buried in a known grave.

I have been to Ambon three times and seen his grave. That was the worst thing I have ever done. Even all of the chaps I have buried and sat with in the prison camp. There was only one, another cobber, he too, that broke me up. Anyhow, ask the next question.

Athol 'Tom' Pledger

They are bound as we are not, they understand what we cannot and they have earned the right to use that word 'mate' in a way that the rest of us simply never will. Their bond is some small recompense for what they lost.

In human nature you saw the very best and you saw the very worst of the behaviour of men. I'm thankful to say the fellows who surrounded me, my mates, they stood tall amongst the tallest, good men. Just men who set an example that you could live by – that's wonderful comradeship. Some men, because of hunger and deprivation and the fact that they were incarcerated, I suppose it's the same as being in a civilian prison, you saw the bad and they became worse, the good men stood up and came through okay.

Lloyd Moule

RAY PARKIN

CHARLIE PARROTT

ATHOL 'TOM' PLEDGER

ROWLEY RICHARDS

FRANK ROY

FRED SKEELS

8

'The will to want to escape is so strong in most people, you just couldn't control it'

To all prisoners of war! Escaping from prison camps is no longer a sport!
All police and military guards have been given the most strict orders to shoot
on sight all suspected persons.

POSTER DISPLAYED BY GERMAN AUTHORITIES IN POW CAMPS IN 1944

Imprisonment divided Australians behind the wire into two broad groups: those who were able to accept that this was their lot, and those who refused to do so. In the first few months after their capture, most prisoners were exhausted and confused, often searching for someone to blame. How had they come to this sad and sorry end? All their dreams of glory, of service; gone. Were their officers to blame? Their generals? Their government? They knew *someone* was and their frustration deteriorated into deep anger. From there, it was a short step to either rebellion or sullen resignation. If it was rebellion they chose, it often began through actions designed to cause as much irritation and annoyance to the enemy as possible.

We agreed, 'Let's annoy them and cause havoc.' And there were lots of things you could do. We learnt how to black-out the whole camp during an air raid. It was blacked out anyway, but you would fuse the electrical system so that their searchlights out on the search towers would not operate and then when they

212

went to switch on the lights after, there was nothing. They would then have to go out and find where the damage was and repair it. Things like that, some of them. It didn't help you to get away but it inconvenienced the Jerry war effort.

RON ZWAR

When a group of people are confined in some way by a repressive authority, they will find ways to assert their independence, even though the rebellion is often conducted in secret. There is something comforting in the knowledge that you're taking an action that *they* don't know about, and if they did, you'd be in trouble. From teenagers in high school to prisoners on death row, secret codes, hidden possessions and clandestine writings of one kind or another are squirrelled away from the prying eyes of their controllers. Australian prisoners of war were no different – they invented and kept their secrets, even in the face of Japanese threats of death if they were caught.

The only place that you could put a diary was between your legs, hold it there, and hope they didn't ask you to move, or didn't give you a hit, because if you had of moved, you would have lost it. But I did keep it in the roof places that I could reach, because the sloping of the roof allowed you to be able to touch the roof in spots and I was able to hide it. I used to hide it in all sorts of places, not always on my person, and luckily I got back to the hiding place every time.

There was a time that we were emptied out of a hut and obviously we were on the move to some other place, and I lined up with all the boys and everything else, and we got all our gear out, the place is empty, and I remembered my diary. So being a foolish young man in those days, I waited till the Jap wasn't looking and snuck back in the hut and got my diary, and got away with it. But they said, 'You are mad, if they catch up with you they will lop your lolly off, you had no right to go back into that hut!' But I did it, and I have still got my diary.

BILL COVENTRY

Diaries were common, though extremely dangerous if discovered. Tools, watches, medicines and money were all hidden from their jailers. In the European camps, one secret that some men delighted in was engaging in illicit sex outside the confines of the camp. Far more of it went on than perhaps anyone suspected.

It wasn't a secret that some of the boys were playing up overseas, either. Even in Germany . . . having intercourse with German women. That used to come out every week. And, of course, those that got caught, they used to shave the girl's head – they used to shave their head and parade them around the village and put the boys in the boob [cell].

I had a Kiwi mate who was caught with a Jerry colonel's missus, and he was put away, down in the dens, and he was there for three months, and I didn't know him when he came out. He had turned as grey as what I had. And he says to me, 'Ray, I will never go.' He says, 'There's no way in the wide, wide world I will ever go back there!' But he got caught.

And we had a sergeant come into our camp not long before our exchange came along . . . now that was over two and a half years he'd been living with a Greek family, on with the daughter of the house and started playing around with the daughter of the house next door, and the first one put him into the Huns. When he came into our camp he told us the story, and we said, 'What a bloody idiot you were! You've had it made for two and a half years and you do something stupid like that.' Christ, he had to be an idiot.

It happens, you know. Us blokes are stupid, and I include myself in that. We're stupid.

RAY NORMAN

For women captured by the Japanese, the fear of sexual attack was especially nerve-racking, given the already established reputation of Japanese troops in China for rape, and their determination to include women prisoners in beatings, murder and humiliation. In Pat Darling's camp, the women knew of the massacre of their fellow nurses on Banka Island and so they held no illusions about Japanese morality. When the command came from the Japanese to present themselves at a 'cocktail party', they adopted a novel solution.

The Japanese had the bright idea that 32 healthy young Australians would be good for prostitutes. So they invited us to a cocktail party. Of course this is when we got to work and did the opposite of making up, by rubbing ashes into our hair, rubbing ashes into our skin and face and washing it all out, as much of it as you can, but to leave it look as though you have a very bad skin and your hair's awful, and I know when I walked in I heard somebody say, 'Who's that?' so I knew I'd done a good job, and one of the sisters of course clumped along in men's boots; we were the most unsightly crew, I can tell you.

. . . We wore our uniforms, of course, to make quite sure that they knew what we were and they had questioned us previously about that, you see, as to what work we could do, and we said there is only one job that we could do and that was nursing, and we were assured that there was always work for women. We knew exactly what they meant . . .

They offered us alcohol, but of course we were very prim and proper and said, of course we didn't drink, nurses in Australia didn't drink alcohol, but we got to work on all the savouries and demolished those. After an hour or it may have been two hours, I can't remember, just talking generally, they were very polite and then they said that four had to stay and four of them did stay and they volunteered to stay.

So we went back to the house, too scared to go to sleep and completely worried about the others, and then about ten minutes, quarter of an hour, it might have been twenty minutes, there was a knock on the windows, 'It's all right, you can go to sleep. We got rid of them.' Of course they were so unattractive, they wouldn't tempt anybody.

. . . Later on a group of women did go out . . . you must remember, there was every section of society in this camp that we were in and probably some of them were quite experienced 'taxi girls', or whatever they liked to call them, and they did go out and from then on we had no further problems about pressure to work for them . . .

We called them 'the girlfriends', and they went out and obviously supplied the Japs with what they needed . . . and as Gilly said, this is Mrs Gilmour, she said to me, 'You younger ones shouldn't look down on them, they are your protection, and this is the only way to look at it.' It was sensible, and also perhaps, they weren't living a very different life from what they had been living, say, in Singapore . . .

'The girlfriends' came back into camp and they were quite well dressed and quite healthy looking, but the advantage of having them back was, of course, that they became friendly with the guards and they were able to get black market food in at night.

. . . When you were nursing . . . if you had to treat somebody who'd been one of the girlfriends, you didn't treat them any differently from anybody else. Just, you know, it seemed pointless. It was their lifestyle, it was their business. As long as we didn't get involved, we weren't going to worry too much about it.

. . . One little girl who had gone out, she was fifteen when she went out and she was Eurasian and the Eurasians were badly treated by both sides, the British sides and the Asian side, and she had had a baby . . . the Japs said to her, that if she gave them the name of the Japanese who was the father that they would arrange a marriage and everything would be respectable, but she was a streetwise little girl and she wouldn't give a nationality, let alone a name. She said, it could be Chinese, it could Japanese, it could be Indonesian or the rest of it.

So she was subjected to what they call *basinado*, which is beating the soles of the feet, the poor little kid, and she was brought back into our camp. She had to be brought back by ambulance, of course, because she couldn't walk, and I was on duty the day she was brought back and Dr Smith said would I go and give her a sponge, which I did, and I must admit it seemed funny to use scented soap and nice talcum powder and all these things and put her into a pretty nightie, but her poor little feet were quite swollen and I soaked those.

When I first walked in with the bowl of warm water to give her the sponge she looked at me with fear and almost like hatred, and by the time I finished she said so sweetly, 'Thank you, Sister, I feel really happy now.' 'Cause I'd sponged her. I didn't treat her any differently from what I would anybody. I mean, you can't blame those kids.

PAT DARLING

Homosexuality did occur occasionally amongst the men in both the South-East Asian and the European camps, but it was infrequent and mostly frowned upon by the majority of men. This was, after all, a time when homosexuality was very definitely not just in the closet, but behind a padlocked door. The men joked about it, adapting their catchphrase 'Home by Christmas' to 'Home or homo by Christmas', but it was generally viewed by them as a dark, murky world, not to be entertained. Still, men like Bert Beecham were able to keep a balanced attitude.

I had the hard word dobbed on me. That would've been 1945, I reckon that'd be. And I had a friend, the sergeant in my unit, we were good mates Keith Mick and I . . . and I used to go across of a night to Mick and have a cup'a tea with him. And in the corner there was two English sergeants. One was an Anglo-Indian, as black as the ace of spades. Gideon was his name. Sergeant Gideon, and his mate was a white fellow by the name Paul White, and they were both homosexuals and they slept together as prisoners of war. And I went over to see Mick this night and, 'Hello', I said. 'What's happened to Paul and Gideon?'

'Oh,' he said, 'they're not talking. They had a bit of an argument,' he said, 'and they split up.'

So a few weeks later I was on night duty in one of the wards and who should I bump into but Basil Gideon and, 'Hello, George, how are you?' he says. 'I'm pretty good, Baz, how are you?' He said, 'What are you doing tonight?' I said, 'I'm working.' He said, 'When's your night off?' I said, 'Not till next week.' He says, 'Well, what about coming down to one of the wards?' he said. 'I think you picked the wrong one, Baz,' I said.

But how's that? Now where was he getting the food from to give him the strength? That's what I wanna know. It must be something about me, 'cause I had only been in the army a short time at Wagga and I'd had the hard word put on me. So I don't know what it was, but I never succumbed.

BERT BEECHAM

The simple fact was that for most of the prisoners, sexual desire declined rapidly along with their health and wellbeing, and the disappearance of their normal sexual feelings caused them all serious concern in the first year or so.

How can I put it nicely? After about eighteen months the food was so poor and for so long, that sexual desire just disappeared. It completely disappeared. And no one could believe it. We'd say, 'Have you had a . . . ?' 'No, not me.' And that, of course, brought up the question, 'Jesus, what's gonna happen when we get back? Can we reproduce?' One bloke says, 'Bloody hope not!'

When it became a general topic of conversation the doctors came in then and they told us, 'Don't worry, it's only a temporary thing. Once you get back on the good tucker you'll be all right. But you'll probably only live till 65 if you're lucky.' Had a shorter span of life 'cause being on bad food for so long, it must shorten your life.

And they were right, because we'd only been home a short time and they were dropping down like flies. Eight of our unit went within the first three months we were home.

BERT BEECHAM

Food mattered more than sex, more than anything. A loaf of bread became far more desirable and attractive than the most beautiful woman in the world could ever be.

When your belly is empty you don't have time to think of what is hanging below, that's about the long and the short of it. Your belly gets number one priority.

LLOYD MOULE

In every camp, the prisoners furiously protected the biggest and most dangerous secrets of all – communication with the outside world and plans for their escape. Radios were a critical lifeline and the BBC news kept them up to date on the progress of the war. Hope was kept alive by a curious collection of tubes, wires and subterfuge.

Ron Zwar was imprisoned in a camp called Stalag 4B, just a hundred kilometres from the German capital, Berlin. A member of the camp's escape committee, it was his task to somehow get the prisoners a radio.

While I was there I palled up with a little German guard and I got him to buy a radio for us. And he got the radio and the way to get it into the camp, we got permission from the Germans to buy a drum, a big bass drum and we had the radio put inside the drum. And the drum was carried into the camp and the radio was inside the drum. So that was just one little way of helping the escape committee.

We had other radios in the camp and some were made in the camp, manufactured. We had our own BBC News each night. The BBC News would come on about seven o'clock – we wouldn't hear it, it would be on a secret radio somewhere. We would take it down in shorthand and then the reader would be snuck from one hut to the next and they'd come in and someone would sing out, 'News up!' and everybody'd be quiet. The BBC News was read out and the fellow would disappear off to the next hut. And that's how we kept up with the news.

And the Germans, they thought they were being smart, on the wall they had a large map of the two fronts. After D-Day, on the 6th June 1944, there was the Western Front and then there was the Eastern Front. And the Germans had a red ribbon down where the Eastern Front actually was supposed to be. Where they wanted us to believe it was supposed to be. But we would go along and from our own news we would alter the pins on their map. And they would say the next day, 'Who did that?' We would say, 'Well we did because that's where the true front is.' They had a fair idea but they never knew – well, they had a shrewd idea how we got to know. They knew we had radios in the camp.

RON ZWAR

Even in some of the Japanese camps, radios were cobbled together from bits and pieces the prisoners either scrounged or stole. What remains astonishing about these primitive receivers is the utter ingenuity of the men who built them. Nothing, it seemed, was impossible for these dispossessed inventors, desperate as they were for good news; or indeed, any news at all, anything that could convince them that the world they had been deprived of still existed.

When the rail line came down they used to bring the trucks, they were Perkins diesel trucks built specially for the line. If the going got too hard on the so-called roads, they'd just take the tyres off and the flanges on the wheels would fit the railway line so that they'd bring them down that way, and these trucks kept coming down.

At the same time the radio's batteries, which they had carted up 200 miles through the jungle, 12-volt batteries, were running very low. They were having trouble recharging them but they solved that problem. When the radio battery was getting flat and these Perkins trucks were coming through, they would arrange to have a bit of a blue straight in front of one of these trucks and they would turn on a fight.

A couple of guys would get in and belt each other up and a few more would get in and the driver would come out, and by that time it was a complete melee and they were having a wonderful time. The driver would get back and he couldn't start his truck, because in the meantime they had taken the truck's battery and had given them the dud battery back. So that's the way we kept the news going for quite a while. They were up to all sorts of tricks like that and they really beat them, the Nips, there was always some way you could beat them.

LLOYD CAHILL

In Bicycle Camp there was a radio hidden away somewhere, and now and again the people who were in charge would get the news, and they would disseminate it amongst the troops, little bits here and there, you know? It might be a week or two old when you got it, but you'd get a little bit of news . . . 'We got news to say that the Coral Sea action had taken place, and that the Japs had lost an aircraft carrier. We had suffered no casualties.'

. . . And so you gradually got fed – you only got fed a little bit because I suppose the officers were always concerned that if we got too agitated or excited by good news, we'd do stupid things, you know? People would try to escape, or some other silly thing, because you could never escape from the islands at any time, because there was nowhere to go, and the natives had a price on your head anyway, you know, all the time.

So we used to get news, even in Burma . . . you only got little snippets of news, but each one was always the good news, you know? They'd tell us when the Battle of Midway – we heard about that, the Coral Sea Battle – we heard that the Japs were getting pushed back on the Kokoda Trail, little bits of things like that. The Germans had stopped bombing England, and we were now bombing Germany, you know, around the clock, and all these little bits would be fed to us.

The Japs all the time would give us – the Japs were always boasting, you know, 'Nippon soon be in Sydney, travelling around the harbour.' And they used to have little snide remarks all the time. They never lost anything, of course.

FRED SKEELS

Just as clever as the construction of the radios was their concealment. The hazardous game of hide-and-seek they played with their captors meant that the radios were constantly being moved and, each time they were, the new hiding place grew in complexity and downright, sneaky cunning. The prisoners in Germany kept one stop ahead of their guards – and were delighted to do so.

I've seen radios, you know the ordinary hair broom with the wooden back, not the plastic ones you've got now, they cut that in half and hollow it out and build a radio in that and *still* sweep the floor. All you needed was a space that big and they built a radio in it.

Another camp I was in they put a false back in the coal box. The Germans used to come around, they knew they had them. They'd come around with radio detectors and everything. But we had too many cockatoos [watchers] out. As soon as you saw the van coming there was no radio on, was there? They'd come in and they'd hunt for them, but the coal box was full of coal – the broom, we swept the floor with the broom.

There's some clever people in prisoner of war camps, believe me. I take my hat off to them. They're clever people.

CHARLIE PARROTT

The German toilet that you sit on was different from the British ones where you just got a pan of water right at the bottom. The German one was a bowl which was solid and actually went up when you flushed it, what you had passed was picked up by the water and dropped down the back. But the base of it, I suppose for economy, was elevated, it didn't go right down so that they only had to use half as much porcelain. So that left a hollow underneath the bowl and by undoing the four bolts that held it to the floor and the plumbers disconnecting the toilet fitting, we were able to put the radio under there, connect it up by wire to the two front bolts, bringing the wire to the two back bolts so we could plug in the electricity to there.

So when the guys came to pick up the BBC news at night, they would just connect the electricity to the two back bolts holding the toilet down, put the headphones on and lift up and connect it to the front bolt. And they could tune in and listen to the news. And if the Germans should come in, in a hell of a hurry the guy writing the BBC news down just whipped his pants down, sat on the toilet and had paper in his hand. And the German went past and opened the door, '*Entschuldigen*,' which means, 'excuse me'. And he would shut it again, and then of course you tear up the news and flush that down the toilet. So yes, it was brilliantly hidden.

GEOFF CORNISH

Occasionally the perilous dance between prisoner deception and jailer detection descended into a farce that was more reminiscent of the American sit-com *Hogan's Heroes* than the very real jails the camps were. From Stalag Luft III, Geoff Cornish tells of a brush with the Gestapo that belongs in a movie rather than real life – except that it actually happened.

We had the radio going secretly at night and took the BBC News so that we were informed of what was going on in the outside world. But by detection, as they do now, the Germans worked out that there was a radio somewhere in our hut. Then Jimmy Higgins, who was supposed to be keeping us in and responsible for all of this but was in our pay, came in. He said, 'Tonight at three o'clock in the morning there is going to be a secret Gestapo search of this hut because we think there is a radio here. They must not find anything or *phht* for me!' We said, 'Relax, Jimmy, they won't find anything.'

Sure enough, three o'clock in the morning *tramp, tramp, tramp, tramp* and there are 30 guards surrounding just our hut so it is absolutely isolated. They keep the far door locked and open this big one at the end of the corridor and in came two funny-looking, little, weaselly Gestapo men in civilian clothes. You would swear that Hollywood had done them up as Gestapo men, they were so typical.

Then they put a small table, like a kid's school desk in the centre of the corridor and we had to file past them, one on this side and one on this side and be strip-searched as you went past, and they did a pretty thorough search and anything they found they dumped on the table.

It was a very hot night as well and after a while they got so hot, because they were working furiously to get through this hut, they took their coats off and hung them somewhere safe where we couldn't get at them over there, and went on searching. And they soon built up quite a big mound of old maps and bits of compasses and things that we didn't particularly want. And they were feeling quite pleased with themselves. But there was some stuff that we did want to get out, including the radio. And different guys had different bits of it secreted on their person.

So we called in 'Bush' Parker, our Queensland stage magician, and when one of the Gestapo was searching Bush he dropped a small round compass onto the floor, grabbed it and the Gestapo man said, '*Geben sie mir!*' 'Give it to me!' And Bush, who spoke perfect German, pretended he didn't understand. The Gestapo man started to prise his fingers open and when he got it open there was nothing there. Bush looked at it, 'Oh, here it is, up here', and produced it out of his hair. So the Gestapo man grabbed his hand and, of course, the same thing happened, by the time he got that prised open it had gone again. And then he is trying to search him.

Bush pretended he was violently ticklish, so the Gestapo man is trying to search him and Bush is finally lying on the floor thrashing around being tickled by this Gestapo guy everywhere. And, of course, he wouldn't stop, so the Gestapo man said to his mate, 'He has got a compass, come over and give me a hand!'

So finally they got the little compass and stood up in absolute triumph, only to find that there was nobody left in the hut at all. While they were fighting with Bush on the floor, everybody with all of the contraband has gone out the other side and they cleared out everything that had been confiscated and re-confiscated it in our own name and the table was bare. They were livid with rage.

. . . And then, they had to put their coats on and come out to the gate to come out. Of course they had to produce their pass to get out of the camp and when they went into their pockets there is no pass there. Nor is the Gestapo identity badge in there, we had pinched that as well. And when they said to the guard, 'Open the gate, we are the Gestapo!' he said, 'No, you pull these tricks continually, I know you are not Gestapo. You can stay there.' 'Ring the commandant, he will come immediately!' 'I will not ring the commandant at four in the morning. I will ring the commandant when he has had his breakfast at six o'clock.' And he refused to budge.

So these little guys have got to walk all around, they were prisoners inside the warning wire, very disgruntled and from our huts, of course, the German speakers were calling out to them, 'You're going to be executed for this, aren't you?' 'You're Gestapo; you've shamed them and let them down.' We could see them swallowing hard and we were hitting home quite desperately. And we kept that up non-stop the whole time until the commandant came up, cigar on and they raced up to him and blabbered away this whole story. 'Hmm,' he said, 'yes, I will retrieve that for you, we know where they hide those things.'

And he walked into the hut and through to another hut and, of course, we gave it all back to him, so he was able to go back to them and give them their wallets with their passes to get out of the camp and their Gestapo identity cards.

But when they got to the gate to show them and opened their ID card, they looked rather like our letters; we were allowed to write three letters a month and two postcards. And each one, of course, was read by the Germans and then marked with a great big stamp, geprüfft, which means 'approved by the German censors Stalag Luft III', with a swastika and a German eagle on top of it. And when they opened their Gestapo passes there was a great big black rubber stamp which we had made from the heel of a flying boot with RAF wings and the RAF crest and the crown on top. And in English underneath, 'Approved by the RAF censors Stalag Luft III.' And there was no way out of it, the German commandant could not take the smile off his face, and he said, 'Well, there are your passes, we won't be seeing you again, will we?' And they knew they were probably, certainly a long custodial sentence as they say. And we never saw the Gestapo again for the rest of the war.

GEOFF CORNISH

Hiding radios and sabotaging the enemy at every available opportunity were all hope-givers in prisoner of war camps during World War II, enabling fighting men to feel they were still conducting a war, albeit a greatly reduced one. But the biggest blow, the coup de grâce of confinement, was a successful escape. There's a good reason why escape stories have lived on longer than any other in the films and books about that war – they appeal to the adventurer in us all, our love of heroism in the face of overwhelming odds. And it doesn't hurt that they're also replete with tension and terror.

Some Australian soldiers began attempting to escape from the very moment they were captured. And they learned immediately that not only would it be difficult, it could also prove lethal.

We were put into cattle trucks again and sent right up through the Brenner Pass into Brenner. The most extraordinary things happened on the way up, because the thing that we found out in prison camps was that everybody always thought about the same thing . . . In every cattle truck, there were 40 men to a cattle truck so you couldn't sit down, you were standing packed. But in every cattle truck, the men realised that if you could cut your way through the floorboards, and the floorboards were about 4 inches thick, some man could get down onto the revolving axle, get onto the step of the cattle truck, unlock the lock of the door and perhaps people could escape. And they did this in every cattle truck without any communication, one to the other.

The Germans had a flat car between all the cattle trucks and when you were going round a bend they would fire along the curve of the tray to deter from trying to get out. So we waited until it was dark and then we had one man unlock the door. We drew lots amongst the 40 to see what order we'd try to get out. And finally people were jumping out when it was dark.

Now realise that going up through the Brenner Pass there's a railway, a road or a river. So your chances of getting onto anything substantial were very remote. And a lot of men were killed when they jumped. Some were drowned when they jumped. But a lot did get finally into Switzerland, which was an astonishing thing to us.

When the Germans found this was happening they wired the loose floorboard to a part of the truck and put a hand grenade between. So that if you lifted the floorboard you pulled the pin out of the hand grenade so you killed everybody. So we weren't able to do any more attempts to escape there.

BILL FORDYCE

Contrary to the Hollywood screenwriter's notion, not every man in a POW camp was keen to leave it. Some sources suggest as little as 5 per cent of the camp communities were committed to escaping. The majority had made a decision to remain disinterested, or were broken by their capture, or were perhaps simply too lazy for the hard and dangerous work that even the planning of an escape entailed. Others loathed all escapees because of the punishments that were handed out by the camp authorities to those left behind.

They argued that very few escapees actually got home anyway, and that the trouble they caused to the enemy was negligible.

A lot of people that were prisoners of war were happy to be prisoners of war. They weren't going to jeopardise their lives. When you're with people for a long time you can practically tell whether a person is going to sit or whether a person is going to try to escape. It's the way they go about things. And also, there's only certain people that you could guarantee may have a chance of getting back. A lot of people can't stand hardship when it really gets hard. All those things came into it.

RONALD WALL

It's not difficult to understand the reaction of the non-escapees when you consider the principal tool of the absconders was to go under the wire – through a tunnel. The tunnels were places of horror that required the utmost courage. Tonnes of earth and clay pressing in on you; cave-ins that left you with a mouthful of soil, screaming silently for help; not enough air to go round and what you could breathe was foul anyway; stygian darkness relieved every now and then by flickering light bulbs if you were lucky or rancid feeble flames from margarine or oil lamps if you weren't. And as for the claustrophobia! There was only one way in, one way out . . . and you had to crawl for the whole bloody length of it.

We were given a room in the major block, which was ideal for a tunnel; it was up a bit, about 10 feet above the ground level outside. So from the end of my bed I cut round the tiles very carefully, we lifted the tiles out and made a hole that went down 10 feet. We made a ladder by taking one bed board out of everybody's bed and then we started off the longest tunnel in the war I think, 136 feet . . .

Going backwards wasn't so easy so we made a turnaround house. I got jammed in that the first time. I went round there because I was longer than the rest of them, and I finally fought my way out of it but it was rollcall and I wasn't there. It took a bit of explaining but I turned up, so I was put in solitary confinement for a while and back to work again. Bob Ross who spoke quite a bit of Italian and looked like an Italian, he was on the gate into our compound and it was his job to hold the guards up, any guards that came through. So he used to talk about their sex life – he was wonderful, he didn't know much Italian, but he knew about the other thing.

We used to make a little digging tool by sharpening a piece of steel that was across the beds to hold them together and we'd just scrape with that. It was sort of a conglomerate of clay and stones and then we'd put that in a Red Cross box, pull a string a couple of times and it would get pulled back to the entrance of the tunnel and then we'd pull it back and fill it again. I used to do the survey work of the tunnel. Found there were too many right-handers. They all worked with their right hand so it kept going round in a circle, so I had to straighten it up again.

. . . The soil that we got from it was always a problem getting rid of it because it was a different colour from the soil on the surface of the ground, so we put it over the top of the carabinieri's quarters which were adjoining my bedroom. The ceiling was badly cracked so we just cut around the cracks, pulled a piece out and that piece went back every time we'd put the soil in the ceiling. Apparently there was an air raid after we left the camp and all the ceiling fell in with the load of that stuff on them.

. . . We used to buy hair oil and put a little wick made out of pyjama cord and just light that. When you came out your nose and mouth were all covered by black soot. Later on when we got about 100 feet we decided that we would have to ventilate it, so the tins that the *pomodoros* [tomatoes] came in were quite big. We got one that fitted inside the other and put a flap gauge on it and a handle across the top and one guy just pumped the whole time, pumped air through cigarette tins that were, you know, Capstan fifties. Remember those? Cut the end out of the lid and the lid fitted, they just joined together like that. Made 100 feet of air, which was good. You've got all day to do something like that. It's amazing what you can do.

. . . When they finally found it we came to this rock which was alongside the tree and went around it, and I poked a rod up through the earth and could see starlight above, so I said we should go that night and the Senior British Officer said no, it was raining and oh this and that, anyway . . . The next morning a woman coming down with a donkey loaded with sticks, the donkey went arse first into the hole and the guards saw it and started screaming and running round in small circles and finally they put a guard in the other end and came out our end in the entrance under my bed and I said, 'It couldn't have been us, must have been the British that were there before us'. So then we got away with it. We weren't penalised or anything. Bad British.

JOHN FITZHARDINGE

And that was the greatest worry of all – that after all their work, all their time and effort, the tunnel would be discovered. It happened again and again, sometime under the most unfortunate of circumstances.

This one day, a Jerry pilot in a JU88, which was a twin-engine aircraft, a very good one . . . they used to fly over the camp now and again and shoot the camp up as we say, without firing a shot, but just low flyover and zoom around and get rid of a bit of adrenaline and so on.

And this day this Jerry fighter came in and came that low over one of our exercise yards that the tail wheel hit the ground, ran along and decapitated a New Zealander's head, chopped his head off, the front of the tail plane just took his head off.

. . . The fighter kept going, full back up, and right in front of it was this 12-foot high fence. And the tail wheel caught in the fence, barbed-wire entanglement. And the fighter was climbing, trying to climb, and he kept control of the aircraft and put on as much power as he could on the two motors and it managed to pull the fence out of the ground and break the strands of wire either side.

. . . So then the next day they had to repair the fence or a herd of fellows would've just swarmed out all over Germany. In the meantime they had six or eight German guards standing there on the outside making sure no one got out through the hole in the fence.

So they got the Italians onto the job . . . and of course they had to dig a new hole, they couldn't put it in the same hole the post was in before, so they dug a new hole nearby. And these posts being rather long, they would've been about 12 or 14 feet long, they were pretty heavy. So what you do with a post like that, you get three or four people to move the end of it over the end of the hole and then they gradually lift it up and as it comes up it drops down with a thud in the bottom of the hole . . . and it just so happened it was right over the second tunnel and it went straight through. The post damn near disappeared in the tunnel.

And, of course, the Italians being a rather raucous sort of people, excited, they're screaming and yelling and running to the Jerries and saying, 'Look what happened!' instead of shutting up and quickly digging another hole a bit further away. They should've woken up to what happened and, but they didn't, so that tunnel was discovered as well.

RON ZWAR

Every escape needed planning and coordination and so in many camps the men formed what they called 'the escape committee'.

Their task was not only to ensure that all escapes received enough planning to have the best possible chance of success, but also to vet all the escape plans hatched in the camp, thus ensuring that one scheme would not scuttle another.

There wouldn't have been more than about ten or twelve on the escape committee, kept very small for obvious reasons of security. Anyone who wanted to escape, if they wanted assistance from the camp, from the escape committee, they had to submit a plan to the escape committee and if the escape committee thought that plan was not practical, they would scrub it, they'd say, 'Well, we don't want you to go but if you go we can't say don't go. But we don't want you to go.'

Because if you get a lot of people breaking out – it wasn't all that hard to get out of the camp, you'd get shot at and so on, you had to take these risks, but well, they were risks you took. But they didn't want too many people milling around outside and a lot of Jerries hunting for them because a genuine escape would then have to get through that extra cordon to get away.

. . . Look, the will to want to escape is so strong in most people, that you just couldn't control it. There were people who just sat on their butts from the day they got in to the day they left. They said, 'Well blow this, I'm here, I didn't want to be here, I'm going to sit here until they come and get me.' There were those sort of people but then there were others who couldn't do that, they'd go crazy . . . and I was one of those who just couldn't bear to just sit there.

RON ZWAR

Ron Zwar wasn't on his own in that respect. Particularly in the camps holding the flyers of the RAF, escape became close to an obsession for these young men.

We never had any other thought but to get out tonight, or at the very latest tomorrow. And that was the overriding consideration or motivating force all of the time. All right, there were one or two exceptions – there were intellectual guys in the camp and they were deeper thinkers and they were inclined to be a bit older and they were less enthusiastic about escape activities. They never denied us that we should do it or could do it, but they didn't enthusiastically join our ranks straightaway. They tended to be apart. Senior accountants, all sorts of people joined air crew and they tended to watch the numbers a bit more than we did. We had no idea of caution or whatever.

GEOFF CORNISH

Nowhere was this passion to get out stronger than in Stalag Luft III, a Luftwaffe camp for captured airmen near Sagan, in Poland, about 160 kilometres south-east of Berlin. The camp's escape committee was led by a South African, Squadron Leader Roger Bushell, probably the most audacious and driven prison leader of the war. His committee began their operations early.

There was no bathhouse in Stalag Luft III, so that once a week we'd be marched down in groups of about twelve or fourteen to a bathhouse, which was probably about a mile down the road. So twelve or fourteen British servicemen with two guards and they'd all march up to the gate. The guards would show their, what we call an *ausweis* – a form to go out of the camp. You'd march up to the gate with that and the guard would read it and then wave us through and we'd march down to the bathhouse. So we used to wear an overcoat with nothing under it. Shoes and socks, of course. We'd have a towel and a bag with razors and soaps and things.

One day someone said, 'Look, if we were to make two good German uniforms and if we were to march twelve men with their uniforms tucked up under their coats and if we were to forge a couple of very good *ausweis* we would be able to march out of the camp.' Sixteen men. So they did this. They said, 'Right we're ready, who wants to go?'

So sixteen men went up to the gate. Two of them in perfect German uniforms. It happens that our battledress is identical material to the Luftwaffe uniform. So it was easy to convert that into a Luftwaffe uniform. So they marched up to the gate. They presented the forged *ausweis*. The guard waved them through. They marched down the road and disappeared round the corner.

And about an hour or so later the escape organisation said, 'Quick, who else wants to go? We've got extra uniforms. We've got extra *ausweis*.' Realise they also had to make wooden rifles that would pass scrutiny from 3 feet away, and they were perfect. The hardest thing we found was making a cardboard sling that looked like leather. 'Cause the rest of it was relatively simple. However, the next lot got ready and they marched out too.

Now I dunno how many thousands of miles from the [English] Channel Poland is, but it's an awfully long way and they were all caught within about a day. But the upset it used to cause Germans was unbelievable.

BILL FORDYCE

Stalag Luft III was the location for what has become the iconic escape of World War II – the Great Escape, as it is now known.

Over 70 men would get out under the wire during one remarkable night. The planning was exhaustive.

It was like an RAF station and the biggest sub-organisation, if you like, was the escape committee. And they coordinated all escape activities, everything to do with escaping. And that was headed by Roger Bushell and he was in our room. So a lot of the planning and a lot of the detail was done in our room. And Roger was a very great friend, he was a South African, brilliant lawyer, and a top barrister and he was working in London in the top law branches there. He spoke fluent German, he was brave and he was cunning. He was the ideal type, and he loathed the Germans. Absolutely and utterly.

Underneath the escape committee there was the security commission who made sure that nobody talked carelessly and gave away anything. They made sure that people didn't glance the wrong way because they knew that some activity was going on. If a lot of people glanced sideways at a certain spot the Germans would know there was something there. So all of those fine details were taken care of in security.

. . . And then we had the German bribery department, that was about five of us, German speakers, and it was our job to get in contraband like special paper for the documents, photographs, whatever we needed; radio valves, because we had our own wireless set and we had to keep that operating. There was a map-making department, forgery department, the tunnel planning department, carpentry, metalwork, to name a few. And there was a team attached to each of those divisions.

GEOFF CORNISH

They dug three tunnels, to give themselves options should one or more be discovered, and called them, 'Tom', 'Dick' and 'Harry'. The tunnels were located an astonishing 9 metres below the surface and were just four-tenths of a metre square – a tiny amount of room for one man to wriggle through. Harry was the final choice, and a long, long night began.

Bill Fordyce was a commercial artist from Kew in Melbourne, who had joined the RAAF and flown with 458 Squadron before being shot down near Gibraltar. He was about to turn 30.

The Great Escape was two days before my birthday. The end of March, 1944, and we'd only been there for less than a year . . . my number was 86 and at the time I had no idea who else was going out. 'Cause nobody told you. Nobody talked.

. . . They had told us that 40 men that we called the VIPs, they had to go. They were the first to go. Then there was some men who had helped with the tunnel. They were to go next. And then anyone in the camp who wanted to volunteer could put their name down. Now I hadn't done much towards the tunnel so I just put my name in with the mob and I was lucky, because there were probably 60 men who were what we called VIPs and tunnel helpers so that the fact I drew number 86 was very good. It was near the front of the mob.

On the night that the tunnel was to break there was about 4 feet of snow on the ground and we had planned the tunnel to break in the woods, which would be about 50 or 60 yards beyond the perimeter fence of the camp. But unfortunately, when they finally broke the tunnel soon as it got dark – and realise, this was midwinter – as soon as they broke it they realised they'd missed the woods by about 20 feet. So that anyone getting out would have to risk the searchlight shining on them as they got out. So the business of getting from the exit to the woods was going to be very, very difficult.

So they relayed back to us in the camp that there was now a rope in the snow from the tunnel exit, into the woods, onto a certain tree. That there would be one man in charge of every group of eight that came out of the tunnel. And that as you came up he would tell you where the light was going to flash and he'd say 'now', and you'd follow the rope into the woods and wait there for the rest of the eight to come along.

Unfortunately, everything happened for the worst. The tunnel was electrically lit from the power supply of the town, and there was an air raid on the town of Sagan that night. We'd never seen one before but that particular night the air force raided Sagan. So that firstly we lost all the electric lights so we had to use those things we called fat lamps. Tiny little things with German margarine and a little bit of a wick in them. And of course the tunnel was air conditioned so that the flow of air through it would blow the lights out. All sorts of problems like that.

You had to lie on the trolley with your arms out in front of you, 'cause if you were any other way you were too wide. Quite a lot of them were broad men. You'd get caught in the bed boards and the tunnel would have collapsed. This happened quite a lot. Several times. So that instead of getting out, I was to go at about ten at night, I got out at about five or six in the morning . . .

The tunnel entrance was about 3 or 4 feet from the bottom of the shaft. Because the people in the shaft would lift the prisoner onto the trolley and he would jerk the rope. Not, as it said in the film, hit it with a . . . that was ridicu-

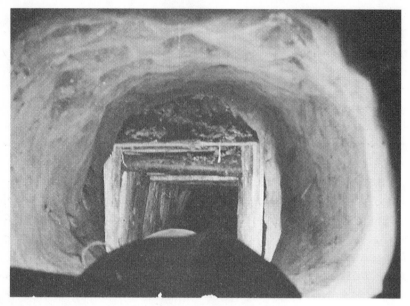

An early tunnel at Stalag Luft III

lous. You'd never make a noise like that. But he would just jerk the rope. The man in the halfway house would tow him along. You'd get to the halfway house. You'd slide over the top of the man who was in the halfway house. Whilst you were lying on him you'd pull the next trolley up to you. He'd help you onto that trolley. You'd jerk the rope and you'd go on to the second halfway house. That way you got to the end.

It was so light that when I got into the entrance of the tunnel they decided that no one else could go through. So immediately I got into it they closed the tunnel down. No one went in after me. And, of course, by the time I got to the exit the Germans had found the tunnel. People were screaming down the shaft to me, 'Get back, the Goons are here!'

Then the German came up and started to shoot with his machine gun down the 30-foot shaft, so the only thing I could do was turn round and go back. And, of course, by this time the system had broken down. There was no one to pull me along the halfway house; men had gone back into the camp. So I just had to scramble and, of course, the tunnel was no taller than the distance from your hip to your knee so you couldn't crawl properly, you had to sort of drag yourself along like this, which meant a risk of pulling in the bed boards.

So I got back into the camp panicking like mad and the Germans still didn't know where the tunnel commenced. Because . . . there were about twenty sandbags put into the tunnel after I got out and the whole thing closed down. Of course, the Germans now knew that there was a tunnel and a lot of men had escaped and there was an incredible panic in the camp. The Germans are going absolutely berserk and firing guns everywhere. They made us strip off in the snow and we stood there with nothing on for a quite a time. Some men were sent to the cooler [solitary confinement]. I wasn't, I dunno how.

So it was a very strange time because we knew that a lot of men had got out. The Germans didn't know. So we were delighted. Just imagine the upset we're causing, and of course, it wasn't for three or four days that the Germans told us that they'd caught them. They said they'd caught everybody and they said that 30 men had been shot whilst trying to escape. The Senior British Officer said, 'How many were wounded?' Because you know, you don't kill everybody when you're trying to stop them. And the German officer said, 'None were wounded, 30 were killed.' So we immediately knew they'd been just killing them when they caught them. About two days later they said that a further twenty had been killed. And we got to the stage where we really didn't know for sure what had happened.

. . . About a day or so after the tunnel broke the Germans came to us and said, 'Look, one of our German officers has crawled along the tunnel to try and see where it began from'. But of course, he couldn't get up because of the sandbags. So they asked us would we open the tunnel. 'Cause he'd crawled along it and didn't have the courage to go back and so for about two days he'd been at the bottom of the shaft. It must have been – I dunno how he survived. Must have been very claustrophobic. So we opened the tunnel and let him out, so the Germans now knew where the tunnel went from.

We got a list sometime later as to the men who'd been shot whilst trying to escape. Some we couldn't account for. They were the ones that were in concentration camps. But we didn't know that they were there. And, of course, this was about a year before the end of the war. So this was in March '44. So life just went along the same old way in the camp.

BILL FORDYCE

Seventy-six men escaped from Stalag Luft III that night. Fifty were murdered by the Germans, including Roger Bushell. Twenty-three were recaptured and just three escaped from Germany. The escape created a ripple that spread throughout all the POW camps.

I didn't know the Great Escape was going to take place. The first we heard of it was when one day in East Prussia, at Heydekrug, we were informed that 50

RAF officers had been shot while attempting to escape, and we had been called out, as a matter of fact, on this particular day, I forget the date now, but we had been called out on parade and when we paraded, this Heydekrug was a camp of about 6000. It was a big camp, but in our particular compound at that camp we were called out on parade and the Germans had not just the usual rifles but some of them were armed with sub-machine guns, and also they had heavy machine guns on tripods planted around the parade ground, about four or five of them, and we realised that something was up. I mean, this was very unusual, it wasn't a normal parade.

Anyhow, the Germans all looked very jumpy and the adjutant came out and stood on a box and read out this announcement that the high command has instructed him to inform the prisoners that 50 RAF prisoners were shot while attempting to escape. Well, you know, that was obviously completely wrong. I mean, anyone would know that that wouldn't happen normally. You wouldn't have 50 officers all escaping and being shot at the same time.

Clearly there was something up which wasn't right, and the mob started booing, they just started booing and there were, I suppose, a couple of thousand of us in the compound there and they just booed and booed and booed, and he couldn't read any more of the notice. So in the end he just threw the paper down on the ground in rage and just marched off, and that was a very, very ticklish point because everyone was outraged. They knew it would be plain murder, couldn't have been just shot while attempting to escape, and Dixie Deans fortunately managed to calm everyone down past the tender point until in the end people realised, because if there'd been a riot there, there would've been hundreds of us killed because of those heavy machine guns and so on.

. . . We remained on the parade ground and then after everything simmered down they counted us, and of course, every time the Germans counted us they got the count wrong because there were all sorts of ways and means of upsetting the count and the main thing was to try and fool the Germans so they never got the count right and never knew exactly how many prisoners, and we were there pretty well all day. They were counting and re-counting and doing all sorts of things, and in the end they hit upon the great idea of getting two ladders and putting them between two huts so that they came together in a vee with just enough room for one person to go through, and they then herded us all together and pushed us through this race as it were, and they had a German just counting as each one was coming through.

Well, of course, it was only a matter of twenty or 30 seconds before some wit started baa-ing and then you had 2000 prisoners all going, 'Baa, baa, baa!' And, of course, they got the count wrong again. So in the end they sent us

back to our huts and that was that, but it was a very nasty day and that was
the Great Escape.

ALEXANDER KERR

Escaping from the Japanese camps involved risks and challenges
that even the daredevils in the stalags would have quailed at. Rarely
did escapes, even in Europe, actually succeed, so the chances of
success in South-East Asia were close to Buckley's and none. And
the men knew it.

Well, what was the point? You were in the jungle, you had nowhere to go, you
had no food to take with you; you had nothin' to ward off malaria, you can get
dysentery and die, get diarrhoea and die. Eight blokes tried it, they all got
caught, they were all brought back and they were shot. Others tried it and they
died in the jungle of starvation and disease. So you just didn't bother, there was
nowhere to go.

There's safety in numbers. You were safer to stay where you were than
to take off. Even from Singapore when they were first captured they tried to
escape. Four got shot, they were brought back. Quite a lot of single ones
escaped and they got killed when they came back. Dunno. It wasn't worth
it. I mean, your skin's the wrong colour for a start, our eyes are the wrong
colour, you're the wrong size, you're amongst the little blackfellas – little dark-
skinned people. You can't speak the language. The only successful escapes
that I know of were a few from Borneo. Six escaped from Borneo. From 2500,
six managed to escape.

BERT BEECHAM

Bert is right. Fifteen thousand Australians went into Changi in
February 1942. None escaped and got home. Elsewhere, others
gave it their best shot – but to bad ends.

Together with other Australian and British prisoners, Herbert
Trackson was sent to Sandakan Camp in northern Borneo. They
were to be used to build a military airfield for the Japanese. But it
didn't take long for him to decide that anywhere would be better
than where he was.

We got to Sandakan, there was very little there, only a few huts and a bit of
stuff we took there with us, a few dixies to cook in and that sort of thing. It
wasn't long after I got in there I started thinking and had seen the camp and

just this barbed-wire fence around and the fallen scrub all round and that, that this would be as good a chance as I was going to get to leave. But no one else was very interested in the idea. As it happened, there's 2000 of them dead and I'm here. It turned out to be a horrific turn-out, after we got out, just the same.

I just went around at mealtimes and that and they'd be sitting around having their meal and sort of I said, 'I don't think we're going to last stuck in this place, and don't you think we ought to do something about making a break for it?' 'Where are you going to go?' 'Out through that bloody fence.' 'Oh, you can't go out there, you'll only finish up out there in the jungle.' I said, 'Well, you may as well die out there as here, what difference?' But this fellow, Matt Carr, he was a bit of a bush fellow, he came from Millmerran, he lived in Mundubbera, and he said, 'Oh, I'll go with you.' So him and I went.

. . . We talked about it for a while and then we went to our two captains, Captain Crozier and Captain Milner, and asked them could they help us. Anyhow, they managed to muster up a few boxes of matches and we got a few dixies of rice from the cookhouse which, I don't know, but what I've heard afterwards, that they paid a heavy price for. Because the Japs were always on us later, trying to make us say who knew we were going and of course, we were definite that the officers didn't know anything about it.

. . . We waited until it was a terrific big storm, lightning and everything. And then we asked some of our own blokes in there if they'd be prepared to hold the wire up a bit so we could scamper underneath, which they did. And we got underneath. Well, as soon as you got through the wire you were into this fallen jungle, with these big logs and that, and we crawled over the top of them and out until we got to the river. And that's all, we didn't have any lights or lamps or nothing like that . . . the Japs knew that we were out there as soon as we knew ourselves. And of course, anyone that went out like that, they straight-away put out a reward notice all around the villages and that, you know, anyone caught helping them, the family would be tortured and so forth.

We got under the wire and out into this fallen jungle, over these logs and made our way through that, but don't ask me how, there wasn't moonlight or anything, until we came to this river. And when we came to this river we knew that the natives would have a boat or something somewhere, and we started to work our way down along the river until we came to this little section of kampongs, native huts on stilts. And underneath we found this boat, pushed it out into the water, and when it got far enough we got into the boat and managed to get along towards the coast, the way the river would run and sort of drift.

Why we didn't get taken by crocodiles is another story, but that's the next chapter.

The next morning we came to an island in the middle of the river, this small island, and we went onto this island and we stayed there this night and then this boat wasn't quite big enough, so anyway we decided that night we'd get another one. We went underneath another kampong and Matt went in and got the boat and brought it out by pushing it along and walking it, and behind him this native was waving a parang, you know, a knife, a native swinging and going crook. But anyway, when he saw there was two of us he went back and we got that one away and that's the one we finished up with. But of course, the natives weren't keen to help you or anything because the word has already gone out that their families and all will be murdered if they're caught helping us. So they were very reluctant to even see where we'd been, wanted nothing to do with it at all.

It was only a canoe sort of thing, but we took that out into the river and pushed it along the bank of the river until we came to the ocean and then we started to move up along the coast. But the boat wasn't very seaworthy, we used to push it along in the night-time, and then rest up in the days. So we took it up into a grass bank area and hid it there eventually because it was no more good to us then. And went along just walking . . . it was somewhere around two to three weeks, I think.

You see we were along the coast a lot, eating coconuts and raiding fish traps and that sort of thing to stay alive. We used to go into the native fish traps and we had a piece of wire netting that we got from somewhere and we'd go in and drag this round like a net and get these little fish and little crabs and we'd take them away somewhere and light a fire and cook them and that's what we were living on, that and coconuts. Besides, when we came to a native garden we'd go in and raid it for pawpaws or taro roots or something like that.

. . . We came to a plantation, a coconut plantation and one of the natives there contacted us and he could talk a little English and he promised to go and get us something to eat. We went into a little hut that was built in this plantation on high, high stilts, it was still raining, and he came back with the food all right but he came back with a company of Japanese soldiers who surrounded us before we could do anything there . . . Matt heard this singing out and he woke me up and anyhow it was the Jap army round there.

At the front door there was this ladder coming up to the door to get in and out, and this Japanese officer was coming up. And anyway, he came up until he got to the top of the steps and he had a revolver in his hand, a 45 or whatever, and the top step broke and he virtually fell into the front door. And I thought this was very funny. But what could you do when there was 30 or 40 others around the hut there?

But anyhow, he got up and he came in and we went with them with no trouble until we got down the boat and they put us on the boat. And when they put us on the boat there were a few of these locals as the crew and anyhow they tried to, I was lying on the deck and they tried to get one of these fellows to give me a bit of a, some sort of roughing up, you know. The Japanese would point to me and you know, show him his hand, but I just lay there and looked at him but he didn't do it.

And they took us back to Sandakan for trial, as we'd become criminals then because we'd escaped from the Japanese Army. And when I was tried by the Japanese, they sentenced me to four years' penal servitude.

HERBERT TRACKSON

For his audacity in attempting to escape the Japanese, Herbert Trackson was sent to the hell of Outram Road Gaol.

And though it may seem strange to say so, he was, in a way, fortunate. Of the almost 2000 Australian POWs in captivity at Sandakan, only six would survive the inhumane treatment and death meted out by the Japanese. None of the 700 British prisoners lived. The murder of those men remains as possibly the most infamous atrocity of the Pacific war.

•

In Europe, prisoners escaped over the wire, through the wire, under the wire and, if they were particularly clever, through the front gate. Some prisoners became almost professional escapees, their exploits legendary, their methods breathtakingly cheeky. The Englishman George Grimson, from Stalag Luft III, was probably the best of the lot. Certainly, he was the most brazen.

Just about everybody who wanted to escape had a plan of his own, how he was going to do it. We had some very good escape artists there. Probably the best known one was a chap by the name of Grimson. He made several escapes, absolutely amazing work.

His last escape, he was dressed as a German *unteroffizier* [corporal], and he had a little black box about that big with a handle on the side which he wound and coming out of it was two wires with crocodile clips on the end, and he waited until some Germans were working on the surrounding wire and they had ladders et cetera there, and they went off to have lunch.

The goons, the workers, had overalls which we called goon suits, and the goons went off to lunch and along came Grimson who spoke flawless German and he took one of the ladders that the goons had left there while they were having lunch, and he put it up against the wire, right underneath one of the lookout towers and he climbed up and he was talking to the guard and he said, 'These stupid individuals, they've gone away and they haven't finished the job. I've got to test these wires for whether they've been tapped or not.'

And so he said, 'I'll just go down and test that.' And he said, 'I think I'll go to lunch myself. I think I'll just pull the ladder over the other side and when the fellows come back tell them they've got to walk out here and get their ladder.'

So off he went and he went in between the two towers and he got up and he put these two crocodile clips on the wires and he had a set of earphones which he put on, and then he wound this, you know. Now, he wasn't content with just doing that once. He came back down and he went along a bit further and did the same thing, and then he called out to the guard, 'It looks as though it's okay.' He pulled the ladder up, put it over the other side and just walked down and he said, 'Don't forget to tell the chaps their ladder's here. They'll have to come around here.' And he just walked off.

He was never seen again in Stalag Luft III, but I believe he went to Poland and joined the Polish Resistance and was caught by the Gestapo and shot, but he did a series of really good escapes. That was his last one which was probably as good as any he'd done.

ALEXANDER KERR

Australians, too, performed extraordinary escapes that one can only marvel at today. Robert St Quentin Hooper enlisted in the Light Horse before the war, then the 2/7th Field Regiment in the 9th Division. He saw action in Tobruk then El Alamein, where his war changed from combat to absconding. And what an absconder he was. Seven, count them, *seven* attempts at escape. He was 21 years old, full of determination and a fierce optimism that could not be extinguished. This man *believed* that he would eventually succeed. And this is how he did it.

Attempt 1

In Benghazi we were put in a camp called The Palms and we weren't given much food, and I said to my sergeant, I said, 'We'll escape from this place. There's a truck come in with our rations at night, we could crawl in under this truck and hang on and escape.' And I had no bread or anything; they used to give us little round rolls of bread every day. And my corporal, he used to save his bread up, in case for rough days and that. I said, 'Give me those two loaves of bread.' I said, 'I'll give you ten pound after the war.' So he gave it to me.

Anyway, all the fellows in the camp were telling their mates, 'Look look!' nudging their mates, 'Look at the fellow under the truck there!' And they caught us, you see. They pulled us out and they took us outside and chained our hands behind our back and put the boots in and that was about it. The sergeant got the most of it, he was a big fellow and they kicked me a couple of times but I pretended I was unconscious and I never complained, and they kicked and beat you up. They got no satisfaction, so they'd knock off if they weren't getting any satisfaction.

And then they took us up in chains, they bought some rope down, they chained us up each side of the iron gate with our feet off the ground and hands behind our back. And the Italian Royalist Guard, they were all right, they put stones under our feet so that our feet were off the ground . . . told us to kick them away if the carabinieri came back.

. . . The next morning I went up and asked this commandant for my two loaves of bread back – I was thinking of the ten pound I had to give the bloke after the war. And he punched me in the cheek there, and he jumped back and he'd bruised his knuckles.

Attempt 2

After a while they shifted us to a camp in northern Italy, near Udine. This camp was called Gruppignano. And when I got there they started to dig a tunnel from there, so they took me in with them. And we dug this tunnel, about 70 metre long tunnel . . . we dug it with an old tin helmet and a pick that we had pinched from some workers.

. . . God, sometimes it would fall on you. And some fellows would help and they were in there for two seconds and they were screaming they wanted to get out, they had claustrophobia they couldn't stand it, see? You understand, when you go 60 or 70 metres underground, head first, and the only way out is to back out and if it falls on you, you're caught. Well, they can pull you by the legs and pull you out. But if it falls behind you, they've got to dig you out.

And there were big rocks there. We had to go around the big rocks and some of them you had to dig out and roll them back to the entrance. When you've got an entrance about 3 foot 6 by 3 foot, and you're in 70 metres, it's a long way in. That's three-quarters of a football field. It's a long way, especially if you're fearful, frightened . . .

We intended to go further out through the cornfield there, but rainy weather set in and we thought it might collapse, so we had to go early. Nineteen of us went through the tunnel and we all got caught in two or three days, I got caught in two days.

I was in the mountains and I came down from the mountains and crawled into a place, I thought it was a barn. And there was chooks and pigs in there and they started squawking and an Italian fellow came along with a shotgun and he took me in. I was wet through and he took me into his room and then he rang the police and said he had a prisoner . . . so the next morning they came and collected me and took me back to the camp in Gruppignano and put us in the cells there and took our boots off and jumped on our bare feet and that sort of thing, beat us up and put us in the cells there for a month on bread and water.

Attempt 3

We were working on loading trains with bricks to go to France and all these trains had little windows in the corner of them and so we didn't lock them, you had to lock them from the inside, we didn't lock three of them from the inside and the other one, jammed a bit of wood in there so it looked as though it was locked.

And we made up our mind we had to escape, so we escaped from the camp, crawled in through these windows, through the window of the wagon, the guards chasing us and they didn't know where we'd gone.

. . . We were in the train for about a week, I suppose, tripped around, 'cause all the railways were getting bombed at that time, in late '42, early '43 I think it was. And we finished up going alongside of Switzerland near Lake Constance there and I said, 'We'll have a go for Yugoslavia, across the Switzerland border.' So we got out of the train and walked across the snow and hid under a bridge until it was dark and when it was dark we went to the Swiss border, we found a bridge, went across the bridge and they caught us with a dogwatch [late night guard].

. . . We didn't get shot, that was the main thing. I had so much clothes on it was so cold, and he said to me, one of the guards said to me, 'Hands up or I'll shoot you, put your hands right up or I'll shoot you!' And I couldn't get my hands up 'cause I had jumpers on and everything I owned on and I could only get me hands up only that far, couldn't get them up any further.

. . . We were just unlucky, they took us back and put us in the jail and we got food and water. And the guard in the morning said, 'You're unlucky. If you'd have gone a mile further downstream,' he said, 'you could have walked into Switzerland.'

Attempt 4

I was sent to a punishment camp, in Austria, they used to call it the toughest camp . . . Anyway, I said, 'We'll escape from this camp.' And the commandant came in and he said, 'Hooper, you don't work on the railway line, you won't work and you won't polish your boots. You know if you work, you polish your boots.' He said, 'Borrow some polish off your mates.' I said, 'I'm Australian, we don't bludge off our mates. Anyway,' I said, 'I'm going to escape from here.' You see. He said, 'Oh Hooper, you're always going to do something.' He said, 'When you're going, let me know, I'll give you an extra piece of *wursten* sausage.'

Anyway, he doesn't know that I'm digging a tunnel. And I've got a string tied to my big toe and my mate used to get up and we'd pull the floorboard up at night and dig it at night, I'd dig it. And when it was all-clear he'd give it one tug and two tugs if it was risky. The guards were around the place . . .

So one night we went. And we climbed, they had a tripwire there about 50 yards outside the camp, we didn't know that. We got chased by a guard, who comes around the corner and fires a shot, fires in the air and we tripped over the tripwire and lost all our bags with our food in, and we climbed over, they chased us and we hid in a bush, and they galloped past us, and then we climbed this mountain all night, three of us, through the snow.

. . . We crossed the mountain, a 400-metre high mountain, and real difficulty getting down the other side. That was harder than climbing up. And you had to go down backwards, 'cause you couldn't walk down it, it was too slopey. I climbed down a rock face at one stage of it and I thought, 'Now there's a beautiful slide down if I sit there, I'll be able to slide all the way down. But I'd probably be going 1000 miles an hour by the time I get to the bottom, and kill myself.' So I had to climb back up that rock wall.

I had my sick mate with me, he was at the top. I knew he couldn't crawl down there. And there was a big gap between the rock face and where I had to step onto the glacier thing and I thought, 'Gee, if I'd slipped down there they would have found me in about 10 000 years' time. There's a body, he was one of the first men or something.' They'd find me body.

. . . We climbed around a big cliff and then my mate slipped down, and he looked like slipping to his death and we were up pretty high and I laughed, it was funny, 'cause he'd wrapped himself around a bush just above the top of it. Anyway, we kept on and just before daylight we got to the other side and hid in a barn. And when daylight came we looked out through the cracks of the barn and here's the camp about 200 yards away. We'd gone up and down the same side of the mountain.

And about seven o'clock that night an old car breezed up and a girl and an old fellow talking in the car and they opened the barn door and she came in with a pitchfork getting hay and throwing it onto the back of the wagon. And getting a bit close, so I leapt up and she let out a scream and jumped up and she said, 'You're the prisoners I heard about.' She said, 'Don't worry.' She said, 'My brother just came home from the Russian Front and he's lost both his legs.' And she said, 'We're Austrians and not very happy about the war.' She said, 'The Germans have got guards everywhere on all the bridges.' There's a lot of bridges and gully and that sort of thing in Austria, and hills. 'I'll go down in the village tonight and see when they're going to take the guards away and how long they're going to keep them.' I said to this fellow, Hilton, 'We can't do anything about it,' I said. 'She might give us up and she might not.'

Anyway that night the barn door rattled about half-past seven, 'Yo ho, it's Ruth and I'm calling you.' And I said, 'We'd better go out, she's probably got the guards here.' And she said, 'They're going to remove the guards tonight, about seven o'clock just after dark.' So we said, 'Right, thank you very much,' and we took off that night at dark and got caught in the mountains. It was nearly daylight, different mountain than the one we climbed up and over, it was nearly daylight and we got caught by a fellow out with his dogs chasing snow rabbits and he caught us and locked us in the cells and then a guard came from the prison we escaped from, the prisoner of war camp we'd escaped from, and took us back.

Attempt 5

So they put us in the cells and I'd hidden in a trough – they used a big thing where you had to urinate in at night – so in there I'd hidden half a pack of hacksaw blades, pliers and a screwdriver . . . so there was five of us in the cell and two of them were too sick they reckoned, to escape, and one, there was an English fellow there, my mate that had escaped with me, Ron Hilton and this other English fellow . . . And anyway all we had was a loaf of bread, when we escaped.

I sprang the door on the cell and then the main doors of the prison were great big oak doors, and they had hooks on the outside of them and they used to put three bars across them too, to hold them as well. But they got careless; they only put one bar across the middle and nuts inside the main doors. They hadn't welded them over, so I undid the 32 nuts. I undid them and then we had to slide the door sideways; we couldn't take the big doors down, just slid them aside just enough to get out.

And we got out there, the three of us, and we started to climb the mountain and this fellow said he was a bit sick, this English fellow, so he said he didn't think he could go through with it, so we gave him half the bread and we kept going, Ron and I. And we lived on snow, when we crossed these mountains. And got down the other side and he was very sick, I think he ate too much snow. So getting down the other side of the mountain was harder than climbing up the side, 'cause it was so steep like.

Anyway, finally got down and we came out near this camp I'd escaped from in the train, before we got on this train from the brick factory and got caught trying to get into Switzerland. So I hid him in a barn and I said, 'I'll go up to the factory at night and contact some of these fellows that were working in these . . . and ask for some food.' So I got one fellow and asked him for food and he said he'd go back to the camp, see if he could get some. And, he said, 'Come back tomorrow night and I'll see what I can do.'

And I went back the next night and he said they had a meeting and, 'Seeing as you escaped from here before, and they weren't allowed to play soccer on a Sunday for six months as punishment, they won't give you any food.' And I said, 'You're in big trouble after the war if you don't give me some food.' And in the meantime he said, 'Well, come back tomorrow night and I'll have another chat to them.' He said, 'I'll give you some. All that I've got is half of some biscuits.' So he gave me half-a-dozen hard biscuits.

. . . My mate was feeling a bit better and then I stole a pushbike from the factory and doubled my mate down to the water and a train used to pull up on the hill and take along water. And we hid in a train; all the freight trains had little cabins on the end of every second or third wagon. When they went through the mountains someone would get in and work on the brakes like, slow them down through the mountains. And we got to a place, what was the name . . . anyway I don't know, it was a big marshalling yard and so we got out there and headed for Yugoslavia . . .

Some American planes came over and bombed the forest we were in. And I don't know why they bombed it, there was nothing in there, they must have thought it was an ammunition dump or something. And then the Germans came in to see what happened and grabbed us again, and took us back, of course. And went through the whole process, interrogation and everything again.

So that was all right, back in, a month in the cells you know – three days on bread and water and one day on good food. And then we went back into the disciplinary compound and the commandant said to me, he said, 'Look, you're not going out to work on the punishment camps any longer. We're going to keep you in here and work in here because you're escaping all the time.' And I said, 'Well it's my job to escape.' And he said, 'It's *my* job to keep you here.'

Attempt 6

There were fellows going out to work, and I asked one of them if I could swap names with him, so I could go out in his place. So I went out in his place on the train and I had another fellow with me and I said, 'I'll tell you what, we'll escape from this train, we'll jump out the window as it's going along.' So we were going along and we go past that place at Treven, in the train. I said, 'Oh that's Treven there, I escaped from there before!'

And we were going along in the train to other places and we'd get to another place, a big station called Rotterman, it was. I said, 'Well, we can't do much here, we'll wait until we get past here.' And I said, 'Get ready to jump out of the train.' So we just get through Rotterman and I said, 'Right let's go!' and I jumped out the train window, landed and rolled down the hill – I hurt my ankle a bit but, you know – and waited for him but he never arrived, I waited for a while. Don't know whether one of the guards grabbed him probably . . . he didn't follow. So I went up and hid in a wheat field and crawled up the wheat field, up the side of a hill.

After a while, I put my foot in a stream at night for a while, then I travelled around, you know, looking for where I could get to. And I got in a train then, another big station, I got out of the train and they chased me, the guards, in one of those wagons, and they came looking for escaped prisoners or something like that. They were probably looking for me, when I jumped off the train. And they chased me and I crossed the railway line and ducked under the trains or anything like that, you know stationary ones, carriages and things like that. Then I find the stationmaster had a nice garden there with all green trees in it. Nice green trees in it, so I hid in there for the rest of the night.

The next day, when I got going again, I was hiding in a barn and a fellow walking along the road, there was no one else in sight. On the dirt road it was, and I had no food and I asked him, I said, 'Can you give me any food?' And he said, 'Are you a *flieger*?' a flyer like, downed pilot, he thought I was a downed pilot. I think he was a Frenchman. And I said no, a soldier, an escaped prisoner, and he said, 'Well stop here', and he brought me a loaf of bread.

Anyway, about two days later I got caught and they took me back to Innsbruck Station and I see he was on the platform there too, but he wasn't arrested or anything like that. And they took me to the interrogation centre and asked me where I got the bread from and that sort of thing. And I said, 'I was in the mountain.' I said, 'And kids were there in the mountains and I asked one of them for bread and they gave it to me.' And they said, 'What were you doing in the mountains, looking for partisans and that sort of thing?' And I said, 'No.' I said, 'As a matter of fact I was looking for an edelweiss to take home to my mother.' Edelweiss only grows in the snow and the highest peaks, there in Austria and those places. And he said, 'Oh Hooper escapes, Hooper escapes.' He said, 'Goes looking for edelweiss!' That's what he said.

Attempt 7 and, finally, success

Then they kicked us round from camp to camp and I struck up with this fellow. We were getting close to the end of the war, and I thought, 'Well, I'm going to get back for my birthday, 22nd March, I'll be free by the 22nd March.' So I said to this other fellow, paratrooper he was, Bob . . . anyway, he was a Scotsman and he was wounded, he was in the hospital with me, same time. He was all right, he was going to escape with me.

So we escaped from that hospital camp and we joined up. We went and we were walking and walking and walking, through shops and that, and we'd dodge wherever the fighting was going on. And we pulled up an American jeep, he was a dispatch driver, and he took us to somewhere in Belgium and we joined up with the Americans there, the air force in Belgium, we stopped there for two weeks . . . got on a British supply plane and they took us back to England.

ROBERT HOOPER

Robert St Quentin Hooper returned to Australia on the *Orion*, the same ship on which he had originally gone to war. He arrived in Sydney the day before the Japanese surrender. Home.

Robert Hooper in London, 1945, after escape

As remarkable as Robert's story is, the escape of over 100 men in Slovenia, led by Lance Corporal Ralph Churches, was the greatest escape by Australians during World War II. And if there's not a film in this story, I've lost my touch completely. It begins in a camp in the small Slovenian city of Marburg, where Ralph Churches and his best mate Les have made contact with the Yugoslav partisans to ask for help to escape. Ralph, nicknamed 'Crow' because he comes from South Australia, was in charge of almost 80 men.

We were put to work at various jobs and finished up on a road-making job. All along I had tried to learn some German and I became quite fluent in German and was elected by my fellow prisoners of war in this camp as their camp leader and so that I remained for two years.

In the meantime, from the road-building job we were transferred to a railway re-ballasting job and the railway line snaked through a bit of lonely country and it was there we made contact with the Slovene partisans.

RALPH CHURCHES

The plan was that four of them would escape, but this number was destined to grow . . . and grow.

So the days went by. They dragged by. Still nothing happened. No word from Anton, no nothing . . . then on the Tuesday night, Les came to me and he says, 'It's on!' . . . So somehow or other both of us thought, 'Well, if four of us can go, why can't eight? We're being sods. These blokes are cobbers. The other blokes are good cobbers.' Sort of two great minds thinking alike. By common consent we told them they could be in if they wanted to. Well, of course they were in like Flynn.

. . . Righto, everybody was primed up. But they had to be there. And so I noticed by two o'clock the first bloke pleaded a stomach ailment and was flat out lying there in the bushes and so forth. Nobody took much notice of him. And one by one I noticed they were missing. So I thought, plenty of time. I'll wait till, say, ten to four. And when I went to move off, one of the guards started following me. A young guard that I knew quite well. So I walked on and he kept following me. At long last I went to where my haversack was. I just, 'Hell, I'm not going to fall at this hurdle am I? What the hell's going on here?' Just a guilty conscience. I wasn't using my brains. He wasn't a wake-up to anything. He just knew that I was good for a cigarette, that's all. So I just pulled out a packet of Capstans. There were two left. I said in my brightest, folksy German, '*Gustl* old boy, have a smoke.' Pulled the haversack out. I said, 'Up there at the cottage there they've got some chooks. Chooks lay eggs, I'm going to have some eggs for tea tonight, *Gustl* old boy, I'll see that you get a couple. How about that?' Eggs were very tightly rationed, I might add. Well he had been on black marketing trips with me. He'd seen me buying eggs before. '*Fancy some eggs?*' '*Danke schön.*' He got one of my fags, lit up and mooched quietly away.

I slung my haversack over my back, walked up towards the cottage, doubled back to the chestnut tree and there they were. Six of them. I made seven. The other bloke wasn't a starter . . . so, seven of us and away we went.

. . . I reckoned we'd gone six, seven kilometres at least and we were out of woodland and getting into meadow-looking country with farmhouses about and so on. And eventually we got onto a decent bit of road. We were marching cross-country. Then we got onto what was a well-used road. We hadn't gone very far, I suppose, and out steps a bloke, one of these *Maid of the Mountains* jobs. He was only a young man, but he had a forage cap on his head with a red star on it and he didn't say, '*Wo da!*' as he would have had he been a German. He said, '*Shtoi!*' which means, stop, halt, checking us out. Anyway, our guide was able to check us out. So we passed on.

. . . He led us to the local inn. There were two blokes, obviously officers because they were very well dressed in made-over German uniforms. You could see a tailor had been to work at them, their britches and everything. Top boots. And they had two red stripes on each of the lapels . . . Anyway, the guide duly introduced us and so forth and they said, 'Nice to meet you. Want a drink?' There was a bottle or Riesling there, so all round we were soon drinking some nice cool Riesling. Nice drop.

And so I opened the batting. I said, 'Well, there's seven of us. Can you get us to safety? I believe it's rumoured that you have American and English liaison officers on mission here somewhere, can you get us here or get us to Italy?' 'Oh yes, all the time. We're doing it all the time. No problem at all. Have a drink.' I said, 'Seven of us, no problem?' 'No, I said have a drink. Don't you realise we're doing it all the time? Your airmen are shot down over Austria. They've got their secret buttons, they can unscrew them and they've got a silk map of Austria and Slovenia. All they've got to do is get down here and we never miss. We get them out.' And actually, statistically that's true. They got 353 airmen out, shot down over southern Germany or Austria.

. . . Well, I thought that was a good idea. Yeah, have another drink. And by now the evening was closing in. It was getting dark. There was a noise going on up the street. It was a musical. And they were having a celebration in the village hall. There's a Cornish orchestra, you might say, floral dance and all that and a lot of stomping. Of course they're great dancing, this clog dancing, what they call *shoe platler*. And there they were making a hell of a noise, this village orchestra . . . I noticed as soon as I walked in the hall a great big lass, partisan's uniform with Mills bombs swinging from her waist. She grabbed hold of me and I was still fully clad. She bounced me round that floor. And oh God, five minutes I had to beg off. It was all very pleasant, very folksy and our chaps were as good as home and hosed.

These blokes were cocky confident, no problem. Then that damned conscience of mine got me. 'What a rotten sod you are. There's 80-odd blokes back in that camp. Seventy-odd of them at least are going to come out and work on that railway line tomorrow. They've given you their confidence. You've been it. You actually have been acting as an officer for two years. They've been doing exactly what you've said. You've been the boss. You're bloody well going to walk out on them.' That's where I thought, 'Come on, Ralph, come on!'

I walked back to the pub. The guide had disappeared. He was a good cloak-and-dagger man, he'd disappeared. But I got one of the locals, plenty of them there; it was near the Austrian border. Spoke German. I fronted these two blokes, and I said, 'Just a minute, you're sure about seven of us?' 'Have another drink. Told you, you're as good as back home.' 'Look, you're very confident. If you can manage seven, could you manage 70?' No, they didn't invite me to have another drink. I moved away from the interpreter and they had a bit of a confab . . .

They came back and asked for details. I explained the train came in at about eight o'clock, disgorged its passengers, guards and civvy foremen and the workers. And then the train choofed off and would call back at somewhere about five o'clock, four-thirty in the afternoon and load up again. 'What's the cover like?' So I explained, 'Well you saw the picture, good scrub, low scrub, plenty of cover.' 'Yes, well, we've decided that we'll do it, but you will have to accompany us.' They wanted a bloody hostage, of course. My German was a bit too good. They were still a bit shady. They wanted a hostage. I knew that. Straightaway I said, 'Most certainly, I wouldn't dream of dragging all your ruffians back there. They'd all jump in the Drau River with fright if you all turned up without somebody to smooth them down. Of course I'm coming. Actually, we'll be acting on a front of at least 100 metres. I think I better get one of my cobbers to come back with me. There'd better be two of us.' So all right, they agreed. All set up.

. . . We got back to the work site [with] about ten minutes to spare. And the commander hived off, I think about 30 blokes as a reserve in case something went wrong, and the rest of us got down in the scrub and cover alongside the railway line . . . I was wearing my slouch hat which I'd preserved all the way through . . . But I remember taking the darn thing off, because it was getting interfering. Just put it alongside me.

Anyway, in puffs the train . . . The guards got out. The civvies got out. My blokes got out and started dragging their feet towards the tool boxes, getting a bit strung out. Then the train went *Hoop!* in reverse gear back down the incline. Back it went and as soon as it got round the corner the commandant nudged me and I nodded my head like that. He jumped up and blew a whistle and they all jumped up.

They were shouting 'Hands up!' in Slovene, German, Italian, whatever. '*Hände hoch! Mani in alto!*' Well of course the dear poor old Germans, these Austrian guards. It was quite comical really. There they were, rifles slung over their shoulders with their hands in the air. My blokes – actually the first bloke up alongside of me was a British regular soldier, I remember. Snowy-headed bloke. I can't think of his surname. I've forgotten most of them, but Snowy he leapt up there and he said, 'Good on you, bloody Crow. I thought you'd be back. Officers don't desert their men.'

. . . In two minutes it was all over. We were back in the scrub going for our lives. It was well after midday before we stopped. We didn't stop for a pause or a puff or anything. And the poor old guards, they just weren't used to forced marching. I think my stocks with them were pretty low. In the war between the partisans and the Germans there were no prisoners taken. None at all. The Germans might capture partisans and torture information out of them, but they would still kill them. There was no quarter given. And I just could not go through the rest of my life – I mean, it's one thing in the heat of battle sticking a bayonet into somebody's gizzard. It's also another one being a party to a massacre. These blokes, when all was said and done were more or less cobbers of mine. The partisans had to give me an undertaking that we would capture the guards, march them with us for two days, take their clothes off – the partisans were always short of uniforms – hand them some rags and turn them loose to walk back to civilisation. And I'm very relieved to say that they did. That happened. So I have nothing to search my conscience about. I'm like Hamlet, aren't I?

RALPH CHURCHES

Ralph's group continued to march to freedom with the partisans, engaging in a firefight with German troops on the way and losing four men in the ensuing chase. They crossed rivers, dodged patrols and were handed from one group of guerrillas to another till finally, they were near Semic, a town in Slovenia where there was an Allied base.

I remember in the middle of the afternoon we went round a shoulder of a hill – oh, biggish mountain I suppose you'd call it – and away in the distance we could see some houses and things, it was a village. And the guides said, 'Semic'. So there it was. Our ragtag mob, we just drooped our way into Semic and that was the end of the road.

A partisan officer who was all dressed up in quite a flash American uniform, stepped out when we got there and started sounding off in English about us being late. We should have been there much quicker. I was in no mood for any nonsense like that. I roared back at him that we had marched 250 kays in fourteen days on very scrappy rations. He didn't look as if he had done 100 yards on the best. It was too bad. We were here and that was the object of the exercise. He choofed off and that was that.

And the next thing I knew, up roared a funny little vehicle. A thing called a jeep. Never seen one before – a jeep. And an American sergeant in it. Very shortish bloke. Nice bloke called Jim, a very genial young man. Made us welcome. Told us that our troubles were over. And he showed us the local school which had been evacuated, of course. And there were hessian bags, palliasses for mattresses. Heaps and heaps of straw to fill them with. So there we are. All we had to do was fill up our palliasses and we'd have a bed. Also, of course, we'd be having a meal pretty shortly. He looked at some of the eating gear and told us, 'So you can junk that gear, you won't need it here.' And we didn't.

We were supplied. We had a really splendid dinner served in nice enamelware. Really, we perked up perceptibly before we went to sleep. But despite the lack of – oh they did find some blankets, but I think we ran them out of blankets. Anyway those that were especially ill clad, they got blankets. And so they slept well.

And that was Semic. Very pretty little village. I've been back to it a couple of times. It's advanced a bit . . .

So there wasn't much to do. Potter around. Oh yes, an English captain – Saggers, Captain Jack Saggers – he came as soon as we arrived. At least as soon as Jim the master sergeant had us down at our sleeping quarters. Came along and bade us welcome. Got the story from Les and I just what had happened. And he considered it all quite remarkable. 'Rather overdoing it, chaps, you know, you should not have gone back. That was really testing your luck too far, chaps.' 'Well we're here, aren't we, Sir?' 'Yes, yes you have justified yourselves. A splendid effort. Really pukka. I am very proud to be associated with you.' Oh he was charming chap, really nice.

And so the days went on. It was a matter then, of course, signalling to Italy that we were there. Could somebody come and lift us out? And yes somebody could . . . I think after about five days, they arranged for us to be flown out from there to Italy. And from there it took two months, but I was repatriated and arrived back in Australia in November 1944.

RALPH CHURCHES

Ralph Churches would be awarded a British Empire Medal for his extraordinary courage and resourcefulness in bringing all those men to freedom. But what he remembers most, is their parting.

We were marched down this very long jetty. And there it was indicated, there was the very same *Edinburgh Castle* that had taken us to Greece. There it was ready to take us to Alexandria and then home. And then the wrench – there was the ship going to Britain. And I thought for a moment, yes it'd be nice to see the old Dart [England]. Be nice. Nah, Ronte's [his wife] calling you, mate.

So the Kiwis and us started going up the gangway on the ship. Poms down there on the wharf. And halfway, nearly up the top of the gangway somebody roared down, 'What about three cheers for the bloody Crow?' So they gave me three cheers. And I still get a little tearful when I think about it. They were really nice guys.

RALPH CHURCHES

And so say all of us, Ralph. So say all of us.

THOMAS SMITH

CLARENCE 'SPUD' SPURGEON

HERBERT TRACKSON

SISTER BERENICE TWOHILL

TOM UREN

HOWARD WALKER

9

'Without hope, we would not have survived'

When war descends upon a nation, upon its defence forces and its civilians, death is inevitable. And while there is no way to prepare a person for the first time he or she encounters death in war time, it is that very inevitability that helps them to understand it, to weave a rationalisation around the hard facts of witnessing life extinguished that allows for acceptance. It also, fortuitously for their country, allows them to keep fighting.

But when a soldier has surrendered there is an equal expectation that, for now at least, the killing will stop. After all, you have no weapons, so you are no real threat to your enemy. You may well have to suffer the humiliation and deprivation that come with being a POW, but for the time being, you're out of the killing zone.

If any of Australia's prisoners of war held that belief when they were captured, they were rapidly disabused of it. For many of them the killing, the death rate, actually *increased* after capture. Charlie Parrott saw more dead bodies in his first weeks of imprisonment on Crete than he had encountered in all his previous battles in North Africa and Greece.

I was transplanting Germans that had been dead a fortnight and it was really blowing. We was putting them in coffins and building a cemetery. Crete was a stench from one end of the island to the other; of dead, there was dead everywhere. The Germans that we were, what's called 'transplanting', were only half covered, and we had to get them out and we weren't permitted to leave that particular area, not even to have lunch. So you couldn't eat lunch. We'd save that meal and take it home. It was tinned food and you'd take it back to the camp and that'd be a bonus for some other time.

We had picks, rakes, all sorts of things to turn the coffins on the side and roll them in. You had to be very careful; if they exploded it was, oh. It's one of the things that still turn me over. My brother was putting one bloke in and he was too long for the coffin. He was a tall fellow. Called the guard over and showed him. So the guard got a pick and bashed him in the shins and doubled his legs up and told him, 'He'll fit now.'

We had spare legs there; we'd chuck an extra leg in with some of them. We had to make a joke of everything, otherwise you'd go mad. Bloke went in with one leg and another one went in with three legs.

CHARLIE PARROTT

Four years of imprisonment later, Charlie was caught between the retreating Germans and the advancing Russians. And death was still stalking him.

When I was in the convent, girls, twelve years old, was coming into the convent for treatment. Blood was running down their legs. Been raped by six to eight Russian soldiers. To me that's not human . . .

One girl, there were six Russians in the street and they was after her and she was running for her own safety. They shot her dead in the street, and I saw that happen. Because she wouldn't cooperate. They're animals. They wasn't animals, even animals don't do that to their own. I've had no time whatsoever for the Russians. People think, 'You should forgive and forget.' I can't forgive and forget that. That was something that's in my mind forever. I can't forget that. When I saw these little girls with blood running down their legs, what else can you do?

The nun, she come and got me, to show me what the Russians were doing. She had tears in her eyes. These things I haven't told a great deal . . . they are things that don't make me feel good to know that people do that. It's shocking what they do.

CHARLIE PARROTT

Around 22 000 Australians went into the prisoner of war camps of the Japanese. One in three would not come out alive. One in three. And they were not all soldiers.

When Pat Darling and the other women prisoners were sent to their last camp on Muntok Island near Sumatra, the war was nearing its end. But the death rate was rising.

The children who had fathers in the men's camp were allowed to visit them. This hadn't happened before, and this was quite all right for children who were old enough to remember their older brothers who, on reaching puberty, had been sent across to the men's camp, but for some of the little ones, of course, when they saw these big hairy men, they just cried. They were terrified of them.

One small family said, 'Daddy just cried all the time when we told him Mummy was dead.' Well, you can imagine the despair. The most tragic people, the most pitiful people actually in camp were the women with young children. There was nothing you could do to help them, except sort of give them moral support because we got so little food, all of us.

PAT DARLING

Death could come from any direction, for no apparent reason. The Japanese moved prisoners to Burma and Thailand, telling them they were going to 'better place, more food', that it was 'a lovely camp'. They lied. And by sending some of them by sea, in unmarked, unidentified ships, they placed them in danger of the cruellest of deaths, from their own forces.

Thomas Smith was aboard a rust bucket sailing from Penang to Japan.

I was in the second ship, I was in the stern hold, and it was nearly all Australians and Americans and Dutch and English, all that mixture from Java, we all went over there together. And they loaded us onboard, I think it was the *Toyohasi Maru*, at that time – I think it had come up from Timor then. By that time it was a rusty old bucket.

And conditions were pretty crook on that. It wasn't very nice. They would only feed us a cup of rice twice a day, I think, and that was about it. Conditions weren't too good. The only toilet they had on board . . . they only let you up in groups of, say, half-a-dozen men, or twelve men, and you had to hang over the side. If the waves were high and the sharks were jumping, it was bad luck. As I say, I was in the stern hold and away we went.

We were a few days out . . . within a day or two days from Moulmein. It was the 15th of January . . . Anyway, it was my turn up on deck this day. And you hung around as long as you could, because it was pretty putrid down in the holds with everyone. There was no room to stretch or lay about. A lot had dysentery at that time; they were pretty crook . . . If you wanted to go or not, you made out that you did. I was sort of lazing around there, hoping I could stay longer.

The next thing I heard this drone, and over came three aeroplanes. Big fellows, [B-17 Flying] Fortresses or [B-24] Liberators. Four-engine planes they were, and a . . . Catalina, flying boat, came over. It was the one that spotted us and these two bombers came over.

Well, while I was there they let their bombs go and they sunk the first boat. The bombs must have gone straight down the hold and sunk it. I watched the thing go down. You could see the old propeller as she went down. It was so quick. By that time, a lot of the chaps in the hold were trying to get up the ladder. It was only a little, narrow thing coming up out of the hold. Of course, the Japs had set up their machine guns so no one could take over . . .

And I thought, 'Gee, my water bottle is down below and that boat is sunk, they're going to have a go at us for sure!' And I looked like going over the side with no water. That was my biggest worry, my water bottle. So I'm trying to get down this ladder to get to a water bottle, and they were trying to push up, which they couldn't do because they had the machine guns on them. Anyway, I finally got down the ladder, weaving my way through to where my water bottle was . . . and somebody had snitched the water. It was empty; it was useless coming down anyway.

It was just as well, though, because those who had stayed up, quite a few of them were killed, because they came back and had two goes at us. And the bombs went off either side . . . they straddled the ship and lifted her up out of the water. All the upper decks were shot to pieces . . . Quite a few of them were killed . . .

To top it off, the Japanese had a little gun out on the stern, right next to our hold, and they fired a shot and knocked out their own mast with the gun. And, of course, the explosions from the bombs set their magazine alight, and their shells were going off right above us. They were coming in and spinning around the hold, bits of shrap. So we was in a bit of bother. I think the ship sank later as it was coming out of port.

. . . On the other ship there were a lot of Dutch. A lot of them were drowned . . . We had a little Pom, an ex-navy bloke, on the ship with us. When the ship was stopped you see, and there was all the Japs and Dutch in the water, he dived over and made out he was saving the Japs, but he was pushing them down and standing on them in the water. He got a few. He made out he was saving them, but he wasn't. He was disposing of them. But no one knew what was going on, you see. It was every man for himself . . . that was our sea journey.

THOMAS SMITH

As the war in Europe came closer to its end, accidental death at the hands of Allied forces became an everyday hazard for prisoners. Tens of thousands of POWs were sent on forced marches away from the advancing Allies and, on the roads, dressed in a bewildering array of uniforms and ragged clothing, they could look just like retreating German troops to the pilots and gunners.

I was marching with Herb Krump, a friend of mine from Adelaide, and I saw these six British Typhoons fly past and we were watching them. You know, there was lots of air activities at that time, aircraft everywhere, Spitfires and so on. Saw these Typhoons go past and then I saw them turn around like that, and I said to Herb, 'They're going to hit us, into the ditch!'

There was a big ditch by the side of the road, and I was in there like a flash, ended up with three or four bodies on top of me and, sure enough, they came down and they strafed our column and they killed 60 of our chaps, and that was what decided me to escape.

I went the next day with Herbie and about ten days later we got through the British lines, but I didn't want to wait for the Russians and I'd already worked out I didn't want to stay in German hands very much longer, and it was the strafing that did it because I figured while we're marching along like this we could easily be the target of another one.

I mean, we did have planes come past, circle us and then waggle their wings and go on as they clearly recognised that we were a bunch of prisoners. We were such a nondescript bunch of fellows, no regular uniform or anything like that, but these six Typhoons, they obviously didn't have a good look, and I found out afterwards they were led by a Canadian wing commander who later found out what he'd done. There are various circumstances, I don't want to go into that, just how he found out, but they were pretty devastated when they realised what they'd done.

ALEXANDER KERR

Friendly-fire events like this were the larger, in a sense, more predictable moments of a war; when ships and planes and weapons of mass death and destruction were in use accidents were inevitable. But many prisoners remember in raw detail other, unanticipated moments of sudden, needless death.

Don't know where they were taking us to, and they moved us about the yard and I have forgotten why. We were standing just on the back of the truck, you know, and I was on one side and he was on the other and I said, 'You are a stupid bugger, Jack!' He hadn't brought any boots with him – well, he didn't know. I don't suppose he knew where we were going. Your footwear wore out and a pair of boots was like gold, you know . . .

But Jack, he was a hell of a nice bloke. I wouldn't say he was exactly vague. For instance, he was a fantastic bloody pianist. I mean, he was a jazz pianist; he could do anything on a piano. He was just a bloody nice fellow but he had a . . . it wasn't that he didn't think properly but he was a bit away with the birds at times and this morning, on the back of this bloody truck and we were going through the yard and our train stopped and there were other blokes kicking around too, and we had to get off and I said, 'We have to get off and go across there.' And I said, 'Not that way, you silly bugger!' And he'd forgotten his glasses this day and I said, 'Well just, I'll tell you where to go.' 'Oh,' he said, 'oh, I'll be right. I'll be right.'

And he . . . the truck's like that and I'm standing on this side and he's standing on the other side, and he gets off this side and I said, 'Now come over towards me across the line. Be careful and don't step on all the stones.' Because I could see he had no bloody shoes on.

And instead of coming across towards me he turned the other way, and I said, 'Now, Jack, come on, just a sec, Jack, for Christ's sake!' And I screamed out and by this time he had stepped onto the next rail and a train was coming and his legs hit me in the face. He died that night and I have never forgotten that. That was one of the worst days I ever spent in the army.

Ross McDonald

The slow deaths were truly awful. The dribbling away of a man's faith, of his will, his determination. Dr Rowley Richards saw all too much of it.

I had always believed that there was a will to live and if that will to live disappeared, well, you died. There's much more to it than that, I'm sure of that. It's a bit like bone pointing, you know. You point the bone at yourself, I guess.

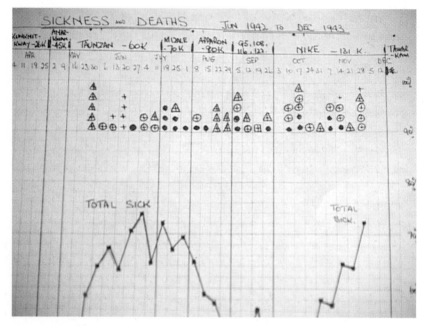

The sickness and death graph Rowley Richards kept in camp

Now I've seen many cases of fellows who have been nigh unto death for maybe a couple of weeks, semiconscious most of the time, being hand-fed by their mates, amazing to still stay alive, and then, when they recover from that and they're starting to be getting better, or think they're getting better, they just up and died on me.

And I think what happened to them was that they would look around and see fellows dying around them and think, 'Oh it's too hard, let me go.' That's purely and simply my own view on that. But I've seen so many of them who didn't *have* to die because of their illness but they had made up their mind they were going to die, and when they were sort of semiconscious and really sick they didn't have enough willpower to, as it were, terminate themselves. But when they got a bit better, they got to that stage.

ROWLEY RICHARDS

Again and again the POWs speak of this strange happening, of men and women deciding that they had had enough, and simply dying. They puzzle over it still, and provide answers that perhaps owe more to their own personality and values than necessarily understanding others. These deaths *hurt* them; sometimes more than the ones that were explainable.

People used to say to me when I came home from the railway, 'Oh, you must have been fit, or you must have been this or that.' But you just had to be darned lucky, that's all. One of the things – and I could do it and a lot could, well quite a few – if you could take a day at a time, it helped. I had several of my best friends in the unit who did marvellous jobs and helped everyone on the railway. But they came to a stage when they thought, 'I've had it, I don't want to carry on'. And if you said that you were dead, there was no doubt about it. I believe you can point the bone at yourself. Well, you could.

There was a chap, Noel Chitty, in my unit, a corporal, who was a 35-year-old bachelor from Melbourne and he did a fantastic job. He carried blokes on the road, a big strong fellow in his own day – and when things were at the worst on the railway, we were working up to eleven o'clock at night from six in the morning, and the monsoon was on, and you were swamping your way back in and we had a bit of a lean-to on a tree, and Noel was with us, he was one of our six or seven, and he came in this night and he said, 'You can have my rice, I'm not going to carry on, there is no one at home, I am not married, there is no one at home who would worry too much about me.'

What we used to do if anyone said that was, we'd beg them not to and then we'd abuse them, really abuse them and tell them they were cowards. And sure enough, he laid down and wouldn't eat his rice and at six in the morning he was gone. What I often said and others said too, 'I wouldn't have the guts.' Fancy, just having the guts to decide you were going to do that. There it was.

JAMES LING

Since Salonika we were losing ten a day to starvation. It's terrible to see your mates. I've got a mate, Jimmy Greer; he died in Salonika of starvation. The thing is that things get a bit tough and blokes chuck in the towel, they give up. You can't pull them back out again . . .

You can usually read them. They'll sit down in the corner and don't want to do anything. Just waste away. This mate of mine used to sit on his right ankle. He could sit on his right ankle all day. Had his foot bent underneath him, he'd sit down on it. He'd sit there all day like that, instead of getting up. This is why I say to anybody today, that if things are not going the way you would like them to go, don't give up. If you give up, you never come back.

CHARLIE PARROTT

Death surrounded them with such closeness and frequency that it became an expected, daily visitor, often an unspeakably intimate one. In Korea, Robert Parker discovered that death also had its uses, even if they were bizarre.

We finally arrived up on the Manchurian border and it was very cold and we were just in these flimsy little clothes, no boots, just bare feet. We ended up in the big camp and in this one big mud hut there must have been maybe about 50 of us. And we all had to lie on our side all together like, and the floor was hard mud and on the word of, 'Okay', everyone had to turn onto the other side. And this is how we slept there.

. . . in the daytime we had to sit up against the wall like that, all around the room, and these Korean houses, they have a kitchen up one end and they have these big fireplaces there and on the top of each fireplace they have a big bowl that they cook rice and millet and other stuff in, normally that happens. Underneath the whole of the hut run these tunnels about so long from the fire, and out the other end they have a chimney going up. So that all of the heat from the fires in wintertime goes underneath the room and warms up the clay floor.

And it was cold and we all used to huddle up there like this, and you had to sit there like that all day. And they would come around to see how many dead. 'Any dead?' We had a few but we wouldn't tell them, they were propped up against the wall so they wouldn't fall down, because if there was any dead they take them away and then they don't give you so much at the one meal a day, they didn't give you so much food. If there was three dead blokes there they give you less, so we ended up with a mob of them propped up there around the wall. Finally, we had to let them go.

This went on for some time and then we got colder and colder, got minus 45 degrees below zero, 45 degrees below zero and that's cold. And it started to snow.

ROBERT PARKER

Death and dying are subjects that many people are uncomfortable with in today's world. We are protected from the hard details of death, the unavoidably unpleasant, physical particulars that are so often a part of a person's end. Yet the POWs speak of the death of mates with a sad, loving remembrance that can, and should, humble the listener.

I have a dear friend; I had. Peter, Peter Van Helmut. He was a Dutchman. He spoke perfect English. He was a Dutch-Eurasian. Indonesian, Javanese, Javanese-Dutch. Major in the Dutch Army, he was. His family were quite a distinguished family in Batavia – had sugar mills and all that sort of thing. He'd travelled the world, all that sort of thing. And we used to sit in the cell; we're watching the door to make sure the guards weren't there. He'd be talking to me, the culinary delights of the pea soup of Holland, of the Peking duck in China, which he'd all prepared, he used to be a gourmet cook of some kind himself. We used to have these banquets of the imagination. We drooled over them. And then, I don't know whether I'll get through this story. And then he died. It's times like that, that get you. I can never, never ever tell that story, but I can write it, which I have done.

About two o'clock in the morning poor old Peter's breathing started to go. At any rate, he died at about two o'clock in the morning. And I put the blanket over him and I waited until breakfast came so I could have his meal as well, and we sat down. And that's the only banquet we had. I sat down and I ate my rice and I ate his, and I went over and called a Jap and I said, 'Peter's dead.' . . . and they come along and a couple of the Chinese trustees come along and wrapped him up in a bit of matting. That's 60-odd years ago and it still affects you. It still affects you.

That's the thing about it; you wonder. You think about all the times that you were close to actually dying. With Peter, it was beri-beri, but the beri-beri went to his lungs, and he actually drowned in his own juices. You could hear the gurgling just as though he was drowning. The moisture was there in his lungs, and he was unfortunate. If he'd just survived a couple more months, medical science would have fixed him up in all probability . . . it went to his lungs poor ole fella. I sat down there with him, I nursed his head and I listened to his gurgling as he died.

BILL YOUNG

Mateship unto death. These two icons, these polar opposites, were intertwined in the camps in a way that we can only partly grasp. These men and women had learned to live together in a world where there was no individual territory, no privacy, not even much internal life available to a person that others did not share or intrude on. They were completely exposed and vulnerable to other human beings, certainly for the first time in their lives, and probably the last.

We were always on the scrounge to get something to bring it back in; it was a challenge all the time, pinch anything. Bring food back for yourself, or your mate, somebody back in the camp who couldn't come out to work and you tried to get him something, yeah. The comfort that we did for each other was, well, it would be surprising.

It is hard for people to understand that if you have got a fellow with his head on your lap and you know he is dying, that is something that has got to come from within you to do it, and comfort him, and tell him that if you live you will be in touch with his mum, or someone like that. That is a sort of deep, deep, deep friendship.

I have just been to Tasmania, and we were hurrying back to the airport, we called back to see my dear friend Lloyd Spender, and I cried like a baby just to see Lloyd again. I might not see him again but we did so much together in the camp. It is all these years, we are both in our mid-eighties now, to go and see that boy again was wonderful for me, so there is something deep that experiences made us be so close together. And you are asking me to remember things that are a bit bitter right now, but to think that you could cradle another fella – for one reason – to give him comfort before he died. And that is something I hope never happens again.

BILL COVENTRY

In conditions like these, suicide was inevitable. But the means were limited and those men who were determined to stop their pain were often forced into humiliating attempts to end their lives.

Our latrines . . . consisted of a big ditch. And over the top of this ditch was a bamboo platform . . . and there were gaps in this bamboo, a couple of feet by 8 inches across so you could squat over and to give a bit of privacy they put split bamboo screens on either side. After a while the smell was absolutely dreadful and the sight was absolutely worse still, but this was the best we could do. Incidentally, no toilet paper.

And this one particular chap committed suicide. This is the only incident that I can recall about someone losing his marbles. He just lifted this thing and jumped in. Then we had to get him out and so forth. But that was the only incident that I heard about. There may have been others along the camps, but this happened in Tamarkan.

One chaplain was asked to bury him and he refused. Another chaplain, in fact the [HMAS] *Perth* chaplain, agreed. The Japanese couldn't care less. He was just another death in the camp. So you just carried out your own burial and recorded it on the record.

GAVIN CAMPBELL

In Stalag Luft III, the big camp, we would have lost two to three people shot deliberately by the Germans. There was, I think, at least two that I know of, suicides where the boys just ignored the warning wire, straight up to the main wire and started climbing over it, and of course they were shot, machine-gunned. We weren't allowed to go and help them or anything. They just died there and then. That was horrible to see. I don't want to dwell on that one, it was awful.

GEOFF CORNISH

The reasons for suicide were as varied as the men who died, and the aftermath as difficult in the camps as it is outside. But the overwhelming emotion expressed by the POWs left behind is compassion, a profound understanding of *why* these people chose to die. Reg Worthington had a mate in the camp in Germany. A mate for whom imprisonment became too much.

I was on the top storey of a two-storey bunk and underneath me was a young Kiwi, New Zealander, Jack Coatsworth. He came from Invercargill . . . Jack Coatsworth was a nice young fellow. We shared things, helped each other as much as we could. He also wrote to his family and I wrote to mine and a lot of the other chaps never bothered writing at all. And some of them never ever received any replies from their family – I don't know the reason, they just didn't.

. . . Some people coped with hardship and upsets much better than others. Jack was one, it got him down. I suppose it could be said I helped him as much as I could because I knew I was coping mentally better than he was. So I helped him as much as I could but then, later on, I moved away from that camp. I was detailed, of course, you don't do anything voluntarily. I was sent out onto a farm camp.

. . . Jack committed suicide. He couldn't take it. As we were marching to the Lazarette every morning, part of the way we marched along a tramline. Jack Coatsworth threw himself under the tram, under the wheels of a tram, coming past him. He just wasn't coping, that's all.

REG WORTHINGTON

We had one fella went mad. I think there was more than one, but this cove was a pitiful case. He got a letter from home, from his mother and sister saying it was a great shame that he hadn't died on Crete instead of becoming a POW.

Few hours later we cut him down. He tried to hang himself. We cut him down and took him down, and we did have a ward there to put the men in and there were a few that had gone that way. So they had him there for oh, five months I suppose, and he came back cured as the doctors thought. And a cove came walking past his bunk one day and thought, 'God that's funny, the way he's laying there with all those blankets up over him.' So he walked back and pulled back his blankets – he'd cut his wrists. So we stopped the blood and sent him back down again and that's where they kept him. Till he came home.

But there were quite a number of army coves – one air force fellow I know tried to commit suicide. He was sent down from Sagan, from the officers' camp for some reason or other. He tried to drown himself. There was a couple of Canadians saw him and they went in and pulled him out. What sets any man off? Or any woman? Just something goes wrong in the mind.

RONALD WALL

Perhaps the saddest revelation of all is that the suicides did not end when the imprisonment did.

Some people got by having an attachment, by having a religion or something like that. That saved them from the quandary. The interesting thing is, I can't think of anyone who committed suicide when they were prisoners of war, but I can think of quite a few who committed suicide when they came home. And there's a thing to cogitate on, the fact that when we have so much, we find that so many people commit suicide. And when death is fearful and so near to you, the last thing in the world, the last thing you want to do is give up your life. You'll fight for it; you'll do anything for it. Because life is precious. When life is in abundance and everything is made easy for you, it's not worth hanging onto.

BILL YOUNG

In the midst of the slavery and death in the Japanese prisoner of war camps, the men fought hard to observe some degree of ritual about another man's passing, to show evidence that this man once walked amongst them. Their efforts were extraordinarily courageous, especially when each of them had so little energy to spare.

One of our mates, Donny McCulloch, he died at the 100 Kilo [Camp]. I helped bury him, poor old Donny . . . over in Zeehan he came from, and he was going to do the township after, but he never got back. Poor old Donny. He sort of gave up the ghost. He got dysentery and he went down. I used to try and talk to him, to encourage him, but he just lost the will to live. He faded away and he died. I know he was crook, but he just seemed to give up.

. . . We were allowed to bury them. At the 100, we had an American, a bugler, off the [USS] *Houston* . . . Because we come from the same place, Maxie Smith, Jimmy Honey and myself, we carried Donny up on a stretcher. He was only just wrapped in rice cloth, rice bag, wrapped up in this bag . . . it was the wet season and it was pouring rain and we had to get him through the creek. We had to hold poor Donny on the stretcher, too, so he wouldn't roll off.

Anyway, we stood to and he played the bugle. It went on all the time. Yeah, it was rather sad when you think of them dying away from home, with no loved ones about . . . it's a terrible way to go. With no support . . . they couldn't get much support from their mates because they were out working, see, so they just died a slow and miserable death. Which is sad. Because if you've got loved ones near you when you're going, it makes it easier. But they died. You'd hear them moaning, you'd hear the death rattles through the night and in the morning you would see so many dead. You'd come back of a night, and there would be so many gone again, some of your mates maybe, it was very sad.

. . . Sometimes they'd make the sick do the burials, who were back in camp. They would pick out the strongest ones of them to do it. Of course, the graves had to be dug and they might put someone who wasn't well enough to go out, but strong enough to dig a hole in the ground. But each one got taken up, every time it was filled . . . graves were dug, and they would always be filled, it didn't matter who it was for.

. . . I think they tried to keep a record, the officers of each *kumi* [section] tried to keep a record of who they were in charge of, how many died. And they did get a fair record, but I don't think they got them all. I think a lot were missed back in those jungles. As we left camps, the jungle would reclaim the camps and reclaim the burial sites, because it would grow so quick. And I know one chap, he was on the burial party, like retrieving after the war, and he said the same thing, he didn't think they got everyone. They got their names and that was the main thing. It would be nice to think that they were back in a decent place, but that was the way it went.

THOMAS SMITH

All of our dead were buried, very shallow graves, probably I suppose, 3 foot would be about the deepest that you would bury them. You'd try and cover the body with some sort of bedding or blanket or rice bags, but rice sacks probably were the usual thing . . . you just bound it up, head and foot around him, and then you just put him into the ground, and that's all you could do.

And the camp administrators, those who were on light duties and that, they'd be making crosses out of bamboo, and they'd put that and try and burn his number and name on it if they had the facilities for doing that. They had to do something to signify who it was, if you could. The Japs used to let us, if you had that in the camp, a bugler, he'd play 'The Last Post'. If there was a padre in the camp he'd probably say service of a few words or something like that. No, I think in all the camps that I've been in and where people have died, you tried to treat them with as much respect as you could, and bury them.

But in Thailand where they were hit with cholera a lot, they just put them on fuel-drum fires and burnt them, on top of one another – had no way of getting rid of the cholera germ, other than by that way, and I think there was, you know, you could have twenty men getting burnt at once on a pile, just to dispose of the body and of the wogs.

FRED SKEELS

I saw Mrs Maddams and she had been one of those absolutely splendid people in our camp. She was a sort of a tower of strength to people and always cheerful, and she was terribly ill and she sat up to speak to me and I was so shocked by her appearance that I could never remember what she said. Anyway, she died the next day and we were told that even the Japs were upset about her death.

By this time the internees, this includes the nuns of course, had to dig the graves and carry out the coffins, and also to make the coffins, and they were given roughly sawn timber and they just made an oblong coffin, and it took twenty people. They used to put them on three poles and have six people on each pole, and one to lead out and one to stand at the back and just support the coffin from the back, because we were always frightened that somebody would stumble and it would possibly slide off, the coffin would.

We were there from November till March and we heard that we were being moved again and one of the cheerful ones had said, when she knew we were going back to Muntok, one of the cheerful ones had said, 'Well, we'll be easy to dispose of there. I suppose that's why they're sending us over.'

PAT DARLING

We tried, on Ambon, collectively, there was an effort made to mark the graves with a proper wooden cross. And a fellow in the camp who was obviously a handyman with wood, creative at making things in wood, made quite respectable crosses with the ends carved and the top bit carved in a sort of diamond shape. And then he engraved into the wood – (goodness knows where he got the tools from) – the fellow's name; you know, rank, name, number and date of death.

And so for quite a while, in the early stages – I emphasise that because there wasn't a high death rate in the early stages – so one of those crosses, and he would polish them with boot polish while the boot polish lasted, that wasn't all that long, but they were a lovely job. I saw some of them before they were actually installed on the grave . . .

So that when we left Ambon those crosses marked a lot of the graves. But as the years went by, and I could talk about how the death rate increased, it was impossible to keep up that supply of crosses. Either the chap ran out of material or he might have died himself, I've forgotten.

MARIC GILBERT

No matter how grandiose the myths have grown, the Australian POWs were not superhuman, not saints in loincloths. They would, in fact, be the first to disabuse us of that notion. But it is their very *humanity* that is so admirable. They gave to each other the only gifts they had – strength of will and strength of body. Their humanity united them, fused them together like metal joined in a forge and the power and compassion of that unity extended right up until a man's last breath. 'Tom' Pledger's story is typical.

Beri-beri is a terrible thing. It is not painful, but your heart and kidneys couldn't take all of the waste material out of your extremities and bring it out, and you pass it out in urine. So it used to start to accumulate in your fingertips and toes and gradually work up and come right up. If it got into your lungs you would just drown and that's the end of you. It is hard to explain. I had it five times. One time if I had have bent my knee like that, it would have split across there and all of this water would start to run down and that would be a sore across there then and wouldn't heal. It is not nice saying this, but my testicles, I used to have to carry them around in my two hands because they were as big as a football. Things like that. And if you could start to urinate, you would be right. I have seen them urinate a kerosene tin full of urine in one night. Once you could do that you were right.

. . . And the only time I ever broke down, no one ever died on their own if you knew they were going to die, and nine times out of ten you did. Other chaps you would be just talking to and they would fall over dead. But we never let anybody die in camp on their own. Somebody always sat with them and talked with them, held their hand, even if they were unconscious, but no one ever died, if we could help it, on their own.

Only one of my cobbers died and afterwards I just went and sat outside and cried my inside out. Excuse me just a little bit. But those who got through had the spirit. Once you gave up that spirit you were gone in a couple of hours. I have seen it happen. Well, I had beri-beri five times, I had amoebic dysentery, I had auxiliary dysentery, paratyphoid, malaria; but I was determined that I was getting home to my family, and that's what got me there. Anybody that came home, it was determination that got them there.

ATHOL 'TOM' PLEDGER

No chap that was there died on his own, he always had somebody beside him. You'd talk to him; you'd do everything you could for him, even though you knew you couldn't do any more for him. But you'd talk to try and comfort him and everything like that. You'd talk about what you're gonna do when you get home. 'You'll be right, mate, don't worry about it. You'll be right, you'll be right.' You know, even though you knew they weren't gonna be right, you'd say, most probably they knew themselves they weren't gonna be right. But, you know, 'We'll be doing this, we'll be doing that when we go home. We'll be able to do this, we'll be able to do that.'

. . . It was hard, it were hard. When you woke up in the morning and went to speak to the cove beside you and he'd gone through the night; shake him, he's dead. You know, because when you went to sleep of a night, closed your eyes, you didn't know whether you were gonna open them in the morning. You just dealt with it; you just have to carry on. It was hard . . . I used to say, 'No little Jap so-and-so's gonna keep me over here. I'm gonna get home, I'm gonna get home, I'm gonna get home!' I used to always say that, 'I'm gonna get home!' And I got home, but I mean it was more willpower yourself, pushing yourself along.

CYRIL GILBERT

Luck is the word many of the POWs use to describe their survival: 'I was lucky', 'it was all a matter of luck', as if their getting out of the camps alive was still bewildering to them. And if death was running a lottery, then some had prize-winning tickets that granted life.

We had one on Timor. He had a hole in his back like that. No, he didn't die . . . and he had an ulcer on his back and you could see his lungs – you could see the bubbles coming out of his lungs and all. And every night they'd put him outside the hut to die, the next morning he would be sitting up there waiting for a feed. He survived. Every time they dug his grave, someone else would fill it, but he survived. I think he got back home even. I don't know what happened to him. But it was that big, right across his back. You wouldn't think it was possible.

And another one of our chaps, going back to Timor, he had a piece taken out of his skull, about that long and about that wide. The bone was taken completely out and you could see his brains, you could see the bubbles coming up out of it . . . the only thing he was worried about was something getting in his head. He was walking around.

THOMAS SMITH

Despite everything – the diseases, the deprivation, the beatings, the deliberate and systematic starvation – the Australians had a higher survival rate than any other nationality in the Japanese POW camps. And they did well in the camps in Europe, and during the Korean War, too. Over the years, historians, sociologists, psychologists and medicos have pondered the reasons why this should be so. Some put it down to superior knowledge about and application of hygiene by the men, others to the discipline of the Australian forces or, in some mysterious way, to 'the national character'. I don't pretend to have the answer either. It's better I think, to let the POWs explain.

A lot of blokes were angry that it was finished. They wanted to carry on, especially the infantry blokes. They copped a hiding but they were prepared to carry on with it. It was hopeless; bit odd. My attitude was, 'Thank God it's all finished. We can get back to normal now.' We thought, foolishly in our innocence, never having been prisoners of war before, that it'll only be a matter of a few weeks and the Yanks'd be on their doorstep gettin' us off it. But they didn't do it. They just left us there. We knew damn well the British couldn't. They had their hands full over in Europe.

We were always confident that we'd get home. Nobody thought we were going to die there. Nobody, no, jeez no. We were, 'Three months, give it six months at the most, we'll be out of this bloody place!' But that was our first mistake, we shouldn't have been so confident.

Then, well, we put it back another six months you see. Six months incre-
ments, until finally we guessed right, we came home. We were always going
to get home. Always.

. . . I was quite sure that we'd get back. No, because of everything that
happened I think we accepted that this six-month idea was crazy, that it's not
going to happen. I think we accepted unconsciously that we'd sit it out, and
we just waited. And there would be periods where you'd be in deep desola-
tion, you know. Then up one day and down the next. I was anyway, and I think
there were hundreds like me. There was always somebody laughing.

BERT BEECHAM

Survival is a funny thing. When you are first taken prisoner you don't care, they
can do anything they like and you will misbehave because you know the war
is not going to be very long, you're gonna beat them. And then the war drags
on and you get a little cautious, you think before you do something stupid, but
it doesn't stop you all the way. But then when things get worse, you tend to be
a bit more careful because you think, 'I've done all this, how long am I going
to have to do this?' And you're prepared to put up with that, and then you come
to the other end where you don't think you're going to survive and you hope
you're going to survive and that's all you've got, just the hope, and if you don't,
well, that's it.

You go through a whole gamut of psychological change, at least I did, and
I've always been a thinker and I've tried to work things out and I've tried [to]
put them into perspective. That is the perspective: you don't care at first, but
then you get a bit cautious, you become very careful and then you get into the
other section, 'Well if it happens, it happens. Not going to take risks to make it
happen.' I think that's a philosophy.

ALEXANDER BARNETT

Morale was always high. 'We'll be home by Easter, or we'll be home by
Melbourne Cup Day, or Christmas', and then it would go the whole cycle again.
We never doubted, despite our condition or so forth. The old motto was, 'the
ticket home's at the bottom of your dixie'. And it was perfectly true. No matter
how abhorrent the food was, how distasteful it was, you had to eat it, otherwise
you wouldn't go home.

GAVIN CAMPBELL

That attitude, exemplified by Australian prisoners of war in both
world wars, did not diminish when the Korean War rolled around.
The Australians who fought there were identical in their outlook.

We were all the same, the four of us that were together there. We used to talk and we used to say, 'Well, don't give in. And if they ask you some questions and if it really doesn't mean anything security wise to our forces or anything like that, just answer that and go along with it, but if it is anything that you don't think it right, we won't answer it.' And that's the way we went. 'If we don't escape this time, we will try another time.' We just didn't want to give in, that's all. How I survived, I don't really know, I survived because I just didn't want to give in that way.

ROBERT PARKER

In some instances, it wasn't the prospect of impending death that eroded the prisoners' wellbeing. In the German camps, the undermining was more insidious.

Boredom is very difficult. One of the hardest things to bear, being a POW, is the uncertainty of how long the war is going to last. That's a big problem. If you knew, possibly you'd go and commit suicide. But if you knew it *might* help you. But the uncertainty weighs heavily on you. You don't know whether you're ever going to see it through. And how long is that going to be? You just don't know, do you? The uncertainty.

REG WORTHINGTON

And, contrary to the strange idea contained in the novel *The Bridge over the River Kwai* that somehow the construction of the Burma Railway gave the men a sense of achievement, is their assertion that when it was over, they were left with less than nothing.

There was no sense of accomplishment when we finished – haven't even today. No, we knew it wasn't going to be useful to them, because we knew that it was being bombed because our own people that were building the line were getting bombed by the Allies, bombing the line. There were still parties of prisoners left on the line to stack wood for the trains, to keep the trains going. And they used to get bombed, the line used to get bombed, so we knew it was being bombed, we knew the Japs weren't getting the value out of it. No, I've never felt that I've accomplished anything, other than my survival, I suppose that was a form of accomplishment.

FRED SKEELS

You had no mind; the Jap took your mind. You did nothing; you just did what he told you. What could you think of; there was nothing to think of. If you did what he said, you knew nothing. There was plenty of rumours but they died out after twelve months. You're stuck in virgin country, in a jungle. You had no food, the food was rotten, what you did have, and you had little of it, and you're working anything up to twenty hours. It was nothing to be out twenty hours. Go home four hours and back out again. See, your mind blanked. The human mind, the human brain must think, when it stops thinking it dies and that's what was happening. It was like you were brain dead. You could talk to somebody or that, but your talk was nothing, it was only of what was around you.

ALLAN HERD

The incessant struggle against despair, against final surrender brought each person face to face with their innermost self. What were they *really* worth? How much could they endure?

The worst experience was seeing so many of our people die on the 100 Kilo Camp. Up till then, little things had happened, you know, but they're only incidental things, like the bombing coming to Burma, traumatic as it was and as scary as it was, it only happened for ten minutes and then it was over.

But we lived with death every day in this camp, and you'd go out working and you'd come home, and your mate's mate had died, and all this sort of thing, and you buried him the next day before you went to work, or whatever. And you'd be out on the working party within earshot of the camp, and you could hear 'The Last Post' being played for someone else, and you probably thought, 'That's Bill, he was not too good this morning when we left.' I think that was probably the most emotional sort of thing that I went through – it was in the 100 Kilo Camp, strange as it might seem.

But I think my darkest moment would have been when I got to Japan, and the first day I went down the coalmines. I'd always had my feet on terra firma except in the navy, and we got to this camp in Japan and the next morning we went out to work and we had to walk down to our coal face, a couple of kilometres down under the earth. I think that was the most frightening experience that I had . . . I didn't like the idea of being down in the bowels of the earth as it were, not knowing what I was doing down there, I had no idea what I had to do when I got there. And I didn't know whether we were being shoved down there to be shot or murdered or whatever. They were the thoughts that went through my mind, and I must admit that I didn't feel too comfortable about it.

But fortunately you were with a gang of other blokes and your cobbers, and you all went down together. But it was still pretty scary and traumatic, from my experience, anyway. And then working down the coalmines after a couple of weeks doing that, well you got used to it.

FRED SKEELS

And there it is, the line that you hear over and over, in one form or another: 'You were with a gang of other blokes and your cobbers.' They came in together and they stayed together. The men did not splinter under the weight of established social class or position, as so many of the British did. They did not have the cultural arrogance of the colonial powers like the Dutch, which prevented them from adapting to captivity. They saw themselves as rightly belonging together and, in so doing, they maintained their strength, stayed united against the brutality of their guards, and somehow, found their way to songs, or the blackest of jokes to keep each other's spirits bloodied, but unbroken. And they stayed aware of mates, of what was needed.

You'd think about home a lot, of course, but not to mention to someone else, you never knew how that was going to affect them and it could affect people badly or nicely. Supposing I spoke to Major George Hooper who, like me, was from Sydney, and mentioned how much I loved the harbour and he might be very upset because he loved it too and he wanted to see it and he was missing it et cetera and he'd be very upset and he wouldn't talk to anybody for three or four days, and that's the sort of thing that could happen.

One thing we always did, if we got angry with anybody or with ourselves or upset, you'd go for a walk and you wouldn't talk to anybody for all day, or two or three days, you wouldn't talk to anybody and everyone would leave you and you're okay. But once people knew you were feeling that way then they wouldn't say anything to you, not even 'good morning'. Leaving you alone was a good thing; at least we discovered it was.

TERRY FAIRBAIRN

Each man found his own way to optimism and hope. For some, like Reg Worthington, it was an almost intellectual challenge.

After I was captured and I saw the strength of the Germans and the great discipline, the German Army is the most disciplined army imaginable. Their discipline is, it's terribly important to them and I realised then with the equipment they had, and the discipline they had, they were going to be a tough nut to crack and it was going to take a long time.

The morning I was captured I realised that this [was] not going to be easy. I was going to learn one German word a day. I set myself that target. One German word a day. And I maintained that for a long time, and that's a big target, believe me, because you don't only have to remember all the other words you've learned, you've got to take in this new one.

And then eventually I became very fluent in German. I could read it, write it and speak it. Using the local dialect, where I was, most of the time, I could talk German to anybody and write it, and I did . . . that way I could get a better idea of what was happening in the world . . . I could read the German papers eventually and I could listen to what the Germans were saying amongst themselves.

I never let onto them unless it was necessary, that I could understand German. I kept that to myself. This was my little secret weapon I suppose you could say. 'I can understand you buggers!' It was good that I did learn it because it did help me in a lot of ways.

I resolved, 'I'm going to see this through.' I was quite determined to see it through. I don't think at any stage I felt like giving up. I was going to hang on, but that's the way it worked out. There were a couple of times especially near the finish when it might have been excusable that I had given up, but I didn't. I wanted to see it through. And I had Iris to come back to and that was a very strong point. Very strong point.

REG WORTHINGTON

For Fred Skeels and his mates, it was the deliberate act of keeping home alive, in their memories and their hearts that kept them going. And again, the fact that many of the units had been raised from the same town, or state, gave them strength.

You'd talk about your mates back home that you knew and that they knew, you'd remember little details as kids, what we did, when we used to go swimming, ride our bikes out. We used to keep our home life in our background all the time, in our minds all the time, and talk about it often.

One of the favourite subjects, of course, was food, always, and we'd all talk about what Mum used to make at home, and how we used to love our, let's say, our plum duff at Christmas time or something. Simple little things like that you'd talk about amongst yourselves. You'd talk about your daily routine in the camp, if anything strange had happened, or something humorous had happened. You know, it could have been any damned thing that would make you laugh, or chuckle about or, you know, even *think* about. And so you talked about home with your mates, more than anything, if they knew what your home life was.

. . . And so that's how you sort of kept your mentality alive, I think.

Fred Skeels

The complete lack of privacy, the impossibility of pretence or false display under camp conditions meant that every man came to know himself intimately. He confronted exactly *what* kind of man he was and in what he believed. Some had previous ideas and understandings of the human condition scoured away.

The Bible was very popular for two reasons. The second reason was that it made wonderful cigarette paper, it was nice and thin and the troops used to be able to split it in two. Split a page like that, it would be quite simple, even the Bible. But that wasn't the real reason.

I read the Bible purely as a book for the first time and, you know, as a kid I used to go to church and we'd read a lesson, verse 22 to 25, from chapter so and so, and little bits and pieces, and for me it virtually was meaningless because it was taken out of context. You know, you need to have the full story.

So for the first time I read the Bible as a book, which I found fascinating, which then intrigued me, so I read the other religions – Islam, Buddhism, Shintoism et cetera et cetera – and got quite a, what shall we say, a broad attitude to religious things, and arising out of it I got to the stage of saying, 'Well, who am I to say that my religion is the right one?' I mean, you've got the Crusades where two people are fighting for the same god on their side and it's all just ridiculous.

. . . Now faith theoretically should have saved a hell of a lot of our fellows, and then you look at it and say, 'Well, he's Roman Catholic – he died, he's a Protestant and he died, so what goes on around here?' And so it goes on. 'He's a Callithumpian, he doesn't believe in anything, but he's still alive! Why?' I guess that it gave one a different slant.

Hope, on the other hand, there's something without which we would not have survived. I mean, you had to have some sort of hope or belief about getting home. For instance, it never occurred to us that we wouldn't get home, despite the fact that you're seeing people around you dying. Now that's somebody else, the poor fellow you know. I've described it as 'disappointment deferred', or

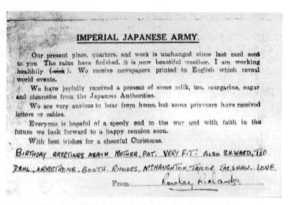

Rowley Richards' postcard sent while a POW

'reason rejected'. You know, reality rejected. In other words, you reject reality, denial just to maintain your hope. You know it's not going to happen but you do all sorts of things mentally to try and con yourself into believing, to maintain your hope . . . you knew bloody well you weren't going to be home by Christmas, yet you'd say, 'I'll be home by next Christmas', when you knew in your own heart there was no way in the world that that was going to happen. But you'd still live in the hope and the belief that maybe you would be. So it's just a self-conning act.

ROWLEY RICHARDS

In his darkest days in Korea, imprisoned by the Chinese, Charles Yacopetti, like many men, found solace in his god.

I was worried how I would be received when I got out. Why hadn't I fought to the death, you know, that sort of thing. But I must admit that was not weighing as heavily on my mind as how to survive. I prayed a lot. It's terribly important to have some religious linchpin to hang onto in these circumstances. And then the task of surviving from day to day takes over. Well the challenge, or, you know, the activity and the thinking required and you think less and less of the adverse side of it all, of the situation. And think more about how you're going to cope with things the following day and so on.

CHARLES YACOPETTI

In prison as in life, there were those who looked for inspiration and explanation in the spiritual and others who took a far more pragmatic view of their circumstances.

There was a type of person, I don't know, but he had something you haven't got. I don't know what it is. Whether it's willpower or – I don't know, but some people can exist under conditions that others can't and I don't know what it is. We used to say, 'Oh, he's dropped his bundle.' What did we mean, he's dropped his bundle? He died. Why did he die? I don't know, he dropped his bundle. He gave up, didn't fight it. I don't know how you fight it, but some people do cave in quicker than others. I don't know why it is, but if it meant the conditions or what it is, I don't know.

But I know this was right because you'd see it every day . . . you see blokes who are really, really crook and yet they'll still battle on, they'll struggle up, they'll carry their own pack. The other bloke that's next to him, there'd be nothin' wrong with him yet he whinges his head off all the time and he [would] get some of his mates to carry his things for him and he'd plod along. I don't know what it is. I don't know what it is.

I s'pose the fittest had the best chance of survival. The fitter a bloke went in, the more chance he had of coming out. A bloke that was crook all the way down the line with diarrhoea, dysentery or something, he's had the handicap right from the start. Had to go out on the line belting rocks around and carrying heavy sleepers and railway lines. Yeah, I s'pose the fittest have got the best chance.

BERT BEECHAM

There were a few older ones amongst us who were petty officers and chief petty officers, who'd been in the navy for ten years or more, and they never survived the traumas of POW life as easily as we did, hardly any of them did survive it.

It was their age, and they all had wives and families at home which played on their minds. They'd get sick and they'd go down a lot quicker than others. And that was one of the mental traumas that many did suffer from. But we were only young kids and we had no problems at home, our mum and dad were still in Australia, you know, and your sisters were there, as far as we knew, they were all quite all right, we had utmost faith in the Japs not getting to Australia. But being as young as we were, I think helped us a lot.

There was 30-odd West Australians came home, 38 I think, off the *Perth*, from the war, and I think there was probably only about six who were older than 26 or 27 by the time we got home. I came home, I was 23 still, you know, I was still only young, and we were all very fit when we got taken prisoner, and I think it helped all of us all the way through because of that.

FRED SKEELS

Then there were those men who were the exceptions to the belief that the older ones would be the ones to die, or the unfit, or the whatever. These blokes, in the finest of Australian phrases, 'you couldn't kill with an axe'. And their mates remember them with a sideways, bubbling laugh.

. . . I knew one chap, Nobby Hughes, from Tassie. I think Nobby's still alive . . . he got a bullet, a bullet went right through his forearm and it was all stiff. The doctor said, 'You will never use that again. You will always have a stiff arm.' He said, 'Don't you worry about that!' But by gee, you'd never know . . . I think they helped him when he come back. But he would get a broom and he would force himself to use that arm. Perseverance. And he got over it.

We had another chap with us. During that bayonet charge, we had a Bill Harper. He got shot through the jaw here, with a machine-gun burst. It shot his jaw off. And Dr Brown said, when they were coming through, 'Oh, leave him. He won't last long. I'll go and find someone else who's better off.' And old Bill said, 'I'll live to drink more bloody beer than you will!' And he did, too.

Poor old Brownie went down on the boat, the doctor; he got sunk on the way to Japan. But Bill got over that. He was still alive two days later, and the orderlies poked a tube down his throat and fed him on coconut juice, so they could get a bit of nourishment into him. Anyway, the maggots got into it and cleaned it out. That's what saved him; they ate all the rotten stuff. He got over that.

Of course, he went up to Burma with the rest of us. And he had his leg off, right up here. Colonel Coates took it . . . right up here, high. It was the highest one they tackled. They put him out in the hut, where most of them were dying anyway; they were expecting him to die. An hour later, Coatesy went out there, and Bill said, 'What about a feed, Doc?' And he said, 'My man, if you can eat something, I'll soon scrounge an egg.' And he survived that, and I think he got back home again, too. You couldn't kill him. He was a tough old man.

Fred Smith

In truth, I do not know how these men kept their faith in each other, or in humanity at large. I can only stand in awe of the strength of their minds and hearts. If I can suggest a small inkling though, of the stuff of which they were made, it is in this story from Ray Parkin. Remember, Ray had been sunk on the *Perth*, captured and beaten by the Japanese; here, he is speaking of his time on the Thai–Burma Railway.

We were right in the middle of the jungle and again, this is where my regard for nature came out – you know, 'How did they do it?' Well, here I was right in amongst it and I couldn't have got a stronger contrast between civilisation and nature than I got up there. I got the worst of mankind coming out on the one hand and the best of nature coming out on the other. Although it seemed inimical to us, because we weren't constructed to live there, it wasn't our business, we didn't belong there. All the other animals were doing fine but, and that showed me how unfit we were really. Only within civilisation could we do anything.

But I did get this feeling. We'd gone into the Siamese jungle, I thought, 'Well for one thing, not many people get into a Siamese jungle. I'd better make the best of it.' So I was observant of everything I could because I realised it as an opportunity; well, people are paying good money to do it now and they're not getting the same. We were getting into the virgin jungle virtually and saw the thing as it was.

I drew a lot of insects, butterflies, all sorts of things like that. Flowers, anything, but also, I had plenty of blokes to help me because as we went out to work we used to find things to discuss, and we would discuss the new flowers that were out, or what was happening. You know, the general state of nature as we went out, and I'd have all the blokes around me collecting butterflies and insects. 'Have you got this, have you got that?' Course I didn't have time to paint it all but still, with the butterflies, course there were millions of them up there, beautiful, in flocks and I couldn't paint them but all the blokes were still bringing them back.

So what we did, we got little slivers of bamboo and made pins out of them and on the inside of the attap hut we'd pin these things on the ceiling. And we had a ceiling covered with these beautiful butterflies and everything and I thought, 'Well, this is better than the Sistine Chapel ever could be!'

But you see, everyone was engrossed with that. With all the suffering and the belting that was going on, we still had this, you know, amongst ourselves, we had other interests and we found interests and we could talk about it. We didn't just go on hating. Well, we didn't like the Japs much but we didn't waste our guts on, you know, screaming, there were other things to be observed as well.

RAY PARKIN

IAN WALL

RON WALL

REG WORTHINGTON

CHARLES YACOPETTI

BILL YOUNG

RON ZWAR

10

'It was one of the great feelings of life'

When a war ends, the emotional outpouring from those who have been affected by it is a complex puzzle, uniquely personal to each individual. Some people explode into elation, dance in streets, kiss strangers, and, caught up by the mob, break every rule of 'proper' behaviour that they have so studiously adhered to for years. Servicemen and women, dedicated for so long to an ugly and exhausting task, can be brought stock-still in a frozen moment of realisation, wondering not only what use there might be for them now, but what do they do about a suddenly possible future. Perhaps the one, shared feeling is an overwhelming, almost tactile, sense of relief. It's done. It's over. Thank God.

For prisoners of war, these emotions can take days after the event to make their presence felt. Dulled by captivity and the daily struggle for survival, most POWs have needed reassurance by others or by seeing evidence with their own eyes before they will believe that peace – and liberation – have finally arrived. When they do accept the fact, it can be as bewildering to them as their original capture, and just as confronting.

In World War II prisoners of the Germans were the first to taste the intoxication of freedom, but not before a terrible ordeal was forced upon them by their captors. Retreating from the advancing Allies, particularly the Russians, German command ordered the prisoners and their guards onto the roads, where they would be used by both sides as a chip in the last dice game of the war.

The long march was a very brutal thing because prisoners were being marched on an empty stomach, many of them sick, being marched in cold temperatures, freezing temperatures, doing 16 miles, 20 miles a day, dropping by the roadside.

There is ample evidence to indicate that many Germans just shot prisoners who fell by the roadside. They didn't give them much of a chance; they'd just shoot them outright. A lot of this went on. It's not known how many prisoners were really killed in that way, but there were also on that long march, many German guards who just deserted and went back home. They didn't want to have anything of it, and there were many instances on that long march of kindnesses by Germans to prisoners who were being marched, Germans who realised how stupid and ridiculous and inhumane the whole situation was, but then there were also many, many instances of absolute cruelty and murderous intent.

. . . So this more than a quarter of a million people roaming in all directions, hungry, diarrhoea-ridden, sick, vomiting, all these people in dire straits were actually pawns in a big game, and Hitler was figuring that he was going to use them for one purpose, and the Allies were figuring that they were not going to interfere with any of their war plans. If the prisoners had known all this it wouldn't have been too good, but we didn't. I mean, a lot of us had our thoughts about it, but anyhow.

ALEXANDER KERR

We marched through snow up to our waist. On my slouch hat, which I had at that time, the snow used to build up and I'd nearly have to almost shake my head to get rid of it, it was starting to pull my head down, the weight of snow on my hat . . . and we just went on, from village to village and cow bale to cow bale. All the cattle over there in wintertime are stored under the houses. And I've wrapped myself around a few, beautiful, big, red beasts, I'll tell you, and aren't they warm, but don't they let off emissions during the night! And it was cold, it was really cold, couldn't take your boots off, they would just freeze stiff, and you couldn't get them on again. But then next morning, you'd be out on parade, 'Fall in, move on!' Then you'd start pounding along, pounding along.

And the column would start tight, but then it would elongate, you know, as the slower ones went to the rear. And that night, those that couldn't go any further were left in charge of the burgomaster in that particular village, as we marched through Czechoslovakia, Sudetenland, down towards Munich. Terrible times.

. . . It was the 30th of March, I remember it well. How could you forget? The bells were ringing down in Biarritz and we were in a little village just up the road called St Johanna's, and you could hear the Easter bells ringing in a foreign land, which reminded us of home, hearing the bells, the church bells . . . and I thought, 'Yeah, bloody German bastards!'

Anyway, it reminded us a little bit we were getting near the end. It was the 30th of March, Mr Rommel had been liquidated and 'Blood and Guts' Patton sent a spearhead up and surrounded our camp at Moosburg, just near Munich. And the planes came over and they went round and round, protecting us all the morning while we were watching the Germans retreating across a valley far away. And then a tank, a big tank came up the gate, pushed the wire down and out pops the Yanks. We said, 'You Yanks?' and they said, 'We sure are, buddy.' We knew it was all over.

And then suddenly, like taking a wet swimming suit off, everything just goes.

RAPHAEL CORBETT

Virtually from Christmas Eve 1944, we were on the road and we'd already experienced what happened on the road. You were expected to keep going, if you fell you got a bayonet stuck in you, or if you moved off the line you got a bullet, if you stole anything you got bashed up. They were pretty adept at using the bayonet; they would put it in about that far and it doesn't stop you doing too much, but by golly it hurts. And we knew what the Hun was like on the road, because he was scared, he was frightened of the Russians and he was coming away from the Russians and we were slowing him up and he wasn't going to be caught in that lot.

. . . On the whole of the march there was no provision of issuing water, it was up to the farmer or the place we were or the village if we could get water. And sometimes you just had to get it out of a stream; course it didn't take long for dysentery to take over, and with very little food and marching every day; you do about 30 kilometres a day . . .

. . . Now the bombing started, like we had bombers when we left Hirschberg, you could count 1000 any time you wanted. They were up overhead and the noise was just there and as you moved and marched the anti-radar metal twisted down on you and the worst thing that could happen was to be hit with one of their auxiliary tanks; you could hear them coming down, they made a horrible noise, but you couldn't figure out where they'd land.

. . . We had beri-beri, the knees were swollen, we were walking along cobbles, every time you walked on a cobble it jars and with beri-beri you get fluid and it swells out . . . your belly was swollen, we had scurvy; red, inflamed mouth and swollen gums. And on top of that malaria and dysentery. It wasn't real good.

At one stage we decided to take our trousers off, and we just put the blanket around us and march like that because you didn't have time to get your strides down. I think I got as far, not quite to the River Rhine because I was moved up and when I got to Duderstadt I found Bill and Dud. Bill was crook and Dud was crook. And Dud had got to the stage were he started to believe things. You resist things that you're told when your brain works properly, but when the Hun says to you, 'Oh we've got a hospital train', you believe it because you want to, and Dud did.

We had a council of war, Dud, Bill and I said we mightn't make it, one of us mightn't get home, one might, so we think it's time to spread – this is our thinking. One has to get home to tell what's happened and we took a chance at one in three . . . Dud chose to go with the RAP [Regimental Aid Post]. He believed, we didn't, neither Bill nor I believed that. Bill reckoned that Duderstadt would be evacuated and he was going to hide in the rubble and take his chance that they didn't get him with a bayonet. And I said I'm going to do the most stupid thing, I'm going to volunteer for a work party, and if you look at it logically it wasn't such a stupid idea because I was crook. How could I work? But I might get somewhere out of there. If I stayed in Duderstadt I would have died.

ALEXANDER BARNETT

Geoff Cornish, not yet a doctor, was given the responsibility for the medical welfare of 2500 men out on the roads, a near to impossible task. Then there was the threat of what the Nazis might do to them as a last gesture of defiance.

At the end of each day's march, when we came to a village, the chief of the German guards was the same rank as I was so I would say to him, 'I want a room in that house for a sick parade for a hospital.' He said, 'But that's the mayor's house!' And I said, 'No?' In other words, 'So what?' And the mayor grumbled all along but he was kicked out.

With the Americans so close, they sent a dawn patrol, an air patrol out to see that we were safe, to see which direction we were going at ground level. And then he went back to the American lines and at midday they would send another one over to check progress and then they would bed down our night position, so they were very carefully monitoring us from a distance.

And I said to the German in charge of the column, I said, 'No funny business and I will see that you are looked after when the war is over, if you act properly.' And in fact I said, 'I am quite sure I can get you a very good position as head lighthouse keeper at Kalgoorlie.' Which is 400 miles from the coast, but he was delighted to be the head lighthouse keeper.

. . . After we finished that march and we were at Landshut, not far north of Munich, the Americans were close behind us. And then we got word from the German guards that the next step was to take the 200 RAF and march just us to Berchtesgaden, to Hitler's secret hideout in the Austrian mountains. And we were to be held there as hostages. It didn't take more than a few seconds to work out that that would be the end of us. If we weren't bombed, because they couldn't bomb Berchtesgaden and not bomb us, if we were going to be held inside it, and so we thought, 'We are either going to be killed by friendly fire, or the Germans will shoot us . . . they are not going to die themselves and let us go free.'

So that was when we really bribed some guards and a couple of the guys got into Munich itself and knocked a couple of heads in, people unconscious, and got into the German radio station and broadcast a message to England saying they were going to march us to Berchtesgaden as hostages.

That night the RAF sent over Mosquitoes, very low level, a lot of them and when we awoke in the morning these A5 white leaflets were like snow right through the camp and all around it. And it said 'Attention!' in German, of course. 'Any man or woman in the armed forces or civilian who moves, or causes to be moved, or takes part in the moving of any prisoner of war from here to anywhere else will be held guilty. Be charged with a war crime. Upon liberation you will be tried by court martial on the spot, the penalty is death and the sentence will be carried out immediately. Signed Harry Truman, Winston Churchill, Josef Stalin.'

We didn't move. A lot of the boys did keep the leaflets as supplies but I had no room for anything but medical supplies in my backpack. But gee, that was lovely to see.

And we were liberated only a few days after that. Patton came in himself, and twenty minutes after the tanks had come in and bashed down the gates, the guards had disappeared, of course, they heard the tanks coming and just vanished. Twenty minutes later they had a doughnut van and we were eating hot doughnuts and were as sick as dogs. After our food to rich American sweet doughnuts and we were scoffing them, you know, gutsing them, you can't call it anything else.

GEOFF CORNISH

Those POWs who were not ordered on forced marches were effectively abandoned by their guards. The German forces, knowing that the Russians were wreaking vengeful havoc as they advanced, were scuttling to whatever protection or hideaways they could find. The prisoners were left to determine their own futures – or surrender to fate. Many refused to lie down and let the war roll over them, and they set off into a world where power lay at the end of a barrel, regardless of which side held it.

The Germans said, 'We are leaving the camp, we are evacuating the camp. All the guards are going. You will be here on your own. You will have to fend for yourselves. You can go into Muleberg or whatever and get whatever supplies you can and look after yourselves, or do you want to come with us? We'll try and cross the River Elbe and get across to our side of the fence, away from the Russians.'

. . . I was in the cooler at the time, I wasn't outside . . . Anyway, next morning the gate of my cell opened up and Pat Thorley, the hut commander, came in and he looked at me and said, 'C'mon you bludging old so and so, come out and do some work.' So he got me out of the clink. And then we were out on parade on April the 23rd at seven o'clock in the morning. We were on parade mainly to count our strength so that we knew what rations to divide up for the day. And we were there facing the west and all of a sudden someone said, 'They're here!'

And we looked around over our shoulder, back to the east and there were the Russian Cossack troops, horse troops. Hundreds of them come madly galloping across the flat terrain and they just swerved either side of the camp and kept going right up to the River Elbe. They didn't know the Jerries had left but just in case there were any around, they would make sure they got them. Only one Jerry refused to go and he stayed in the camp, and we heard a rattle of machine-gun fire and a Russian knocked him off and did a nasty thing. He tied a rope around his leg and tied the rope to the pommel of his saddle and just galloped down the main road of the camp with this Jerry dragging along behind him. So there we were, we were released.

And then the Russians said, 'Now, if you want to eat, you go find your tucker. We're not going to feed you.' So then a mate and I, a chap from Wagga Wagga and myself, we teamed up between us and we went on walkabout for about ten days and lived on farms and so on.

We moved around Germany, still having to be careful because the Russians were more dangerous to us than the Germans had been. The Russians would shoot at you as quick as look at you just for fun, for the hell of it. See how fast you could run or how high you could jump. Especially if they got drunk, which they did quite often. Their discipline wasn't that great.

. . . The people looked after us – we had beds to sleep in, food cooked for us and they were living quite well. They were getting food out from different places. Tinned meats out of the top of a piano and so on where it was hidden and things like that.

And one place we went to the lady of the house asked us in, gave us a hot drink and said would we stay there with her. We said, 'Well, no not really. We want to move around.' And she said, 'Well, we'd like you to stay because the Russians come. If there's no men here the Russians come and they can be violent.' And with that, two of her daughters came in; they'd been hiding out in a field, a big rhubarb patch . . . and she said, 'My two daughters would be safer if you were here.'

We stayed there overnight and then we went on the next day. We had a chook we'd caught and killed and she cooked the chook for us, and we went on like this for about ten days and then we went back to the camp. And the Americans came in with a convoy of trucks to take us out. And they lined us up on the parade ground. We were stationed in a big permanent army barracks, German Army barracks, and these trucks were lined up on the parade ground for us to hop on board and they'd cart us out. And the Russians wouldn't let them; they sent the Americans away again. They said, 'No, you're going, you're not taking these prisoners.' They wanted their own people back on their side before they would release us. We were the bargaining tool.

RON ZWAR

After leaving his mates Bill and Dud, Alex Barnett joined a working party, as he had planned, but malaria and dysentery had left him helplessly weak and he had to plan again. Like so many Australian prisoners of war, his resourcefulness was his best weapon, but he could never have imagined that his days as a maths teacher would mean his survival. He was 24 years old.

When we arrived in Hanover, we arrived at the railway station and the rumour was true, we were to clear the railway line at Hanover, but there was nothing there really, it had been bombed. It was shocking, it was the worst bombing I had ever seen and I was crook. I was really crook and I was at the end, I was desperate, but I still had my brain working and it's your brain that you need, not your brawn.

I heard from a Hun that was marching, one of the guards, a whisper that there was a hospital train going to leave Hanover and I thought, 'Yep, I've got to get on that train, if it's true.' So I asked the guard to parade me to the higher-ups, the colonel in charge. He just laughed and told me to go chase myself and so I thought, 'Oh well, I'll do a trick.' You know the old trick? You're working and you pick up something, walk around with it and look as though you were working? I did that.

And I went along the station and I saw an office open and a whole heap of reasonably ranking officers arguing and chatting and whatnot and I recognised the colonel and I said, 'Herr Obst, do you speak English?' And he said, 'Yes.' And I said, 'I heard that there's a hospital train, I'm really sick. I've got malaria with dysentery and if I don't get on the train I won't last.' And he said, 'You're not British?' And I said, 'No.' And he said, 'What are you?' And I said, 'Australian.' He said, 'What the hell are you doing over here fighting in my country?' I thought, 'Oh God, I've really picked one here.' And I said, 'All our relatives live in England and we call England home and what happens to England happens to us, that's why I'm here.' He said, 'What do you want?' I said, 'I want to get on the train.' 'You? Who came over to wreck my country?' I said, 'Yep.' He said, 'No, you can go to hell and back.'

And I looked over and they are all working away like steam at a mathematical problem, and there's paper everywhere and they were in a frantic mood . . . and I said, 'You seem to be having trouble with your mathematics.' And he said, 'What would you know?' I said, 'I might. I notice that you've got an integral stuck there.' He said, 'We've been working on this for two days and we haven't got it.'

And I looked at it, and in the bad old days of calculus, to solve some integrals, they weren't solvable. You had to know the answer and you had access to the answer and you kept it in your brain. It was one of those. So I said, 'How important is it?' He said, 'It's very important.' I said, 'I don't want to know what it's all about, but it looks as though you're not doing any good at it. If I solve it, can I get on the train?' And he laughed. 'You can have a go, not that you'll ever get near it. We've the best brains in Hanover working on this.' And I said, 'Give me a piece of paper and a pencil.'

And it was one of those things that came out in five lines, and he looked at it and he said, 'But you come from Australia. What do you know about that?'

And I said, 'Well I solved it, didn't I? Can I get on the train?' Then he barked an order and I was escorted to the train and lifted onto it.

And we sat on the train, and it wasn't a hospital train, it was a train carrying wounded and they were on flat trays and carriages and I was sitting in the yards there, it was in the days when they had Mitchells [fighter planes] up over the top and a locomotive came along and the moment it came it was hooked and down came the Mitchell and blew it off, that happened twice. And just as nightfall came they got another one and it took off.

From there somewhere between Hanover and Hamburg I lost consciousness and I woke up in a holding camp like a *lager*, which I have deduced as being part of the Fallingbostal complex and there I laid on the stretcher until the British 7th Armoured Division burst through with a tank, picked me up. I lay on the tank side and was taken out. That's how I was rescued. From there we went through pockets of resistance until we eventually got to Brussels and from Brussels to England . . .

That was the first time we'd ever met DDT [insecticide] and they puffed it all over us and we had a bath. And I remember stripping off and I looked at one of the blokes I was with and I said, 'God, you ought to see yourself. You haven't got any buttocks!' And he said, 'You want to have a look at yours.'

. . . They put me on the *Mauritania* in a stretcher and the Pom in charge, a major, said, 'Are you an Australian?' And I said, 'Yeah.' And he said, 'I don't like Australians.' And he said, 'What are you in for?' And I said, 'I've collapsed, with my liver.' He said, 'Are you a POW?' I said, 'Yes.' He said, 'I don't like POWs. You're discharged, go onto the deck.'

I was discharged out of hospital and did duty all the way home on the *Mauritania*.

ALEXANDER BARNETT

Treatment with DDT for lice and various kinds of bugs became a lasting memory for many of the POWs after their release. It seemed that they had to be cleansed, disinfected and drenched in clouds of powder before they could be thought of as ready to join their countrymen . . . and women. Bill Fordyce had been in the famous Stalag Luft III.

As soon as the British troops saw us, it was very obvious we'd been POWs and they said, 'Well, you were prisoners of war. You must have lice. We have to delouse you.' So they would have a thing like a big bicycle pump, they'd shove it up your shirt and down your neck and up your trousers and so on, and pump

DDT powder through. And when they'd finished, they'd paint a big purple spot on the back of your neck to show you'd been deloused.

So we then walked on in our groups of four or five towards the Channel, and as soon as we saw another lot of British soldiers we'd get out our tinned powered milk and dust ourselves over with this so it looked as if it was DDT powder. And then I'd get out my tin of paints and paint everybody purple on the back of the neck, and we'd say we'd been done and they'd just wave us through.

So we finally walked right through to Brussels and then there was the most incredible airlift. There were thousands of Lancasters coming into this aerodrome nose to tail. All round the perimeter there were tens of thousands, maybe hundreds of thousands of prisoners, in rows of sixteen, 'cause that was the number a Lancaster could take. The traffic was so intense, the flying traffic, that one airman told me after the war that if you missed the circuit you had to go back to England to get back into the circuit. It was incredible.

A Lancaster would come up, taxiing very slowly. They'd drop a ladder, sixteen men would come and climb into the bomb bay. I can't talk about this. And the Lancaster would then turn, take off, and go back to England.

. . . We went back to a place in the south of England called Dunsford, and as the aircraft pulled up and we got off the aircraft each man was met by a WAAF [Women's Auxiliary Air Force] officer. And I grabbed this girl by the arm. I hadn't seen a woman for over three years and I was terribly impressed. And I thought to myself, 'I'm going to take this bird out tonight.' You know, I had that filthy uniform that I'd swum the Mediterranean in, that I'd been wearing for the last three or four years and the chances of going out with no money were absolutely nil, but I thought and everybody did, 'We're going to take this woman out tonight!'

She led me across towards the hangar. She said, 'There's a wonderful meal for you, set up in the hangar.' And I thought, 'To hell with the meal. Concentrate on the girl!' Finally, halfway across towards the hangar there was a little hut with a Red Cross on the roof and she led me across to this and she said, 'Oh look, just go in there'. And I said, 'What's in there?' And she said, 'Don't worry, everybody has to go in there.'

And when I got in I found it was a man with one of these big bicycle pumps prepared to cover me with DDT powder. And I saw this and I said, 'Oh I've been done!' And he said, 'You're going to be done again.' So he covered me with this powder and I went out the exit feeling very stupid, dusting myself down. And the girl said, 'Look, don't worry about it. They're doing it to everybody.'

And we went across and sat down at this table where this immense meal was laid out, which we couldn't possibly have eaten.

There's one thing I didn't tell you. Years before, the Germans found that when we were issued with uniforms in England we all were given what was called a fly button compass. This, of course, was before the days of zips. So that the top button you took off and it had a pivot. The second button sat on top of it, was a perfect compass. When the Germans found this out they cut all the buttons off everybody's flies so that you could always tell the air force. They were going round holding up their trousers. So that when I arrived, sitting next to this WAAF officer in the hangar at the food table, I had no buttons on my fly. And the man had just filled me up with DDT powder so I sat down to do a line with this girl and I crossed my legs and out of my gaping fly came a great puff of white powder. And I thought, 'This is a horror of war. First woman and I can't even do more than a puff of white powder!'

BILL FORDYCE

While the end of the war in Europe was a protracted affair, war with Japan ceased with a suddenness that left everyone scrambling for control. The dropping of the atom bombs on Hiroshima and Nagasaki meant that in some prisoner of war camps across South-East Asia, the question of whether or not the war was *really* over took a long while to be answered. For the prisoners held in Japan itself, though, the Emperor's declaration of surrender was immediately apparent. Des Mulcahy was the warrant officer in charge of a camp near Kobe, and he wasted no time in asserting his new authority over his jailers.

We posted our own guard and hunted the Japanese men and their officer outside and told them not to come back inside the camp unless I sent for them. The first thing I sent for was the old chap and got him to get us a wireless . . . We then got a message from [General] MacArthur who said if we wanted any food for the welfare of the men, we could commandeer it and sign for it and they would pay for it, so we got that organised.

I am down in the kitchen this day and a runner came down and said, 'Quick, you are wanted up at the main gate.' I said, 'What is the trouble?' He said, 'The guard has gone up on the road and he has stopped a big Jap truck and he has brought them down here. He said he has a full bullock in the back; you had better go up and see what you can do with it.'

So I went up. They had a dressed bullock about 300 pounds weight in the back of this army truck, these two Jap corporals. I said, 'Open the gate and send them straight down to the kitchen and tell Jack Nichols to get the bullock out and cut it up as quickly as he can and get it into the soya pits to get it cooking. The faster he can do it, the better. Then bring it back here and wait here for me.' I went over to the truck and I said, 'Right-o you two blokes, you can get out and walk back to your barracks. I am keeping the truck. I might want a truck later on. Some unknown reason might crop up and I might need a truck.'

So away they went and, of course, they lost face, they lost their army truck. They went back to camp and we could smell the meat cooking and the boys were all walking around with their nose in the air, with this beef. We hadn't had beef for two years.

Another runner came down. He said, 'Quick, come up, there is a car load of senior Jap officers up there [who] want to see you.' I walked up. I could see they were pretty senior men so as I went past the guardhouse I said to the sergeant, 'Have four of your men out here with rifles standing ready, something might develop here'.

I went on out. I saluted this bloke, he was a full colonel, and he saluted me back. He spoke good English. He said, 'Excuse me, Sir, but you have confiscated the week's ration supply for my 1000-odd troops. They will not have any meat all this week and they will be very disgruntled.' I said, 'That is bad luck. I have 200 men here who haven't seen meat for two years.' I said, 'They have been disgruntled for two years and I have put up with it.' I said, 'If I were you, I would advise you to get in your car and go home and leave the meat here.' I said, 'If you put a song and a dance on I'll confiscate your car and you and your officers and friends can walk home and lose face too. Now you make up your mind what you want to do.'

He blinked his eyes a few times and looked around and saw I meant it; he saw the four blokes lined up there with rifles, so he saluted and got in the car and went away. I never saw a sign of them afterwards.

DES MULCAHY

The Allies were faced with enormous logistical problems in recovering and repatriating their POWs. Intelligence reports towards the end of the war had made it clear that the men under Japanese control had suffered terribly and were in no shape to effectively take care of themselves. The first priority was food and medicine, and the quickest way in was from the sky. In Des's camp, as in others, they painted huge white letters, 'PW', on the roofs, so the pilots could find them among the destruction of a bombed Japan.

The next day they came in dropping food and what they had done, they had two 44-gallon drums, the top and bottom of them cut out, and they were welded together into an 88-gallon drum, and they just tipped all the stuff into it and put a top on it with a board across it, with nails to hold it, and they dropped it out in parachutes. But they were too heavy and they snapped all the ropes of the parachute and these great big 88-gallon drums came hurtling down into the camp. There were blokes going in all different directions. We didn't have any injury there, but one of the camps nearby, it fell and hit one of the buildings and killed an officer inside.

There were four planes came in; the first three dropped this food on the camp and the fourth bloke could see what was happening so he dropped his into a little lake beside us. It was a much bigger lake than we had at Kobe but only a shallow one. The boys swam out to it and they were there for a long while. 'What are you blokes doing?' 'We have all the tea and sugar and coffee here and we are having a great time!' So we gathered up all the broken tins we could find.

That night we had bully beef, we had Spam, we had meat and veggies, we had cake, we had everything. It was all put into the kitchen stores to be cooked up where we ate everything. They gave us another drop after that and we had it pegged out with parachutes. That was a good drop, they dropped everything in cardboard cartons, four cartons to a flag and down it came and it just floated down nicely, it didn't damage anything at all.

We had a little bit of medicine sent in. We had four medical officers in that camp . . . Sweeney was one and Carter was the other and we had two Dutch surgeons. They had nothing to operate with. When they opened all this stuff up they got some of the boys in who had cysts on their arms and they had a great go there. They sterilised one little room, and they had chloroform around the place and the blokes were popping in getting this out and that out and something else out. They couldn't do anything major, of course, but they could only just do superficial wounds.

DES MULCAHY

In the chaos that was Japan in those first days after surrender, an organised and decisive man like Des Mulcahy became the law, even if it was not a job he wanted.

One night, we were in camp and I got called up to the guardhouse about eight o'clock. They said, 'There is a Chinaman up here wants to see you.' So I went up to the office and this Chinaman is there, he turned out to be a Korean but could speak English. He said he was from a work party down the line and they had just killed their company commander and they had taken to the bush because they feared the *Kempeitai* [Japanese military police] would come and kill them all because they helped them.

I got five men with rifles and said, 'We will go back in and get things organised for you.' So we walked back down the line and I said, 'Now you tell me when we are getting close to where your men are, I don't want to get into a fight with your men. You tell me when your men are here, close by.'

We got to a certain stage and he said, 'I think we are getting pretty close to the men.' I said, 'Well, you go ahead now and if your men are there, tell your men I want them all to come out and stand on the railway line where I can see them. To stop there because I want to come down straight through the middle of them, I won't hurt them, I'll come straight down through the middle of them and I want to lead them back into their camp.' So he did this and he came back and he said, 'The men are all up . . . Sir!' We walked down through the middle of them; and they had pickaxes, they had crowbars, they had baseball bats – you name it, they had it, anything they could find to use as a weapon, they had it on them.

We marched back up to camp and I said, 'You form your men outside and I will go inside the camp and have a look.' . . . I went down and the camp commander was lying in the middle of the parade ground, bashed to pieces with baseball bats. Other than that the place looked quite good, well kept, cleared and tidy, so I came back up and I said to him, 'I want you to march your men down and number them off, I want to count them'.

He marched his men in and formed them up and numbered them off and I think there were 135 he had. And the story was, I found out afterwards, the Japs had brought him over, as a young fellow, treated him like a little god for about six months, sent him back to Korea to tell his mates what a great place Japan was so he would recruit these blokes and bring them over and they would put them straight into the coalmine. All these young blokes came over and thought they were going to get treated well by the Japanese and instead, they got stuck straight into a prisoner of war camp and put into the coalmine so they were very anxious. The commander was still left in charge so that is why they killed him. He got them into trouble so they did away with him.

While this is going on, this car load of *Kempeitai* rolled up – he wanted to take control of the camp. I said, 'No, you are not taking control of the camp. I am in charge of the camp.' He said, 'What rank are you?' I said, 'I am a warrant officer.' He said, 'I am a colonel!' I said, 'I don't care what you are, I have the weight behind me here and I am in charge of this camp.' I said, 'Don't you do anything that will fringe on that.' I said, 'Have you got any lower NCOs with you?' He said, 'Yes, I have got a warrant officer.' I said, 'You get him out of the car and I will let him stay here, but you senior officers have to get off the scene as quick as possible, I don't want you around. I want that body taken away immediately and the rations increased by 25 per cent for these men.'

He saluted and got into the car and he left the corporal with me. I took his pistol and gave it to the officer, then I took him in and I showed him where he could sit and where he could move, and he wasn't to go past a certain thing. Then I did a tour of the camp and down in one of the back rooms I found there were eleven people minus legs and arms and that from accidents in the mine, and they were put down there and they only got half rations, the poor things. I had to keep a guard on that camp then, right through for the next week until we got a call to leave.

DES MULCAHY

Eventually, Des and his men were relieved of their duties by the occupying American troops and they began the awkward task of adjusting to a world they had not encountered for a very long time.

We got word to catch this train and move down to the Nagasaki wharf. We loaded up and got on the train and down we went, and I got out of the train and walked over and saluted the senior Yank I could see there. And he looked a bit perplexed, this bloke, and I said, 'What's the trouble, Sir?' He said, 'You gave me a fright.' I said, 'What do you mean?' He said, 'I was sent down here to meet a trainload of Aussies and when you got off the train I thought it was black Americans.' I said, 'We've had 82 days in the coalmines, Sir, without a break.' I said, 'And no soap and no hot water.' I said, 'You will have to bear with us for a while.' He said, 'All right, we will fix all that up.'

And they took us over and lined us up, and we went to a little bloke and he was sitting at a table and you had to take your watch off, if you had it, and put it in a bag and then it was fumigated . . . You went into the next tent, you took off all your clothes, you threw them in a heap in the middle because they said they wanted to burn them all, they were all lousy. We went into the next hut and there were all hot showers, about 30 or 40 hot showers around the wall and we had lashings of soap and hot water and we had a fantastic time with this. It was the best bath I had ever had, I think.

They said, 'When you have finished with the towel, do the same thing, throw it in the middle of the room because we are going to do away with that too. When you have finished that, go into the next room and you will be equipped with your equipment.'

So we went into the third hut and the Yanks had all this stuff lined out to fit everybody, ready to wear. You put your new clothes on and when you came out the other end we were like Paddy's market. The bloke on the outside had our watches and he said, 'Now, the girls have some doughnuts and coffee down there at the wharf if you would like to go down.' Now I had some blokes there that had joined the army when they were fifteen and hadn't seen a white girl for three and a half years. You had a job to get them down there; we almost had to frogmarch them down. But once you got them down there and got them started, they were right.

DES MULCAHY

Slowly, camp by camp, the prisoners were located, and if the Allied commanders could not get troops to them immediately, they delivered supplies. In China, the civilian POWs had been expecting the end and were prepared. In Howard Walker's camp:

The word got around the whole camp that Germany had surrendered. And this was, I think it was about May or June 1945, something like that. So that, of course, was a sign that things were going very well. We thought, 'Well surely now with the heat off the European sector they'll be able to bring all the American troops over to the Pacific and finish things off here.' And so we became a lot more optimistic after that.

But then we became more worried, particularly the adults, about what was going to happen at the end of the war. That was a continual worry all the way through. What will the guards do when they find they've lost the war? Will they just kill us all and kill themselves, or what will they do? They were capable of anything. And that was a continual worry.

And then the word got around that the Americans had dropped two gigantic bombs on Japan and they were so gigantic they might end the war. And very soon after, I think it was days, wasn't it? We had another note came around to say that the Japanese had surrendered. And I must admit that whatever negative or ambivalent feelings I had about atomic bombs later, at that stage we were very, very thankful for the American atomic bombs ending the war so suddenly. And then to our amazement and delight, the Japanese guards just disappeared, they just melted away. En masse. One day there's guards, the next day there weren't any guards.

Of course we had camp administration which had been planning for some time for this contingency, so they brought this contingency plan into play. And they just took over the whole running of the place, which they had been doing internally anyway. Their main worry was the supplies, particularly food, which we needed daily, and of course medical supplies, which we were short of. The food was coming in through the Japanese, of course that stopped . . .

Probably the next day after the Japanese disappeared, big American planes flew over and dropped leaflets saying, 'Food is on the way and supplies; we will be dropping this down to you.' And a day or two after that these great big American bombers came over and dropped on some vacant land next to us, it must have been hundreds and hundreds of big 44-gallon drums full of food and supplies.

Some of these, the parachutes gave way and they came down and smashed and we ran over to them and all this wonderful food fell out, chocolate and cheese and honey and things we hadn't tasted for years, and medical supplies. And that then kept us going. I think there may have been more drops too, so that there was so much, there were 1000 people in the camp at Pu Dong and there was enough to supply us all and kept us all fit and happy.

HOWARD WALKER

Allied command was not certain of the location of all the camps. Some Australian troops had disappeared into a black hole from which no news had come in years, and there was no certainty that anyone was still alive. Ambon was such a place and the prisoners there suffered the indignity of having to convince their own forces of their identity.

. . . [The interpreter] said to us, about a week after the war had actually finished, which we didn't know about, 'We are going to . . .' I'm paraphrasing this, I don't know exactly what he said but it was to this effect, 'We're going to get you ready to go to your homes. Are there any things that you need?' Well, of course, our doctor had a whole list of medications that he wanted, including vitamin B injections. So from the very next day, every day we got a vitamin B injection, you know, which started to make a difference almost instantly. The food ration went up quite sharply. Rice, I can't quote figures, but actually almost more than we could actually, literally, stomach, because I can remember the pains of hunger were being replaced with terrible indigestion pains. Our stomachs had shrunk to that extent and here's a whole sack of rice we only dreamed about having and we were now getting without any trouble and we just couldn't digest it all.

They fitted us out with Japanese marine shirts and shorts because our clothes were generally in tatters, nothing on our feet. And there were no more work parties, we weren't sent out on work parties any more. I said, 'The war *has* to be over.'

So one of the American officers, you note that I'm saying one of the *American* officers, not one of our officers, started to browbeat the Japanese authorities, the interpreter and even the camp commandant, telling them that they had to make available a radio transmitter so we could tell the outside world come and get us: 'We're here, come and get us!'

And that took a while for the Japs to do anything about that, but they eventually relented and took this American officer plus two American wireless operators that happened to be in the camp, to a wireless installation down in the nearby village, Galala village. And they made contact with Morotai and, of course, Morotai couldn't really believe what they were hearing at first, the people at that end.

And I believe they were quizzed. Well, one of the fellows must have been one of our fellows because one of the questions I heard that they were asked was, 'What's the pub on the corner of Flinders Street and Swanston Street in Melbourne?' And they answered, 'Young and Jacksons.' 'Yeah and what's it really noted for?' 'Oh, for Chloe.' You've heard about Chloe? So that established their bona fides, so quickly the powers that be arranged for four corvettes to come down and take us off.

. . . They came down and signalled to the Japs and the Japs made sure they directed these ships through the minefields that they had laid across Ambon Bay and on the 10th of September 1945, this wonderful sight came down Ambon Bay – four corvettes of the Royal Australian Navy. And I'll tell you their names: the *Junee*, the *Cootamundra*, the *Glenelg* and the *Latrobe*. I will never forget those names. I was on the *Junee*. And they tied up at Ambon wharf and in the meantime we were taken in by trucks . . . into the wharf where we were assembled. Our own officers here had us lined up and we were assembled and greeted by these fellows on the corvettes, and well, it's very, very hard to really to put into words our emotions at that happening, it was just so wonderful. They had baked a whole stack of bread on board and handed out loaves of bread to us. They could see how emaciated – we were still fairly emaciated, of course. They were shocked because there were a lot of stretcher cases, fellows who were not much more than skeletons. They were on the wharf too, and they

Maric Gilbert

had to get them on board and look after them. They were shocked I know, because I met a lot of them at a reunion years later and it was something to hear them tell of their feelings and reactions when they saw us on the wharf there. It is something that will stay with them for all their lives, I'm sure.

MARIC GILBERT

There had been rumours about the existence of Australian nurses in a prison camp somewhere, which were denied by the Japanese. An Australian war correspondent, Hayden Lennard, began searching for them. His persistence was rewarded and the camp was found. Pat Darling and her mates were going home.

Japan surrendered on the 15th of August '45. On the 26th of August we were told that the war was over. That was the day [Commandant] Siki made his announcement. I might add that Siki was sentenced to fourteen years' imprisonment with the War Crimes trials.

   We just hugged one another and laughed and cried and were quite hysterical with joy. It was such a relief and then the men came over from the men's camp and they took on the heavy jobs. They did the cooking, they did the carrying out of the coffins, because people still continued to die, which is very sad, and the native people came in with chickens to sell and dried fish and that sort of thing, and the Japanese actually opened the stores which had held the Red Cross supplies which had been sent to us, and they'd never been delivered, and most of them had deteriorated in quality anyway, but a few of them were quite, you know, they could be eaten.

. . . We were absolutely amazed that no one was being released from camp . . . and it was only afterwards that we learned that the Japanese had vigorously denied that they had any army nurses, any Australian Army nurses as prisoners, and it was due to the diligence of people like Squadron Leader Madson and one of his pilots, Ken Brown, and another man who was a reporter, they were determined to find out, they knew we were there and they were determined to find us.

They landed their plane on the aerodrome at Palembang. They didn't know whether it would have been mined or whether there were any booby traps there or not, and there they met an ex-prisoner of war who said, 'Yes, there are Australian nurses and they are at a camp at Lahat'. We were at Loebok Linggau, and that was how we were found. And then it was on the 15th of September, which was a month after the Japanese had unconditionally surrendered, that we Australian nurses and three very sick women were taken to Singapore.

. . . Eventually we saw a plane arriving and it landed and the first person off was a major, he was a doctor, Dr Harry Windsor . . . and we of course, always travelled in our uniforms in case anyone could see us . . . and he looked at us, we were the only standing people, and he said, 'Where are the Australian nurses?' And we laughed and said, 'We're here!' 'Cause we were dressed as best as we could be, and then following him were two women dressed in safari suits with boots and gaiters and the whole works and pips denoting their rank. One was a senior colonel and one was a captain, and the senior one, of course, was the Principal Matron of the Australian Army Nursing Service . . . and Matron looked at us.

Somebody said, 'But who are you?' And she said, 'I'm the mother of all of you and ever since I've had this position I've wanted to find out where, I was determined to find you.' And she said, 'Where are the rest of you?'

And of course there was silence for a moment then a voice, I don't know whose it was, just said, 'They're all dead.'

PAT DARLING

Harry Windsor, the doctor who wondered who the nurses were, was so angered by the appearance of the survivors that he made a recommendation in his report concerning the fate of the guards and all those Japanese who were involved in the treatment of the women. His words burn still, all those years since 1945. He said they all 'should be forthwith slowly and painfully butchered'. Pat and the other nurses had no idea of this at the time, of course, as they were making their own joyous way back into civilisation.

Of the 65 who were on the ship, on the *Vyner Brooke*, 24 of us came home, and of course, when we arrived at Singapore and we were greeted by the Red Cross people with cups of tea and by a lot of the war correspondents and . . . we were taken to St Patrick's . . .

We arrived there and you know, it was all so unbelievable. I shall never forget having a wonderful hot shower. I think it's the best shower I've ever had in my life, and toothbrushes and toothpaste – much better than a bit of coconut husk and a bit of charcoal, and the nurses who hadn't known us beforehand found us a little bit surprising I think, because we were in such high spirits. Because they had been given lectures on the way over, which was fair enough, and they were told that there was a possibility that we would be resentful and uncooperative and sullen and all the rest of it, but instead of which we were flying high, higher than kites could fly, and in terribly high spirits.

It was funny when we went to bed, I can't remember what time, couldn't have been too late, and we were given nice nighties and things like that, wonderful, and about the middle of the night I felt water pouring down through the roof. It was raining and there must have been a hole in the roof somewhere, so being a practical person, I hopped out of bed and pushed the bed out of the way of the rain. Sister was shocked, she said, 'Sister, you'll wake the whole ward!' I didn't care two hoots who I woke. And somebody, I could hear a sleepy voice saying, 'It's raining on Pat'. And another one laughed and said, 'She should be used to that.'

PAT DARLING

In all the areas that the Japanese had occupied, prisoners were progressively found and released and happily re-entered the real world. They were stunned but delighted at the rapid change in their fortunes, though, as many noted, if imprisonment brought them strange and curious moments, their freedom was completely surreal.

One day I'm on the surface, not working, beautiful day, and I looked from the south shore of Honshu across the inland sea to Kyushu, and I'm looking straight down at Nagasaki, not realising it particularly at the time and it was a beautiful blue – clear, blue sky with a row along the southern horizon of like little cumulus clouds, like a flock of sheep, you know, going along and then I heard a rumble and I thought, 'Oh, that's ack-ack [anti-aircraft fire] over at Moji', which was only fifteen miles away and it used to get regularly bombed.

And then out of these clouds down there it started to form an anvil, like the thunderheads that form in clouds, and I knew, 'Oh yes that's a thunderhead, it must have been thunder I heard not ack-ack.' But this cloud, see normally that takes at least half an hour to form and I saw this cloud going up, it was out of proportion. I thought, 'What's happening?' Something, I couldn't explain it. Anyway, it went up and it came out in a plume at the top and I thought, 'Well, that's the best meteorological observation I've ever made, I'll remember that. I'll tell them about thunderheads.'

And then it was later, when these aircraft came over they started to drop some newspapers and we found out that I'd watched the cloud of the Nagasaki bomb. But not knowing what it was at the time till later.

But the amusing thing was, when the papers started to arrive, course we'd been out of communication with the real world for a long while or the unreal world I will say, and we didn't know just what had happened. But there were three major things that happened. The atomic bomb, jet propulsion, we did see a couple of jets come over, and the third one was the biro pen. Oh, here was a pen, oh they said at the time, you don't have to refill it, it'll write for two years! Bullshit! That's the one thing we wouldn't believe, was the biro pen. That was impossible.

RAY PARKIN

I think the first white lady we saw was Lady Mountbatten. She took a risk, coming through all the hostile country. Some of the Japs were still pretty hostile, and they hadn't laid their guns down then. But there was two truckloads of guards, and she was in a jeep, and she came out to see us, that far out. And she went along past everyone, and went through the sick hospital, and she said to one chap who had dysentery pretty bad, she said to him, 'How does that affect you?' What a question to ask anyone.

But he was pretty quick on the uptake. He said, 'Well, I travel a greater distance quicker than I normally would.' She was a great old stick, though.

THOMAS SMITH

We knew nothing, we knew nothing. We knew something must have been happening because the planes weren't going out at all and they'd stopped.

There was still a few machine-gunning, going on from our side. We knew something was happening and it must have been coming to an end. They didn't tell us. Then all of a sudden, one morning we heard this 'Cooee!' on the top of the mountain. So we 'cooeed' back.

. . . Everybody went mad, everybody. I have pictures there. Looking for something to make an Australian flag and we had to put up the flag and that was made and we found something and put it up. There was great rejoicing. There was a journalist there and he took all of our names and all our addresses and everything else. He said, 'That will go straight home to your people and say that you're alive.' And they did that, they did that straightaway. But my mother was not alive.

SISTER BERENICE TWOHILL

The Jap commandant came back, and we were told by officers to line up, and he was going to address us. And this little Nip got up on his little soapbox and told us the best way he could in English, that the war was finished, and we were all free, and 'Nippon your friend!' That was good. So that was it.

From then on we were told about putting these PW signs up everywhere – we put one up on the roof of our hut . . . and after a few days the Yankee B29s came over and they parachuted food and clothing and stuff down to us. Amongst some of the paraphernalia was medicine . . . we didn't have a doctor in our camp in Japan, we had a Dutchman, he wasn't a doctor, he was a sort of medical orderly equivalent, I suppose, in the Dutch Army . . .

But anyway, they dropped this medication, and amongst it was some little white tablets called phenobarb, which is, I don't know what, an antidepressant of some sort, and he dished these out to everyone. I don't think he knew what they were for really, but we all got handfuls of these given to us, and of course we promptly took them, thinking they were good for us in some way or another. But they put us all to sleep and we were getting around like zombies for two or three days, these damned things, we took so many, some of us. You know, you'd take half-a-dozen of these little white tablets, 'They're good for you, take them'. And you'd be like a zombie for two days . . . So eventually someone must have woken up to this, so we stopped taking them.

It's a wonder it didn't kill half of us, you know, these damned antidepressants. Penicillin was dropped to us, he didn't know what it was, no one knew what it was, hardly.

FRED SKEELS

Sheila reads from her diary:

Wednesday 12 September 1945. This morning, most of the camp turned out to watch the victory parade. It was the formal surrender by the Japanese officers to Lord Louis Mountbatten on the steps of the Municipal Offices. The padang was packed, it looked like the whole population of Singapore was there. Planes, flying boats, transport planes, bombers (you name it, anything that flew), flew low and zoomed here and there. The army, navy were assembled on the Padang together with the band; the marines did look smart in their 'whites'. What a lovely sight – we cheered and we clapped and we hugged each other and cried and laughed and then cried again! The atmosphere was unreal.

Those who were specially invited were in the Municipal Buildings. I was on one of the balconies with the others. The POWs were there too. Lord Louis arrived in great style – how we cheered and waved our hands. The band played and he walked round, inspecting and talking to the army and navy – one sailor fainted and had to be taken away on a stretcher. Seven Nip officials then arrived – the Chinese roared their anger and wanted to rush at them but were kept at bay by the MPs.

After the ceremony was over – they came out again and were taken away. The Flag (our beloved flag), was hoisted while the band gloriously and thrillingly played *God Save the King* followed by French, Dutch, Chinese and American anthems. Heard speeches – had photos taken. We cheered and danced and cheered ourselves hoarse. There was dancing in the streets – we were mad, gloriously, madly happy – Time stood still as we let our hair down – for a moment we forgot those three and a half years as we went into a frenzy of dancing, singing – 'we are FREE, FREE, FREE! AT LAST!'

That was the moment that we knew we were free, it was a wonderful moment, and I don't think it will ever be repeated again.

SHEILA BRUHN

The momentary madness of freedom wasn't confined to World War II. When the truce was finally called in Korea, appropriately for the so-called Cold War, it was politics that dominated the prisoners' liberation.

We were called onto parade and it was announced that an agreement had been reached and that we would soon be informed the details for our departure . . . the commandant summoned me up to his office and told us that in the next two or three days the vehicles would turn up, and to mark the occasion . . . he had acquired some Japanese saki whisky, rice whisky. But he called it peace wine and that he would like to celebrate the occasion by giving

Charles Yacopetti on his return from Korea

all the soldiers a little sip of a glass of peace wine, and he expected me to say what wonderful treatment they had given us et cetera, well at least I understood that's what he wanted.

. . . They paraded the whole 50 of us and the guards had a little table; all the soldiers were taken from the parade and filed past and they picked up their glass of peace wine and went back into line and I stood up and I proposed a toast to Her Majesty. I suspect that the English I used couldn't have escaped the interpreters but whether they understood enough as to what that might have meant, and that in fact, it was almost an affront to them, for what I said was, 'Well, we can't deny that we have been reasonably treated but we look forward to the next war when in fact, as a result of our experience, we will make sure that the roles are reversed and they will be the captives and we will be the captors'. That, I think, escaped them.

CHARLES YACOPETTI

The Chinese started these lectures on Communism and capitalism and all of this sort of thing. They tried to teach us that capitalism was no good, we were no good, and we should be Communists and all of that. But we didn't get much sense . . . we used to call it the Pyok Nong University. And we were only drop-outs.

. . . All of a sudden they started putting up POW signs on the camp and taking us down to the village to have a bath in the big pools they had down there, and they gave us some more clothes and everything. Because the peace talks had progressed, and they were putting POW signs on the camp to let the aeroplanes know there was POW inside.

. . . So things went on like that and it suddenly finished and they put us in trucks to the railway and then put us in these goods vans and took us down to the – where they had set up a demarcation line sort of thing. It was a big section across the 38th Parallel and it was no-man's-land in between there, between North Korea and South Korea. So they had this bridge that went across from North Korea to South Korea and they called it 'The Freedom Bridge'.

And so they took us from the schoolhouse that they put us in, and gave us cigarettes. I had a couple and started to go dizzy, and they gave us things to eat and razors and all things like that. We left our moustaches on, of course. And they drove us down to this Freedom Bridge and we were in the back of

Robert Parker with his mother upon return from Korea, 1953

this truck with a mob of Pommies and here is this Australian journalist [Wilfred Burchett] that had come and visited us up in the camp on the Yellow River. He wanted to talk to us and he just got drowned out because he was a Communist and he was on the Chinese side.

. . . They exchanged us and then sent Chinese prisoners of war back. There was lots of Chinese prisoners of war that didn't want to come back, they stayed there. But there was a lot of diehards that came back and threw their gear, took their clothes off and threw them at reporters and reckoned they had a hard time in the South Korean prisoner of war camp. Which they didn't. Any hardships they brought on themselves.

. . . We spent a couple of nights there and we got sprayed and disinfected. And we spent the night with a mob of Kiwis at this place there and they all got drunk and we didn't. We hadn't drunk for years, two and a half years or something and it didn't affect us but they were all flaked out when we left.

. . . And then they flew us from there to Australia via Taiwan.

ROBERT PARKER

The irresistible question people ask any POW about the end of their captivity concerns the desire for revenge. After all they suffered, all they endured, it seems inconceivable that they did not want immediate vengeance, some kind of retribution. Their answers, and they are many, are surprising.

After a week or so we decided we would take our chances. We wanted to get into Singapore, down to the wharves, because we knew that boats were coming in. So we were bumming lifts in trucks, of course, and we went into Singapore. The first lot I went with, the remaining six or seven mates went in and we went straight down to the wharf area. If you went right into the city there are wharves that are right there, and there is a beautiful little park there where in the old days they used to play Test cricket and tennis.

Anyway, the day we went in we could hear this noise, this terrific noise of shouting and yells and it was from down this park, this beautiful park. We got down there and here is this whole line of Japanese POWs lined across, and across them was a line of Chinese and the Japs were there to clean up the park, and they were cleaning up bits of papers and rubbish and whatnot and the Chinese were behind them, tearing up papers and dropping them, and guarding them was a complete company of Gurkhas with their bayonets out.

We stood there for a while watching them. And one of my mates said, 'We don't want to stay here watching this, do we?' And I said, 'No, I don't think we do.' I was very proud the way our Australians behaved after. We had said, for years naturally, we were going to get our own back. Well, of course, when the Japanese took Singapore Island, the way they behaved, they killed 30 000 Chinese in the first three or four weeks. There were heads on every pole round Singapore Island, severed heads of Chinese and brutality going on all the time.

Well, we said we would get our own back. We decided, sort of collectively, that we weren't going to be like them. We just ignored the whole thing. I never saw an atrocity committed. In several instances that I knew of, and I didn't blame the chap, was when he went up and jobbed a Japanese who had ill-treated him. Some of those who'd been at the *Kempeitai* jail and had been tortured. But there was never one thing from Australians collectively. And that was pretty good.

JAMES LING

We ran into this German battalion, or the remnants of it. It might have just been the remnants of the company, and this German sergeant pulls up alongside us and we couldn't escape. We had to, you know, we had to stay there. There was no use running away or anything.

So we just sat down on the side of the road, took out our cigarettes and lit a cigarette each and he's got a *panzerfaust*, what we called a bazooka, on his bicycle, you know, for destroying tanks, and he stops and he says, 'Who are you fellows?' 'Oh, we're a couple of escaped prisoners of war.' 'Yeah? Can you spare one of those cigarettes?' 'Yeah.' So we give him a cigarette and [ask], 'How are things going?' 'Oh, not good at all.' 'Where are the Americans?' 'Oh, right behind us.' 'What about your fellows? What are you going to do?' 'Oh, as soon as night falls all my fellows are going to disappear into the countryside.'

So, that was the feeling. And they looked exactly as we did on Crete and on Greece, you know. 'We're being beaten.' You can tell a beaten man by the way the soldiers are going past and their heads are down. A couple of them are dragging their rifles on the ground, that kind of thing. You could see they were beaten men.

KEITH HOOPER

The fact that we were taken to Japan, we lived the last twelve months with the ordinary village people of Japan and they were wonderful. They were sympathetic people. They were good people and they had nothing to do with the rest of it. Now, how can you go and blame those people? They'd been there; it's the bastards up top that do all the damage, not the Japanese people. And when we left Ohama, those people were there, genuinely wishing us *sayonara* and I felt closer to those people.

When we got down to Wakayama, the Yanks were there – oh chuck every-thing away, we've got everything, we'll give you the world, and all the rest of it, you know. And they had petrol on everything, burning it up and we had things we wanted to save, that we didn't want to go on the heap.

. . . I genuinely felt closer to the people of Ohama then than I did to the Americans at that moment. We'd been conditioned to that. In other words, I'd shared more with those people in the Japanese village than I'd shared with these blokes that had done it, out amid all this opulence.

RAY PARKIN

So now the long journey home began. Their first contacts with their countrymen and women were the doctors and the nurses who fed them, treated their wounds and their diseases, and did what little they could for the broken and shattered thoughts that lay inside them before they sent them further on. None of the medical staff that worked in the repatriation hospitals will ever forget those days. Eileen Fisher was serving at a hospital in Labuan.

The people that came to us were the ones that were too sick to make the trip home. They had to come and see if they could recover enough to make the long trip home. It was the most surprising time in my nursing and, of course, you must remember that there were some people in the hospital that knew that they had relatives in the camps so they were always on the lookout for somebody that they might know. I can remember one of the sisters, she had a brother that turned up and when he found out that his sister was at the hospital, not having been in a duck before, and if you know it, this amphibious vehicle, it's about 8 feet off the ground when it's on its wheels and it's travelling; in his excitement at seeing his sister, he jumped off the duck and he was emaciated, with no muscles in his legs, and broke both his legs.

So that was a sad greeting, but it was an exciting time because we were able to say, 'It's all over for you. Now all you have to do is get your strength back and we'll send you back home.' Of the British patients that came in many were civilians, because the rubber plantations were mainly run by British or Dutch and we had a number of elderly gentlemen that had had rubber plan-tations that had spent three and a half years in a concentration camp and they were in a very bad condition. We had lots of nuns that were in Catholic ministries there, we had Dutch priests that really looked the part in their dark tan surplices and their hair cut like the priest you've seen of old, a particular haircut, all very humbled and all in terrible condition. Their condition was equally as bad, especially the Catholic nuns who had been abused, the young nuns had been terribly abused by the Japanese.

One young nun that was in our hospital was completely off her head, mental case, with the treatment she'd had. And the children that came in with the Dutch parents, a lot of those came through our hospital. There were children as young as three and a half, where the mother had been pregnant when she'd been taken a prisoner of war and they were all very scared coming into another situation where many of them didn't understand the language. I had a word or two of Dutch that I'd learnt on the *Oronya* that came in very handy. But when I went around the wards to view them and they were under mosquito nets, the children would tend to huddle at the end when somebody walked in, they were so frightened. So it proved that they had had very rough treatment. It was heart-rending to see the kiddies in that condition.

And the stories that were told by the POWs of how they'd been treated and what had happened and the friends they'd lost during the time they were there, and the doubt whether their sons and fathers had survived because they were all divided into male and female and sent to different camps, and many of the mothers had no idea whether their sons and husbands were still alive. But it was over and that was the wonderful feeling, that it can't get worse, it must get better from now.

. . . The psychological damage, I think, was far greater than the physical damage, where with good food which we gave them, that was graded. When they came in they could only have a very, very light diet and then gradually they had a seven-point plan that would go to, say, a roast dinner, because the body would reject it if they suddenly ate everything. So it was done to benefit them, but some of the patients didn't appreciate it. They were so hungry they thought they should be allowed to eat everything and anything, and some of them had very sly ways of getting food and you would find empty tins near the bed where they'd cut them open and eaten what was inside because they were so hungry. And I can remember one Welsh gentleman, on the end of the food line, he would race to the front, have his plate filled, he'd only take a couple of paces from the line, he'd gobble it all down and get on to it again and try and get another plateful. You see, this was very dangerous, if you couldn't control their need for food. So you had to take them very, very gently through that graded diet to the full diet.

. . . Some of the Japanese officers after the war was over, they committed suicide by falling on their sword, or in one case, the 2IC in the camp couldn't get to his sword to fall on, but took a knife and cut his throat, because the tradition in Japan is never to give up, otherwise you're labelled as a coward. It's always an honour to die for your country, and that was one thing that the army had to be sure to do, to try and take the officers before they took their own life. Colonel Suki who was in charge of one camp took his life, and Colonel Nakatiri's 2IC cut his throat and we very quickly stitched him up and gave him good Australian blood which he was not happy about, and he was in my ward.

. . . It was a sad time because we were meeting the enemy for the first time. For years we'd been frightened of the Japanese and we thought they were all villains and, of course, we hated them, and suddenly here they were amongst us, those that had been taken. They were in camps and our boys were getting them to do road work and other jobs and I was given two young Japanese boys in my ward to help with some of the small chores and I found out that neither had ever been in Japan. They'd both come from Sumatra. They had been in a Catholic village and they were Christians. They had had to join up when the Japanese Army came through because they were of Japanese parents, they were just taken into the army, and I began to realise how unfair it was for them. They didn't want to go to Japan and be demobilised, and we began to talk to each other and I formed the opinion that they were very nice lads.

One unusual circumstance happened on a Sunday when the Roman Catholic priest was giving mass to the boys and they were all kneeling in the chapel tent and he was working his way down through them giving them the sacrament, and one of these Japanese boys looked out of the window or out of the tent flap more correctly, and he saw the mass being given and he had such a look of longing in his eye. I said to him, 'Go out if you want mass.' And he said, 'I'd be too frightened to.' And I practically pulled him to the door of the tent and said, 'Go out!'

He timidly walked out and he knelt about 3 metres from the last man kneeling and the padre, I watched as the padre came down to the last man and gave him the sacrament and looked out of the tent and saw this young Japanese boy kneeling. He didn't hesitate, he walked out, he gave him the sacrament. How foolish can we be, hating people we don't know? And that is why war is such a shocking thing.

EILEEN FISHER

Food, medicine, kindness, words of compassion – small jewels of human contact that were clutched deep in the hearts of these men.

It was the first time I had ever seen any nursing sisters cry. And when they took us up that gangplank, tears were running down; we were emaciated, you know, bones were sticking out everywhere. I was lucky I wasn't, I still had some beri-beri so I was filled out a little bit. That was that.

. . . Well, firstly, have you ever tried to talk to a woman if you haven't seen one or spoken to one for nearly four years? It is hellish hard, to find, 'Hello', to find something to talk about. It was them that talked more to us than we talked to them, I suppose. Of course, we didn't know about the atomic bomb, we didn't know about what had happened from the day we were taken prisoner hardly. Anything they could tell us.

Even when she took your pulse, it was nice to have a woman touch you. If you have been a prisoner and amongst men for nearly four years and before that you had women friends, well I had Jess, it was so hard. I can't remember what we said or what we did. They were so good to us. They seen that we were well looked after and well fed and didn't overeat, they were marvellous to us

ATHOL 'TOM' PLEDGER

Tom Pledger had made it through Ambon, he'd made it through Hainan and now he was going to make it back home. This is the letter he wrote to his fiancée, Jessie, as he sailed back to Australia.

Dear Jessie,
Well love, at last we have said goodbye to that land of bad reminders, a land fit only for Asiatics, not white man. It is gradually disappearing in the wake of the ship. This morning we were awake before daylight to sit around and get a glance of the hospital ship. It is called the *Jerusalem*. It is a British ship and has British sisters on board. They have been wonderful to us; it was a big moment of my life to be able to once more talk to a white woman. One sister started to cry. And believe me; I couldn't stop crying myself as the nervous strain is too great.

But just think of it, dearest one, that day when we will be together again after all of these years of separation. They are just broadcasting a church service and I have just said a prayer thanking God for our delivery and hoped he has watched over you all as he has watched over me. We are bound for Manila and then transfer to the *Wanganella* and then straight to Sydney.

I won't sleep tonight because we have nice mattresses and just think, white sheets. And pillowslips. It seems a shame to get between them. I saw an Aussie paper the other day and saw photos of the streets of Sydney on peace day. Gee it must have been a great day for you all at home.

Well dearest, my love hasn't altered one bit. And my memory of you and my folks has often been the only thing which has kept me going through these last three years. But, dear, we will make up for all of it when I get back, which should be about the end of the month. Give my love to everybody, cheerio dear, I can't settle down to write, lots of kisses and hugs,

Yours forever,

Tom

Tom and Jessie were married for 51 years.

•

Perhaps the last word on freedom should go to Bill Young, who had been sent to the infamous Outram Road Gaol for attempting to escape. Release from Outram Road was like a pardon from execution.

It was tremendous. It was one of the great feelings of life. When they let us out the door. As soon as I saw them without swords. None of the guards had a sword on, and even the warden didn't have a sword and I knew then, I said to my cobber Jimmy Brown, he's a pessimist, I said to him, 'It's finished now, Jimmy, this is it!' And oh, he said, 'No,' he said, 'you've been saying that for a couple of years now.' And when they led us up and said, 'We're going to send you back to Changi,' it was beautiful, it was beautiful.

. . . The first night out was a beautiful night. And we hadn't seen the sky or the stars for two years, and we went down to the beach, there was a little beach at Changi, at the jail, and we went down and we sat there all night, we just sat there, the group of us. We just yarned occasionally and just looked and there was the stars and this huge moon come up, and the ocean was at peace as well and it was just lapping into the shore on the sand and we just sat there all night. That was the most perfect night. It lasted so long, all through the night. It wasn't just a moment, it was a whole night, and it was beautiful.

That night was Bill Young's birthday. He turned 19.

11

'I saw life at its best and worst'

When World War II ended, the Australian government, through the army, navy and air force, put all its available resources into the huge effort to repatriate prisoners. The prisoners of the Japanese, that is. The prisoners of the Germans, released first, came home in dribs and drabs, mostly by sea, and they generally arrived without any public fanfare or fuss.

But the prisoners of the Japanese, numbering as they did in their thousands, were an entirely different matter. For a start, the war had ended and the nation now had time to concentrate on these men and women. Their recovery from captivity was seen as a symbol of sorts of the Allied victory. Then there was the almost visceral hatred of the Japanese that had developed in Australia, inflamed by the prisoners' physical condition – emaciated, shrunken, aged. The public, and the government, wanted them home *immediately*. What might have been best for the prisoners was not considered.

We are all back in Changi to get organised into different groups, who lives in Victoria, who lives in Tassie, who lives in New South Wales, getting them all together, putting units together, putting names in newspapers, sending it back to Australia. And we are in Changi, and the Australian Army has taken over their section, the Pommy Army has taken over their section et cetera. And they put up a big army truck, a closed-in vehicle, and on the top of it they have got loudspeakers, as we call them . . . big speakers, and that's for entertainment and so forth. And the first music that was played over the loud speakers was 'Don't Fence Me In'. Bing Crosby singing 'Don't Fence Me In'. I have always thought that bloke that did that had the most wonderful sense of humour.

. . . So then we all formed up at different times and we were taken to the wharf in Singapore, which was a fair way away from Changi, we were taken on trucks to the wharf. And then, of course, it was hours and hours of standing on the wharf with the ship there, waiting till you got your name called and name written down 555 times and everything else, and then finally up the gangplank, with what little gear you had, and on board the ship we came.

And they brought us back to Darwin first, and for some reason or other I was loaded off at Darwin. And a terribly embarrassing thing, they took all us fellas out of prison camp and brought us onto the barracks for the day, or the night, or something like that – I don't know why they did – the ship, the whole bunch of us, and brought us into an army camp where there were a whole lot of girls, army girls, and put on a dance. Well gee whiz, to see a girl was a bloomin' fright, let alone trying to make her dance at a party! That was torture to me.

BILL COVENTRY

After the isolation of the camps the adjustment to public display was asking a lot of these men. They had no defences against the natural curiosity of other people and no real idea of their importance as icons. There were some moments in the public gaze, though, that the prisoners cherished. Reg Worthington, the boy from a farm near Murwillumbah, was chosen, after four years of captivity, to visit royalty.

They wanted some volunteers to go through a testing period for a visit to Buckingham Palace. I volunteered. We were drooling. You were checked out from every possible angle and I was one of the twelve that was still there at the finish. So off I went with these other people to Buckingham Palace.

. . . We went by bus or something and pulled up at Buckingham Palace and we walked – no you don't walk when you're in the army, you march – through the portals of Buckingham Palace into the great, big backyard. Big lawn area, must be 5 or 6 acres of it, beautiful big lawn. And that was in June 1945. June in England is their nicest month, I think. Beautiful.

There were a lot of people. Mainly troops, both sexes, from various parts of the Empire – there was an Empire then. And there was a certain number of medals dished out and I saw one chap being decorated with the VC [Victoria Cross] and I think his name was Brown. He was an airman from Canada. He was in a wheelchair and he had no legs. I think he would have swapped that VC medal for a new pair of legs.

We met the King and Queen. We had afternoon tea at Buckingham Palace. The Queen Mother, who just died not so long ago and King George VI, who was not a brilliant type of person, or he wouldn't have got above the rank of lance corporal if he had been in a real army . . . And the Queen stopped in front of me and asked me a few questions and I answered as best I could and we talked for, I suppose, a couple of minutes, quite a little bit of a chat you could call it. But I've always said of the Queen Mother, she was a lady. I don't know of any reason to change that at all. She was the pick of the royalty bunch as far as I was concerned. It was just typical everyday stuff. Nothing very intimate or anything like that. Just how I enjoyed being clear of the war behind me and so forth.

. . . It was a unique experience, especially for me. I've never been a great believer in royalty. They're the cause of me going to Greece. But that's beside the point, it's not their fault. Oh yes, I always thought that we were sent to Greece because of the connection between Greek royalty and English royalty. At least I think so. I might be wrong . . .

The present Queen, she was there, about a 17, 18-year-old, and Princess Margaret was there. She's just passed away too I believe. I wrote in my diary, 'Princess Lizzie looks all right but Margaret is bow-legged!' That's my comments.

REG WORTHINGTON

The sadness and disappointment of the camps was not yet over, however. Disease and despair resided in many a prisoner's body, and both would claim more victims.

The sad, sad thing about it, a couple of boys died on the ship on the way home – gone through all that and then plug comes undone on the way home. But the getting over it was a difficult period; it took us years to get over it. Our families, our families welcomed us home and gave us the Australian wonderful roast dinner and meals . . . that nearly killed us, 'cause there was no advice. Advice should have been given, 'Feed the boys on rice and gradually let them eat'.

We got taken from the wharf onto one of the British ships and they sacrificed their ration to feed us, because we looked so sick and so ill, and they fed us sausages and mash. And the boys lay on the ground and screamed with pain, because what it did to your tummy so, you know, the tummies had shrunk to such an extent. See a 12-stone bloke was down to 6 stone.

BILL COVENTRY

Counselling was unknown, hurtful ignorance was displayed by military and civilian authorities alike, and there was no *time* to try to come to terms with the upheaval in their lives. The only wonder is that more prisoners did not die immediately after their release. Some treated themselves in the only ways they could manage.

A few of our chaps, when they hit England, they went off the deep end altogether. They did all the wrong things. You see, we were suddenly in possession of money. All our wartime pay was stored up and we were able to get it and I didn't draw much, because I wanted money for when I got home. But some people as soon as they got the money, they did all the wrong things.

There is one chap I will talk about, Greg. Now Greg was the first Aussie that escaped from our farm camp. When he arrived in England, I didn't see this but I heard from his own cobbers, the first thing he did was spend money and he got himself a woman. He was with this female on the street and somebody, an Englishman, made a comment about the Aussies being over here 'pinching our women'. Words to that effect.

And Greg turned around – he was an aggressive bugger – he turned around and smashed this bloke and broke his glasses. It cost him a lot of money in the local police court. That's what some of them were like. They didn't know how to control themselves under a different set of circumstances. All of a sudden they were free. They couldn't handle it.

REG WORTHINGTON

The Australian repatriation camp was at Eastbourne on the south coast of England and the air force one was at Brighton, just along the way. And we had a number of suicides. I can't recall how many. It might have been ten at the most. And I was called in. My original company commander was then the colonel in charge of the camp and because I'd been a cadet journalist and knew shorthand, I was called in as the court recorder of some of these suicides, which were very sad. All the fellows that did suicide, they were treated as killed in action or killed on active service. They were never listed as suicide.

They included a very good friend of mine, a journalist who got himself discharged in London, as you could, and for some reason went around to the home of a woman journalist one night, a famous woman journalist of a big magazine, and he suddenly, they're having a glass of wine, he suddenly pulls out a whole bottle of pills and swallows the lot. Suicides in front of her. I have an idea why he did it, but it's hard to say with some of these fellows.

Some of these fellows just couldn't cope with being free again. That's why I say I can always understand why a man comes out of jail and commits a crime – not because he wants to but because he wants to get back to jail. He's become conditioned to living in jail and that's the life he wants and he'll go back to it time and time again. Recidivist, time and time again. It's an incredible thing and no different to being a prisoner of war, you see. The only thing about being a prisoner of war, you know that the war's going to end some time and you're going to come out. But not everybody will feel that way.

KEITH HOOPER

Still, nothing was going to dilute the joy felt by so many Australian prisoners on returning to a home they had often thought was lost to them forever; a home that for a time, gathered them to its heart in relief and triumph.

We boarded the *Highland Chieftain*. It came down very slowly from Singapore, and they fed us on milk arrowroot biscuits and condensed milk, to put a bit of fat on us. It fattened us up pretty quick, because we laid around the decks all day. It was a very exciting time when the captain said, 'You can now see the first point of Australia. You're home.' And there wasn't much said, but we were back, we were home.

They brought us down the channel, down through the Coral Sea, down through all the coral reefs. Being close, it looked like you were going to hit a cliff, but they went slowly, and wended their way around, until we came to Brisbane. And that was a very exciting time, in a way, coming up the river. All the tugboats were firing their water cannons, and there were bands out there playing on these boats, and people cheering. We were just standing still, like zombies, all lined up along the side of the boat. It was really overwhelming to get this welcome home. We weren't allowed off the boat there, but the welcome was tremendous.

Then we set sail for Sydney. We sailed into Sydney and we were stationed out at Ingleburn. They put on a trip, by coaches . . . and they paraded us through Sydney. Well, you've never seen anything like it. All the ticker tape was coming down from all the buildings in the main street. And the buses had a job getting through the crowds. There was a lot holding up placards, 'Have you seen so-

and-so?' And 'Do you know so-and-so?' People were anxiously waiting to find information of their husbands and fathers and that sort of thing. It was very, very exciting.

THOMAS SMITH

Late on, I guess it would have been the Wednesday afternoon, we came into Sydney Harbour and there was the sun setting behind the Harbour Bridge. A glorious sight. Wonderful. We were back home again. We had completed the circuit. I like to call it, 'Around the World on Five Bob a Day'. But it was great to get home.

REG WORTHINGTON

We were naturally wildly excited, but a little apprehensive, and that was very definite because we didn't know how we were going to be greeted. Our first thoughts were, 'We surrendered and nobody would want to talk to us.' These other people had been in a war for three and a half years, all the people that we knew, and we really were apprehensive. It wasn't talked about publicly, but amongst ourselves we were all feeling much the same way. We just wondered whether we would be welcomed back to the country that was our home.

Of course we had only, well, first of all to see the people that were on the wharf. Our relatives were not allowed to come to the ship. That was guarded right off, Woolloomooloo was, and it was only army personnel. The band was there and so on and a row of double-decker buses, of course, waiting to take us. So it only took us to get down through Martin Place in the double-decker buses to begin to think, 'Well, perhaps people do want to see us!' The place was packed. There was ticker tape, which we had never seen before, every-where. People were racing out trying to hand us bottles of beer through the doors and the welcome was absolutely overwhelming. And that happened all the way out to Casula.

JAMES LING

There were curious undercurrents to the official celebrations. Just before Singapore fell, and even as the surrender was being negotiated, General Gordon Bennett handed over command of his division, escaped from the island and returned to Australia, leaving his men to be taken into captivity. Some of his men supported his actions, but his claim that he left so he could pass on knowledge about how to fight the Japanese – particularly given that he'd failed to engage them – was not convincing. A military enquiry after the war found he was not justified in leaving Singapore.

When the ships carrying the men of his 8th Division arrived in Sydney, Bennett was there to greet them, and the way the men behaved towards him on that day is typical of the controversy that still surrounds him.

We came down through the Barrier Reef and came straight to Sydney, to Woolloomooloo Bay, and I'll never forget the greeting there, all the brass in the wide world were there. And there was this little, bald-headed man in civilian clothes down there and it was Gordon Bennett, and the chaps on the boat, on our boat in particular, battalions and that, they went roaring mad, 'We want Gordon Bennett!' Ignored all this brass down there.

JAMES LING

We got in and eventually got up the harbour and, of course, it was quite amazing, extraordinary experience . . . Bennett got on the ship. He got on the ship to welcome us back and we were told to go up to the front to see the great man and they just went up and they turned their back on him. They gave him the raspberry. It was pretty grim. So he was talking more or less to nothing.

DR LLOYD CAHILL

Many of the men carried with them small keepsakes of their captivity, little things that they had treasured during their imprisonment, or that had, in some way, contributed to their survival. Some had Bibles, or wrinkled and faded photographs of a girlfriend, a wife or a mother. Others carried their dixie, the dish that had held their paltry rations. One souvenir that the Changi men brought home with them surpassed all the others.

The concert party in Changi got a piano fairly early in the piece in Singapore. A working party was cleaning out homes and that sort of thing, that had been badly bombed, and there was a piano in one of them and apparently they struck a sympathetic Jap who knew the concert party had got going and he allowed them to bring the piano back, which became the Changi piano . . .

Anyhow, it was on our boat coming home and when we got into Woolloomooloo Bay the idea, of course, was to get the piano off the boat and the blasted wharf labourers, they went on strike and refused to allow the crane to be used. And the fellows in charge of it were a chap called Jack Boardman who was our top pianist, beautiful pianist too, and there was a fellow named 'Happy' Harry Smith who was a comedian.

So they went up and saw the captain and told him the story and the next thing that happened the wharf labourers, there were eight organisers, all came aboard and the captain took them up. He'd sent down a message that they were all to come up, that he was sympathetic with their strike and he had unlimited bottles of beer up there for them; they all came up and while they were up there we got the crane going and got the piano back and that's still in use, that piano.

JAMES LING

After the ticker tape and the cheering crowds, however, the men were immediately gathered up into the unforgiving embrace of the armed forces, and the prisoners of war of the 2nd AIF, the great volunteer army, suddenly remembered all the things they hated about petty bureaucrats and jumped-up NCOs.

I was asleep on a bunk somewhere and they said, 'Come on, up you get, you are on the move!' Course we were used to that. And it was cold so far as I was concerned, because I didn't have any clothes, and I grabbed a blanket off the bed, thank goodness, and a little bit of possessions that I had . . . and they put me on a bomber plane, a Liberator or something, to fly us down to Adelaide.

And I don't think I have ever been as cold in my life, sitting on the bare aluminium of an aeroplane, and the bomb bays, and the cracks in the bomb bays. And you could look down and watch the land go underneath it, and I saw the brumby horses and everything else. And the pilot went as low as he possibly could because he knew it was freezing cold back in that bloomin' aeroplane – thank God, as I say, I had a blanket – and we were nearly all day flying down to Adelaide.

We had a rest in Adelaide and somebody gave us some sandwiches, and I was a bit doubtful about the sandwiches but I had the sandwiches, and they flew us to Melbourne. I got to Melbourne in the dark, was picked up with a utility, a driver and an officer. I had to sit in the back of the utility, and they took me to the last address that I had, which was an aunt's place in Kooyong Road, Caulfield. They said, 'Righto, this is as far as you go, report to Heidelberg Hospital tomorrow.' I got out and went up and rang the front door bell, they didn't even know I was in Australia!

Got out to Heidelberg and tried to tell who I was, and the matron said, 'I can't do anything with you, you have got no papers, you have no pay book, I don't even know if you are telling me you really are a soldier, we can't deal with you.' And I went back to that bloomin' Heidelberg Hospital for three days, and I got the same story every day. All they did was give me lunch.

. . . I went to Albert Park and was in civvie clothes and they wanted to know what I was doing in civvie clothes, so they issued me with a uniform . . . I was there one day and the smartypants fellow came up to me and I had . . . palled up with half-a-dozen POWs, we were all in the same position, nobody knew what to do with us. And the bloke said to me, 'Righto, you fellas, come with me.' So I went with him. And he said, 'Now, see that stack of tent floorboards?' He said. 'We want those to be moved across there to there and put there.' I said, 'You are joking!' And he said, 'No.' 'These fellows are not going to move anything.' I said. And he said, 'I'm not . . . are you disobeying an order?' I said, 'If you think I am.' 'I will go and get the officer!' I said, 'I don't care who you bloomin' well get!'

So with that he went and got the officer. And I said, 'These men, and myself, are five days out of prison camp, Japanese prison camp and you want us to move those floorboards that are there, and I have refused.' Well, did that bloomin' upstart of a young sergeant get into trouble. I was very pleased, here's this . . . I am almost grey-haired by then, aren't I; I have been in the army so long. I told him to go and jump in the river.

So gradually we went through the discharge process, which is a joke, you know, because medically they didn't know if there was anything wrong with us or what to do about it, they just discharged us as medically fit. We weren't fit. Full of malaria, full of everything else, and they sent us home to go to bed and shiver and shake, because malaria used to come back on us so much. And then after we had been home a while we went to doctors and went to Repat because we were called up, and they said, 'Oh,' the doc, smarty pants, 'Oh, you can't get malaria, you have been six months out of the territory, you won't get malaria.' No, we got malaria for a long time afterwards.

. . . I can remember going to Princes Bridge and standing there crying like a baby, it was just too much. I got to the city of Melbourne for some reason, I don't know when and so forth, but I got across Princes Bridge, and those little alcoves on Princes Bridge, I got into one of those and I was a mess, and then I got on a tram.

I got very sick in Swanston Street once, I was terribly ill, and my vision all went and I got migraine and I got everything else, and I got a tram and the connie [tram conductor] thought I was drunk and wanted to put me off the tram.

. . . But gradually we went on, and I got married and, you know, slowly you battle back. It was terrible, I couldn't work when I first came home, I tried so hard but you couldn't do a full week's work, you just fitted in where you could and so forth.

BILL COVENTRY

We finally got back to Sydney . . . they sent buses down to pick us up from where we landed. Took us to the showground. It was I suppose, half past nine when we got out there. By the time we got our ration coupons, our leave passes and that, was about half past eleven. I looked at the leave pass and I just turned around to the bloke behind me and I said, 'Jeez they're giving us nothing,' I says, 'This starts this mornin. And the day's almost gone!'

And there's this WO2 [Warrant Officer Class 2], standing within earshot. He said, 'What's the problem, Corporal?' I says, 'This leave pass, at least we thought it would have started from tomorrow.' Just like that he says, 'You're going to remember you're back in the army now, son. You're not sitting on your arse in Germany!' I says, 'I realise that.'

Ian Roberts, who'd been our OC [Officer Commanding] and didn't get taken prisoner, he'd been up to New Guinea, got malaria and come back and he was issuing the ration coupons. And he heard what this WO said. And he come over and he says to me, 'Right,' he says, 'don't take any notice of this bloke. He's never moved out of the showground in two years.' He says, 'He wouldn't know what it is to be in the army.' And he turned around to him and he said, 'And if ever I hear you talk to one of my boys again,' he said, 'I'll make bloody certain you're up in New Guinea!'

RAY NORMAN

First of all we were taken into a hut area and we were sprayed really, as we walked through it, because they were still uncertain how we were . . . they wanted to make certain that we were deloused of anything. So we went through there. A funny thing happened. Some of our boys spotted that there were shirts and singlets in a store at the back of this hut. And we forgot that our loved ones were outside. We stole anything that we could. We didn't even need it – because that is what we had been doing for three and a half years. It is funny isn't it?

JAMES LING

'Tom' Pledger, having sent the first letters he had been able to write in three and a half years, was desperate to see his parents and his fiancé, Jessie. But, as with seemingly everything associated with these POWs, getting there was going to be a challenge.

My mother and father didn't know, until I got home, that I was still alive. They didn't get word back from the government that I had been found until after I got home. The first thing they knew I was alive, my brother-in-law, he was in the army and he was on the train going into Central and he was reading the *Herald*, or the *Telegraph*, one of them, and there was a list of recovered POWs and there was my name. So he got off at the next station and he went to the nearest phone and he rang my mum and he rang Jess to tell them. That was the first they knew of where I was and that I was alive.

. . . I knew she would be there; she was that type of girl. She told me she would nurse until I came back. She wasn't a trained nurse but she was in a private hospital, she was there for ten years. And she always said that the day I got back she would walk out. I had a photo of her, the photo is still in there on the dressing table, a copy of it, I have still got the other one in an album. And I had that with me all of the time and I had the letter she wrote; things like that meant a lot. That would lift your ego up straightaway and they were the things that kept us going.

. . . When the ship landed here in Sydney, that we came back on, they took us out to Ingleburn and as soon as I got out of everything, I raced to the telephone and I rang Jess up and the first thing she said, 'Oh, you have still got your tongue!' And I said, 'Yes why?' She said, 'There have been rumours around that the Japs have been cutting the tongues out and that was the only thing I was worried about, that you had your tongue cut out.' So anyhow she said, 'Well, I am going straight in now to resign. I can't get a train until tomorrow morning but I know your mum and dad are on the train from Brisbane coming down now.' So she said, 'You meet them tomorrow morning and I will meet you at seven o'clock tomorrow night.

. . . I got three away from the x-ray machine, three or five, and it broke down. They wouldn't give you leave, they wouldn't give you pay, they wouldn't give you *anything* until you were x-rayed. So I heard them talking, there was a lorry going into Marrickville from Ingleburn to get some of the locals x-rayed, so I grabbed my papers and I said, 'I am going on that truck no matter what you say!' so another chap and I got on the truck, we got x-rayed, we never got back until seven o'clock to Ingleburn, in the meantime I had to get a leave pass, I had to get my pay, I had to get outfitted in uniform and everything, and it was about half past eight before I got through.

I raced into Liverpool on the train and into town and at Central they used to have a cloakroom there you could put your stuff in for soldiers. So I went there and put all of my stuff in and talking to the woman when I was putting it in, and I told her I had been a POW and I was going up to the Peoples Palace, and she said, 'Oh we have a phone here, why don't you ring them up?' So I rang them up and they said, 'No one by the name of Pledger here.' So I said, 'Oh, they must have left a note then or a message?' 'No message.'

I didn't know what to do. Jess's train was in and gone. So the woman said, 'I would go up there and put your foot down, there must be something.' So I got out, you know the ramp from Central down to Pitt Street? And I am walking down there and who should be walking up out of Pitt Street but Mum, Dad and Jess! They had had tea and thought, 'We had better go up to Central and see if he is there.' And that's how I met my future wife. In the middle of Pitt Street.

I was discharged from the army on the 29th of November '45 and we were married in Taree two days after, on the 1st of December '45 and Bruce Gordon who also went right through with me, he came up and was my best man in Taree . . . Jess couldn't get any wedding clothes because of the coupons. Some friend made her a dress, and she came to DJs, came all of the way to Sydney and bought that hat. It's a funny looking hat now, but it looked good in those days.

She said she never had a honeymoon with me. She had it with Gull Force . . . all of the time we were out every day with some of the prisoners of war.

ATHOL 'TOM' PLEDGER

Australian POWs of World War II returned to a country that was grateful to have them home, but was neither culturally nor medically equipped to deal with their mental state. The best medical advice on offer at the time was to avoid confrontation with their 'neurosis', and it would somehow go away. The families of prisoners were literally advised to 'avoid mentioning the war if possible', or to, 'change the subject'. In a sense, they need not have worried. The ex-prisoners didn't *want* to talk.

I had mixed feelings, mixed feelings. This might sound snobbish, it's not meant to be, nor is it . . . I was somewhat aghast at the Australian accent, having been in a prison camp, mainly with RAF guys, and having been away in the UK for so long. I found out since, most of my friends, when we landed in Melbourne and started talking to our next of kin. The first thing that hit us was the Australian accent, it is a harsh accent, whether we like to admit it or not and it was very different. And I know that when I met my father and he said, 'G'day, son, how are you?' I sort of went, 'Oh!' you know, it was unexpected but it was I guess, a natural reaction, but believe you me, you get used to it very quickly.

. . . I will willingly admit when I came home I was fairly wild in some ways. I found I couldn't sleep, was one problem, I don't know whether you know where Brighton is, but it's about 10 miles from Melbourne and quite often I would get out of bed at two in the morning and I'd walk into Melbourne, then I'd catch a tram back to Elsternwick which would be about four to six miles from our place and then walk home and go to bed and Mum would come in and say, 'C'mon it's time you went to work yah yah yah.' and I'd say, 'No, no, no, I'll get up later.' and sometimes I didn't and sometimes I did. And that worried my family, I know that, but I didn't know at the time, the old man used to try and have a few words with me, I couldn't hear him or he couldn't hear me, I'm not certain which. And that was a bit of a problem.

I went along to the Department of Veterans' Affairs at Dad's insistence and spoke to them, and the Doc did me over there and they came up with a diagnosis that I was suffering from Nervous Dyspepsia.

REX AUSTIN

When we came out of the prisoner camp into England we were mental. There was no way in the world that we could sit down and talk to a civilian. We didn't know – they started talking about what they went through – we just got bored and we'd turn around and walk away. Didn't matter about manners, they bored us so why listen to the fools? We were definitely in type of a mental stage I'd say . . .

. . . You could understand another POW in respect of where he was. Because what he'd tell you, you knew could've happened. But a civilian couldn't know; there was no way in the world they could know or understand. I suppose that's one reason why I didn't talk to my family, but you're not the first one that's asked that question. I've been asked that question a lot by a lot of people whose husbands have been POWs. Members of family. 'Dad never talked to us. What we know is what we overheard him talking to a friend about.' Well how could you? You couldn't understand it.

RONALD WALL

They needed each other, not just because they were mates, but to ratify their lives, to help them believe in the reality of what they had undergone. Unfortunately for some, the only place where they could comfortably meet was the pub.

You'd hit the grog, you do to a degree but you drink with your mates and you're not talking about anything, you're just talking to your mates, it's very hard to understand that, some boys, the grog got them. And you do use it as a safety valve I think, and it gets you into trouble.

ALEXANDER BARNETT

You'd go into town and meet all your mates, and stay in town all day, yarning and talking and drinking with one another. I think it was very important; unconsciously it probably was one way in which we got a lot of things off our chest. Found out a lot about one another and what had happened to each of us, because we'd scattered over the whole universe of the Asian nation as prisoners, where you'd met one bloke when you were first a prisoner, and hadn't seen him for another three years, could have been anywhere. So that was very important that you did that, and I think that probably helped you get rehabilitated yourself, you sort of did it to yourself, you didn't have counsellors.

. . . People looked at you differently, they did, that's honest, even in my own family, my parents, they didn't know whether I might be mad, or going mad, or I'd suffered something like this, it was funny, you could feel it that they didn't know how to make you out. It was all very deep, it wasn't on the surface, they were very happy to see you and they'd talk to you, but you could see them sort of thinking and muttering with one another.

I know the first night I got home, I went upstairs in the house where my parents were living at the time, where the bathroom was, and I went up and had a shower, and while I was under the shower my dad came in and looked me up and down, and never said anything. He just looked me up and down and never said anything.

FRED SKEELS

It is hard not to feel sympathy for those families who watched one man go away and so often, another return. And while there was a natural curiosity about what the prisoners had seen and what had been done to them, their loved ones could not help but trip and stumble if they tried to find out.

I used to hate Sunday nights as I wouldn't go to church, but all the others would come in and they would never want to know the nice things that had happened. They'd always want the gory, horrible bits. I did burst out of the house one Sunday saying, 'You're a lot of ghouls, let's talk about something nice when I come back!' Hard to overcome, but the family were family again.

JOHN MATHEWS

The insensitivity displayed by some to the prisoners' problems was best exemplified by the society matron who, at a function to welcome prisoners back, pompously informed them that the reason they survived, and, in her view, were so healthy, was because of their rice diet. Ray Parkin encountered another fool.

Where my mother and father lived, in Ivanhoe, course all the neighbours knew and everything, and so they had an open house and people were streaming in and out of the house, you know, congratulating me on being home and all that and the local butcher he came up to me, and of course these people were asking me questions and I just gave answers, for the time being, I couldn't tell them the whole story. And this butcher got alongside me, he didn't want to know what I had to tell him, he was telling *me*, he said, 'Oh,' he said, 'while you were away you've no idea what it was like here.' He said, 'Even tea was rationed!' I said, 'God, I'm glad I wasn't here!' That's how some of the people were, you know.

RAY PARKIN

Thomas 'Fred' Smith had enlisted at 19, leaving behind his beloved Huon Valley, in Tasmania. He'd been part of Sparrow Force on Timor, and after capture, had endured Selarang, Malaya, Burma and Thailand. Many times he thought the railway would kill him, but he'd made it. Or at least, he thought he had.

We were taken into Launceston. The parents were there, and my younger brother and sister, were there to meet me. That was our reunion. Because they didn't know where I was for two years. They didn't know whether I was alive. They only received one card back from me that I was allowed to send. That was two years later after they found out where I was.

. . . We were going to travel around to Queenstown, where we were living, by bus, but the younger brother had got a V8 coupe car. During the war, they couldn't buy tyres or tubes, they were pretty hard to get hold of, they were rationed. So the tyres and tubes he had in there weren't very good. And there was about five or six of us in this little coupe, to try and get back to Queenstown. We got halfway back and the jolly tubes blew up. We finished up having to jam the tyres full of dry grass, build them up with dry grass, jam that in. So we got home about four o' clock the next morning. The people next door got their house ready for a welcome home, they had the 'Welcome Home' up, but it was about four o' clock in the morning, so it all fizzled out. We had a welcome home the next day.

That night, I went into this nice soft bed, I couldn't sleep in it. I had to pull the blankets onto the floor to sleep. I was used to the hard bed. On the soft bed, I just felt like I was floating and that was no good. So I pulled it onto the floor. The first meal, Mum dished up a nice hot roast dinner, roast potatoes, carrots, all the sides, lovely. And I cut up a bit of meat, and I went to put it in my mouth . . . and I couldn't eat it. Couldn't get it past my lips. My tummy seemed to revolt against it. I suppose it was the smell or . . . it took me quite a while before I could back into eating anything. Well, she wasn't very happy. She couldn't understand why I couldn't eat. But my dad knew, he knew what was going on, because he'd had pretty tough times himself. Probably tougher than I had, in Gallipoli and France.

Mrs Coulthard was a tremendous worker during the war. Organising parcels for the boys, and all this sort of thing, doing welcome homes and doing everything she could. She was a real hard worker. She had organised this welcome home, and there was about two other POWs and the others were returned soldiers. She put us up on this stage, which I didn't want. But I only went because she had done so much.

So I went up there, and all the bigwigs got up there and said how much they should help us and all this big talk. And I wasn't very much impressed with it. And of course, then, when I did start work, I couldn't settle down very well at all. You can imagine being . . . all those years, those three and a half years, living on a knife edge. Four years away from home, living amongst all those people, then coming back to a dull job.

Up there your life expectancy was any time, and coming back to a job like that, it was just nothing. I couldn't settle down at all. So I got a job, a transfer . . . I'd already got this job off this foreman, I thought I could do this truck driving, in the mines. I thought that would be better than what I was doing. So I had to go to the general office, to the manager, to get this transfer, and he was one of the bigwigs that had said, 'We've got to help these boys all we can, because they've had a tough life.' So when I approached him about the transfer he said, 'No, we're not transferring anyone, you've got to stay where you are.' He wiped me off like a dirty rag, I thought, 'Well, that's it.'

THOMAS SMITH

Virtually all servicemen and servicewomen have difficulty settling back into society and employment after a war. Sometimes it's because of the dreams of their old life that they have nurtured for so long that have no chance of being realised, or it may be due to the rejection of their achievements by those who stayed behind. For the POWs, it was doubly hard.

Most people who lived back in Australia felt the hard life in the wartime with coupon rationing of sugar and butter, and clothing rationing, and all those sorts of things, and having to work hard. There was a great deal of antipathy to us those who had been in the bank before the war and had gone away and their jobs had been taken over by girls, practically all the appointments during wartime were women. They were tellers, ledger clerks, posters, postage clerks and even people who occupied the role which is now an accountant in the bank. When we came back they were emptied out down the scale and they resented it bitterly and things were not at all happy.

. . . People were telling me how hard it was to be a civilian in Australia and of course having seen 200 men die in a matter of two and a half months around you, with the prospect that your life, even when you got home was not going to be very long, the hardship they put up with. I said, to one girl, 'Yes,' I said, 'But your war effort is bearing interest at four per cent whereas mine has probably taken four years off my life.' Oh, shock horror and she went and reported me to the manager.

. . . We didn't care about the sympathy of people; we wanted a fair deal, that is what bugged me about the Vietnam veterans. We had suffered far worse casualties, far more traumatic conditions, far tougher conditions all the way through, for a longer period, because a battalion in Vietnam was only there for a matter of months and they were relieved and then another battalion took their place . . . Certainly they were militia serviceman and hadn't volunteered to go there, they were being sent, which does put a burden on them and I freely admit that.

I do feel that we were badly treated by society and the Department of Veterans' Affairs in the very early stages. There was a modicum of shame in it, you did feel if your uncles had fought and won a war and suddenly you go to war and you let the whole side down.

WALTER HICKS

Some men managed by deliberately and consciously removing their POW experiences from their daily lives. It rose up on them again and again, but they fought it down, refusing to acknowledge that it could or would, hold them back.

I had terrible nightmares, terrible nightmares where I was back in the camp again and I experienced all sorts of things and you know, I'd wake up screaming or amongst sweat or something, but they were difficult. But I was very strongly resolved to get back into civilian life and to find a wife and to start a family.

And I found a wonderful girl at a dance who became my wife and she was my wife for 43 years before she died of cancer. She was a tremendous strength in that I wouldn't have recovered as quickly as I did if it hadn't been for her wonderful understanding, her patience with me, because I wouldn't have been all that easy to live with in many respects, especially if I was waking up screaming during the night, which she would have found terribly distressing. But she supported me all the way through and we had three wonderful kids and so on, so that was a big factor.

The Repat were very, very good too. I drank bottles and bottles of great big bottles of cod liver oil extract for months and months and months after I came home. I used to have to go into Repat and collect those. But it was a slow, gradual process.

I possibly differed from your average returned digger in as much as I didn't think it would be healthy to be put, or to see myself in a special category because I'd been a prisoner of war, so much so that I was not at all interested in joining an organisation which was formed in Melbourne called Ex POW and Relatives Association. I didn't like that idea in principle because I wanted to put that behind me and get on with my life and I didn't think it was healthy mentally, to adjust again. I mean it was probably a minority opinion but that was the way I felt then. And I'd never been a member of an RSL, mainly because I wasn't interested in going to a club that had a licence and who seemed to think of nothing else but grogging on, that wasn't my scene so I didn't bother with the RSL. I'm not disputing that they've done and still do wonderful work for ex service people in many areas but it just wasn't my scene.

Nor was Anzac Day, I marched the first year I came home, 1946, it was the natural thing to do and have the cheering thousands, you know, first Anzac Day after the war then. But at the end of it I thought, 'This is not for me. I don't really enjoy this adulation, I don't really like it.' I never marched again, never marched again. I've tended to look on Anzac Day; it may be wrongly, as a glorification of war. Now I know my mates would jump on me and most RSL people would jump on me and say, 'Nonsense, it's not.' But that's how I felt about it for many, many, years up to fairly recently. I'm not sure that I've even got rid of that attitude about Anzac Day, I tend still to think it's a glorification of war which is something, you know, I absolutely loathe and detest and I've grown to loathe and detest all forms of violence, I really have. I've written letters to the paper about it even.

MARIC GILBERT

Like Maric, many men had marriage as their goal once they returned home. And it wasn't as if they didn't have the courage to face up to the challenge. It was just that for some, the path was a little bit rocky.

When I landed back in Sydney, most of the family were there to meet me, but poor mother had died, I missed her, still miss her actually. This is one of the fallacies of war – you go, 'You must expect things to be different when you get back.' But overall I came out really well.

I became engaged to the girlfriend from the Tocumwal camp. She became a Shire Councillor, head of the council at Cootamundra; she was the head in the office . . . But then I had my jaws broken eight times in the prisoner of war camp and they were badly out of alignment, my teeth The army had spent a couple of days on them and they did a reasonable job, but I still didn't have proper occlusion.

My favourite cousin had married a dentist while I was away and he had set up business in West Wyalong, so he invited me out and said he wanted me to spend a week and, 'I will give your teeth a good go-over.' I said, 'Right.' So out I went and went down this morning and got in the chair and looked up and this little vision sort of poked its head around and I said, 'Where did you come from!' She said, 'I am the assistant.' The next morning she was there again and I said, 'Where do you live?'

I switched horses and became engaged to her, cancelled the other one, became engaged to her and married this one. It was a very happy marriage; we just missed 50 years before she passed away.

DES MULCAHY

I didn't really have girlfriends, I think I got a Dear John letter from one in the Middle East, but that was par for the course. I had always admired this woman; she was older than I was, but there was no way in the world I was going to do anything before I went overseas.

But when I came home the first thing I did was find my little black book and there was her telephone number, the first I rang and she said, 'Oh, I thought you were dead! I couldn't find you.' I said, 'What are you doing?' She was a schoolteacher, correcting exam papers. 'Good,' I said, 'Sammy and I are coming around. We've got a dozen bottles. We'll help you correct the exam papers.' Sammy was Sammy Fry, Sergeant, 2/24th Battalion. He was the head of the Teachers College of Victoria, so Sammy and I did the examination papers and we passed all the kids and we got Lois tiddly and ourselves that night. I didn't miss a night, except when I had to go to Ballarat for discharge.

We went out and then I said to her, 'I'm crook. I'm no bargain but I'd like to marry you.' and she said, 'I'd like to marry you but I can't, because I'm engaged.' And I said, 'Go and break it off!' She said 'What?' She said, 'I'm not keen on him.' I said, 'Well go and tell him, or I'll break his bloody neck.'

Next day she rang and said she had broken it off and I said, 'Good enough. We're engaged. When are we getting married, tomorrow?' And she said, 'No I can't, I'm teaching.' She was teaching at Upwey, she was teaching English and she was teaching with Bill Woodfull, the test cricketer, and he is a very nice bloke, and his son's a very nice bloke, he's a dentist now. And she said, 'I couldn't let Bill down.' 'Oh well, when do you finish, the 20th of December?' I said, 'Right, that's the day we get married. I'll meet you on the train.'

And I picked her up with a train full of flowers and I took her home, you're not supposed to see your bride on the day but I did, gave her a big cuddle, then went home and got dressed and we got married at St Marks.

ALEXANDER BARNETT

It is impossible not to admire the women who took on the responsibility of these men. As Alexander Barnett says, I'm crook. I'm no bargain. What did they think of their husbands, these men with their arms curled around their plate at mealtimes, so as to protect their food, with their night-time horrors and their cold sweats, their malaria and their precious mates, their silences and their all too obvious pain? That they loved them there can be no doubt, thousands of families in Australia bear witness to the depth and strength of that love. That they saved them though, *that* is the miracle.

If it wasn't for my wife I wouldn't be here. Because a POW has got a lot of things tucked away that you don't know you've got, and the first inkling was, we lived in East Camberwell and I was walking with her down Monomeith Avenue and they had white picket fences and I could still see the movement on the picket fence as a car came around and the noise it made, it sounded like a tank and it looked like a tank, and I kicked her feet, fell on top of her to protect her. She still married me. And then I had malarial comas . . .

I didn't know what post traumatic stress was, I didn't want to know, it was 'war neurosis', that's what they called it. And I'd seen what happened to the blokes, they were given uppers and downers and that was wrong and I said I wasn't going to tell the doctors, I picked one up by his collar. He reported me. He told me that everything, I'd been vomiting I had a lot of pain, and I thought it was my liver that was playing up again. And he said to me, 'With you POWs, it's all in your head.' I just leant over and picked him up by the collar and he was only a little squirt, and shook him, put him down, and didn't go back.

. . . We didn't tell them, they didn't believe it, it didn't happen: 'European! He's telling lies. We know what happened, they were all out on farms while the Germans were away and getting nookie and all sorts of things and it was the Japanese prisoners, they suffered. You couldn't have suffered like that!'

You didn't go to the POW meetings after a while because one of them would taunt you and of course a fight would start, and you learnt to shut up, and the wife suffered because she was told that nothing happened to me.

ALEXANDER BARNETT

Counselling? All of these chaps land back from a war, here one day and they're out for counselling. We never had a counsellor. Straight off the boat, discharged and that was it. Nobody worried about it. Go to a doctor, they have got no idea what was wrong. They had no idea what we went through. The first one I went to about these pains in the tummy, it was Repatriation then, not Veterans' Affairs. I went to him. Now he was a doctor in his fifties or sixties so he should know something about doctoring. And he said, 'What's wrong?' And I was telling him about these terrific pains I was getting in the belly, and I told him I had been a prisoner of war and the diet I was on and everything, and I blamed it on that. And after he examined me he come back and said to me, 'There is nothing wrong with you, you're only bludging.' And that's when I saw red. I hopped up, and my papers were on the table and I ripped them in two and I threw them right in his face and I said, 'You can stick your bloody Repatriation!' And walked out.

ATHOL 'TOM' PLEDGER

Oh yes, some got depressed. I had one in particular, in Tasmania; he shot himself, killed himself. People don't commit suicide when there's a war. When life is threatening you hang onto life. When life is in abundance you can let go of it in a blink of an eye . . .

The fellow I know seemed to be as happy as Larry when he went out and shot himself. Why he was happy, he had decided, made a decision to do something, the decision to kill himself was horrifying to us, but to him it was satisfying, quite peaceful, all that load, whatever it was affecting him, all the memories of the prisoner of war days and everything was gone. He went off quite better than I'd seen him for a good while.

BILL YOUNG

By far the most hurtful matter for the prisoners was the comparison made by many people between the POWs of the Japanese and those who were prisoners of the Germans; a comparison that astonishingly continues even today. Why would anyone choose to do this? As if pain and suffering were like weights and measures in a grocer's shop and you can somehow discern who suffered the most. It's madness – but it happened.

My father asked me if I would help out with meeting some of the air force POWs who at this stage were just coming out of Japan, out of Asia anyway and I of course volunteered to do so. I had the privilege of meeting two RAAF ex POWs from the Pacific War, and I found I couldn't help them at all; these guys were so traumatised by what had happened to them and what was happening to them that they really didn't need any assistance from me. It was an extraordinary experience, one that I value very much, but I had to turn round to my father after only a couple of days and say, 'Look, Dad, I'm sorry, I'm wasting my time, I'm wasting their time, they can't be helped.'

. . . They'd been POWs in Singapore, they'd been prisoners much longer than I had, they didn't really appreciate anything that had gone on in Europe in terms of POWs. I rather think that I probably didn't appreciate anything that went on in their war and we had nothing to talk about; there was just nothing that one could . . . no common ground at all with them. It was a case of both these guys were airmen and it was a case of get them uniformed, get them back into uniform again and leave them to their own devices, and I think they appreciated that I was doing that too.

. . . They didn't seem to be happy to be home. As I say, I think they had been traumatised to the extent that they were living in a bit of a world of their own, if I can put it that way. Perhaps because we had time to recover in England and the boat trip et cetera, I think we came home excited to be home, looking forward to being home, and we'd had the opportunity rehabilitating our mental thoughts whereas these guys hadn't had that, I think they both been flown home, in fact I'm pretty certain they had, so they hadn't had that experience. No doubt in time they'd have come completely good the same as we were, it was too early. I think that's the result in a nutshell.

REX AUSTIN

We just intermingled, we weren't kept separate. We just intermingled, and where a division seems to have crept in between European and Jap POWs was they spoke of their atrocious treatment and the public knew of a lot of it and had their sympathy. And some of them were flown straight out of POW camps or within a day or two, came back here living skeletons. They looked horrible. Whereas we'd had three months in the UK fattening up, a month's leisurely trip home on the boat, four months, nicely sun-tanned and you know, we were 'people who had dodged the real war'.

The European war, later in life, was not *Australia's* war, that was England's war. Australia's war was up here in the islands. And that's how we were victimised in that, it wasn't our fault, we had no choice where we were being sent, most of our POWs were taken prisoner of war before some of the people who were Japanese POWs had enlisted!

RON ZWAR

We didn't talk to the other POWs. We didn't really you know. We'd both been prisoners of war. Alright, I'd been in Germany, you'd been in Japanese hands. I think in a way, and this is interesting; we fellows who were in German hands and there were 7800 of us, were always reluctant early in the piece to talk about our experiences after we'd learnt what had happened to the fellows in Japanese hands. And there were 22 000. And a third of them died so it made a big difference. No, no, no, no, no.

KEITH HOOPER

Slowly, life embraced them, and, for the most part, hope and optimism returned. Families were started, jobs taken up, futures planned. And if the nightmares still occurred, at least now they were a little more manageable. But for 'Tom' Pledger, there was to be one last demand on his courage, one last journey back.

In 1947 I had been into Uralla and had my appendix out and Jess was home with the two babies and I came home and I had about a fortnight convalescence at home. And during that fortnight I got a telegram from the army to see if I would be prepared to go to Hong Kong to give evidence on the war trials. And I said no. Well, at the time I said no, because I knew Jess had had those two little kiddies nine months old, trying to look after twins on her own, and I thought it was too much.

Anyhow we talked for about a week about it and Jess said, 'Look go. If you don't you will regret it all of your life. I will close the house up,' we had just moved in, 'and I will go up to Mum and Dad's on the farm at Taree.' I still wasn't decided and then she talked me around to saying yes, I would go. But it was only to be for three weeks. I was away three months at these damn trials.

. . . We had our own solicitors looked after us. And they took us out and showed us, it was a big old shed, where the trials were at Kowloon, where the trials were going to be held. They showed us all of that. Then they went over our evidence with us. And they just said, 'Tell it as you see it.' And so that's what we did.

And when my turn came to give evidence I started off and got up to a certain point and I forget what it was now, but I gave a point of view on some

Japanese officer in witness box, War Crimes Trial, 1947

medical thing. And they hopped up and said no, I couldn't do it, because I wasn't a medically trained person. So then they had to adjourn the court while the court then decided. It went all day, deciding whether I could give evidence or not. And so the next day they brought me back in and they said they had decided I would be allowed to give evidence.

. . . I could tell them what food they had, what drugs were received from the Japanese. Who died. What the verdict of their death was. How many had beri-beri, how many had dysentery. All of that sort of thing I could tell them. So I was mainly in there to give all of that evidence. What was our weights, our average weights? What was the food we got and how many calories we were living on, how many grams of stuff, I had all of those figures down, see, so I could tell them all of that. Didn't have to be a medical doctor to tell them all of that sort of stuff see?

And they might even ask me, 'You had an operation there where the chap died, why did he die?' 'Well,' I said, 'in the doctor's opinion, which he told to me, he died because there was no anaesthetics. We didn't have enough vitamins to treat him beforehand. We didn't have this or that drug.' See? So it was all of that.

. . . To tell the truth I could only recognise one Japanese and they just looked like humble, little, old men. That's what they looked like, just little old men. I didn't have any feeling for them whatsoever. Only I could picture what they

Japanese accused at War Crimes Trial, 1947

looked like in the camp, like the doctors and that. How their doctor brought a visiting lot of people into the camp into the hospital. And here is all of these blokes bloated up with beri-beri, another bloke is that thin you could see through him. And they all had a good, old laugh about it. Well I could tell them those things see? 'That's him there; he was the one that laughed.' But he didn't go back and send us anything to treat those people. So that was mainly what it was all about.

. . . I looked after so many people that had been bashed for no reason at all by the Japanese, and so many of them had died from malnutrition; I felt I had to have my say about that before a court. I felt I had to, because they were my friends who had been hurt, killed even. That's why . . . I wanted to see the death penalty. At the time, yes. I had no qualms about it in those days. I have now, but even now I am not sure about it. If anybody takes a life knowingly and for no reason whatsoever, I think they haven't got a right to live. Well that's what they did to us, they took our lives, knowingly in our case.

ATHOL 'TOM' PLEDGER

•

At the end of all these interviews, each ex POW was asked to reflect on the life they had led, the paths taken or discarded, and what stayed with them still about their imprisonment, their war behind the wire. I want to end this book with just a few of their answers, to leave you with this lasting memory of their worth, for in them I think, lives the best of us, as a people, and as a nation.

It changed me definitely, because I was just a young Sister. I saw life at its best and its worst. I saw what human beings could do to each other, what hatred could do, and yet what faith could do and what kindness could do. That's what we are here for, to help one another. I saw how useless all this is, when people go on hating one another and killing one another. How someone lives with that I don't know, lives with themselves I mean. When you have just massacred a whole lot of people, how would you feel? I don't know. We are all born with animal instincts in all of us. War brings it out in so many. In war it makes some men, men, but others – it just makes them animals.

SISTER BERENICE TWOHILL

I must admit, I think being a prisoner of war must have affected me in many ways. When I first came back, the first party I went to was down to my surf club at Palm Beach, and there I ran into an old friend of mine, John Deakin. He was at school with me and John said, 'Oh heavens above,' he was in the air force, he said, 'come out here and tell me, come, we'll get a beer and come outside and tell me.' And I was still in army greens, 'Tell me what it was all about.'

So we went outside and after about 20 minutes I'm talking away and he's just listening, and he just suddenly stopped and he said, 'You know, Lloyd, I think it probably did you the world of good to be a prisoner of war. You were a terrible bastard before you went away.' So there you are. So I always think of John Deakin. Maybe it did me good. He thought so.

. . . I think that nature is very kind for most people in any case. I think you kind of forget some of the bitter parts and the really nasty parts and remember the funny parts and the amusing parts, and I think of all the wonderful fellows that I met and still have been my friends all my life. Unfortunately there's not many left now. But they were wonderful guys; wonderful fellows and I think I did learn a lot.

LLOYD CAHILL

If I had known what I was going into I wouldn't have had the guts to face up to it, but having done it, I wouldn't have missed a minute of it. What I learnt and the friendships and all those things are absolutely invaluable. And I've been involved in ex-service activities ever since the war.

Our unit association was formed on Anzac Eve, 1946, and I was recovering from a bout of malaria on that particular night and I got there late, I was sitting up at the back of the hall and they were calling for nominations for president and somebody nominated one of the officers, 'No, he's a bloody officer!' and so it went on, 'Nominate somebody else.' 'No, he's A Troop,' or 'He's B Troop,' you know, the parochialism was just absolutely incredible and then somebody lit their eyes on me up the back and nominated me.

Now the troops saw me as neither fish nor fowl. I was not sort of one of the officers in authority, I suppose. They didn't identify me there. They identified me with somebody who was trying to help them. So I became president and I still am.

ROWLEY RICHARDS

What I would like to say, before we finish, that it is through the family, my wife and family that helped me survive all these years. I was in a big, black spot and I could never have done it without them. I love them all dearly and they've been a big help and I wouldn't part with them for the world. And all the friends I've had, too.

I've had a lot of friends during my life and I regard them as true friends. You know your true friends. When you're in a position like that, you get to know people's character and who you can trust and who you can't.

My family, I love them. When I'm gone, they can look back and say, 'He did his best.' Which we've both done, we both worked hard. With five kiddies, you've got to keep your nose to the grindstone. We've worked hard, both of us, and we've both done it together. When I'd come home from work, the meal would be cooked, and when we'd all had our meal, I'd either do the dishes while Daphne put the kids through the baths and cleaned up, into their nighties or pyjamas, then we could all sit down together. And this went through the years, we've always done it . . .

We've had our hard times; we've had our good times. Now we're having our good times. We can sit back and have a lot of fun. There was quite a lot of bad times with all the stitching up and so forth. But you've got to look ahead, think positive, and keep mixing with younger people. It's a big must, is to keep in touch with the young people.

THOMAS SMITH

Some fellas have got it, some fellows haven't, and I think that is the only reason why I am telling you stories today, because you were determined that they weren't going to beat you. And you have got some funny determination thing.

Now that I am an older man and I think back a little bit, I probably had that determination all the way through. But as long as you rule your determination with gentleness, you can fit into society, and that is what I have tried to do. I am no hero, I'm no anything else, but you just try to do it gently. So, you make it or you don't make it.

BILL COVENTRY

I probably got more sense, you know, I'm sure. Certainly not perhaps immediately after I came home, but over the years have gone by I've – as I said earlier, I think it was a learning period of my life, you learned a lot about life, you learned a lot about the human side of it, you learned that people can put up with a hell of a lot and still stay alive, people can put up with a hell of a lot and still be human to one another. Yes, you learn all these sort of lessons, and I think it changed me to the point where, with the help of Bonnie after we got married anyway, she helped me a lot I think, get over a lot of troubles.

FRED SKEELS

I got my greatest lesson in philosophy up there you know. We'd been working up on the railway which was up on the steep hill side, about a sixty degree thing and we were cutting along the side of it and putting in bridges and cuttings and so forth, and to build the bridges we had to have some cement for the base.

So four of us were sent down one day from the railway to the river, where the engineers were, to get a barrel of cement. And, of course, we were bare-footed and in g-strings and all the rest of it, and it was about, I suppose about four miles away . . . we got the barrel of cement, and the only way to carry it was to put two wire slings on it and put two poles through and carry it on our shoulders. Well, that's an awkward thing anyway, but when you're in bare feet and the tracks are ditched in the centre and they're slippery, it's a very awkward thing and we said a few things about it in our disapproval.

But when we got a little up the track, it was sometime during the wet season, and one of these storms was coming over, and the jungle there, there's these straight-trunk trees which go up fairly high, then they spread their canopy of big leaves, and when these rainstorms came over, it creates such a din that you can't hear yourself shout underneath it, it's just bedlam. So, we had to take shelter and there was a lot of wind with this too.

So we took shelter and the only shelter you could take was your back up against a single tree and just hope for the best because it was so violent that there were tops being brought off trees and whole trees were coming down and it looked like the end of the world, and here we were just with our backs against the tree and hoping. And I thought, 'This is it, or could be it.'

And I happened to look up and there was a bit of a branch above me, with a number of leaves on it, big, flat leaves, and I looked up and underneath one of them was a mosquito, a single mosquito. Probably one of the frailest things in the jungle and here it was, riding it out as if nothing was happening outside its orbit.

And I just looked, and the contrast of all the commotion that was going on outside and this frail insect up there, found a niche and would weather the storm and a thought struck me then, I thought, 'Well,' I knew it was a rat race outside and I thought, 'Well, when I get out there, I am going to find meself a leaf just like this mosquito and weather it out.' It was the beginning of me philosophy I suppose.

RAY PARKIN

Notes

All quotes from the following people are from their Australians at War Film Archive interviews, as numbered below.

Rex Austin	#0382	Bill Fordyce	#0523
Alexander Barnett	#0781	Cyril Gilbert	#0821
Bert Beecham	#0119	Maric Gilbert	#0746
Francis Binstead	#0716	Phil Greville	#2455
Sheila Bruhn	#1998	Ernie Granland	#0744
Lloyd Cahill	#0662	Colin Hamley	#0642
Lawrence Calder	#1842	Allan Herd	#0712
Gavin Campbell	#0047	Walter Hicks	#0807
Thomas Canning	#1699	Keith Hooper	#0654
Ralph Churches	#1094	Robert Hooper	#0693
Raphael Corbett	#1718	Alexander Kerr	#1489
Geoff Cornish	#1388	Malcolm Keshan	#1364
Bill Coventry	#1677	Arthur Leggett	#1413
Pat Darling	#0005	James Ling	#0015
Ken Drew	#0065	Ross McDonald	#0496
Wilton Eady	#0987	John Mathews	#2035
Terry Fairbairn	#0913	Athol Moffitt	#0799
Eileen Fisher	#0029	Lloyd Moule	#1285
John Fitzhardinge	#0932	Des Mulcahy	#0025

Ray Norman	#1137	Herbert Trackson	#0732
Robert Parker	#1378	Sister Berenice Twohill	#0177
Ray Parkin	#2552	Tom Uren	#0728
Charlie Parrott	#1402	Howard Walker	#1418
Athol 'Tom' Pledger	#1705	Ian Wall	#0674
Rowley Richards	#1144	Ronald Wall	#1013
Frank Roy	#1936	Reg Worthington	#1990
Bob Simonson	#0195	Charles Yacopetti	#0578
Fred Skeels	#1553	Bill Young	#0032
Thomas Smith	#1697	Ron Zwar	#1981
Clarence Spurgeon	#0937		

Photo credits

All the 'then and now' photographs of those whose stories are included in this book came from the Australians at War Film Archive, and thanks for this are due to the Department of Veterans' Affairs.

Thanks are also due to the following, who provided other photographs used: Sheila Bruhn (p. 98), Lloyd Cahill (p. 128), Raphael Corbett (pp. 81, 83 and 89), Geoff Cornish (p. 232), Ken Drew (p. 80), Bill Fordyce (p. 8), Maric Gilbert (p. 204), Robert Hooper (p. 247), Malcolm Keshan (p. 182), James Ling (p. 199), Des Mulcahy (p. 56), Ray Norman (p. 143), Robert Parker (p. 311), Athol 'Tom' Pledger (pp. 342 and 343), Rowley Richards (pp. 262 and 280), Sister Berenice Twohill (p. 79) and Charles Yacopetti (p. 310).

Index

EB